Social Aspects of Education:

A CASEBOOK

Edited by
Edward T. Ladd and
William C. Sayres

The complexities of education in action are demonstrated in this casebook through twenty-two vivid and instructive reports of actual school experiences. The major challenges of significant school situations—both in and out of the classroom—are graphically presented.

These authentic case histories are filled with such problems as school discipline, controversies over school organization, and curriculum change. There are extensive accounts of the events following the racial desegregation of a high school, of the partial non-grading of a city elementary school, and of several conflicts between local groups and state education departments seeking to improve standards. Their challenging overtones lead into sociology, political science, and law.

Through the case studies the social and cultural aspects of education can be seen clearly, with fresh insight into the realities of education. The reports, all authentic, are printed here for the first time.

PRENTICE-HALL EDUCATION SERIES
John J. Finlanbee, Editor

Social
Aspects
of
Education

A CASEBOOK

PRENTICE-HALL EDUCATION SERIES

John S. Brubacher, Editor

Social
Aspects
of
Education

A CASEBOOK

Edited by:

EDWARD T. LADD
Division of Teacher Education
Emory University
and
Department of Education
Agnes Scott College

WILLIAM C. SAYRES
Division of Research
New York State Education Department

PRENTICE-HALL, INC.
Englewood Cliffs, N. J.

1962

© 1962 BY
PRENTICE-HALL, INC.
ENGLEWOOD CLIFFS, N. J.

LIBRARY OF CONGRESS
CATALOG CARD NO.: 62–8574

PRINTED IN
THE UNITED STATES
OF AMERICA
81548—C

Preface

          This book is designed primarily for advanced undergraduates or beginning graduate students studying social and cultural aspects of education. The cases lead into many fields of study, but their primary emphasis is in sociology, political science, and law.

    In our view the basic purpose of a casebook in teacher preparation is to offer concrete, realistic, challenging materials suitable for both inductive and deductive study. There is much to be learned through inducing generalizations or principles from specific cases; at the same time there is also real value in the deductive application of generalizations or principles to specific cases.

    While the book was still in the blueprint stage, the publishers were kind (and prudent) enough to ask a substantial number of educators how *they* might use such case materials. At least six ways were reported:

1. The initial use of cases to bring out or induce the issues, questions, or hypotheses to be studied systematically.
2. The supplementary use of cases to illustrate—or provide problems for the application of—issues or principles already formulated. (The reverse of 1.)
3. The use of a case to motivate the study of a single principle or issue which it dramatizes especially clearly. (A rudimentary variation of 1.) The instructor and students can refer back to the case as often as appropriate during the course.
4. The use of a case as an integrating focus for a case-conference type of discussion, for which various students have prepared themselves by exploring various dimensions—psychological, legal, economic—of the case.
5. The use of cases as a review device.
6. The use of cases as a basis for examination questions.

    Educators who noted these uses attested that case studies were vivid, dramatic, practical and instructive demonstrators of principles in action; that they could be applied to experiences with which students were or would become familiar; that they could be instrumental in strengthening reasoning and analysis; and that they established convincingly the interdisciplinary character of educational problems. With all these affirmations we wholeheartedly concur.

All the cases in this book are authentic: only such identifying details as names have been changed. While we say this with some pride, we have no wish to belittle other case collections; these latter have been so few and far between that all such contributions are welcome. Nevertheless it was not solely the scarcity of available case materials that led us to make the present collection. In our opinion, a serious drawback to other case compilations has been their tendency to feature fictitious or idealized cases, often so obviously contrived and pat that quite a misleading impression of the nature of case evidence is given. We suspect that readers trained on such cases are likely to be sadly disillusioned when, later, they try to reach conclusions and make decisions in situations where comparably ideal data cannot be obtained. Cases which, for example, conveniently reveal the inner thoughts and motives of the *dramatis personae* at critical moments can hardly be expected to prepare the reader to deal with related problems in real life where such revelations would be, to say the least, exceptional.

In some instances case studies have appeared which are "based on" true incidents. That is, they are not outright fictions, but they substantially embellish or supplement known truth in order to present a tidier, more complete story. While such studies have a fascination and appeal all their own —and we shall continue to read them with interest whenever they are offered—we must confess our misgivings about them also. There is too much tidying up, too much concern with giving the reader easy-to-take capsules regularly fortified with the prescribed quota of pedagogical vitamins and minerals. A few loose ends often constitute the most intriguing and challenging part of a case, and we find ourselves less than grateful when the author ties them up for us.

An important function of the case method is to sensitize the reader not only to what *was* reported, but to what was not. If we truly seek to foster growth in judgment and analytic discrimination, we must not encourage the reader to approach life looking for self-contained situations with all pertinent cues and clues at hand. Rather we must encourage them to consider not only what is given but what is not given; to weigh the known against the unknown; to arrive at operational conclusions and decisions on the basis of accessible evidence, while tempering these with an awareness of the ways in which additional information might modify them; and by relating the insights and gaps in one case to the gaps and insights in another, to build up an increasingly comprehensive body of perspectives and precedents as a guide in a variety of situations, without ever reaching a point of final closure prejudicial to further learning and growth.

The cases in this book represent reported truth. The materials do not include all that anyone might wish to know about a given case; rather they include the knowledge that was available at a particular time to a key observer, decision-maker or assessor. The basic criterion for inclusion of evidence is historical. The cases characteristically involve a real problem or "forked-road" situation, calling for decisions to be made and/or conclusions to be reached; accordingly only information accessible to the decision-makers at the time of decision is presented. Interpretations and arguments for or against prospective decisions are offered only as they comprise part of the case evidence; the student must learn to weigh the subjective along with the objective. Thus we have sought neither to augment case evidence with fictitious data or information unavailable at the time, nor to remove from the evidence observations which are not strictly objective but which provide relevant shadings and overtones.

In looking at cases like these, many readers will promptly try to decide who was right and who was wrong, and what should have been done. This tendency, one which is natural and is found even in professors, makes for great interest in the events described. But it may subvert the scholarliness of one's examination of the case. In using cases in our own teaching, we have found that we had to exert ourselves constantly to get students, before passing judgment, to ask themselves the neutral questions which lead to understanding: Why did these things happen? What issues were involved? What were people's motives? What assumptions were they making? What further information would best illuminate the episode? And so on. Those interested in the editors' views about ways in which the cases in this book might be used in teaching may obtain upon request from the publisher a teacher's manual.

Since one purpose of the book is to encourage the reader to discover for himself such social aspects and concepts as social control, social change, and social class, identification of these with specific cases has been reserved for the teacher's manual. The table found on the front end paper of this book is presented as a quick guide to various topics of educational concern.

Readers interested in more extensive expositions of views about the use of cases in professional education may wish to look at two books which have emerged from the use of cases at Harvard University.

Andrews, Kenneth R., ed., *The Case Method of Teaching Human Relations and Administration.* Cambridge, Massachusetts: Harvard University Press, 1953.

Sargent, Cyril G., and Eugene L. Belisle, *Educational Administration: Cases and Concepts.* Boston: Houghton Mifflin Company, 1955.

The cases range from the more sensational to the more prosaic. Some have dramatic appeal of headline proportions; others deal with the relatively unspectacular type of problem students will later be called on to deal with all too frequently. Of course, we expect that cases exciting and absorbing to some readers will be of passing interest to others, and vice versa. In our own perusal of them, we have found that successive readings also make a difference; some cases, though we recognized their pertinence, did not really excite us until the second, third, or fourth reading. We certainly hope that wherever appropriate the reader will be encouraged to seek the same experience!

This book was conceived and began to take shape while the editors served together as staff participants in the Master of Arts in Teaching Program at Yale University. The original impetus came from a fellow participant, John S. Brubacher, who had long been a forceful advocate of the case approach to learning. In all fairness to him, we point out that this may not be the book he was waiting for, but we are grateful to him nonetheless.

This book is obviously the product of the efforts of many persons, to all of whom we are grateful. Brief though many of these accounts may seem, collecting the materials for them, writing them, and responding to the importunities of the editors proved to be much more work for the contributors than most of us had imagined. The contributors and editors alike are grateful, too, to the anonymous informants who gave us their time and their documents, as well as to the publishers who allowed us to quote copyrighted materials without giving due credit. Although the editors are responsible for the lists of Selected Readings, here too they received the help of many people. Above all we are grateful to the Yale Graduate School's Master of Arts in Teaching program of 1955–58, with whose support and under whose aegis this book was begun, and to its Director, Edward S. Noyes, now with the College Entrance Examination Board.

North Chatham, N.Y.

E. T. L.
W. C. S.

Table
of
Contents

<table>
<tr><td>CASE 1</td><td>

Rating the
Superintendent

</td></tr>
</table>

The minutes of a meeting of the city Education Association's Representative Assembly, Tuesday, February 8, 1949, included the following paragraphs.

> As a basis for a better working relationship between teachers, through the association, and the administration, the executive secretary suggested that a rating of the superintendent be made in regard to his personnel practices as they have affected the morale of the teachers.
>
> A motion was made that the executive secretary, together with a committee of his choosing, prepare and send out by mail a questionnaire addressed to each member at his home. . .
>
> The motion was seconded and carried (unanimous vote).

Thus without fanfare began a series of events testing the relations between the teachers and the Superintendent of Schools. The three months that followed saw not only a clash between the representatives of the teachers and the Superintendent, but also dissent among the teachers themselves, and quarrels involving the PTA, the newspaper, and the public at large. The unanimous decision on the part of the Representative Assembly was a last resort before open rebellion. It was

1

described not as a Declaration of Independence but rather as an ultimatum that demanded an appraisal to be used solely "to develop a better understanding between the administration and the teachers' professional organization." (Excerpt from the February 8th minutes.)

Although unanimously carried in an open meeting of the representatives of teachers from every building in the school system, the motion had not been spontaneous. It was the result of a recommendation from the Association's Board of Directors, a group which comprised eight representatives of the teachers, plus an Executive Secretary employed by them. It consisted of a president, first and second vice-presidents, a treasurer, two representatives from the elementary schools, one from the high schools, and one from the principals' and supervisors' group.

Of the 1,060 teachers in the system, 1,008—or ninety-five per cent— were members of the professional group calling itself the Education Association. The Association had a long history of collective effort to improve the profession of education. Its membership reflected the full range of qualities generally associated with pedagogues—some inspirational, some creative, some conservative, some liberal, some radical, some indifferent, some careless, some lazy, some cynical.

Representing this aggregate as its attorney, and employed as its Executive Secretary, was John Thornton. Mr. Thornton, a man in his forties, was native to the city, having received his formal undergraduate and graduate education at the city's university. He had great patience, an easy-going manner, enthusiasm for progressive ideas, tolerance of variety and even opposition, respect for the teaching profession, and courage. He was not liked by all the teachers, nor were his policies always supported by all of them. Nonetheless, his ability was such as to carry conviction to the majority.

What had brought about the unusual recommendation from the Association's Board? What did the Board hope to accomplish?

During the previous two years there had been a growing dissatisfaction among the teachers, contributing to a lowering of morale. This dissatisfaction centered more and more upon Superintendent Charles Harrison.

In the two years since his arrival in the city, Superintendent Harrison had gained a reputation for being intolerant of inefficiency. He was forceful in his administration, not always polite in his denunciations, or even in everyday parlance. He was spoken of as one not given to conferences but to monologues, sometimes to diatribes. He was often

RATING THE SUPERINTENDENT

scathing in condemnation of members of his staff. He was a tireless worker and a fearless representative for public education. He was unrelenting in the pursuit of his educational objectives.

Since his arrival Harrison had attended only one of the Education Association's business or social meetings. This had aroused considerable unfavorable comment among the teachers in the system, as had other changes attributed to him. The noon hour had been shortened; the school day had been lengthened; a new system of attendance and census reports had been introduced, adding to the teachers' work; and time had been cut down or eliminated at semester end for making out and submitting administration-required reports. Furthermore, there seemed to be unnecessary delay in arriving at salary agreements, so much so that at one time the teachers did not know what salary they would receive until the Saturday before the autumn semester began.

Harrison appeared to have no use for the Education Association, its Representative Assembly, its Board, or its Secretary. When he and the School Board revised a manual of rules and regulations for teachers, they did not ask the Association's advice or assistance. Indeed, the Superintendent organized his own "Advisory Council," composed of representatives from the schools to be elected by the teachers, stipulating that no one should be elected to it who was also elected to the Education Association's representative assembly.

During this two-year period, however, Superintendent Harrison and Mr. Thornton had worked together closely for a state amendment to give state support to the schools. Thornton had also helped in getting a higher mill levy through the state legislature. But there had been two recent examples of failure to work together. The School Board had secured the introduction of a bill in the state legislature changing the wording of the teacher tenure law. According to the new version, "indefinite contract teachers," that is, those having met all professional requirements for maintaining their positions, would have to sign annual statements of acceptance of their appointments before April 15th. Such a bill ran counter to custom and distressed the teachers under "indefinite contract." The second instance occurred when the School Board secured the introduction in the state legislature of a less acceptable retirement bill after another bill to improve retirement provisions had already been introduced at the request of the teachers.

Gradually the teachers came to say among themselves that their professional organization was to have no voice in any matter pertaining to them or to the profession itself, and that Mr. Harrison considered their elected representatives and Board *personae non gratae*. They began asking themselves what possible actions remained open to them. How could they represent their point of view to the Superintendent forcefully, clearly, and specifically, without stirring up the public to take sides in what was actually a problem entirely within the profession itself?

The city in which they worked was a mid-western city of over 200,-000. In it were two universities, one public and one private. The population consisted of persons of many national origins, including Slavs, Germans, Scandinavians, English, and Italians. Its economy was based on agriculture, mostly food processing and meat packing. It had neither great wealth nor widespread poverty. It had little to attract tourists to visit or the youth to remain. It was not a union city, nor was it opposed to unions. Historically, it had been a frontier town, a railroad center, agricultural hub, and eventually a minor military center. Its cultural predilections could be assessed by the fact that legitimate theater companies from New York played one-night stands, while rodeo and ice shows played a week or more. However, by dint of much cooperative enterprise there were a symphony orchestra and an amateur community theater. At that time school salaries were near the bottom of the scale for the forty-eight states: 1947, minimum $1,260, maximum $2,790; 1949, minimum $2,340, maximum $3,780.

Within a week after the unanimous vote of the Representative Assembly authorizing the Executive Secretary to draw up a questionnaire rating the Superintendent, the Elementary School Principals' Club, by majority vote, resolved as follows:

> We respectfully request the members of the Association Board and Assembly to reconsider their decision to ask members of said organization to "rate" the Superintendent of Schools.

In transmitting this request to the Association, the Elementary Principals' Club gave as reasons the belief that such action would fail to promote a better relationship between teachers and the administration, would result in serious differences of opinion among the Association members, and would expose the profession to unfavorable public opinion. The Board met with the officers of the Elementary Principals' Club, and the two groups agreed to abide by the results of a referendum sent to all members of the Association.

A letter was written explaining that approval by a majority with regard to appraising the Superintendent was desired before the Association and its Board went ahead with a questionnaire. A copy of the letter was sent with a ballot to each member. The ballot asked simply, "Are you in favor of the proposed appraisal of the Superintendent?" with space for a "Yes" or a "No" mark. The returns indicated that a decisive majority wished to go ahead with the appraisal. However, the Elementary Principals' Club and its president continued to criticize the appraisal plan and to try to organize opposition to it.

Although members of the Association's Board issued no reports to the newspaper, the issue became publicized, and people outside the profession began taking sides.

The city's newspaper began to publish items concerning the proposed appraisal. On February 24, 1949, the paper wrote:

> . . . Public school teachers Thursday were deciding whether to 'grade' their Superintendent. . .
>
> Some teachers have found fault . . . because of pension legislation which he favored. The measure would have given teachers smaller pensions than they are seeking, but would have eased the pension load on the . . . taxpayers.

The President of the School Board was quoted as comparing the rating to one which school children might give their teachers, and saying it would mean as much. In a letter published in the newspaper, a high school department chairman rebutted the School Board President's remark, calling it "insulting" to liken the intelligent opinion of the teachers to that of children, and describing the President's comments as being in "poor taste" coming from a man in his position.

The Council of Parents and Teachers, which included no teachers, but whose vice-president was an elementary school principal, sent a letter to the President of the Education Association over the signature of its own President, requesting answers in writing to the following questions:

> 1. What policies of the Superintendent have proven detrimental to the educational progress of the children?

2. What specific policies are against teacher welfare?
3. What use is to be made of the rating sheets?

The PTA Council asked for a reply within six days.
Within two days the Association President replied:

> . . . We are not privileged to answer your questions about the appraisal of our superintendent's personnel policies and practices. We have felt that our purpose could best be accomplished for all concerned by keeping this matter confidential within the profession.
>
> We have not released any publicity about it and if any of our members as individuals have discussed the matter with you or your council they have had no authority to do so. . .

Another newspaper story gave publicity to the President of the Council of the PTA, who claimed the great majority of its membership favored the Superintendent. A letter from the Council, read before the School Board meeting of April 4th, expressed appreciation for the Superintendent's program. The article quoted her as saying, "That was our way of telling the . . . Education Association we didn't like its appraisal. . ."

Some persons opposing the appraisal wrote letters to the Education Association Board calling the appraisal "disloyal, unwise, and presumptuous action," or saying, "For God's sake, why don't you grow up?"

However, the appraisal form was worked out and on or about April 8th was mailed to the members of the Education Association. With it went a letter stating that "every effort has been made to keep this appraisal on a high professional level." A return envelope stamped and addressed to the Education Association's downtown office was supplied, since many teachers had reported that their principals might use coercive or repressive measures against any teacher known to favor the appraisal. The form is given below.

Appraisal of Administrative Practices

> Teachers do not want to run the school. All they ask is that when there is a question that concerns their work, they be consulted about it and given an opportunity to express their disapproval or their acceptance of it. In short, they want to be felt as personalities in their places, not robots. And that is

not too much to ask in a democracy.—NEA's *Democracy in School Administration*, December, 1948

This appraisal of the superintendent's personnel policies and practices is being made in an attempt to help the Education Association develop a better understanding of a practical working relationship between the superintendent and the teachers through their local organization.

This action comes as the result of two years of increasing unrest among teachers. Many groups and individuals have registered complaints with the EA office which show that teachers have felt driven and insecure in their jobs.

Constant repetition of the same complaints indicate that this feeling stems for the most part from two sources: first, the introduction and changes of policies which have been put into effect without due regard for the opinions of the people those policies affect; and second, the confusion and uncertainty in the minds of the teachers as to what part teachers and their welfare actually have in the superintendent's program for developing and maintaining good schools.

This appraisal is divided into three main areas. At the beginning of each there is a general statement on which you are asked to express your opinion. Under each general statement there are substatements so that your appraisal may also be directed toward specific points.

Two factors will determine whether this appraisal can accomplish its purpose: 1) the returns must represent the opinion of a large number of the profession, and 2) each individual opinion must be the result of honest and unbiased consideration.

Since we are not interested in individual opinions except as they contribute to a group profile, it will not be necessary for you to sign your name.

Please use the five-point scale—1, 2, 3, 4, 5. 1 will designate that the superintendent's personnel policies and practices are highly superior. 3 is considered average. 5 will designate that they are undesirable. Circle the number that best represents your opinion of the point under consideration.

I PROFESSIONAL LEADERSHIP

Local, state, and national education associations have always been principally concerned with the improvement of education for children through raising the standards of the profession and working to make it attractive to the best type of teacher.

1. To what degree does your superintendent show
leadership in working for these general objectives?   1 2 3 4 5

The EA is concerned with the problems of securing adequate tenure, retirement, sick leave, salary, and a reasonable teacher load.

To what degree do you feel that your superintendent shows leadership in working for:

2. Adequate sick leave   1 2 3 4 5
3. Adequate retirement benefits   1 2 3 4 5
4. Adequate tenure   1 2 3 4 5
5. Adequate salary schedule   1 2 3 4 5
6. Reasonable teacher load   1 2 3 4 5

II DEMOCRATIC ADMINISTRATION

It is the intent of the administration that the assumption of the responsibility and the transmission of suggestions for the improvement in the operation of
schools shall be a two-way relationship. It is the
function of a teacher, a clerk, a custodian, or a staff
member, in a democratic organization to make his
recommendations to as well as to receive instructions
from the central office. This two-way interchange and
flow of recommendations and suggestions for the improvement of the schools is the responsibility of the
whole staff.—City Public Schools, *Handbook*
(1948), p. 2

7. How successful in actual practice is this "two-
way interchange and flow of recommendations
and suggestions"?   1 2 3 4 5

To what degree do you feel that the democratic
procedure—"this two-way interchange and flow of
recommendations"—was used in these changes of
policies and practices:

8. Lowering educational qualifications for teachers
entering the system   1 2 3 4 5
9. Lengthening the school day for teachers   1 2 3 4 5
10. Shortening the noon hour for teachers   1 2 3 4 5
11. Introducing a new system of attendance and
census reports which add to teacher load   1 2 3 4 5
12. Cutting down or eliminating time at the end
of the semester for making reports   1 2 3 4 5

13. Introducing changes in legislation which affect
teachers   1 2 3 4 5
14. Introducing changes in curriculum   1 2 3 4 5

> In order that such a two-way flow of administrative
> suggestions may function, an advisory council of
> teachers organized for the purpose, will meet as
> often as necessary to consider the general administra-
> tive and supervisory problems of the Public Schools.
> —City Public Schools, *Handbook* (1948), p. 2

15. How successful is the advisory council in maintaining a "two-way flow of administrative sugges-
tions"?   1 2 3 4 5

III PERSONNEL PRACTICES

The greatest asset of any school system is a cheerful, optimistic, and
enthusiastic staff. The superintendent, more than anyone else, is
responsible for creating and maintaining this spirit.
16. How successful is your superintendent in cre-
ating and maintaining high morale?   1 2 3 4 5

Judging from the information that you have received from such
sources as the Superintendent's Bulletin, the Handbook, committee
meetings, building meetings, the advisory council, and from personal
contact, what impression have you received of your superintendent
in regard to these particular qualities as they affect his personnel practices (the first four items have been adapted from the scale on which
teachers are rated)?

Sympathetic Understanding
17. He is approachable, friendly, and obviously
sincere and understanding in his dealings with
teachers.   1 2 3 4 5

Emotional Stability
18. Calm and even-tempered, he shows poise and
maturity of action under most circumstances. He
responds well to criticism.   1 2 3 4 5

Judgment and Tact
19. He senses probable outcomes of situations and
makes reliable decisions. He works among teachers
without arousing resentment. He promotes understanding rather than antagonism by knowing what
to do and say at the right time.   1 2 3 4 5

Cooperation and Dependability
20. He works well with others. Whether leader or
follower, he carries his full share of responsibility.
He is reliable and finishes what he begins.   1 2 3 4 5

Loyalty and Trust
21. He is able to inspire loyalty and confidence in
his staff; he shows that he has faith in them.   1 2 3 4 5

Delegating Authority
22. He delegates responsibility to individuals or
committees and accepts their recommendations.   1 2 3 4 5

Working Conditions
23. The providing of pleasant working conditions
and adequate equipment do much toward developing high teacher morale. He strives to provide
pleasant, well-lighted classrooms and other modern
facilities.   1 2 3 4 5

Books and Supplies
24. He strives to provide the best textbooks and
supplies available for the various departments of
the schools.   1 2 3 4 5

IV ADDITIONAL APPRAISAL OR COMMENTS

1. _____   1 2 3 4 5
2. _____   1 2 3 4 5
3. _____   1 2 3 4 5

Mr. Thornton did not give a copy of the questionnaire to the press.
Nevertheless, the local newspaper printed on the front page an excerpt
from it, and beside it a story in which Harrison was quoted as calling
it "blackmail" but as saying that he was perfectly willing to be rated.
"I'm rated every day by the community and the School Board. My
record will stand up."

The following day the newspaper quoted members of the School
Board:

. . . I can't understand it . . . I have the highest personal and
professional regard for him.

. . . We ought to put a stop to it (the appraisal).

They (the teachers) are very foolish. . .

I don't like this rating at all. It may mean that salary negotiations will bog down. If we can't have harmony with the teachers, we can't have harmony in the classroom.

. . . Mr. Harrison should not be subject to this personal attack. If the Association members have any grievance, they should submit it to the School Board and not try to undermine the school organization by such political tactics.

Typical of the negative comments on the appraisal was the comment by the President of the Elementary Principals' Club: "His fine work here certainly doesn't merit any appraisal."

On April 12, 1949, there appeared a lead editorial in both morning and evening editions of the city's newspaper. An excerpt follows:

For years . . . school principals have "rated" the teachers who serve under them. The principals indicate the qualities in which they believe the teachers are satisfactory or superior, and those in which they could improve. The method is intended to give the teacher an objective appraisal of her teaching skills, and to help her "grow." The "rating" system, used in many cities, is considered a valuable tool in improving the quality of teaching.

A willful group that appears to be in control of . . . an organization of teachers, last week seized upon and perverted the "rating" method in a sort of guerrilla war on Superintendent Harrison. . .

The guerrilla war apparently stems from the fact that Mr. Harrison as executive officer for the Board of Education, has undertaken to carry out the Board's decisions and policies, and has not adopted and fought for all of the demands of the Education Association's ruling clique in matters of salaries, sick leaves, pensions, etc. . . . .

On all possible grounds the "rating" is preposterous. To begin with, most of the teachers do not know Mr. Harrison well enough to "rate" him; they can depend only on hearsay. More, the "rating" system was never intended to be reversed. Teachers, for example, are not asked to "rate" their principals, nor are children called upon to "rate" their teachers. . .

Precisely what the . . . . clique proposes to accomplish by its "rating" is not quite clear. It has been suggested that, when the results have been compiled, a secret committee will wait upon the Superintendent and inform him of his weaknesses. Such effrontery would never be tolerated in any private organization, and it ought not to be tolerated in the schools.

That same day at a special meeting the School Board offered Harrison a new three-year contract increasing his salary one thousand dollars each year, from $12,000 to an eventual $15,000. The Board adopted a resolution of "implicit confidence" in his "abilities, judgment, loyalty, integrity and leadership." The Executive Secretary of the Education Association expressed his congratulations, adding, "I have great respect for him. There have never been any personal differences between us." Harrison declined the offer for "personal" reasons, at least for several days. A short time thereafter he accepted it.

In a letter sent to all members of the teaching staff, the Board of Education stated that it was unanimously opposed to the appraisal of the Superintendent. It said that the appraisal was "a personal attack upon the Superintendent of Schools and an effort to discredit the Superintendent and this Board" which "can only result in increased confusion and uncertainty in the minds of the people."

> The Board directs attention to the fact that ten of the first fifteen questions in the "Appraisal" are directed at policies and practices of this Board of Education, not policies and practices of the Superintendent. The others are outgrowths of the application of policies and practices approved by this Board.

The letter stated that Point 10 falsely implied that the Superintendent had caused the noon hour for teachers to be shortened, whereas he had simply enforced a Board rule made long before he was hired. Point 11 similarly dealt with the enforcing of a state statute concerning attendance and census reports made prior to the Superintendent's arrival, and adding $52,000 to the schools' income. Point 13, changing of legislation affecting teachers, the Board claimed to have had done under its own direction.

> In respect to Point 14, we direct attention to the fact that no curriculum changes have been made except after and upon recommendations of committees of teachers and principals.
> . . . We have found a very considerable body of opinion, on the part of many responsible people whose judgment is not to be dis-

carded lightly, that there has been a deliberate, subversive effort, on the part of a small coterie dominating . . . policies and practices, to create unrest among teachers and undermine their morale.

The letter continued by stating that the Education Association tried, "rather futilely, for over a decade to increase the income of the public schools so as to make possible better salaries," but did not succeed until Harrison "gave intelligent and experienced direction to the community's efforts." It mentioned the increases in salary already given, but expressed doubt as to the justice of automatic increments to teachers "without any provision for rewarding excellence and achievement and without regard to individual differences in ability, effort, cooperation, understanding and loyalty—a salary schedule in which attitude is immaterial."

We sincerely believe that the vast majority of you are loyal, reliable, responsible people of mature judgment, devoted to your work and motivated by the highest purposes. We believe that most of you are professionally minded, and have concern for the dignity, honor and efficiency of your great profession. To all such we give our assurance that our faith in you continues, and that the "Appraisal" action of the Education Association will not be used against you.

The newspaper gave considerable space to reporting the School Board's letter.

The Education Association Board wrote a rejoinder and mailed it to its members. It was much shorter. It reminded the members that the Representative Assembly and the Board had acted only after numerous complaints had been registered to them, that it had polled its membership and acted after a decisive majority had voted in favor of appraising the Superintendent's administrative and personnel practices, and that it had always maintained dignity and decorum by not publicizing its activities with respect to the appraisal. It reminded the membership that only their unity had made possible such gains as those mentioned by the School Board.

There should be little question in any . . . member's mind about the accomplishments of the organization during the past few years. Every gain has come through the hard work of the total group working

together. Who does not remember the fight for the single salary schedule? The many campaigns to raise the mill levy? The Saturday mornings the teachers spent at the courthouse examining tax records, the
beginning of a movement that has increased tax valuations which now
bring in more than a $1,000,000 additional revenue each year. Who
does not remember the battle in 1943 to get teacher tenure which for
the first time guaranteed, under state law, security for the teacher?

. . . As long as members of the Education Association stick together, we can continue to make gains for the improvement of the
city's schools.

The Board of the Education Association wrote a letter to the School
Board saying it desired to discuss the problem frankly with it, since it
appeared that the School Board "failed completely to give any recognition to the problem that the . . . association is trying to solve,"
namely, that for more than thirty years the Education Association had
been the official representative of the teachers, but apparently now was
deemed by the Superintendent not to be.

Unusual significance was now being attached to the forthcoming
election of officers and members of the Education Association's Board
of Directors, scheduled to take place in May.

"In accordance with a constitutional provision of the . . . Education Association, the following teachers filed in person for election."
Thus began a letter sent out on April 15th to all members of the staff;
a slate of candidates for the eight elective positions followed. "It was
inevitable," the letter went on to say, "that the ill-advised appraisal
action" would divide the membership and threaten the survival of the
organization. The "expected reaction" had come when more than fifty
members had gathered, effected an organization, defined purposes, and
collected money "for a more professional concept" of the purpose of
the Education Association.

The letter continued as follows:

We repudiate the leadership of the present Education Association
Board because it has—
    —failed to define clearly the problem of which it complained.
    —violated the confidence of the membership by its unprofes-
    sional approach to the alleged problem.
    —allowed personal differences to endanger the unity and the best

interests of the teaching staff.

–jeopardized gains made by the Education Association over a long period of negotiations with the Board of Education.

We affirm our support of both a rededicated Education Association and the forementioned candidates who have pledged themselves upon election—

–to serve diligently the best interests of the Education Association membership by conducting full and free discussion of any contemplated action involving the prestige and welfare of the whole group.

–to restore the confidence of the community in the professional quality of its teaching staff through a positive educational program.

–to work for an informed membership.

–to promote unity of purpose among all who would improve the welfare of teachers and educational opportunity for the children. . .

The letter ended, "Your support of this move is earnestly solicited in the election, May 3."

As the election approached, the Board of Directors of the Education Association agreed that it should nominate candidates representing a favorable attitude toward the appraisal, since the present Board had been responsible for its conception and circulation to the teachers. (In accordance with the Board's original intention, no results of the questionnaire had been made public either to the membership or at large.) The Constitution of the Association prevented the incumbent President from succeeding himself. The person nominated for that office was the high school journalism instructor and English department head who had called "insulting" the School Board President's likening the teachers' rating the Superintendent to children's rating their teachers. Two more were nominated in addition to five members of the present Board. For all practical purposes the slate was as definitely pro-appraisal as the opposition was anti-appraisal. The opposition had chosen the name "Professional Unity" for their ticket. The pro-appraisal candidates called themselves the "Loyalty Ticket."

On April 30th the "Professional Unity" slate sent out a second letter and sample ballot, addressed—as was the first—from the addressograph in the offices of the Board of Education. It spoke of the "mis-

sion" of the slate and asked the electorate to weigh the issues "thought-
fully" before voting. It asserted that "public confidence must be regained," and that no slate created by the present Association Board
"could negotiate successfully with the Board of Education in the face
of public opinion."

The Association Board has drawn overwhelming rebuke from the
Board of Education, the PTA, the general public—the very people
who hold the power of decision for teachers.

Second, a positive, constructive program must be revived by the
Education Association. . .

Third, desirable gains for teachers and pupils must be pressed fear-
lessly and unitedly.

The election took place on May 3rd. The next morning's newspaper
headlined the election of the pro-appraisal slate. In the largest vote in
the history of the Association, with 967 of the 1,008 members voting,
the results were as follows:

	Pro-appraisal	Anti-appraisal
President	817	141
1st Vice-President	784	171
2nd Vice-President	752	187
Treasurer	763	167
Grade Schools' Representatives (2)	491	97
	470	98
High Schools' Representative	259	37
Principals' and Supervisor's Group	54	5

What about the appraisal itself? What had it revealed? How would
it be used? Would the results interest the Superintendent?

True to its purpose from the beginning, the Association Board and
its Executive Secretary never released the results of the poll to the
press. It maintained that its own purposes were best served by treating
the problem as one strictly within the educational profession. However, a graph of the results was constructed. Later, after the end of the
spring term, when the hue and cry had subsided, the Executive Secretary met with Superintendent Harrison and showed him the results,
which are reproduced on pp. 17–19.

It would not be correct to say that Harrison made an about-face in

Question 1: To what degree does your superintendent show leadership in working for these general objectives?

Question 2: Adequate sick leave

Question 3: Adequate retirement benefits

Question 4: Adequate tenure

Question 5: Adequate salary schedule

Question 6: Reasonable teacher load

Question 7: How successful is this two-way interchange and flow of recommendations and suggestions'?

Question 8: Lowering educational qualifications for teachers entering the system

Question 9: Lengthening the school day for teachers

Question 10: Shortening the noon hour for teachers

Question 11: Introducing a new system of attendance and census reports which add to teacher load

Question 12: Cutting down or eliminating time at the end of the semester for making reports

Question 13: Introducing changes in legislation which affect teachers

Question 14: Introducing changes in curriculum

Question 15: How successful is the advisory council in maintaining a 'two-way flow of administrative suggestions'?

Question 16: How successful is your superintendent in creating and maintaining high morale?

18

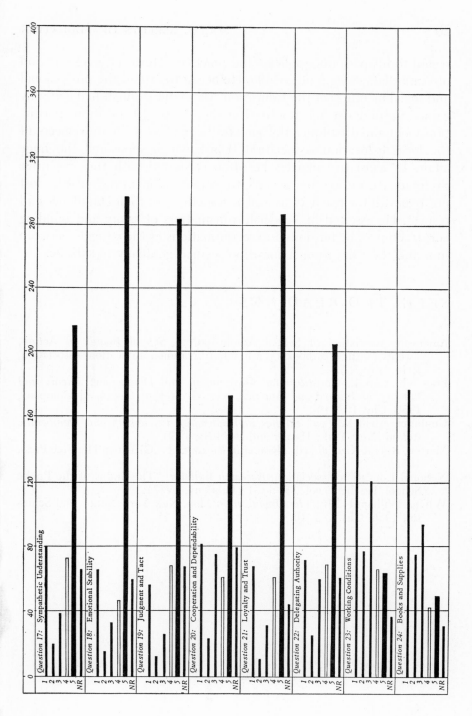

regard to his personnel policies and practices. However, over a period of years changes were noticeable. He began to attend the professional and social meetings of the Education Association, which had certainly gained in solidarity and resolve. For the National Education Association Centennial banquet the Superintendent sat with the officers of the local Education Association Board, which sponsored the huge affair. In legislative matters he often conferred with the Executive Secretary. According to observers, the Superintendent regained his lost prestige with the teachers, as well as something of their confidence and respect. He asserted his leadership in matters of salary and building construction. The tensions and recriminations of the struggle between him and the Education Association seemed gradually to subside.

SELECTED READINGS

American Association of School Administrators, *School Boards in Action,* Twenty-fourth Yearbook. Washington: National Education Association, 1946. Chs. 3, 5.

Friedrich, Carl J., *Constitutional Government and Democracy: Theory and Practice in Europe and America,* rev. ed. Boston: Ginn and Company, 1950. Chs. 1–2, 19.

Gouldner, Alvin W., ed., *Studies in Leadership: Leadership and Democratic Action.* New York: Harper and Brothers, 1950.

Merton, Robert K., et al., eds., *Reader in Bureaucracy.* Glencoe: The Free Press, 1952.

National Education Association, *Research Bulletin,* "The Status of the Public School Teacher," vol. 35, no. 1 (February, 1957).

Whyte, William H., Jr., *The Organization Man.* New York: Simon and Schuster, 1956. Chs. 1–5, 10.

CASE **2**

The
North Hanford
Case

At a public, bipartisan, political forum on Thursday, October 3, 1957, candidates for election to the North Hanford Board of Education heard the president of the Taxpayers Association,[1] a Mr. F. Donofrio, declare that Leo Wolf, a junior high school science teacher, was a subversive. Mr. Donofrio read, from a 1955 *New York Times* news clipping, statements to the effect that Wolf had "taken the fifth" before an investigating committee when accused of being at that time the national director of the Labor Youth League, an allegedly communist organization.

The candidates one after another pledged themselves, if elected, to be in favor of having Wolf removed from the school system if he were a subversive.

On Friday, October 4, 1957, Wolf, whom a nearby school system had turned down for "political reasons," admitted to a reporter that he had been a communist party member. He claimed that prior to his appointment as a teacher in the school system he had discussed the matter fully with the Superintendent of Schools. Wolf said he knew

---

[1] The Taxpayers Association was composed of four people: Mr. and Mrs. Donofrio, a widowed banker, and the wife of a service station operator. Through the device of a printed letterhead they were able to solicit information from various sources, including the Subversive Activities Control Board.

21

it would be a problem and "wanted to keep it in the open in order to retain his self-respect." One newspaper, *The Urban Herald*, printed immediately a front page story about Wolf as an "alleged Communist."

On Sunday, October 6th, one day prior to the election, leaflets were found under the windshield wipers of cars in North Hanford. The leaflets carried pro-Democratic Party statements and presented questions concerning the management of the school system by the Republican-dominated Board of Education.

NORTH HANFORD VOTERS

ARE OUR CHILDREN BEING SUBJECTED TO COMMUNISM??

It was disclosed at the Public Forum held on Thursday, October 3, 1957, in the North Hanford Junior High that the Board of Education had hired LEO WOLF as a science teacher in the North Hanford School System. WOLF, it was disclosed, was a prime mover in the LABOR YOUTH LEAGUE—A RED FRONT ORGANIZATION. According to a *New York Times* news release of February 16, 1955, (page 16) which stated:

> "The LABOR YOUTH LEAGUE was organized in Chicago on May 28, and 29, 1949. A prime mover was LEO WOLF of New York. The Subversive Activity Control Board said he was NATIONAL YOUTH DIRECTOR OF THE COMMUNIST PARTY at the time. He became NATIONAL CHAIRMAN of the League and still holds that position."

MR. WOLF was the teacher who was hired to replace the teacher displaced by the board.

We, the Democratic Party demand to know:

1. Why didn't the school board investigate this teacher before hiring him?
2. What are the Board's policies on hiring teachers?
3. What are the reasons the Board dismissed the teacher WOLF displaced?
4. Why did First Selectman Hallson claim the "North Hanford School System is Rotten"?
5. Why did the Superintendent of Schools declare he would assume all responsibilities on hiring WOLF?

6. Why did Mr. Gail, the former Chairman of the Board of Education, ask the members of the Board to take an oath of secrecy concerning WOLF?

7. How long do we have to subject our children to an EDUCATION of the type that is now being offered by the BOARD OF EDUCATION?

We, the DEMOCRATIC PARTY, hereby pledge to add the following to our platform:

"THREE: TO PURGE THE NORTH HANFORD SCHOOL SYSTEM OF COMMUNISTIC AND SUBVERSIVE INFLUENCES."

VOTE FOR THE PARTY WITH A PLATFORM

OUR CHILDREN NEED OUR VOTE

OCTOBER 7TH—6 A. M. to 6 P. M.

VOTE DEMOCRATIC   PULL TOP LEVER

Many residents, as well as Board of Education members, reported receiving anonymous telephone calls late Sunday night. They were accused of being pro-communist if they aided Wolf in his scheme to "foul the tender minds of children." The callers were never identified.

On Sunday afternoon the Board of Education met in secret session to draft a letter to the State Board of Education asking that Wolf's temporary emergency certificate be revoked.

On Election Day, Monday, October 7th, at 2 p.m., the principal of the school handed Wolf a letter indicating that he was temporarily suspended. Three reasons were given for the action. First, it would serve the best interests of the school; second, it would serve the best interests of Leo Wolf as a person; third, it would allow an investigation to begin. Mrs. Wolf had previously learned of her husband's suspension on a noon radio news broadcast. Upon telephoning her husband, she discovered he had not yet learned of it. She stated that the radio news reporter asserted that the State Police were on the scene and investigating.

On Monday afternoon, after school, two thirteen-year-old girls circulated a petition seeking Wolf's reinstatement. That night the father of one of the girls reported anonymous calls asking him if he knew his daughter was "trying to help that Communist."

In the election that day the Democratic candidate supported by Mr.

Donofrio and the Taxpayers Association was defeated. With four Republicans and two Democrats having been elected, the composition of the Board of Education remained the same. (The state law provided that not more than four of the six might belong to one party.)

*   *   *   *   *

A month earlier, before school had opened, the bi-partisan Board of Education, meeting in executive session, had given unanimous approval for Wolf's appointment to the school system. They had written him a letter wishing him "every success in teaching." The Superintendent of Schools had told Wolf privately that his prior membership in the Communist Party would probably be less of a handicap in his adjustment to the community than the fact that he was a Jew. The Superintendent had not known at the time of appointment that Wolf had been a member of the Communist Party as recently as 1955. He had told Wolf that there might be "rough politics" during the fall, but that he should "just do your work in the classroom and the job is yours." Wolf had been appointed to teach general science and mathematics.

On October 15th the state chapter of the American Civil Liberties Union sent the following statement to the North Hanford Board of Education.

STATE CIVIL LIBERTIES UNION
AN AFFILIATE OF THE AMERICAN CIVIL LIBERTIES UNION

October 15, 1957

To the North Hanford Board of Education:

This is about the case of Leo Wolf, consideration of which was postponed, at your prolonged meeting on Oct. 14, to Oct. 16. After observing your careful deliberation of other matters at the Oct. 14 meeting, I am persuaded that, if you considered this case with equal detachment, you would reinstate Mr. Wolf, and proceed no further toward terminating his contract.

Our state has been singularly free of the excesses of anti-Communism. Repressive legislation of all sorts has been avoided, and our teachers have not been subject to the humiliation of special oaths and investigations. Does this mean that we in this state are "soft on Communism"? Certainly not; it means that we understand the weakness of its evil doctrines in the face of democratic teachings and examples.

It was in this spirit, I am sure, that your predecessors on the Board acted in deciding to employ Mr. Wolf. If the material facts about his past Communist connections and his present position were laid before your Superintendent, and if, advised by him, your Board first made and later confirmed this appointment, you should be commended, and not condemned. You will have given Mr. Wolf an opportunity to redeem himself, and to fill a useful place in the community. This is an admirable way of demonstrating, to our school children and indeed to the world at large, the precepts of charity and of neighborliness that we would like to guide our lives, in contrast to the ruthless brutality of totalitarian systems.

Suppose, on the other hand, that you give way to the pressures that have been put upon you, by people who unthinkingly ignore these precepts, and that you take steps to dismiss Mr. Wolf. What legal cause can you establish? Unless he made material misrepresentations to your agents, I suggest that you have none. His past Communist connections do not disqualify him, especially since your Board knew about them. His resort to the Fifth Amendment before an investigating committee in 1955 does not disqualify him; this is clear from recent decisions of the Supreme Court. You may say that, good cause or not, passions have been stirred by this episode, so you will simply break the contract and expose yourselves to a lawsuit. This would be a poor example of law-abiding conduct to hold up before your children.

The honorable course for your Board is to live up to your contracts and your responsibilities. Those responsibilities include providing a competent science teacher for your junior high school, and science teachers are hard to find. Give yourself an opportunity to appraise Mr. Wolf's performance in that post. Tell your critics the reasons for your actions; then stick to your guns. Point out to them that all of us would like to see the miserable remnant of Communist followers in this country change their allegiance. But what hope do we offer these people, if, on escaping the nightmare of communism, they find that the free world is also a nightmare?

Sincerely yours,

Ralph B. Washington
Chairman

On Thursday, October 17th, *The Suburban Weekly* carried this front page story:

Accused Teacher Says:

"POLITICS CAUSE OF SUSPENSION"
INVESTIGATION NOT YET STARTED

North Hanford—"I have been completely truthful and frank at every stage, from beginning to end. In fact, there has not been a single charge against me nor any accusation against my integrity and I firmly believe I would be teaching today if it were not for the recent election campaign." This was the statement of Leo Wolf, suspended science teacher at the North Hanford Junior High School, to a Weekly reporter this week. Thus, Wolf, whose situation continues as a major topic of conversation in this area, condemns the action taken recently as little more than a political maneuver. Wolf was suspended October 7 (election day) by the North Hanford Board of Education following the charge by F. Donofrio, at a public political forum, that the teacher had been closely aligned with Communist youth activities and had taken the Fifth Amendment as recently as 1955.

It has been reported in other papers that Wolf was suspended pending the outcome of an investigation. However, a representative of the State Department of Education said Tuesday, "This department does not enter into a local matter until either party (the teacher or the local board) makes an official request for some action."

The State Police Department said, also on Tuesday, "We have nothing to say and know nothing about the case at all." A check with the Brooke barracks of the State Police revealed that no such investigation is underway.

Meanwhile, at the meeting held Monday of the Board of Education, other matters were considered. Action on the Wolf case was postponed.

The previous evening, however, October 16th, the Board of Education had met again. It had been told the results of its communication to the State Department of Education: Since North Hanford had never in the first place asked for even a temporary emergency certificate for Wolf, he apparently held no valid certificate, and no certificate could be revoked. (The State Board of Education was not otherwise involved, since its policy, while not allowing the appointment of current members of the Communist Party as teachers, did permit the appointment of ex-communists.)

At this meeting the Board had then voted officially to dismiss Wolf from the school system.

*   *   *   *   *

North Hanford was a rural suburb. It was perched on a ridge, fifteen miles from a moderately large (170,000) industrial-educational urban center and eight miles from a small (20,000), very old (1636) shore town in New England. Over half of the 3,000 people in North Hanford lived and worked in the small community; the others commuted to the urban center.

A drive through the village revealed a few stores and four churches. Eight bright yellow school busses could be seen parked around and in the barns of Williams Brothers Farms; three hot-rod stock car racers were parked across the street.

Bond issues for schools and other civic improvements were notoriously unsuccessful in North Hanford. It was dubbed by a new resident as "the realm of cesspools, carpools, and country schools."

But the community was changing. Its population grew an estimated 50 per cent—from 2,000 to 3,000—in one year. The percentage of college graduates was rising. A turnpike recently completed was expected to swell the number of commuters even more.

Leo Wolf had been born into a family of working people five years before the stock market crash of 1929. During the Depression both his father and his mother had been members of the Communist Party. His first and dominant impression of social ills came, he said, when he was eight years old during the 1930's, as his father was being severely beaten by police during a strike. Leo never knew a time when he was not a Communist by family affiliation. When he left the party in 1955, he said, "I cannot do a complete about-face and reject all of Communism. That would mean rejecting my father and mother completely. My father is not an ogre; he is no beast; he is a timid man."

Leo Wolf worked his way through college and earned a B.S. in chemistry. He worked as a research chemist in a tire factory and was judged by his superior to be doing satisfactory work. He was told, however, that if his communist affiliation was ever exposed, he would lose his job. When this in fact happened in 1955, Wolf decided he might like to try to become a teacher.

Warned against education courses as an undergraduate, Wolf had never prepared himself to teach. He learned that the shortage of teachers, and of science teachers particularly, might make it possible for him to qualify for a teaching post with a temporary emergency teaching certificate.

Wolf went to summer school and took twelve hours of work in education. He did well as a student, making three A's and one B. He said he was particularly challenged by a graduate course in educational psychology. Given a choice between the typical question-and-answer final examination or writing "A Defensible Concept of Teaching," Wolf took the latter and wrote the following on his final examination paper.

The Challenge of Teaching
by Leo Wolf

My concept of teaching is one that requires defense: first, because it will be attacked from a variety of quarters; second, because I have tried to make it economical, not seeking to answer every anticipated objection so that the central ideas are blurred and it falls of its own weight.

The objective of teaching should be: To awaken the individual to his full potential for learning, searching out and helping to provide for those experiences that will best equip the learner for constructively changing himself and his environment.

Rather than spell this out in all directions, I will submit its worth as a concept or definition to several tests.

1. Does it in fact clash with, and thus exclude, other concepts of teaching which I would consider negative? Does it arouse any opposition or can it mean all things to all men, and therefore nothing to anyone?

a) This concept rules out, in my opinion, behaviorist approaches to education. Its emphasis is on cognition, awareness, understanding, not on reaction a la the whole range of associationist, stimulus response theories. Its emphasis is on the potential for learning of the individual, not on subject matter in a narrow sense. It rejects the idea that the purpose of teaching is to "impart knowledge." Its concept of learning is through experience, not by virtue of repetitive drill.

b) This definition also challenges what appears to me to be a very prevalent defeatist conception toward the job of the teacher. It would be attacked by many teachers whose outlook on teaching really is help-lessness; those who claim that the teacher is hemmed in by impossible obstacles and resign themselves to a view of teaching as a secure job which one can settle into for the better part of a lifetime. (If I do not go into this here, it is for lack of time.) While it may be argued that this attitude of resignation and cynicism should not be graced by regarding it as a "concept," my guess is that the dead weight of these ideas and the conditions that generate them is a more negative factor than any particular behaviorist or traditional approach to learning. In fact this is the inevitable path of least resistance leading to the mechanical clinging to status-quo, outmoded drill methods.

c) The concept I favor will also, I hope, be attacked by those who place the main emphasis of teaching on "adjustment," those who see the job as one of helping every individual "find his place in society." These critics would be very suspicious of my use of the word "change" —"changing himself and his environment." There! You see! The early behaviorists also speak of changing the individual rather than helping him to find himself; they believe the job of education is to "drive the animal out" so that the human can emerge.

But this, of course, is not my concept of change. Wherever learning takes place change occurs both in the individual and his environment. Perhaps, under some circumstances, behavior is modified in the direction of adjustment. But that is not and should not necessarily always be the case—and certainly it is not the chief aim of education. The history of progress is a history of struggle against "common sense" and against "adjustment," for the weight of society is generally against new ideas and for conformity. It might be said that those who speak glibly of "adjustment" and make that an end in itself have more in common with behaviorism (as to ends, not means) than I. The behaviorist squeezes the learner into a rigid mold; the "adjuster for adjustment's sake" guides the learner toward a contour mattress. But the result is conformity and the failure to awake the individual to his full potential for learning and for change. In fact, it can be said that in the extreme, adjustment negates learning because it seems to minimize the element of frustration. . . .

2. Is my concept in harmony with modern scientific views on the learning process, or does it contradict them?

In my opinion, it is in harmony. The emphasis on learning through experience has already been mentioned.

Nor does it contradict the concept of needs as essential to learning. The individual's awakening to his full potential for learning is, in a sense, a process of awareness of his personal and social needs and the never ending assertion of new needs. If needs are the motor of learning, then the individual's "horse power" for learning is an awareness of needs. Probably the most challenging thing in teaching is the realization that you are helping to arouse consciousness of needs and even contributing to the process of growth toward new needs.

The principle of parsimony is expressly stated in my concept ("best equip") and, of course, a recognition of retentivity and sensitivity is implied here. The stronger the need and the individual's thirst for learning, the more developed (within limits) would be the characteristics of retentivity and sensitivity.

Above all, my concept does not limit itself to intellective factors, for if the sights are set on the full potential of the individual rather than on the narrow subject matter, this presupposes created [sic] the best atmosphere and emotional environment for learning.

Time does not permit a discussion of each aspect of the learning process. But it would seem to me that the realization of the objectives I have indicated, requires differentation of process and achievement, an understanding of the learning curve in respect to maximum and minimum potential for any given learning experience, maturation factors, etc. The emphasis on experiences also bespeaks an approach to motive incentives corresponding to need.

3. Has the concept number two any obvious *pitfalls?* Yes, it has. Any concept does. For if emphasis is put one place, onesidedness and oversimplification readily arise. The main pitfall I think would be the tendency in striving for high goals (the awakening of the individual to his full potential for learning) to run ahead and not be sensitive enough to the problem of levels of aspiration. Of course too high standards *imposed* by the teacher will frustrate and disintegrate learning potential. In my opinion, "teacher dominance" is detrimental, not helpful, to the objectives advanced in this paper.

4. Does my concept help establish definitive criteria for distinguishing "good" and "bad" teachers.

To my mind it does. Given the objectives put forward, what kind of teaching qualities are essential? I would put a premium on two, without both of which failure would be assured:

first,—love for people, and I fully agree that this means putting the needs of the learner foremost. Without this the high goals set would be a mockery. Full potential means *emotional,* not only intellectual health.

second,—the spirit of challenge. The teacher must be willing to challenge and be *challenged.* Put in another way, the teacher must be a *learner* in every situation. His curiosity, respect for ideas, refusal to cater to icons and articles of blind faith is his most important teaching tool.

In addition to these *sine qua non* qualities, three others should be encouraged:

a) growing knowledge of one's own field, an unwillingness to simply pass on old "truths" (this is a matter of almost criminal negligence in the way science is taught in the schools).

b) growing knowledge and examination of the learning process, in truth learning from the learner.

c) growing knowledge of and curiosity about the environment in which the learning situation is set (the community, culture, home, etc.).

5. Can these criteria be measured? Within limits, yes. They would easier be measured in existing classrooms and teachers, rather than in candidates.

But first I would say that one should not arbitrarily demand all these qualities to the same extent in all teachers. That's why I put the first two, first. If a teacher or teacher-candidate has love for people and a willingness to challenge, to learn, everything else can follow.

There are three approaches to measuring these qualities that I can think of:

first and most important, frequent and lengthy exchanges should be had with candidates under as relaxed and unthreatening circumstances as possible—their attitudes, prejudices, curiosity, feelings for people can be estimated (*not judged*). Tests are possible, but frankly I am unconvinced about them at this point. Oliver's experience I believe was as much a measure of the inadequacy of his test as of the real contradiction among teachers between theory and practice or rather claim and deed. Tests and discussion probing should not be abstract —it should point to particular attitudes relating to particular settings —e.g., depending on the setting of the school situation (e.g., basic attitudes may be just as important wherever the individual goes, but the determination of them in a rural setting, a ghetto area, etc., etc., may be quite different).

The best thing would be to observe the candidate in a teaching situation. One month of work with children should tell more about the teacher than any discussion or test.

Finally, (for lack of time and writer's cramp) I would look for teachers who can be won to a flexible outlook, who can be helped to recognize prejudice and bad teaching qualities in themselves. For if we only look for those who already "qualify," we will probably have few teachers indeed.

If this is written as if in considerable assurance, it belies the hesitancy and trepidation with which I consider my own possible involvement with the theory and practice of teaching.

Wolf taught school only one month. It is difficult to appraise his effectiveness as a teacher in that short period of time. Reportedly, however, he was liked by his students. They stuck by him during the two days, Friday and Monday, when the news broke about his prior communist status. Wolf said, "The kids were great; they weren't nearly as hysterical as some of their parents."

The Chairman of the Board of Education met several times with Wolf to determine whether he would accept an out-of-court settlement of nine weeks' salary. Wolf refused, and he hired Richard Hatt, a lawyer, to take the case to court.

In response to an inquiry from Hatt, the Secretary of the North Hanford Board of Education wrote as follows:

October 17, 1957

Mr. Richard L. Hatt
Attorney and Counselor at Law
35 Center Street

Dear Sir:

RE: MR. LEO WOLF

At a special meeting of the North Hanford Board of Education held in the Junior High School on October 16, 1957, the following motion was voted unanimously:

> For the best interests of the North Hanford school system, in lieu of the notoriety that the controversial matter of Mr. Wolf's background has received most recently, and because of the possibility—the very real possibility—of future friction in the school system, and further, in view of the questionable status of his certification, I move that Mr. Wolf be discharged.

Very truly yours,

NORTH HANFORD BOARD
OF EDUCATION

Secretary pro tem

LMM

At the Board of Education's meeting on Friday, November 1, the Town Counsel, E. B. Rand, said that, according to his interpretation of Section 938 D of the General Statutes of the state, since Wolf had neither a "regular" teaching certificate nor a "temporary emergency permit," he was not entitled to the rights of a public school teacher.

On November 7th Hatt reported having received a letter from the Board of Education denying a public hearing on the Board's action to dismiss Wolf. The Secretary of the Board stated that Wolf was not considered eligible, since he held no temporary teaching permit. Hatt noted that the letter also made it clear that a public hearing would not have been granted even if Wolf had held a permit, since the Board does not feel a teacher is eligible for such a hearing. "A public hearing for Leo Wolf would force the North Hanford Board of Education to divulge the reasons for its action," Hatt stated. The attorney added that, although Wolf had been present at the meeting of the Board on October 16th, he did not consider that the meeting constituted a public hearing.

On November 14, 1957, a lead editorial in *The Suburban Weekly* was entitled "Fight It With Democracy."

Fight It With Democracy

Leo Wolf was fired from his teaching position in the North Hanford school system because of what was called his background in communism. Furthermore, he was denied a public hearing on the dismissal by the Board of Education. The basis of the Board's refusal was Wolf's status (or non-status) as a teacher. He does not, according to the Board, hold a certificate which would entitle him to rights and privileges normally granted to qualified teachers.

Does not this denial of a basic right somehow resemble the totalitarian aspects of the governmental form with which the teacher has been linked? In notifying Wolf's attorney of the denial action, the Board also made it clear that a public hearing would not have been granted even if the teacher were the holder of the proper certificate. It is apparent that the Board does not want the matter to go before the public; for reasons that only its members know.

The history of the Wolf case is interesting. The school administration had evidently found the teacher qualified to fill a vacancy in the Science department—with or without certification. Following a charge that Wolf was national chairman of the Labor Youth League and that he had taken the Fifth Amendment in 1955, the Board suspended him. This took place on Election Day. The timing of the action, of course, is significant. At a later meeting it was voted to fire the teacher.

While it is true that communists constitute an endless threat to the American educational system, it is equally true that they must be dealt with democratically if there is to be an effective result. Making it impossible for the accused to present his case at a public hearing is, in our mind, little different from the process which would be employed in the Russia of today. This "eye for an eye" procedure may appeal to many as being completely justified; it does not, however, demonstrate that Americans are willing to practice what they preach all over the free world.

We hold no brief for Leo Wolf at this point—either as a teacher or as an American citizen. If what he has been accused of and fired for is true, he does not deserve to hold a teaching position in a public school system in the United States. Nevertheless, he does deserve to be heard publicly. He deserves an opportunity to report to the parents of youngsters he taught. And, we remind the Board of Education that he deserves the rights of an American even if he does not "qualify" for the rights of a teacher.

It is just as dangerous for America to resort to the tactics used in communism as it is for this nation to condone the employment of teachers who subscribe to such political beliefs. We happen to believe that the best weapon against communism is democracy. Let's fight with that.

After Wolf's dismissal a representative from the State Education Association met with him to decide whether the teacher was being wronged, and whether he needed the legal support of the organization. Wolf was asked to sign a statement that he would support, in toto and without reservations, the general policy of the SEA. Part of this policy stated that no teacher who is a member of a communist organization is qualified for support. The SEA wanted to investigate to determine if Wolf was in fact qualified, as an admitted ex-communist, for legal counsel paid for by the SEA. Wolf, however, declined to accept the support of the SEA, because "I do not want to be 100 per cent bound by any organization—that is why I left the Communist Party." The SEA returned Wolf's yearly dues and dropped the matter. Following are excerpts from two SEA publications.

Excerpt from "Communism and Education"

A. As a measure of defense against our most potent threat, American schools should teach about Communism and all forms of totalitarianism, including the principles and practices of the Soviet Union and the Communist Party in the United States. Teaching *about* Communism does not mean advocacy of Communism. Such advocacy should not be permitted in the American Schools.

B. Members of the Communist Party shall not be employed in the American schools. Such membership involves adherence to doctrines and discipline completely inconsistent with the principles of freedom on which American education depends. Such membership and the accompanying surrender of intellectual integrity render an individual unfit to discharge the duties of a teacher in this country.

C. At the same time we condemn the careless, incorrect, and unjust use of such words as "Red" and "Communist" to attack teachers and other persons who in point of fact are not Communists, but who merely have views different from those of their accusers. The whole spirit of free American education will be subverted unless teachers are free to think for themselves. It is because members of the Communist Party are required to surrender this right, as a consequence of becoming part of a movement characterized by conspiracy and calculated deceit, that they shall be excluded from membership in the State Education Association.

D. The SEA affirms its confidence in the profession itself to protect our schools from subversive influences and to maintain our devotion and loyalty to democratic principles and the American way of life.

Excerpt from the "SEA Handbook"

Under the state law (Section 938d of the 1955 Supplement to the General Statutes), a three-year probationary period of initial employment is set up during which time a board of education may terminate a teacher's contract by notifying the teacher in writing prior to March first in one school year that his contract will not be renewed for the following school year. Such teacher may, upon written request filed with the board of education within ten days after the receipt of such notice, be entitled to a hearing before the board to be held within fifteen days of such request, and at such hearing the reason or reasons for the nonrenewal of the contract shall be made known. The teacher has the right to appear with counsel of his choice at such hearing.

Beginning with and subsequent to the fourth year of continuous employment by a board of education, however, the contract of a teacher is continued under law indefinitely and may not be terminated by the board except for cause. As stated in the statute, such a teacher may have his contract terminated "at any time" only for "one or more of the following reasons: (1) inefficiency or incompetence; (2) insubordination against reasonable rules of the board of education; (3) moral misconduct; (4) disability, as shown by competent medical evidence; (5) elimination of the position to which the teacher was appointed, if no other position exists to which he may be appointed if qualified; or (6) other due and sufficient cause."

Prior to terminating such a contract, the board of education must give the teacher concerned "a written notice that termination of his contract is under consideration," and, upon written request filed by the teacher with the board within five days after receipt of such notice, the board must "within the next succeeding five days give such teacher a statement in writing of its reasons therefor." The law provides further that "within twenty days after receipt from a board of education of written notice that contract termination is under consideration the teacher concerned may file with such board a written request for a hearing, which such board shall hold within fifteen days after receipt of such request. Such hearing shall be public if the teacher so requests or the board so designates. The teacher concerned shall have the right to appear with counsel of his choice at such hearing whether public or private. A board of education shall give the teacher concerned its written decision within fifteen days after such hearing." The board of education retains the power to "suspend a teacher from duty immediately when serious misconduct is charged, without prejudice to the rights of the teacher as otherwise provided."

The term "teacher" is defined in the new act as including "all employees of a board of education, below the rank of superintendent or supervising agent, who hold a regular certificate issued by the state board of education." The provisions of special acts regarding the dismissal or employment of teachers prevail over the provisions of this act, in the event of conflict.

*   *   *   *   *

Among teachers and principals in the area much discussion of the case ensued. Most of the teachers had been informed by the Principal about Wolf's past. One teacher commented, "Wolf was a marked man from the first. If he had done anything out of line, we would have known it immediately. He couldn't have been more conspicuous if he had worn a sign on his back." Another teacher, in disagreement with the first, said, "He may say he's an ex-communist, but he may not be one. We all know the communists are taught to lie if it will better serve their purposes." And a third teacher added, "He may be a communist. He may not. But I lean toward the theory that what the world needs is more *ex*-communists. I think he deserves a chance to make good if he has changed his mind."

Some teachers had questions about how the case was handled. One said, "Look, we're really all in this thing together. We have to see that he's treated fairly; next time it might be one of us. What could happen to one could happen to all." Another teacher added, "In times of crisis, men's pasts are combed for unorthodoxy. Every society punishes truth. Whatever the crisis, we must stand for disciplined inquiry, and seek the truth no matter how touchy the situation is."

Viewing it differently, a principal in another school stated the issue in this fashion. "Two questions appear here. One, what are the limits to job freedom? And two, who may set these limits? Whoever is in authority must set the limits—and if the limits are that you must be co-operative, then that means that you must not be insubordinate. If you must be competent to teach, then that means have a certificate and good character. It seems to me that Wolf failed on both counts."

Wolf himself summed up his experience by saying, "I would like to teach. All I wanted from the Board was that they be as fair with me as I with them. But my views are different. Because of this, I was fired. Every teacher or administrator will present his own prejudices. The question is, do they try honestly to fight against prejudice?"

*   *   *   *   *

A change in superintendents had complicated the issues. The superintendent who had appointed Wolf, Jacob Abelson, was known as a "rural superintendent." That is, he worked with a number of schools, each one having no more than thirty-five teachers. Since North Hanford, during the transition time from August to September, had come to need more than thirty-five teachers, a new superintendent, Charles Custer, had been brought in. It was Abelson who had appointed Wolf, and Custer who, with the help of the Board of Education, had refused to keep him on as a teacher.

Abelson was fifty-two years old and Jewish, had been educated in the state public schools and university, had rejected offers from city systems, preferring the rural superintendency, and had a reputation for being liberal—he was a Democrat. Custer was forty-one years old, was a Protestant and a Republican. He had been educated in the public schools of Maine, a private college in Maine, and the University of New Mexico (where he received his advanced training in education). He had been a coach, then a school principal in Maine, and he was accepting his first superintendency at North Hanford. His speech contained an unusual mixture of New England ("sawr" for "saw") and the West; he confessed that he found the basic attitudes of the people in the West to be more open and friendly than those of the New England states, where family, cultural heritage and social institutions seemed to dictate a conservative reaction to newcomers.

Superintendent Custer said he first became alerted to some difficulty with Wolf when the Board of Education told Custer it thought there "might be more to the Wolf case than meets the eye." "I think," Custer said, "the Dean of the College of Education telephoned a friend in the State Department." Custer went directly to Wolf and got the full story; Wolf told him that he had been a member of the Communist party as recently as 1955.

"I think," Custer said, "I got more from Wolf than Abelson did; I think Abelson thought Wolf had been associated with the communists during the depression and had left the party in 1936—but obviously Wolf was too young a person for that to be true."

Custer then went to the Board of Education. "The Board called Wolf in and agreed to keep him on, but not if he became 'a public issue.' We didn't know two things at that time: we didn't know Donofrio and his group—you know that Taxpayers Association is a farce—were going to make such an issue of things. Some of their fliers were quite rough. And we didn't know that Wolf didn't have a temporary teaching permit." Custer said he realized that they had an "out" when, three or four days after Wolf had actually been suspended by the Board, Custer received an application form from the State Department of Education. This form is one the Superintendent has to sign stating that he is unable to find a fully qualified and fully certified teacher for the post. "I refused to sign the application form, because the Board had already indicated it did not want to keep Wolf."

The Board of Education settled with Wolf out of court. It gave him six months' pay, minus what he had already collected. The Board actually paid $200.00 more than it needed to. Wolf had been collecting unemployment insurance money, which alters the amount the state has to pay in such situations. In addition, the Board gave Wolf what he requested, the following formal public statement.

> The North Hanford Board of Education and Mr. Leo Wolf both agree that the publicity surrounding his presence as a teacher in the North Hanford school system impairs his effectiveness as a teacher and that therefore it appears to both sides that the best solution would be to compromise the present litigation and the same has been done by adjustment of salary and withdrawal of his action.
>
> At the same time it should be made clear that in his relations with the Board of Education Mr. Wolf has been at all times co-operative and truthful.
>
> Any misunderstanding that may have arisen as to Mr. Wolf's status is not the fault of Mr. Wolf, Supt. Charles Custer or the Board of Education.
>
> Dated this 18th day of December, 1957.
>
>   Plaintiff, Leo Wolf
>   By
>
>   _____
>
>   His Attorney
>   Defendant, North Hanford Bd. of Education
>   By
>
>   _____
>
>   Their Attorney

Later Custer said that he felt Wolf was not a communist, but that he should not have tried to get a teaching post in a community so near his home town, where the name Wolf had for so many years held bad connotations because of Leo's parents. Custer felt that the community was not "big enough" to keep Wolf as a teacher.

> I didn't dodge any issue, but I did realize that either we had to keep the thing as minimal as possible or else make a big case and carry it all the way. There's no use to borrow trouble, you know. I didn't

really start with Wolf, so I felt no compulsion to make a big thing out of it.

What did the pupils learn from the incident? Superintendent Custer thought that they lost a little time in science. "We had to have a substitute teacher for a while, then Mackey took over; but they didn't lose much." Custer said he thought Wolf really wanted to be "a friend with the kids." "He was very cooperative and probably knew what he was doing because of his youth league work."

What did the teachers learn from the incident? "I think the teachers would not support Wolf," Custer said. "As a matter of fact, Wolf had not asked the local teachers to support him." The teachers, said Custer, were aware of Wolf's former communist status and were suspicious of him. "Wolf really was working in a boiler room—some parents had already started to ask me to get their children out of Wolf's class."

Superintendent Custer said that the Board was trying to follow a policy of hiring young teachers fresh out of teachers colleges who were fully certified. "I know one thing; this board is going to be very, very careful from now on, especially with any people with temporary emergency permits."

The North Hanford Board of Education seemed to be under the direct domination of one man, Harold Plant. He was a lawyer and an elected representative (Republican) to the State Legislature. Educated in the public schools, the state university and law school, he was a local boy who was still "making good." He seemed to pride himself on being responsive to his constituents; yet with the lawyer's concern for both sides of a case, to recognize that the minority today (the Democrats) might easily become the majority of tomorrow. As the case proceeded beyond the deliberations of the Board of Education and into the law courts, Plant had shown himself to be an able supporter of due process of law (as an officer of the court) and an able defender of the point of view of the Board of Education in the litigation. The town counsel, E. B. Rand, had actually defended the Board in court, since much of Plant's time was being taken up by the sessions of the House of Representatives.

Plant later said:

> Frankly, Wolf was suspended because adverse publicity was not good for North Hanford, and also because of the possibility of untoward incidents. What I mean by that is, suppose the man is still a

communist—might he not subtly and insidiously indoctrinate our children? Let us take a case that is not so loaded with emotional overtones. Suppose a teacher of reading were to fail to teach a class of youngsters to read. The next teacher would have a much more difficult task trying to catch up. It might mark those children for life. The same thing can be said about Wolf. He might scar some of those children; we can't afford to take that chance. Science can be a factual, seemingly innocent, subject until you realize that the dialectical materialism of the communists is really a kind of scientific materialism. It is not a far jump from science to the basic philosophy of the communists. And since Sputnik, we know that they are good scientists.

Plant outlined the case from beginning to end.

We had an executive meeting in which we invited Wolf and his lawyer (Mr. Hatt) in. We asked Wolf directly: "Have you told us all?" He said he had. He was very adamant on that point—he wanted us to think he was being honest and above board. But I think Wolf did not tell Abelson everything, that is, about his most recent communist activities. We held a public hearing, although Hatt thought it was only an "open meeting." It was on the strength of this hearing that Hatt brought legal action against the Board of Education for "improper procedures."

We were told by Wolf that he had cut cleanly from the communist party. But some things still bothered us. First, of course, was the public ruckus. We have had plenty of newspaper publicity on this case —too much for the good of the people. Secondly, we were bothered because Wolf seemed unwilling to repudiate communism. He said he still had friends in the party, for example. Also, his parents are still communists. He refused to accept the professional teachers' code, which of course states that communists may not teach in our schools, although ex-communists may teach. Thirdly, Wolf was not officially certified. We could easily have been open to suit from an irate parent, as well as cut off from state aid if even one teacher is not certified. Finally, the outcome of this incident has led us to adopt a new policy. We, that is the Board of Education, now interview all new teachers. There aren't too many, of course. But we ask each one this question: "Are you now or have you ever been a member of the Communist Party?" The person who does not answer takes his chances.

A few months later Leo Wolf received a fellowship to pursue a doctorate in chemistry at one of the nation's top universities.

SELECTED READINGS

Beale, Howard K., *Are American Teachers Free? An Analysis of Restraints Upon the Freedom of Teaching in American Schools.* New York: Charles Scribner's Sons, 1936.

Crossman, Richard, ed., *The God that Failed.* New York: Harper and Brothers, 1949.

Ehlers, Henry, and Gordon C. Lee, eds., *Crucial Issues in Education: An Anthology,* rev. ed. New York: Henry Holt and Company, 1959. Part I.

Gross, Neal C., *Who Runs Our Schools?* New York: John Wiley and Sons, 1958.

Hook, Sidney, *Heresy, Yes—Conspiracy, No.* New York: The John Day Company, 1953.

Kennedy, John F., *Profiles in Courage.* New York: Harper and Brothers, 1956.

Stouffer, Samuel A., *Communism, Conformity, and Civil Liberties: A Cross-section of the Nation Speaks its Mind.* Garden City: Doubleday and Company, 1955.

Yarmolinsky, Adam, ed., *Case Studies in Personnel Security.* Washington: Bureau of National Affairs, 1955.

CASE 3

Can the Mayor Be a Teacher?

Robert Mayer was a high school science teacher in the city of Lakeland, a city with a population of 19,000. He was in his late thirties, unmarried, and by all indications vitally interested in teen-age people. He was president of the A.F. of L. State Teachers Union and secretary to Operation Lakeland, a board set up to attract new industry to the city.

Mr. Mayer did not limit his interests to science and young people. He was greatly interested in government and politics and followed closely the state legislative program for teachers.

In the fall of 1955 Mr. Mayer ran for mayor of Lakeland on the Democratic ticket. One important item in his platform was a proposed referendum on changing the Board of Education of the Lakeland School District from an appointed to an elected one. He was defeated for the position of mayor. He got the referendum, but when it took place the voters rejected his proposition.

Mr. Mayer continued his political activities. He kept a watchful eye on the recommendations for state legislation on education, especially on teachers' salaries. When one of these was accepted and made law, he immediately asked the Board of Education for the $100 differential in salary it allowed for those with master's degrees—as distinguished from 30 semester hours' study beyond their bachelor's degrees. The Board, in accord with an opinion from the legal division of the State Department, refused Mr. Mayer's request. Mr. Mayer then took legal action against the Board, seeking to force it to adjust his salary schedule on the grounds of alleged additional qualifications.

On September 30, 1957, the State Supreme Court directed the Board to pay Mayer a total of $87.50 due him from December 1, 1956, to November 25, 1957, together with costs in the amount of $30. Mayer was supported in this action by the A.F. of L. Teachers' Union. The case was closely followed by boards of education throughout the state, many of whom made immediate adjustments in the salaries of teachers holding master's degrees.

In the 1957 local elections, Mr. Mayer again ran for mayor, this time on the Liberal ticket. No mayor had ever been elected from the Liberal Party. When asked by a reporter before the election, "Who is behind you?" Mr. Mayer answered:

> I feel I am the people's candidate, and that the people are behind me. They want a change and I am asking for the opportunity to give them that change. My support is coming from the ranks of Republicans, Democrats, Liberals, and independents alike. It is gratifying to see the rallying of these forces to the cause I've been fighting for two years for our city.

Two further questions and answers concerning his campaign appeared in *The Lakeland News*, the only local daily newspaper.

> Q. Why are you running for office?
> A. Government is everybody's business. Each must make his contribution to good government as he sees it.
> Q. What are some of the points in your platform?
> A. 1. Put the Board of Education back into the hands of the people by an elected board. Appointed boards are taxation without representation.
> 2. Return powers to the Commissioner of Public Safety and avoid the police-chief-dominated city.
> 3. Give a dollar in services for a dollar in taxes. Cut the waste, the featherbedding, the inefficiency, the vested interests.
> 4. Fair property assessments. Give a Board of Appeals and a fair distribution in this respect when assessments are raised.

5. Set up a commission to sell water to surrounding communities and keep down the rates in our own community. Water is our most abundant, and should be our cheapest, commodity.

6. Revise the milk laws so that the people are protected and so it no longer becomes the property of practically one man in our city.

7. Provide for adequate recreation with a minimum of waste. I'm especially interested in a Teen Center and adequate swimming facilities for our community.

8. Industrial expansion and harbor development. I feel my experience on the Board of Directors of Operation Lakeland and Secretary for four years will be invaluable in this respect.

9. Push for Permanent Personal [voter] Registration.

10. Investigate completely the Civil Service Commission.

11. Equality before the law. Eliminate the special privileged few in administration of the law.

Mr. Mayer's opponent in the 1957 Democratic primary and in the election was Mr. Gerald Fisher, a member of the five-man Lakeland Board of Education. In answering questions concerning Mr. Fisher and the Board of Education, Mr. Mayer pressed the attack:

Q. What about his record on the Board?

A. He says it is Republican dominated and is trying to blame them for the errors. But he cannot divorce himself from his own voting record. Each time when the Common Council and the Federation of Labor have petitioned the Board to have a referendum for an elected board, Mr. Fisher never voted nor said a word in defense of having such a referendum. The vote was always 5-0 for tabling the resolutions.

Q. What about your case against the Board of Education?

A. For Mr. Fisher's information, the courts ruled in favor of the teachers which shows that we had been discriminated against by Mr. Fisher and the rest of the Board. This case will affect thousands of teachers in the state but it amounts to less than $80 for me, less than I've already spent on the case. An important principle was involved and we won in court. Now Mr. Fisher is part of more waste and fighting against the teachers' basic rights in pursuing the case to a higher court, where the Board is going to lose again but is spending more money to fight the case.

On November 5th Mr. Mayer was elected Mayor of the City of Lakeland.

In his statements to the people following the election he announced that, since he was a bachelor and had no obligations other than to himself, he would continue to live on his teacher's salary of $5,500 and would donate his mayor's salary of $5,050 to help set up a Teen Center for the youth of Lakeland.

While Mr. Mayer was accepting congratulations and making his plans for taking over as mayor, the Board of Education was consulting the State Department's Division of Law on the legality of his holding both positions.

On December 20th an opinion arrived by mail from Mr. Samuel Rose, Director of the Division of Law: "No person may hold the position of high school teacher in a city school system where the mayor appoints the Board of Education, and at the same time hold the office of mayor." Mr. Rose explained in his letter to the Board that:

> This is clearly incompatible under the principles of common law, in that there is a clear conflict of duties between that of teacher, who is an employee of the board, and that of mayor, who appoints the members of such board. Consequently it is our opinion that the person in question will have to resign as teacher or will need to resign as mayor.

At a special meeting that same evening the Board met in executive session. Mr. Mayer was then invited to appear. He was handed the following statement by the attorney for the Board:

> I now hand you this paper on which are set down the statements which I am about to make. This is not a hearing; therefore, discussion is inappropriate. The board's sole purpose in requesting your appearance this evening is to advise you of a legal opinion which the board received today (Friday) from Samuel Rose, State Department of Education, law division, and to carry out the suggestions which George Clark, counsel to the department, made to certain members and other officials of the board a few weeks ago. Those suggestions were that if the department should rule that in its opinion this board could not properly continue your employment as teacher in the local public school system after you assume the office of mayor, the board should in such event, advise you of that opinion and of its intention to terminate your employment, if it so decided.

Mr. Mayer thanked the Board and left without further comment. Once outside he distributed a prepared statement:

I feel that to run for office is the highest duty of citizenship. I have run and the people have chosen me to govern their city for the next two years.

I owe it to the teaching profession, to the students whom I teach, and to myself to fight this and protect the rights of teachers who seek to fulfill a public duty by entering the field of government and serving their fellowmen there. They should not be penalized nor their job jeopardized. My fight is to encourage my colleagues to enter the field of community service through politics.

The question of my ability to teach and serve as mayor, does not seem to be within the jurisdiction of this board.

As a teacher I possess tenure. I have violated none of the tenure requisites.

As Mayor the question arises that I shall be appointing members of the Board of Education. The implication is that any such appointments would be to favor me as a teacher. The implication is also that this mayor is of less integrity than any other mayor because he would appoint people of biased views. Any abuses which arise, however, are inherent in the very spoils system by which a board is selected rather than elected, and not out of the one who does the appointing. The following points are to be considered as invalidating any argument of incompatibility:

1. The board is fiscally independent, therefore the mayor can control no monies nor bring pressure upon the board or its members from this point.

2. Once the mayor appoints a board member he has absolutely no control over him. The board members receive no direct pay for their functioning either, so this cannot be held out as an inducement.

3. The mayor appoints only two of the five members in any given term of office, a minority number.

4. There cannot be even a question arising until the mayor actually makes the appointment which will not happen until a vacancy occurs next June.

5. The board can relieve itself of this question by listening to the mandate of the people and having a referendum for an elected Board of Education. The Mayor is put in the incongruous position of appointing board members and then not being responsible for the acts of those members by having no control over them. The board members should be directly responsible to the people by election.

On December 29th Mr. Mayer presented the following statement to the Board:

First, in asking that you hold any action in abeyance concerning me until further study can be made of the entire question, may I point out that Mr. Rose has been contacted personally during the past week and he stated explicitly that his was merely an opinion and has no judicial value.

That any action which this Board takes is its own responsibility and that the state would not interfere if the board chose to either retain me as a teacher or dismiss me. Thus if the board takes no action, there is no action and the responsibility for any action rests squarely upon the Board of Education, and not on the State Education Department. We are getting this in writing.

Second: There is no question of legality since neither this case nor any like it has ever appeared in the courts to our knowledge.

Third: This is a grave and serious decision to deprive a man of his tenure rights and requires full consideration by the board to even bend over backwards to protect what has been accumulated in the way of rights.

Fourth: That any action other than to hold this matter over for further study will act to demoralize teachers, go against the will of the general citizenry of our city, and interfere seriously with the education of those students whom I teach.

And fifth, that my feelings on an elected Board of Education are as strong as ever and I will continue to fight hard for this one principle, irrespective of what course the board may take. I am sure the Board of Education will act in a fair and favorable manner. I merely ask for justice without vindictiveness and that the board take no action until this serious matter is given full consideration and studied more thoroughly.

On December 30th the Board held a special meeting at the home of its President to discuss Mr. Mayer's statement. During the 45-minute discussion, Mr. Mayer and his attorney were asked to leave the room. When they returned, the Board's lawyer informed them that upon assuming the office of mayor Mr. Mayer would be served with "charges" setting forth the reasons for his dismissal as a teacher. A meeting of the Board would be held on January 28th in order for Mr. Mayer to be heard on the termination of his employment.

Speaking for Mr. Mayer, his attorney said that he had conferred with Mr. Rose in the capitol and that the latter's opinion was not binding on the Board. "There is no question in my mind that it is up to the Board members to decide on this issue." He further pointed out that he and his client thought there was nothing illegal about holding the two jobs, and if "there is a criterion of appointing Board members, it can't be used until the appointments are made."

Mr. Mayer himself reiterated that it was in the Board's power to make the decision, asked a delay in any action, and said that if he found that he could not do justice to both jobs he might request a leave of absence.

"You're not asking for a leave of absence tonight, are you, Mr. Mayer?" Eric Sands queried. He received a negative reply. When someone suggested that the Board should wait to see if the mayor-elect made any appointments to the Board, Mr. Sands remarked, "Aren't we to assume that he will carry out his office, functions, and duties to the best of his ability? The Charter of the city provides for these appointments. Are we to assume that he will break this oath before he has taken it?" Mr. Mayer replied that he thought it "distasteful" to make appointments, and that the Board should be elective.

"I want to interrupt this to say that several members of the Board attended a meeting with Dr. George Clark, chief counsel for the State Department of Education, and it was his opinion that was expressed by Mr. Rose. Your opinion that we received an opinion from an assistant is not right," interjected the President of the Board.

The attorney for the Board explained that the "charges" with which Mr. Mayer would be served would not be a reflection upon his integrity nor would suggest that he was unfit to teach. "They are just the facts that he may not properly be employed as mayor while a teacher, period."

After Mr. Mayer and his attorney left, Louis Alden said, "We don't want to do on injustice to the people of Lakeland, the students, or Mr. Mayer. Why must we act at this time?"

"The incompatibility arises when he takes office. That's why we must act now," replied the attorney for the Board. He further answered a question of Alden's by explaining that although their ruling was not based on a specific law, it was based on "common law"— general rules and principles which have been laid down over the years. In response to a query as to why the Board asked for, and acted in accordance with Mr. Rose's opinion, Gerald Fisher said:

> We asked for an opinion because the people of Lakeland asked our position on it. We've no axe to grind. We're not out to crucify Robert.

We have two opinions from the capitol from men whose job is to do this type of thing, and I think we should take their opinion.

The attorney concluded the discussion by getting an affirmative answer from the Board. "As I understand it," he said, "it's full speed ahead."

On Wednesday, January 1, 1958, Robert Mayer was inaugurated Mayor of the City of Lakeland. During the ceremonies he was presented a gavel and block on behalf of the teachers of Lakeland High School. The inscription on the gavel's band read:

> Robert Mayer, Mayor of Lakeland
> First term Inaugural, January 1, 1958
> Government is Everybody's Business
> With Best Wishes
> Your Co-Workers—The Teachers of Lakeland High School

In accepting this gift the science instructor said:

> This gift touches my heart deeply. First and foremost for it comes from those with whom I have been associated for the past 10 years. And secondly, for it comes from the profession I love so well. . . . I shall return.

On Thursday, January 2nd, the high school reopened after its winter vacation. Mr. Mayer reported to the office of high school principal Russel Conover and signed the teachers' register. Then in a completely amiable exchange, Mr. Conover said, "Bob, what are your intentions?"

"It is my intention to assume my teaching duties at no compensation, and I believe the education of the children is of the utmost importance," came the reply.

"I have been directed by the Superintendent of Schools and the Board of Education that you are not to teach or take over your home room—even without compensation," Mr. Conover said. Without hesitation Mr. Mayer said he would go to his room and pick up his personal effects.

One of a group of students then approached the Principal and said, "If Mr. Mayer goes, so do we." Mr. Mayer himself said to them, "Don't do anything foolish. *My* main concern is your education, and that should be yours. We will take care of these things by due process of law."

Nevertheless a number of students did absent themselves from school. When Mr. Mayer spotted them in the downtown section of Lakeland, near the City Hall, he invited them to come to his office and there talked with them. He than escorted them back to school, where the Principal marked them "tardy," rather than absent.

That evening Mr. Mayer made a public statement attributing his discharge to "politics." He asked the Board to allow him to continue to teach until the end of the term. The Board refused the request but did not cancel the hearing on the matter scheduled for January 28th.

Meanwhile Mr. Mayer's supporters began circulating petitions asking the Board to reinstate Mr. Mayer and also to agree to another referendum on the question of changing the Board from an appointive to an elective one. By January 24th over 4,000 residents had signed the petition, and the Board officially authorized the city council to schedule such a referendum.

On February 4th the Board considered Mr. Mayer's dismissal and voted to reaffirm it. Mr. Mayer then took the matter to court. On Saturday, March 29th, the State Supreme Court issued a ruling to the effect that the duties of teacher and mayor did not conflict, and an order to the Board to reappoint Mr. Mayer. The Board promptly appealed the order. On Tuesday, April 1st, Mr. Mayer returned to his teaching position. He taught one class and was then told by the Principal to leave.

April 1st was also the date of the referendum. The vote was 3,970 to 1,028 in favor of making the Board of Education elective. That same evening Mr. Mayer appeared before a meeting of the Board and demanded that it reappoint him, which it did. On the following day he resumed his school duties.

SELECTED READINGS

Foff, Arthur, and Jean D. Grambs, eds., *Readings in Education.* New York: Harper and Brothers, 1956. Chs. 2–4.

Hamilton, Robert R., and Paul R. Mort, *The Law and Public Education; with Cases.* Chicago: The Foundation Press, 1941.

Lazarsfeld, Paul F., et al., *The People's Choice: How the Voter Makes Up His Mind in a Presidential Campaign,* rev. ed. New York: Columbia University Press, 1948.

Lieberman, Myron, *Education as a Profession*. Englewood Cliffs: Prentice-Hall, 1956.

Mead, Margaret, *The School in American Culture*, the Inglis Lecture for 1951, Harvard University. Cambridge, Massachusetts: Harvard University Press, 1951.

National Education Association, *Research Bulletin*, "Status and Practices of Boards of Education," vol. 24, no. 2 (April, 1946).

White, Leonard D., *Introduction to the Study of Public Administration*, rev. ed. New York: The Macmillan Company, 1939. Chs. 36–37.

Whyte, William H., Jr., *The Organization Man*. New York: Simon and Schuster, 1956. Chs. 1–5.

CASE **4**

After Desegregation at Southville High

On Monday, August 20, 1956, twelve Negro students were among the 700 or so who registered at Southville High School for the school year that was to begin the following Monday morning. Southville High had always been an all-white school in a southern state with a long tradition of racially segregated public education.

The change did not come unheralded or unplanned. The Henderson County school board and its school administrators had been fighting the case in the United States courts for nearly five years, when, in January, Judge Edwards of the District Court had ordered them to desegregate the county's three high schools "not later than the beginning of the fall term of the present year." Although the Board had taken no explicit action, J. D. England, Principal of Southville High and one of those named in the court order, had announced that he would proceed to admit Negroes to the school. The Board had appointed a committee of the school principals and the PTA presidents to help prepare the public, and England had worked closely with the local weekly newspaper editor to inform the public about the matter. The court decision and its significance had been discussed not only in the

PTA, the civic clubs, the well-established churches, and the newspaper, but also in forums conducted by the students at Southville High School. England had arranged, too, for the teachers to assign the students themes designed to make them aware of their responsibilities in the situation.

In May the weekly Southville *News-Times* had reported full details about the impending change, and on August 9th it had again reprinted the court order. That same day its lead story had recounted details and background, including the school's policies with regard to social events and athletics. In a publicized conference with Negro parents England had promised equal treatment for the Negro students. On the eve of registration day he had stated:

> There's been no trouble here at all. The people may not like this by choice, but they realize it's a court order and it's what we have to do. I'm not expecting any trouble.

When school opened on Monday morning, August 27th, a number of persons, some teen-agers, some adults, variously estimated as totalling from 60 to 150, were gathered close to the entrance to the school. Six white students, all boys, paraded up and down carrying makeshift signs with messages such as the following:

StRIKE AGAinSt INTERGRATiON OF SouThvillE Hi

Later the six sat under the trees on the school lawn, and then two of them went into the school to attend classes.

Of the 791 white students registered, only 715 reported to school, and a good number of these did so apparently against their parents' wishes. Some parents later came to the school and took their children out. Of the 15 Negroes, one had apparently decided to drop out of school, and two stayed away to "wait and see what happened." Six boys and six girls turned up.

All seven local policemen were on hand, and the crowd was orderly as it heckled the arriving students, especially the Negroes. "Niggers. . . coons . . . go back to Africa," they shouted. "You'll never stay in that school!" Billy Lines, a Negro senior, led the Negro students as they filed through the crowd, and he took the brunt of the heckling on what some of them later called "the longest journey of their lives." One told a reporter later in the day, however, "It's hard to say how we felt. But we weren't bothered at all. We came on in as soon as we could."

As school got underway, home rooms were organized. In one junior home room the teacher invited Mary Sue Brown, one of the Negro students, to tell the rest of the class something about herself and her ambition to become a doctor. The class listened closely. A few minutes later they elected Mary Sue vice-president of the home room. According to one of the white student leaders in the group, the school's FHA president, the choice had not been an act of tolerance or kindness: "It's just that Mary Sue is so pretty and smart and has such a wonderful personality. Anyhow, she had to be good to get elected; she ran against a member of the football team."

In another home room a Negro girl was chosen secretary.

No incidents between Negro and white students in the school were reported.

During the lunch break, however, when the Negroes and some of the white students walked a few hundred yards to town for their noonday meal, there were some minor difficulties outside. The crowd was still close to the school. A Negro student and a white student engaged in a brief fight, and an adult member of the crowd tripped and kicked a Negro girl student. Another member of the crowd attacked an elderly Negro woman. The police interfered promptly and restored order. They took a knife away from one Negro student. They made no arrests.

That same day the Henderson County court refused to issue an injunction stopping the desegregation, an injunction which had been requested six days earlier by a state segregationist organization on the grounds among others that in the absence of explicit instructions from the school board England had "no authority" to desegregate the school.

On Tuesday morning the school registered full attendance. Although the crowd outside the school was noticeably larger, the police were more active, and no incidents were reported. As the morning wore on, most of the crowd dispersed.

On Wednesday morning, however, the number of white students reporting to school was down somewhat. Again, as they entered the school, they were heckled by a group of adults and teen-agers, the latter group conspicuously including stay-away students. For the first time the Negroes used the side entrance to the school. As time went by, the crowd grew in size, and the police kept it off the school grounds entirely—except briefly during the morning, when a visitor to South-ville, George Meyer, precipitated an incident that caused some stir.

Meyer, a segregationist leader from another state, had arrived un-invited in Southville early the preceding Saturday. He had immediately started a door-to-door campaign, trying to arouse the opponents of desegregation to action. He had found a number of supporters and, notably among the town's leaders, a number of opponents. On Sunday afternoon he had held a pseudo-religious antisegregation rally, in which he had repudiated the United States Supreme Court and invited the citizens to assert their right to block desegregation. That evening the County Sheriff had arrested him on charges of vagrancy and inciting to riot, but on Tuesday morning the county court had tried him and released him for lack of evidence.

On Tuesday evening Meyer had spoken to a crowd on the court-house square, again arguing against desegregation and attacking the Supreme Court. Many in the audience had cheered him on. "One court is higher than the Supreme Court," he had said, "and that is the people." He had strongly criticized local officials, especially J. D. England. "England must go!" he had shouted. At this point the con-siderable number of high school boys standing at the fringes of the crowd had heckled him. The crowd was variously estimated at from 200 to 600; there was disagreement, too, as to how many of them had concurred with the speaker, and how many had been there out of curiosity.

By Wednesday morning, at any rate, Meyer was well known in Southville and was acknowledged as the leader of the opponents of desegregation at the high school. During the morning he appeared at the school. Followed by part of the crowd, he made for the front door. The police stopped him but sent for England. When England arrived, Meyer demanded that he eject the Negroes or resign. England explained the court order under which he was acting and said that while he was principal he had no choice but to keep the Negroes in the school. He said he would be willing to resign, however, whenever 51% of the parents and students wished him to.

Meanwhile the students were responding to Meyer's arrival at the school. According to an account by one of the school staff:

The children inside listened and watched. They discussed what they would do should he lead his group into their school.

The Negro children sat and waited. They looked straight ahead, with almost frozen expressions. And strong white boys moved near the doorways, and edged over and managed "conveniently" to find seats in front of, to the side of, and behind the Negroes.

England went back to his office and called an assembly. When the students had come together, he told them of Meyer's ultimatum and asked how they felt. The president of the Student Council took the chair, and the school staff left the room. The students voted 614 to 0 in favor of England's staying. England then asked the students to poll their parents on the same question and report the results to him the next morning.

Outside the school the crowd grew. At lunch-time a white teen-ager attacked a Negro student, and some 50 or 75 persons chased several Negro students and other Negroes through the streets. The students were rescued by members of the school's football team. Sporadic disorders continued during the day, by the end of which the police had made a number of arrests. At about 2:30 p.m., an hour before dismissal time, the County Sheriff slipped the Negro students out of the school through the back door to protect them from the crowd in front. "There were about 500 people outside, and I thought somebody might get hurt," he said.

During the afternoon five Southville citizens, including England and one member of the school board, requested Judge Edwards, whose chambers were in Jonestown, seventeen miles away, to issue an injunction restraining Meyer and others from interfering with the operation of the desegregated school. The judge prepared a temporary order, and it was handed to Meyer that evening by five United States marshals, just as he was beginning to address a second evening rally on the courthouse square. Despite the injunction, Meyer continued with his talk, which was listened to by some 800 persons.

Meanwhile the County Sheriff was meeting with the Negro parents and offering to drive the Negro students to school in Jonestown himself if they would withdraw.

On Thursday morning the number of picketers at the school was up to 300 or 400, and the number of students in attendance down to 600.

England announced the results of the overnight poll of parents: 447 for his remaining, 6 for his resigning, 19 ballots returned stating no opinion.

Apart from the fact that a woman hit Billy Lines with a stick as he entered the building, the crowd outside the school was orderly during the morning. Meyer stayed away "because of this injunction they have against me." At 1:00 p.m., when he reported to the court, he was arrested and held on a charge of contempt of court arising out of his speech the previous evening.

That afternoon the crowd in front of the school became disorderly. Although now prohibited by the police, anti-integration posters were displayed, fist fights broke out, Negroes were pelted with tomatoes, and several arrests were made.

In the evening several hundred persons gathered at the square for a third rally which had already been called by Meyer. In his absence as many as twenty persons came forward one after another to speak against school desegregation and "mongrelization" of the white race, and to attack local, state, and national leaders.

On Friday morning school attendance was down again, this time to 436 whites and 10 Negroes, the latter arriving again in cars. (One of the absent Negroes was ill; the other was testifying in court.) Absent white students made up a large part of the crowd outside the school, but there were many absentees who presumably were being kept at home.

On that same day Judge Edwards found Meyer guilty of contempt of court and sentenced him to a year in prison.

As the Labor Day weekend started, and the Southville High students headed for the football stadium for an evening game against their arch-rival, many persons were saying that the worst now seemed to be over.

The events of the succeeding 48 hours did not bear them out. That same evening a fourth segregation rally was held, at which 1000 persons were addressed by a segregationist leader just arrived from a neighboring southern state. The crowd got out of hand, and the return of the spectators from an 18–0 football victory contributed to its wildness. Scores of persons marched through the streets chanting, "We want Meyer," some of them threatening to dynamite the Mayor's house. Cars of Negro tourists were attacked. The local police were powerless against the mob; the Mayor tried to appeal to the Governor of the state for help but could not reach him.

The next morning the city council declared a state of emergency and formally requested state help in restoring law and order. At the insistence of the mayor's son, who was the attorney for the school board, and another lawyer, the council authorized the formation of an auxiliary police force of 35, consisting largely of prominent local citizens. As a crowd of 2000 gathered for another evening rally, this auxiliary force used tear gas to break up a threatened attack on the courthouse. Then someone shouted, "Let's take their guns and kill the nigger-lovin' sons of bitches!" A pitched battle seemed about to break out.

Just at that moment 110 state policemen in 39 police cars with sirens wailing and red lights flashing made a melodramatic entry and took over. The police allowed the speakers at the rally to say their piece. Those who spoke all disavowed the use of violence, and merely urged parents not to let their children go to the desegregated school. When the speeches were over, the crowd drifted apart. (Some of the credit for this was given to a thunderstorm.)

At 12:35 p.m. on Sunday 633 National Guardsmen in 60 vehicles, including 7 tanks, arrived to patrol Southville. Nevertheless, that evening there was another rally, this time with 3000 persons. One Negro had to be rescued from a mob in which someone had shouted "Kill that nigger!", and a cross was burned on the school grounds. At about 9:00 p.m. a defiant, taunting group was driven across a curb line by guardsmen with fixed bayonets. "Order and a resumption of mob action hung in a precarious balance for two hours," one reporter said. Then the organized opposition seemed to melt away. A large crowd stayed around for some time, many of them until 1:00 a.m. But the National Guard commander noted that it contained a high proportion of women, children, and teen-agers, and he described them as seeming "to be a happy crowd, jubilantly happy."

On Monday, Labor Day, the National Guard imposed a ban on all meetings, outdoor gatherings, outdoor speakers, and the like. Southville was quiet and orderly. Perhaps some of the violent segregationists had gone off to take part in a race riot in a town some 20 miles away.

On Tuesday morning, September 4th, Southville High School opened its doors for the second week of school. A United States marshal stood on the school steps and read aloud a new order from

Judge Taylor enjoining the entire citizenry of Southville from interfering with school desegregation. While small groups close to the school grounds jeered, 257 white students and 9 Negroes entered the building, the Negro boys using the front door for the first time. As they went in, several white boys said "Let's don't go to school" and walked off. As the Negro girls went in the side door, a white boy was heard to shout, "What are they going to do in school today by themselves?" Shortly afterward, some 20 white students standing near the front door went on into the school when advised to do so by the National Guard commander and the football coach.

Most of the absentees were rural students; the attendance of students from the town itself was fairly good. Two white girls who stayed away said they "didn't want to go to school with Negroes." "Some of the students are too yellow to stay out," one said. They, however, were going to stay out "until we get the school all white."

England received "75 to 100 calls from frightened people" who were concerned about reports that there would be violence at the school. One widespread rumor was that a bomb had been placed under the building—which was promptly searched. The next day England told the press that there was "a campaign of fear going on." "People are being intimidated," he said. "It's perfectly obvious." Two mothers had come to him with tears in their eyes saying they had been warned that unless they kept their children out of school, their homes would be dynamited as soon as the National Guard left. Newsmen found evidence of many such threats. They, like England, attributed less of the absenteeism to deliberate boycotting than they did to parents' fears for their children. (As late as the following Monday England was to receive telephone calls from parents asking if it was now safe for their children to return to school.)

Attendance figures for the first eleven days of school are shown in Table I.

On Wednesday morning, as the twelve Negroes returned to school, white persons lined the walk, but—except for a quiet "Here they are!"—were silent as the Negroes filed through. The attorney for the Board of Education announced that the next day a list of absentees would be drawn up, and the Executive Committee of the Southville High School PTA issued a statement urging parents to send their children back to school.

Table I

Attendance at Southville High School
August 27 to September 11, 1956

	White	Negro	Totals
Total Registration	791	15	806
Attendance, Monday, August 27	715	12	727
Tuesday　〃　28	791	12	803
Wednesday 〃 29	c.738	12	c.750
Thursday 〃 30	c.588	12	c.600
Friday 〃 31	436	10	446
Tuesday, September 4	257	9	266
Wednesday 〃 5	312	12	324
Thursday 〃 6	382	12	394
Friday 〃 7	407	12	419
Monday 〃 10	517	12	529
Tuesday 〃 11	578	12	590

According to a press report, England "strongly hinted" that he would resign if the white students did not return.

On Thursday a citizen's group survey of the reasons for students' absences led to the results shown in Table II. The columns of the *News-Times* were almost entirely filled with news about the school crisis, and an editorial said, "We must stand together in Southville, obey all laws (whether we like them or not) so long as they are laws, and see that others do the same thing."

Table II

Results of Survey of Absentees From Southville High School
September 6, 1956

Absent because of desegregation	83
Absent because of fear of violence	58
"Playing hookey"	27
Absent for undetermined reasons	134
Transferred to other schools	12
Total	314

On Monday, September 10th, England gave the County Superintendent's office the names of 257 students still absent from school. By the next day the number of formal withdrawals seemed to be stabilized at 36.

The first National Guardsmen were allowed to leave Southville for their homes as early as Thursday, September 6th. After that the detachment was quietly reduced in strength until the following Tuesday, when the last guardsmen pulled out. Meanwhile the local police force had been enlarged to 12 members. The Sheriff had expanded the auxiliary force into a stand-by force of some 200, many of whom had been given anti-riot training, and had made efforts to arrange for more rapid obtaining of state help should that again prove necessary. He had also communicated with the United States Attorney General, requesting that 10 deputy U. S. marshals be named. He announced that Southville could now deal with "any situation."

In the streets and the courthouse square of Southville order had returned. On September 19th the Chairman of the County school board declared the issue closed.

*   *   *   *   *

What was happening inside the high school? How were the students themselves responding to desegregation?

A reporter interviewing a large number of the white students found not a single one who said he actually wished to attend a desegregated school. But he reported all the white students apparently resigned to the situation. Seating in the classrooms was alphabetical, and only one white student placed next to a Negro had asked to have his seat changed. One 16-year-old boy who had been accosted by Meyer before school had opened had laughed in his face and told him he was going to school not to fall in love with a Negro girl but to get an education.

"I don't think there's any of us who really wanted to go to school with Negroes," said one girl. "But now that they're here, we might as well make the best of it." "They have got to have an education like everyone else," she said.

Another white girl said, "I think it's all right as long as there are only twelve of them, but if more come in—and you know there will be more—I think the county ought to build a high school for them."

Asked about a white parent's statement that the white students were "beginning to feel sorry for the Negroes," a senior girl said, "I don't think anybody's feeling sorry for them exactly. But I think if anybody tried to push them around in the hall or anything, the other white students wouldn't let them." In class, she said, the Negro students had been "mostly ignored" by their classmates. "They've answered questions and things like that in class. The teachers haven't made any distinction at all." Other reports indicated that there had been no social contact at all between the groups.

In the middle of the second week of school a white girl said, "It's just like we've always been going to school with them. We don't bother them and they don't bother us."

One Negro girl told a reporter that there had been "no trouble of any kind" in the school building, another that the white students hadn't treated her "too badly."

Most of the Negro students told the press their wish was above all to go to desegregated schools. They did not especially want to be together with white children, but they felt that only in previously white schools could they get the caliber of schooling to which they were entitled. Billy Lines, the quiet senior who had led his fellow Negro students in the mornings and had waited every afternoon until they were all safely out, pleaded with his mother to be allowed to stop going to Southville High—he didn't want to be hated by his neighbors. His mother insisted that he go through with it for the sake of his younger brothers and sisters. Before going to bed, after sitting brooding and trembling, Billy would take an aspirin and pray for God's help in getting "through that line in the morning."

These were some of the comments the Negro students made to reporters:

"I just want to get an education."
"White folks don't bother me. I went to school with them in three states."
"Once you get inside school, it's fine."

* * * * *

As September wore on and autumn came to Southville, the issue did indeed seem to have been settled. No one in the County responded when the Board of Education, after considering the desegregation situation for an entire meeting on October 11th, quietly announced its readiness to arrange for any of the 12 Negro students' families to transfer their children "to any other school within a reasonable distance." Nor was there any apparent response to a Ku Klux Klan demonstration two evenings later, which brought 125 carloads of hooded klansmen from a wide area driving through Southville, holding a rally in the country nearby, and burning four crosses.

Some 35 students, it was estimated, stayed away from the school for good because of the desegregation; an unannounced number applied to the school board for transportation to a nearby all-white school, a request on which the Board refused to act at its November 8th meeting. At the school itself, to quote England, "everything went smoothly." The Negro students reported that the white students had grown more friendly, asking "about my homework, did I have it done, things like that." The members of the football team went out of their way to talk with him, Billy Lines said.

* * * * *

During late August and early September both county and federal authorities had brought Meyer into court. Having appealed his contempt conviction to the Circuit Court, he was still at liberty. Now it was the state's turn. On September 24th the state's attorney general filed charges against Meyer for inciting to riot (a misdemeanor) and for violating a statute which made it also a misdemeanor to

> . . . Wilfully and intentionally utter seditious words or speeches to instigate others to cabal and meet together to contrive, invent, suggest or incite rebellious conspiracies . . . to contrive the ruin and destruction of the peace, safety and order of the government.

Meyer's trial on these charges was set for Monday, November 5th, in the Southville County Court House. Owing to several recesses, the trial lasted until fifteen days later. During that time the prosecution brought 10 witnesses against Meyer, and the defense 58 on his behalf. As the trial began, pro-Meyer pickets in the courthouse square suggested that he had been framed and that the trial would not be fair. Soon the courtroom, which seated 200 people, became a gathering place for Meyer's supporters, most of the audience coming from the rural areas. His trial turned into a forum for what was probably the longest string of racist speeches ever heard in the area.

It was also during the first days of November that little anti-Negro incidents began occurring in Southville High School. There was a sudden increase in the number of insulting and bullying remarks made to the Negro students. During the next weeks ink was poured into one Negro girl's locker, and eggs smashed on Negro students' books. Knives were flourished before their eyes. Two white boys reported that they had been offered—and refused—$5 and $50 respectively to start fights with Negro students.

A faculty member reported that in the hallways one could hear such shouts as, "If you come back to school, I'll cut your guts out!" Foul language was constantly whispered where it could be overheard by the Negro students. One day during a study hall in the auditorium, white students inconspicuously whispered filthy names to a young Negro girl. They kept it up for some time. Finally, "one boy looked like he was going to touch me, and I left." As she walked out of the auditorium, the white students applauded their triumph. Later, after a lecture from the Assistant Principal, some of the white students apologized. Others looked back at the Assistant Principal "with blood in their eyes," whispering "nigger-lover."

During the week of November 19th a national magazine published an article about the Southville situation under the title, "The Ordeal of Billy Lines." After that a number of the white students seemed to make him the special target of their harassment. A group of other white boys quietly organized themselves to watch over him in case he should actually be attacked.

A member of the school staff said it appeared as if 40 or 50 students had embarked on an organized campaign to make the Negro students' life unbearable. According to a November 24th press report, England said that the segregationists were now trying "to scare the Negro children out of school [and] force me to resign." A reporter said that school authorities were unable to punish the offenders because they could not obtain incriminating evidence against individuals—this being due partly to the unwillingness of other white students to testify openly against them. He did obtain from some of the troublemakers themselves the statement that they were being encouraged by "men in town."

For some time England had been receiving numberless insulting and obscene telephone calls; altogether he changed his unlisted number four times. KKK crosses were burned in front of his home.

> But now they're trying to hurt me not only by threatening me, but by boycotting the stores where I do business, and threatening the

faculty and trying every other means of intimidation they know. It makes a man feel terrible when he sees his friends hurt because of him.

Few, if any, of England's fellow citizens offered any tangible support.

> How can I feel the same way towards people I knew all my life as friends when they refused to stand up for what is right and found the nearest hole and said, 'I hope it doesn't hurt business'?

England began to express openly his view that the law-abiding majority, including all but one of the members of the County Board of Education, were largely to blame for the worsening situation.

One member of the Board was willing to be quoted as agreeing with England. The Chairman, however, said the Board had done everything it could to conform to the federal court order. "I don't think the Board ever gets into disciplinary problems," he said at a meeting on November 29th. "The matter of protection for the Negroes is outside the Board's jurisdiction." It was a matter for the Principal to handle.

A local observer was quoted by a press correspondent as saying that both the general citizenry and the Board had been proceeding

> . . . On the theory that the safety of the pupils outside of school was a matter for the police and that their well-being inside school was a matter for the school principal.

The *News-Times* repeatedly criticized the apathy of the people of Southville toward the situation.

On November 19th, the day before Meyer's trial was to end, the Henderson County Registrar of Deeds issued a charter to an organization called White Youth of the State, which was affiliated with a state-wide organization dedicated to maintaining racial segregation. The group's president was a 17-year-old Southville High School girl. According to the officers, the organization had been formed the previous week and now had 107 members in Southville High School and two nearby high schools. The granting of the charter was the occasion for a newspaper story and photograph.

WYS badges began to appear in school, bearing the slogan, "Keep our schools white." One girl wearing such a badge frequently went out of her way to sit near Negro students. When a teacher asked her to remove the badge, she replied that it was her "legal right" to wear whatever she wished.

The WYS launched into a series of semi-secret meetings in back rooms and off alleys, at which KKK literature and pictures of Negroes kissing white girls were distributed. One of the boys who went to these meetings said later:

> We talked about how we would hate Negroes and the people who take up for them. . . . We just talked. Sat around for hours and hours. I got tired. They didn't tell us exactly what to do, just said a lot of things.

Throughout accounts of the meetings ran the recurring words "hate" and "mongrel," and the slogan "Yesterday-Today-Forever."

A member of the school faculty asserted that the students who joined the WYS "were never quite the same afterward." Before long the WYS began to harass white students who refused to join.

The Negroes began staying closer together again. They were now only ten; two had dropped out the previous month, one to move to the north.

On Tuesday, November 20th, the arguments in Meyer's trial ended, and the jury recessed. Forty-five minutes later they returned and reported their verdict; on both counts not guilty. The crowd in the court room cheered loudly.

Meyer stayed on in Southville and set up a White Citizens Council headquarters on a highway outside of the town. He now launched a campaign to get the state legislature to adopt strong segregation laws at its next session. Local elections were to take place in Southville in December, and the WCC openly backed a candidate for mayor of Southville and a candidate for one of three positions on the city council.

At Southville High incidents of intimidation and harassment continued to multiply. On Monday, November 26th, rocks were thrown at Negro students outside the school. It was reported that an FBI agent had been sent to talk quietly with England about the situation, and a week later a press agency was to report that the FBI had "a volume of information" about the organized harassment and intimidation.

On Tuesday, November 27th, two white boys threw eggs at three Negro girls, and Negro students were cursed and tripped in the corridors. That same day one of the six Negro boys told England he was "tired of being molested," and with England's permission he and another Negro boy left the school. The faculty decided upon a policy of firmer discipline: no type of misbehavior was to be excused, and, wherever justified, there would be expulsions.

But on Wednesday no Negro students came to school. One of the Negro mothers said,

> We'd had all we could bear. We wanted some assurance our children wouldn't be harmed before we let them walk into that school again.

Mary Sue Brown, one of those who had been pelted with eggs, told a reporter, "We just decided to stay away from school today. We may go back tomorrow." There was no organized boycott, she said. "Everybody just made up his or her own mind."

Another girl said that whether she would stay in school would be up to her mother. "I'd rather stay," she said, "but we can't be treated any more the way we have."

When asked by reporters for a statement, England said that he had been instructed to say nothing about any aspect of the desegregation situation.

The Superintendent of Schools said, "In the light of all the trouble we've had, everybody feels like it is best that we say nothing further at this time."

The Chairman of the County Board of Education said he did not know of any instruction to England not to talk about the matter.

On Thursday morning six Negro students left their homes and walked toward the school together. As they approached the school building, they saw a truck, a car, and a number of people. They feared they were to be attacked, they said later, so they turned back and did not attend school that day. The police, who checked the situation immediately, reported that the car had stalled, and the truck was a tow truck sent to haul it into town. The police chief described the Negro students as "a little frightened, a little on the shaky side."

As Mrs. England entered the school—she was one of the teachers—she was struck by two eggs.

England called a school assembly. According to pupils, he said in firm tones,

I want to give it to you straight . . . I'm not going to tolerate any misconduct. . . . And I mean it.

A meeting of the County Board of Education was scheduled for that evening. But when the Chairman was told by "at least one Negro parent" that if the Board would agree he would request transportation for his child to the segregated school in Jonestown which Southville Negroes had previously attended, he moved the meeting up to 1:00 p.m. Although the Board had received no actual requests for transfers, it again went on record as being willing to "make all necessary arrangements" for transfers for Negro students.

During the day Mary Sue Brown's father said, however, "We're standing pat. Personally, I'm not asking for anything of the kind."

One of the other Negro girls said, "I'm planning on going back in the morning with the others. [It's] the only thing for us to do."

The father of one Negro boy said his family had received an anonymous, obscene telephone call, in which he had been threatened with "bodily harm" if his boy returned to school the next day. The Negro minister, too, had been given a telephone warning that the Negro students would be physically attacked.

Reporters predicted that what happened at 8:30 a.m. on November 30th would decide the fate of desegregation at Southville High.

That evening the Negro parents held a meeting. They agreed that none of them would request transfers, but that they would keep their children out of school until the school board gave them assurances of their safety. Apparently there was some talk of asking the Board, if it could not guarantee their safety, to instruct them in their homes.

The next morning, Friday, November 30th, as time for school opening approached, five men sat in three cars parked half a block up the road down which the Negro students would have walked. A police car was parked nearby, its occupant watching the five men closely. When asked by a reporter whether they belonged to the White Citizens Council, the men refused to answer. After the time for the opening of school had passed, the men drove off.

At the school, in 25° cold, about 15 white boys had stood outside the entrance. When told by England at 8:25 to come into the building, they had done so.

During the day the school board Chairman issued a statement, reportedly in response to pressure from constituents in a nearby town, where he doubled as mayor. He said the Board would give Mr. England "any support he feels he needs" for putting a stop to the disturbances at the school. "I'm sure the Board will grant any request," he said, "from this man who has done such a magnificent job."

As the week ended, the County Superintendent asked a nearby school system for permission to send Negro students there should they request it. A teacher was quoted as saying, "It looked like everything we had built up here was falling apart."

On Saturday England conferred for two hours with the federal district attorney. The press reported the latter's attitude to be in effect: "It's your problem. You'll have to handle it." But he agreed to refer the matter to the United States Attorney General. This information was made public.

It was also revealed that England and about half of his faculty were talking seriously of resigning in January if the Board and the public did not give them greater support.

On Sunday, December 2nd, word leaked out of a secret, unofficial meeting of the members of the Board, at which the situation was discussed. At the meeting there was talk of closing the high school entirely. Then it was agreed that at its special meeting called for early on Monday morning the Board would adopt a resolution asking the United States Attorney General for help.

At two of the town's prominent churches the sermons that morning were devoted to the importance of law and order.

At 7:30 on Monday the school board met in extraordinary session. Before school opened an hour later, the following letter had been sent to the Attorney General of the United States, with copies to the United States District Attorney in the area, Judge Taylor, and the Governor of the State.

> The School Board of Henderson County has conscientiously done all in its power to comply with the direction of the U. S. District Court in Jonestown, which ordered the integration last January 4th.
>
> This has been done, contrary to our convictions on the matter and in the face of constant criticism and harassment from our fellow citizens. . . .
>
> The Negro children in Southville High School have asked us for protection in attending school. The board does not have legal authority to give this protection nor does it wish to assume it.
>
> The only penalty which the board can apply to the present prob-

lem is to expel students, an action which obviously was designed to enforce routine school regulations and not to enforce a Federal Court mandate.

The board's position is that it has complied with the law in opening the school to all children and it is the responsibility of others to enforce the injunction if it is to be enforced.

The board feels that its duty is to obey orders of the federal court, not to enforce them. The situation now existing in Southville High School is not simply a disciplinary problem. For the authorities of the federal government to retreat to their impregnable position or assume, or take the position, that the carrying out of such an order is a "local problem" would seem to be the height of absurdity and wholly inconsistent with reality and other federal government policies. . . .

The Henderson County School Board must know whether the Department of Justice intends to continue lack of enforcement of the federal court injunction. If so, it might become necessary to close the Southville High School so long as we are under court order to abolish segregation.

It is imperative that we hear from you within five days, so that we may plan accordingly.

After the Board meeting England held a press conference, at which he described the Board's action as "the strongest action it could have taken." (Later in the day the news wires reported a comment from lawyers at the Attorney General's office which—by referring to a similar case in another state—seemed to say that a more appropriate source of help would be Judge Edwards, who could again institute contempt proceedings.)

England also publicly blamed the WYS for the recent difficulties, saying that about 40 students were responsible. No Negroes came to school that morning, and England said, "I believe they will stay out this week."

It was the last day of the municipal election campaign in Southville. Interest in the race mounted, as the White Citizens Council distributed handbills with information about the candidates' stands with respect to its platform.

On that same morning the Reverend Peter N. Baker, who for eight years had been minister of the all-white Southville Baptist Church, sent word to the Negro children that he was willing to escort them back to school the next day if they so wished. They accepted his offer.

Word spread quickly around the town, and Mr. Baker received a number of threatening telephone calls. On Tuesday morning, December 4th, accompanied by an attorney who was Chairman of his church's Board of Deacons and by an accountant at the town mill, Baker went to meet six of the Negro students—one of the girls was hospitalized. He escorted them down the road to the school, past some 50 hecklers, and, at 8:35, into the school. A reporter went along, and a policeman was on hand. Baker asked the latter to take down the names of those who were heckling him, which he did.

A few minutes later Baker started down the street, followed by the crowd. Fearing what he called a "trap," he stopped at the police station and asked for help. The whole force was on duty at the school. He went back out and headed again for his office. Four men closed in on him. According to one report he pushed one of them away. At any rate he was grabbed, tried to escape, then fought back but was forced to the ground by seven men and two women. Someone shouted, "Kill the - - - - nigger-lover!" Another man hit him several times in the face. Storekeepers and the police rushed up, and the assailant was arrested. Witnesses who told the story to reporters asked not to be identified by name.

During the morning several white youths, none of them a student, showed up in the school. Two of them, one a recent drop-out from the freshman class, stopped a student in the hall and demanded of him, "Where's the niggers? We want to get them." Mrs. England left her classroom and went out into the hall, but just then England himself appeared. The two youths ran, one nearly knocking Mrs. England over. The rumor spread around town that he had attacked her.

That day England expelled from school a white student who pushed a Negro student.

As these events became known, the Board Chairman polled members individually as to whether the school should be closed. All agreed that "until further notice" it should. The six Negroes were dismissed early and escorted home by police. When the other students had left, the school's doors closed.

Late in the day the twenty-five member high school faculty addressed a lengthy statement to the public. Its first four paragraphs contained a quotation from, and a reaffirmation of, a three-year-old declaration of the faculty's "beliefs as to the purposes of education." The statement went on as follows:

As conscientious citizens, teachers, and parents, we have attempted to live up to these purposes. A minority group has tried to prevent us from carrying out our professional obligations. Despite this, for the sake of the children of this community, the principal of this school and the staff have continued since September under almost unbearable circumstances at times.

We feel that we would have succeeded, and were making progress until George Meyer's acquittal and the organization of the White Youth Council. The activities of this small group in our school have been of a vicious nature, obviously prompted by a mature person.

This vicious undercurrent has brought about the closing of Southville High School, whether deliberate or unintentional. We are now faced with the fact that this minority movement is depriving more than 700 children, some of whom are our own children, from receiving education to which they are entitled.

As teachers of your children, we call upon conscientious parents of young people and all interested residents of this county to investigate the current activities of this minority group which is rapidly bringing about a breakdown of respect among the young people for law and order, contributing to delinquency, and an overthrow of authority, which results in mob rule. We make this statement because we feel many parents and citizens are unaware of the type of leadership to which the children of Henderson County are being exposed.

We believe there are enough people who are interested in law, order and the education of the children of Southville that they will come forward and make known publicly their feelings on a matter which affects the whole future of their children and our democratic way of life.

We give the principal of the Southville High School, Mr. J. D. England, Jr., our unlimited support for having done an excellent job under distressing conditions. Only a person dedicated to the welfare of the youth of this community and the principles of a democratic government would have undergone such personal harassment as he has received.

For the sake of the children of this community, and the people who believe in upholding law and order, and our democratic way of life, the Southville High School faculty unanimously goes on record as being willing to continue to teach the children of Henderson County who are interested in receiving an education and have a sincere desire to learn.

The Southville Faculty (Signatures)

Word spread around town that by that afternoon the FBI would arrest 18 trouble-makers, and the Board Chairman told the press, "We hope it will be possible to reopen the school within a few days." He said the Board would decide at a meeting later in the day and would rely heavily on England's recommendation.

Mary Sue Brown's family announced that it was moving away from Southville later in the week. "I hate to go," the girl told a reporter.

> At first the girls at school were real nice to me, but later one of my best friends was named an officer in this White Citizens' Youth movement, and it seemed like she changed overnight. She hasn't been so nice to me since.

"Things are getting worse here since this school situation came up," her father explained. He had not been able to get regular work for three years.

> White folks live across the street from me, and before this we all got along real fine-like. Whenever the white folks wanted something of mine, they just came over here and got it, and when I wanted to borrow something from them I did the same thing. . . . Things have changed.

England and several other Southville citizens and the U. S. district attorney met with Judge Edwards at his chambers and reported on the recent events. The district attorney presented evidence "showing in my opinion a violation of the injunction Judge Edwards made permanent September 6, 1956," and asked Judge Edwards to "order the arrest of certain parties." Edwards said he expected to act on the matter the following day.

During the day the Board's appeal for help was received in Washington, as was also a request from Judge Edwards for an investigation by the FBI.

That evening the United States Attorney General wired the Board that at Judge Edwards' request he was instructing federal agents to

> . . . Ascertain the facts and bring before the court for proper process all persons who may have wilfully violated the order of the court. . . .
> The Department will also institute any additional proceedings that may become necessary in the future in order to secure observance

of the court's order and to protect those who obey it from interference.

The Department of Justice has a duty to assist the Federal Court by apprehending and prosecuting those responsible for wilful violation of court orders and the Department will continue to discharge this duty. . . .

The Attorney General reminded the Board, however, that "the primary responsibility for keeping law and order. . . rests upon the state and local authorities."

Perhaps it was a coincidence that the new outbreak of violence had come on the morning of Election Day. There was some comment later in the day about the unusually heavy afternoon voter turn-out which brought the total number of those voting up to double the previous record. Three statements made later to reporters may help to explain what happened.

You might call Peter the catalytic agent we needed to bring this whole thing into the open. The whole White Citizens' Council ticket for mayor and aldermen was defeated four to one. People who'd been afraid to speak up before spoke out with their ballots.

Somebody had to do it. And it wasn't going to be my husband, and it wasn't going to be any of the others that have businesses here in town. Most of us had shaken our heads over the Citizens' Council and what it stood for, but we'd gone right ahead pussy-footing and passing the buck. Peter Baker stuck his neck out for all of us.

Remember, we're not called the Bible belt without reason. Baker wasn't just anyone getting mauled. He was a symbol, too. What happened, happened to us all, and it waked us up.

The man who was elected mayor by 1,344 votes to 353 had previously served several terms in the office and had also been a judge. He had strongly opposed desegregation. Now he stated that he would "abide by the law and expect everyone else to."

On Wednesday Judge Edwards issued criminal contempt warrants against sixteen persons, including the local Chairman of the White Citizens' Council. Before nightfall seven U. S. marshals and three special deputies had arrested all of them but the one woman, who was still being sought. They were arraigned, being charged with "one or more" of a lengthy list of violations of the court order forbidding interference with the desegregation at Southville. They denied the charges, promised to abide by the law and stay away from the school, and were released on bond. The White Citizens' Council Chairman told the press,

> All I've been doing is saying what I believe in. The way I under-
> stand things in this country is that every man has a right to have his
> say.

The County Board of Education held a three-hour meeting, stated that it was "gratified with the progress of federal and local authorities," and said that it would not reopen Southville High until it was safe for students to return. But it was "hopeful of reopening" the school the following Monday. It invited the whole school faculty to a luncheon meeting on Friday, "to coordinate efforts of faculty and board with federal and local authorities for the orderly reopening of the Southville High School." The Board invited a federal official to join them at the luncheon, "to give the teachers an opportunity of advising them of any conduct on behalf of the students within the school that might be considered a violation of the federal injunction."

The President of the school's PTA told the press,

> I think [the school] should be reopened by all means. I just don't
> see any point in shilly-shallying around any more about it.

Polls of parents indicated general agreement with this position.

On Friday the school board's luncheon was held. It was a closed session, lasting three hours. The Board announced that it expected to reopen the high school on Monday, "barring any acts of violence" over the week-end. England said he expected no trouble when the school reopened. Those present agreed on the importance of handling the students with caution and patience and using "an educational approach."

The Police Chief promised the Negro students full protection, and the Board of Education said it would expel any students caught harassing them. Most of them indicated they would return to school. Several prominent citizens expressed the desire to be allowed to talk to the students about the importance of law-abiding behavior, but it was agreed that the county attorney should read to the whole student body the text of the September injunction and explain where the line was drawn between ordinary misbehavior and violation of the court order.

It was reported that half a dozen FBI agents were investigating 72 persons, including 17 students at the school.

On Monday, December 10th, Southville High reopened. A total of 583 white students, about 70 fewer than the previous week, and 8 Negroes entered its doors. The latter walked to school, chatting with newsmen and newsreel camera operators. There were fifteen white students and three or four adults near the door, but no demonstrations of any kind. The student body was reported to be in a "jovial" mood. At 8:45, after attendance had been taken, England opened an assembly, amid loud applause and, according to a reporter, three boos. He urged the students not to be restless because of the television cameras. He then introduced the county attorney, who said he was there at the request of the Board to tell the students in his official capacity not how to think or what to believe, but how they must behave as long as they were students at Southville High. He read the court order, explained that it applied to minors, and that it forbade "gathering outside the school" when Negro students were arriving, "messing up lockers, filthy language, pouring of ink on books, and anonymous letters to teachers." He suggested that students cease wearing WYS badges. England declared that the injunction made it "perfectly clear where we all stand," and said, "I hope we can forget our differences." Both men were loudly applauded.

The whole day—and the days following—passed with no disturbances. England reported that "generally the attitude of the students toward the Negroes has been wonderful." Prosegregation buttons and stickers virtually disappeared.

On December 11th a state segregationist organization requested permission to address a student assembly on the students' constitutional rights. No action was taken by the school board until five weeks later, when the request was unanimously denied with the explanation that such an address would be "anti-integrationist" activity.

Christmas vacation came and went, and the second semester started. Some of the white students continued quietly harassing Negro students (putting tacks on their seats and so on). On the first Monday in February, just after the end of school, a 21-year-old Negro senior was reportedly warning a white boy to stop bothering one of the Negro freshmen. Whatever was said led to the older Negro's hitting one white boy and then pulling out a pocket knife as if to threaten others nearby.

The Negro boy, whose school record was characterized by England as "poor," was suspended. The white boy was withdrawn by his parents, who said his studies had been hurt by desegregation. They described themselves as preferring to let the Negroes take over the school, and have the boy work on a farm "where he won't come into contact with all that stuff."

In the middle of February England described some of the students as "still very unhappy" about attending school with Negroes, but said that all in all it was "pretty much of a dead issue within the school now."

No further incidents of any magnitude occurred in the school during the rest of the year. In May England resigned his position, to accept a teaching fellowship and to work toward a doctorate in school administration at a university in another state. That same month Billy Lines quietly became the first Negro to graduate from the school.

For two years there were incidents in the community involving the discovery or the detonation of dynamite. When in February the home of one of the Negroes had been badly damaged, the whole community had collected money to help rebuild it. And when, early one Sunday morning in October, 1958, the high school building itself was dynamited, the citizenry reacted with prompt determination. An abandoned building nearby was cleaned and refurbished by hundreds of volunteers. "They did in three days what it would normally have taken weeks to accomplish," said the Principal. Then a new high school was built.

All organized opposition to desegregation at Southville High had ceased.

*   *   *   *   *

What was the setting in which the events we have described took place? Southville itself, an old town, had a population of 3,712, according to the most recent census. As a shopping and government center, it served a population going beyond Henderson County's 60,000 inhabitants. Despite the relative backwardness and poverty of many of the rural areas upon which it depended for its livelihood, Southville was a prosperous and proud community. In 1949 the average family income in the town had been estimated at $2,833, well above the average for the state. Its chief industry was a textile mill employing about a thousand workers. Workers commuted to the mill from homes throughout Henderson and four other counties.

Of Southville's population a young lawyer said, "We're more urban all the time. . . . Around the courthouse there are very few left of the old sit-whittle-and-spit crowd."

Southville lay in the eastern part of the county, and it was from this rural area that some one half of Southville High School's enrollment came. It was primarily a farming district. Recently, however, two large federal government installations, six and nine miles respectively from Southville, had attracted many laborers of various levels of skill. The latter were mostly whites from parts of the Deep South where old patterns of farming were disappearing. However, between 1940 and 1950 the county's Negro population had also grown—from 484 to 1,813.

The northern and western parts of the county, where mining was the chief occupation, were sparsely settled and had been less affected by change. Many persons in this section of the county were well acquainted with dynamite and its use.

The county's Negro population was scattered, with many districts having no Negroes in them. Except for those at one of the government installations, the largest group of Negroes in a single place consisted of the 220 living in Southville. They were maids and janitors, or held other service and unskilled jobs, most of them at the government reservation. At Southville they had two churches and a segregated elementary school. The school was operated by the Southville Board of Education, which was separate from the County Board. Their high school age young people had always traveled by bus to schools outside the county.

A prominent white resident described Southville's Negroes thus:

> These aren't like the Deep South Negroes. We haven't had integration, but they've never been like the bowing-down ones, always tipping their hats and stepping aside on the street corner. These are people who vote, who call us by our names, and who have self-respect.

They were not people with high school educations, however, nor did their community contain any professional or business persons. Many of them told Negro interviewers that before desegregation race relations in the town had been good. They mentioned the custom of exchanging choirs between Negro and white churches, and the fact that occasionally whites had attended Negro church suppers. At the same time all the evidence indicates that Southville's Negroes as a group strongly favored the desegregation move.

As to Southville's white citizens, few if any favored the desegregation. Positions of civic leadership in Southville tended to fall to persons whose families were of long standing in the community or who were themselves important in its business life. Mr. England's family was well-known in Henderson County, and among other relatives of his known in education in the county was his father, a superintendent of schools not far away. The Chairman of the county school board was owner and manager of a creamery in the nearby town where he also served as mayor. One board member was the Southville Chief of Police. The board's attorney, who at a young age had already distinguished himself in the state legislature, was son of the mayor, who co-owned and ran Southville's biggest department store. His wife, by the way, was a public school teacher. The newspaper editor's wife was a member of the Executive Committee of the PTA. Most of the community's leaders attended the Southville Baptist Church.

Almost to a man the white leadership, England included, had joined in court battles and other, informal efforts to head off school desegregation. But, according to the editor of the News-Times, "not a single businessman or political leader or community leader" took any part in the attempts to interfere with it once it had been ordered by the court. The editor himself, who until the court spoke had urged resistance to desegregation, over and over again appealed to the public to obey the law, and explained the facts and the law of the case. Just before the Negro students first entered the school, the press had quoted England as saying that "with the exception of one or two" the white parents had accepted desegregation. One citizen told a journalist, "I'd say 90% of us are for abiding by the law."

In November, by way of contrast, a city official was to speak of the white community in these words: "We're broken off into different groups that eye each other with distrust and suspicion and are fighting each other."

Meyer's following was estimated at from 250 to 350 persons. The lawyer for the school board said this about them:

> There are a few sincere segregationists in Meyer's group, but I'm afraid that they're mostly people opposed to anyone who has achieved

a little material success. . . . These people aren't so much for segregation as they are *against* something. It happens to be integration, but they're against authority and looking for excitement. . . .

Two years later the same man had this to say about "those Meyer people":

For a while it was big for them, they belonged, and they were running things, and they were important. Then it just died. . . . They went back under the rocks or wherever they came from. You know, you never see people like that unless there's trouble. You know how they were on me, just standing up there and hating me as hard as they could in those days. Well, of those fifteen that were tried in Jonestown afterwards, six came by to see me as their lawyer when they got in trouble. . . .

And my father, you know how much trouble they gave him when he was mayor. Well, the other day three of them, maybe not Meyer's top men, but sure-enough fellow travelers, went down to Dad and tried to get him to run for mayor again.

One old-time resident, reflecting upon the composition of Meyer's following, said this:

Southville had its share of the hoodlums in that mob, but the whiplash was carried by the miners from the hills, some of the canned heat and moonshine goons who are regular week-end guests at the town pokey.

The description hardly seemed to fit the Chairman of the local White Citizens Council, which was organized after the events of September, 1956. He was a machinist inspector at a federal government installation, who had moved to a rural home in Henderson County in 1953, after having spent most of his earlier life in the Deep South. He said this about himself:

The FBI checked on me for four months. I don't smoke; I don't drink. I don't claim to be an angel, but I am a whole lot better than some of the people who have arrested me.

What they've got against me is that I keep right after them—legally. They've tried to change the time of school board meetings so that I couldn't make it and protest against things.

During the heat of the controversy one of the active opponents of desegregation had this to say:

> The trouble was, a lot of people thought they were better than we are. When one bunch rules the roost too long that's bad, and history shows . . . [he trailed off without finishing the sentence].

As one segregationist leader called for a boycott of the entire Chamber of Commerce, he characterized that body as filled with "integrators, traitors, and radicals."

A Negro doctor well-acquainted with the situation said simply, "It's the poor folks against the rich folks, and the rich folks have laid down the law."

SELECTED READINGS

Allport, Gordon W., *The Nature of Prejudice*. Cambridge, Massachusetts: The Addison-Wesley Publishing Company, 1954.

Benedict, Ruth F., *Race: Science and Politics*. New York: Modern Age Books, 1940.

Ehlers, Henry, and Gordon C. Lee, eds., *Crucial Issues in Education: An Anthology*, rev. ed. New York: Henry Holt and Company, 1959. Chs. 2, 5.

Hill, Herbert, and Jack Greenberg, *Citizens Guide to Desegregation: A Study of Social and Legal Change in American Life*. Boston: The Beacon Press, 1955.

Key, V. O., Jr., *Southern Politics in State and Nation*. New York: Alfred A. Knopf, 1950.

Myrdal, Gunnar, *An American Dilemma: The Negro Problem and Modern Democracy*. New York: Harper and Brothers, 1944.

Tipton, James H., *Community in Crisis: The Elimination of Segregation from a Public School System*. New York: Bureau of Publications, Teachers College, Columbia University, 1953.

Wey, Herbert, and John Corey, *Action Patterns in School Desegregation: A Guidebook*. Bloomington: Phi Delta Kappa, 1959.

Rinks
and
Soshes

West High School had an enroll-
ment well over 2000 in a building about 30 years old. It served an
area of the city inhabited largely by business and professional people.
It was a three-year comprehensive high school, with relatively high
academic standards and an enviable scholastic record. More than 70
per cent of the graduates later enrolled in college. Nowhere in the district was there an area of poor dwellings or slums. In fact it was regarded by many as one of the most desirable residential districts in the
city.

Teachers liked to teach at West High. They found the students for
the most part eager, and the patrons interested in school affairs.
Because of the community's strong academic tradition in recent years
the teachers and the four full-time counselors had found it increasingly
hard to meet the needs of slow learners. These students appeared to be
left farther behind in the growing emphasis on mathematics, science,
and other "difficult academic subjects."

The students of West High had always cooperated in school government, and through the years the student council and courts had taken
a larger share of responsibility for student behavior. There was no
shortage of activities for any student who wished to take part. The
PTA sponsored dances and ski trips. The school had a strong and

successful athletic program including intra-mural sports. Dramatics and music were well developed, and there was a wide array of interest clubs in areas such as science, languages, and art. Students were described as eager, well-dressed, and socially competent.

Some West High students were said to be "over-privileged." The term "sosh"[1] had been coined by their fellow students to describe members of this group. To call a boy a "sosh" was to suggest that he was supplied by his parents with a liberal allowance, good clothes, and an up-to-date car, and that he did not have to take his studies seriously if they interfered with his skiing.

"The Inn" had existed for several years. It was one of three "beaneries" across the street from West High. It had once been a medium-sized grocery store, and its cavernous interior was furnished with a few booths along one wall, a juke box and counter opposite them, and a large area of littered floor in between. At noon it teemed with students buying quick lunches, but during other hours of the day the adult visitor commonly found at the Inn only a small group of boys and girls, who appeared to regard him with open suspicion. This was the hard core among the habitués of the Inn. They were nondescript in appearance and habits, but they had one common denominator. All of them clung to the companionship and security they could find there and nowhere else. Other students called them "rinks."[2]

The Vice-Principal of West High visited the Inn at intervals to round up students who might be skipping class. He often found a boy or girl who on the school records appeared to have been legitimately excused from classes because of illness. "I felt better," he was typically told, "so I came over to the Inn."

During class hours one might also see there students who were under suspension for disciplinary reasons and a few older "alumni" of the Inn who dropped in for a pleasant hour. Almost without exception those students who had police records of serious delinquency were found at the Inn.

Male "rinks," who outnumbered their girl counterparts four to one, were often conspicuous in tight jeans worn precariously low on the

---

[1] The "o" is long as in "socialite."

[2] The term "rink" appeared in teen-age jargon during World War II, when roller skating rinks became meeting places for service men and school girls. There is also an adjective "rinky," a synonym for "cheap," used to describe dress or conversation.

hips. Many had elaborate haircuts. Their most consistent badge was the impression they gave of resenting all authority. They appeared to constitute a minor sub-culture within the teen-age group.

Two blocks east of West High School the ground rose to form a low ridge which had become known as "Sosh Hill." Here many of the socially active students parked their cars and ate their sack lunches at noon to the dismay of householders who sometimes found their driveways blocked or their lawns littered.

During the summer of 1956 summer school classes were held at West High School. Hundreds of students from all over the city who had received failing grades during the year arrived daily for a half day of classwork. The Inn stayed open and did a good business.

On July 12, 1956, two girls were reported to have been molested in a nearby park by a group of boys who had followed them when they had started home from the Inn after school. In the active police investigation that ensued, the proprietor was warned that loitering at the Inn must cease. His first move was to prohibit smoking, which had been permitted for years.

"When school opened in the fall the kids were like bees who return to find the hive gone," declared the Vice-Principal. "Not angry, just bewildered and lost." They clustered around the door of the Inn and completely filled the sidewalk. For the first time in the school's history, motorists and nearby residents were treated to the sight before school, after school, and at noon of a crowd of carelessly-dressed and often insolent-acting boys smoking and lounging about near school. Public reaction was immediate, and complaints poured in from citizens already alarmed by reports of "blackboard jungles" in other cities. The Vice-Principal went out to talk to the boys on the sidewalk.

Within a day a delegation of teen-age patrons of the Inn called on the Vice-Principal requesting that the school outfit a room as a smoking lounge. They were informed that such a project would be a violation of state law and totally unacceptable to the public. The Vice-Principal commended the delegates for their thoughtful approach to the problem and urged them to work to protect the reputation of the school and of teen-agers.

When the delegation returned to the Inn they called a mass meeting of students to hear their report on their failure to obtain a smoking lounge in the school. The larger group responded by loudly demanding a smoking room in the Inn even at the expense of building and policing it themselves. Some of the more ambitious ones began at once to draw plans and to collect sheets of used plywood.

At this point the proprietor acted to clear the proposal with the fire chief's office, and was forced to tell the boys their plans could not meet the building code requirements. Resigned to defeat, the boys returned to the sidewalk.

West High School had a long-established and effective student government. The Vice-Principal next took the problem to the Student Cabinet. The outcome was a three-step program of enforcement by the students.

> 1. Around the school a no-smoking zone with a two-block radius was set up.
>
> 2. A patrol of popular student leaders including several star athletes was assigned to mingle with the crowd on the sidewalk and urge individuals to move away if they wished to smoke.
>
> 3. After a week during which the issue was to be thoroughly aired in home-room discussions, violators were to appear before the student court.

For some time the plan appeared to be working. The crowd dwindled somewhat, and public complaints became fewer. Then the patrol reported, "We cannot cover the entire area effectively without feeling like cops. What is more, lots of the smokers enjoy being caught. They become heroes when they blow smoke in our faces."

Meanwhile violators pleaded in student court, "All we want is a place to smoke. Smoking is not a crime. Rich kids smoke in their cars. Don't be hypocritical." This logic began seriously to weaken the Student Cabinet's position. The smoking-free zone was reduced to a one-block radius, and patrolling continued sporadically.

While the onset of winter reduced somewhat the amount of conspicuous loitering, it seemed also to reduce the ardor of the patrol boys proportionately. With public education generally under fire, the administration struggled with the problem. Suspensions proved useless. As often as not the suspended boy would then spend his whole day at the Inn. Parent conferences seldom were effective, since parents of "rinks" seemed often unable or unwilling to discipline their children.

Snow was rare enough to occasion excitement among West High students. On January 9, 1957, five inches of snow fell during the day. In front of the Inn a loaded city bus was having difficulty drawing away from the curb. It was after the close of school, and there were students on the bus and on the sidewalk. They began a snowball fight. Mrs. George Leary, who lived in a second-floor apartment nearby, opened her window slightly and called, "Stop that, you bad boys!"

At this moment the bus got under way, and the boys on the street, including some who were not students, turned their attention to Mrs. Leary. As snowballs shattered her window, she retreated with her baby to another room. Snowballs continued to pour through the window and to smash against walls and furniture. George Leary, her husband, hurried to the street and grabbed the arm of the first boy he met, Ed Wesley, 17 years old. Witnesses, all teen-agers, stated that Leary struck Ed first. However it may have happened, within a few moments the adult was knocked down in the snow, the snowballing had stopped, and the crowd was melting away.

Police were unable to find witnesses to disprove Ed Wesley's story that he had merely been walking by when Leary attacked him, and that he had not been involved in the snowballing. Leary did not press charges, saying he was afraid of reprisals. "I might have expected Ed Wesley to be guilty," stated the Vice-Principal. "He has a quick temper and strongly resents authority. His home is very unstable." Wesley was later dropped from school for an accumulation of offenses.

Mrs. Leary sent the bill for replacing the window glass to the school for payment. It was returned.

A little more than a month later, on February 12th, a few minutes after 8:30 a.m., another incident occurred. Sixteen-year-old George McArthur, his lip cut and bleeding, left the Inn and ran to the home of his grandmother for a butcher knife with which to "protect" himself from further attacks by three "soshes" who had invaded the Inn. George's younger brother Bob ran after him to reason with him, and a frightened girl named Susan burst into the office of the Vice-Principal wailing, "Please stop George before he kills somebody. He's awful mad." She identified the three aggressors by name and referred to them as "soshes."

The Vice-Principal called the accused boys from class. The leader was a handsome, well-dressed boy known to be a good and well-be-haved student. "Sure, I started the fight," he admitted readily. "I told him a week ago to get his hair cut. I can't stand these 'rinks' with long hair."

The Vice-Principal called the two chief belligerents and their parents to his office, but when it became clear that what had been violent animosity had quickly turned to mutual disdain, he placed both boys on probation and sent them back to class with the threat of suspension if further trouble developed.

On March 12, 1957, police Patrolman Charles Wendell was on motorcycle duty during the noon hour. Responding to a report of a fight, he pulled up to the curb in front of the Inn. It was a pleasant, sunny day, and the sidewalk teemed with high school boys and girls. As the officer dismounted and began to push through the crowd toward the door, he met unusual resistance.

"The kids pressed tightly around me," said officer Wendell. "Everybody was cheerful and pleasant. One boy with a sandwich in his hand observed that I was a fine-looking officer, but that my badge was dusty. He took out his handkerchief, polished my badge, breathed on it, polished it again, and then pretended to see his reflection in it. Another said, 'Your cap is messed up, sir.' He took off my cap, admired it, and replaced it carefully. When I got to the door there was no fight and no one who remembered seeing a fight. I made my way back to my motorcycle. It wouldn't start. The spark plug had been disconnected. We are not permitted to lay a finger on a minor unless we see him commit an act of delinquency. These kids know that. One man alone is helpless."

On March 15th, in the course of questioning a girl who had been skipping class, the Vice-Principal learned of the formation of a club within the hard core of the Inn patrons. "It is called the 'Stilettoes'," said the girl, "and some of the boys have gravity knives." [3] She was persuaded to name two members. One of the boys, Don Framan, 16, was on parole from the state correctional school and could be expected to talk freely.

"We got up a club," said Don, "to buy an old car and fix it up. That way we could afford it. We aren't rich like a lot of the kids around here." He stated that the gravity-knife charge was just "big

---

[3] "Spring-blade" knives were prohibited by state law, but "gravity knives" do not have spring blades. A gravity knife opens downward of its own weight and can be snapped into cutting position with a quick wrist movement. Pocket knives with blades over three inches long were considered dangerous and banned by city ordinance. Any and all pocket knives were banned from schools.

talk." The Vice-Principal discussed with them the serious consequences of forming an armed gang. Two weeks later he was informed
that the club had broken up.

During the spring at least three fights occurred between individual
"rinks" and individual "soshes." In each case, as in the one previously
discussed, the "sosh" was the aggressor, and his excuse was little more
than his general dislike for "rinks." According to the school's practice,
all students who fought were given quick suspension until their parents could come in for conferences.

As a group "soshes" gave school authorities very little trouble. Some
of them belonged to sub rosa fraternities or sororities, but only occasionally did they come to the notice of the Principal. The following
was an example:

Ronald Smith was the son of a prosperous retail merchant. Ron
had his own late-model convertible. He belonged to a "social club"
(fraternity). His social needs were met very well outside of school, and
although he had intentions of attending college, he did not work
more than the minimum in his classes.

On May 13, 1957, Ron and two friends brought beer to school in
Ron's car. They drank it at noon on "Sosh Hill" and were suspended
until their parents could come in. Ron's mother seemed aghast at his
behavior and promised to see to it that it would never happen again.
"We give him everything he wants," she said, "I don't see why he has
to do this to us."

STATEMENTS

William H. McAvoy, Principal of West High School, 41 years in public schools, 17 years a high school principal:

> There is a growing tendency among educators to become deeply
> concerned with the out-of-school phase of a child's life. I will not
> deny that much needs to be done for these children who cluster
> around the Inn, but we must be careful that we do not lessen our ef-
> fectiveness as an educational institution. Much of the time spent on
> these unwilling learners might better be used to improve our prac-
> tices in teaching the willing ones.
>
> The simple fact is that the school is 30% overcrowded, and this
> combined with growing demands for more training in science and

math is a real challenge to school administrators. It cannot be met if we extend our supervision across the street and after hours. Until schools can find added lunchroom space to accommodate the increased load (West High School has 608 stools in its lunchroom and now schedules 2400 students into three lunch periods of 30 minutes each), students must be allowed to leave the school grounds at noon.

For the most part these children are not friendly to school work. They earn a high percentage of failing grades; they take up a major share of the counselors' time; and they disturb class morale by their unwillingness to participate. In a very real sense their problem is social rather than educational, and perhaps we should find another agency better fitted to serve them.

I do not regard it as a proper activity for professional educators to patrol adjacent streets. The strongest force these children know is the approval or disapproval of their peers. A steady campaign through the student council and home rooms urging good behavior as a means of protecting the reputations both of the school and of teen-agers is the best practical answer, although obviously not a completely satisfactory one.

I. J. Stephens, proprietor of the Inn:

I like kids. My own two kids are in college, and we have always had a crowd of kids around our house. My wife and I ran a string of popcorn and candy counters in theaters for years, but we moved here so we could quit the night work and have summers off. The business is paying off, but I'm always uneasy. I wish my place would draw some of the better class of kids who hang out at "Maggie's." [4] I've tried giving better service and bigger servings of food, but they stay away.

Cutting out smoking helped inside the place, but it raised hob with the neighboring merchants. Now the kids who smoke grab a sandwich and head for some sheltered doorway up the street to eat and smoke. It's bad for the other guys' business. Customers, especially women, don't like to push through a crowd. These other merchants want me to allow smoking inside again, but there I'm stuck with the law. On the other hand, things are better in here. Used to be a kid would sit on a counter stool for an hour with a dime coke and a cigarette. Now he drinks fast and heads out the door. It leaves more room at the counter.

---

[4] "Maggie's" was the oldest of the eating places near West High. It was clean, pleasant, and carefully operated. Smoking was not permitted and had never been a problem. The place was shunned by "rinks" but teemed at noon with good scholars and student leaders.

Another problem is the litter on the sidewalk. I have to clean up the whole block after lunch. I had the Sanitary Department put a trash container by the door, but someone set it afire and they moved it away.

Sergeant George Blanco, Juvenile Division, City Police Department, fourteen years' work with juvenile delinquents:

Beaneries are a problem all over town. Every high school seems to have one place like the Inn where the rejected kids hang out. Loitering is the only real difficulty. Sometimes there is a little gambling, pitching pennies, some dice, a little poker. A lot of these kids steal cars for a joyride and abandon them. In fact, a car seems to be a symbol of independence to them. Sometimes I have doubts that car stealing by a fifteen-year-old is crime in the ordinary sense of the term. These kids can read; they know that adults consider cars a badge of success. Some of these kids who steal cars would walk a mile to return your wallet. The great majority of "rinky" kids grow out of it when they meet with adult success like getting a job or serving in the army.

It is illegal to open a tavern near school, but some of these beaneries can be a bigger headache to police than any tavern. These places cannot be closed unless the owner breaks a law or fails to comply with fire and sanitation codes. Of course they are careful not to sell cigarettes to minors, but lots of these kids belong to naval reserve units and can get all the smokes they need at the P-X. Trying to enforce an unpopular anti-smoking law would get us nothing but trouble. We're understaffed as it is.

J. R. Scoville, counselor at West High School, twenty-four years in public high schools, father of four children:

"Rinks" run about five-to-one boys. They are usually pleasant, ineffectual youngsters who have failed to find a place in any high school group. They don't participate in activities, and they don't succeed in class. Perhaps girls tend to find more personal satisfaction in school work because at this age they do better than boys in hand skills such as typing, handwriting, and notebook making. Girls tend to be a little more submissive than boys to routine and order. The few girls who are among the "rink" group are very poor students and seem to be in a state of angry rebellion over home conditions or rivalry with better-dressed, more successful girls.

Suppose we start with the whole student body; then take away the average and better students whose sights are on college. Next, take away the athletic set who reap a harvest of adulation. Take away the student government leaders, the actors, the singers, the radio hams, the musicians. Then take away those who feel secure because of clothes, or car, or spending money. At the end of this process you find a little residue left, the youngsters who have never succeeded in any acceptable way. These can easily become "rinks," because identity with the "rink" group is easy. All one needs is an undersized pair of jeans and an open dislike for organized school activity.

The fact is that this community has accepted the tradition that every youngster should have a high school diploma, and the child who is not academic-minded finds himself more and more outcast.

Special classes for these unwilling students have not had much success. It is commonly thought that a program heavy with manual arts subjects will meet their needs, but many of these youngsters lack the self-direction to complete a project, and their resentment of authority gets them into trouble early. Actually the most effective thing we can do for many of them may be to help them to see their problem and then wait for them to grow out of this stage, as some of them do.

Art Edwards, Vice-Principal of West High School, fifteen years teacher of biology and journalism at West High.

It is important not to think of this as a "blackboard jungle" situation. These children tend somewhat to like and respect their teachers. They like school, but hate school work. I have tried suspending them to look for work. Almost without exception they return and ask for re-admission. They seem especially to like whoever is vice principal. The man who previously held this position received a pair of golf shoes as a going-away gift accompanied by a hand-lettered scroll signed by "The Gang at the Inn."

I have enjoyed similar respect and confidence. After all, the vice principal listens to their problems, he gives no exams, and he can, by the quick surgery of suspension, bring relief when the pain of class work becomes too much to bear.

I have noticed that each time the "rink" group attempts to organize, as in the case of the "Stilettoes" or the smoking-room project, the organization falls apart. Perhaps the boys and girls who find it so hard to live under classroom authority rebel in similar manner against the discipline of any group.

During the summer of 1957 another beanery, the "Corral," opened its doors, and when the proprietor of the Inn returned on the opening day of school he found that his "rinks" had deserted him. New competition and trouble with health and sanitation authorities soon caused him to close the Inn for good, and the crowd moved to the sidewalk in front of the Corral.

SELECTED READINGS

Cohen, Albert K., *Delinquent Boys: The Culture of the Gang*. Glencoe: The Free Press, 1955.

Gordon, Calvin Wayne, *The Social System of the High School: A Study in the Sociology of Adolescence*. Glencoe: The Free Press, 1957.

Hollingshead, August B., *Elmtown's Youth: The Impact of Social Classes on Adolescents*. New York: John Wiley and Sons, 1949.

Reissman, Leonard, *Class in American Society*. Glencoe: The Free Press, 1959.

"X" Marks
the Initiate

CASE 6

It was 7:30 on the morning of May 22, 1957. As Art Edwards, Vice-Principal of West High school,[1] crossed the waiting room on his way to his office, he stopped short at the appearance of two boys waiting in chairs near the door. Each had a broad "X" cut in his hair with clippers. One leg of the "X" reached from the forehead over the top of the head to the nape of the neck; the other over the top of the head from ear to ear. One boy, trying to disguise the "X" mark, had apparently cut his remaining hair with scissors, leaving tell-tale snip marks and ledges. "Mr. Nyles wouldn't let us into woodshop with these haircuts," they told him.

"Wait here," said Mr. Edwards.

In the office he found Miss Stark, the secretary, with her hand over the mouthpiece of the telephone. "It's Mrs. Jones, mother of Ronald," she said. "She said there's been an initiation. She doesn't want to send Ronnie to school with his hair clipped the way it is."

Mrs. Jones sounded distraught and on the verge of tears. "They took the boys to Silver Beach Park last night and clipped their hair," she said. "They made them take off all their clothes. Then they painted their bodies with something that burned and irritated and turned the boys loose to find their way home without any clothes at ten o'clock at night." She stopped a moment; then she went on. "Mr. Edwards,"

---

[1] West High School, which is the scene of this incident, is described in some detail in the preceding case.

she pleaded, "Ronnie just couldn't take it. It is five miles home clear across town. He didn't have any clothes at all. It was cold, and he was itching and burning all over. Ronnie went to a house where he saw a man watching television; he tapped on the window, and the man came out. The man got a blanket and brought him inside and gave him a shower. Then he telephoned me, and I went and drove him home. He won't be at school today because he is covered with calamine lotion. Ronnie is a little allergic anyway. Mr. Edwards, what are West High School kids coming to?"

"Well, in the first place, Mrs. Jones," said the Vice-Principal, "let me say how sorry I am that this happened; I will try to get to the bottom of the trouble. In the second place, I hope you realize that social clubs have nothing whatever to do with West High School."

Ronald's mother interrupted, "He says they give dances, and that you have to belong to a club like this if you want to go. The crazy thing about it, Mr. Edwards, is that after they have done all this to him he still is glad that he joined. I have forgotten the name of the club."

"Let me read you a list of them," said Mr. Edwards, "and perhaps it will come to your mind. Moonlighters, Voo Doos, Baronetts, Grenadiers, Cavaliers, Stardusters, Twilighters, R.M.'s, Tri-W's, K.R.'s."

"That's it," said Mrs. Jones, "K.R.'s is the one he mentioned."

"Good," said Edwards, "when Ronald is ready to come back to school I want you to come in and we will talk this over. Meanwhile I will investigate on my own."

In the course of questioning the two boys who had been waiting, the Vice-Principal was told a story essentially the same as Mrs. Jones'. Two social clubs, the K.R.'s and the Baronetts, had held a joint initiation at Silver Beach Park. The boys had indeed been stripped of their clothes, painted with irritating dye, paddled severely, and told to find their way home. After the "pledges" had wandered for an hour in fright among the paths and byways of the park, the senior members had returned to pick them up. They had found all except Ronald Jones. Members of the two clubs had searched the beach and the wooded hillside behind it for an hour before concluding that Ronald had started off to find his way home.

The initiates were eight boys from West High School, all sophomores and juniors, aged sixteen and seventeen. The older members of the clubs were in their last year of high school. Combined membership of the two clubs was about 60, but only a small fraction of the membership had participated in the initiation and hazing.

Armed with the names of the initiates, the Vice-Principal checked the morning attendance. Three of the initiates were absent from school pleading illness. Edwards immediately suspended them and the others from school until they could bring in their parents for complete airing of the problem.

The term "social clubs" was used in Pacific City to describe organizations which were regarded as thinly disguised fraternities or sororities whose aims and activities were sometimes "anti-school." According to state law:

> The State Board of Education shall have the power and it shall be its duty . . . to examine and accredit secondary schools provided that no public high school or private academy shall be placed upon the accredited list so long as secret societies are allowed to exist among its students.

Precisely what is meant by "secret society"? Pacific City school administrators had tried to phrase a satisfactory definition that would distinguish what they regarded as harmful associations from such adult-sponsored organizations as DeMolay and YWCA. They had adopted the policy of mailing the following statement to parents of boys and girls known to be members of "social clubs":

> School authorities recognize that many parents wisely desire to provide for their children a carefully supervised club program to satisfy the normal social need of young people and to provide a wholesome outlet for their energies. Clubs to which high school students belong outside of school are often classified according to their principal aims as being either *character-building* or *social*.
>
> So-called *character-building clubs* are sponsored by adult character-building organizations such as the Y.M.C.A., Y.W.C.A., Masons, Knights of Columbus, Churches, Camp Fire Girls, Girl Scouts, or Boy Scouts. Responsibility for the actions of club members falls upon well established and highly regarded adult groups. The schools also provide a variety of sponsored clubs.
>
> The term *social club* can be applied to any organized group of boys or girls whose activities are largely social and who are not sponsored by an adult character-building organization.

Despite its desire to keep hands off, the school district finds itself involved in the activities of *social clubs* in two ways; first when citizens connect in their minds the activities of a certain club with a certain high school, and second, when club activities appear to violate state law.

The following activities, when participated in by a club which is not sponsored by a reputable character-building organization, are considered by Pacific City schools as presumptive evidence of violation of the state law:

1. Using Greek letters in its name.
2. Having pass word, grip, or other secret sign.
3. Being affiliated with any local or national school or college fraternity.
4. Having initiations of any character whatsoever or stunts.
5. Conducting rushing parties.
6. Holding meetings without an authorized adult sponsor being present throughout the entire period of the meeting. The name of such authorized adult sponsor to be on record in the principal's office and such sponsor to serve until another has been substituted and reported to the principal.
7. Conducting parties without proper chaperonage.
8. Wearing at school any special garb, haircuts, or insignia designed to distinguish members from other students.
9. Failing to file a full membership list and roster of officers with the principal each semester or to report new members as they are added to the list.

These standards define the conditions under which a social club is clearly illegal in the eyes of the School Board. Membership in such a club is an infraction of Board regulations. The conditions quoted above are designed to help parents insure their children against unwholesome club activities.

While a majority of social clubs have high standards, there is a tendency for non-secret clubs to become more and more secret and occasionally to develop unwholesome characteristics such as vicious and harmful initiations, drinking, unchaperoned dances, or rushing parties. In 1941 a local boy died folowing an unchaperoned social club initiation.

This letter has been written so that you may better understand the problems that social clubs occasionally present. Hardly a semester goes by without reports from distressed parents of dangerous initiation practices, heartbreak of girls who are "rushed" but not chosen, improperly chaperoned dances, or severe paddling of new members.

The fact that you have received this letter *does not* mean that the school believes that your son or daughter belongs to a club of questionable nature. It is being sent to the parents of all social club members whose names are on record in the principal's office. Prohibited activities are listed here in the hope that you will join the schools in making sure of a wholesome atmosphere in the clubs to which our boys and girls belong. You are invited to telephone the principal of your school and discuss with him any concern you may have about your son's or daughter's club activities.

There were in West High School three boys' social clubs and three girls' social clubs whose membership was made up exclusively of West High students. In addition, there were five city-wide clubs whose members came in part from West High and in part from other schools in Pacific City. Social clubs tended to ape university fraternities and sororities, though in general they were careful to avoid open disregard of school policies. Students seemed proud to be asked to pledge social clubs, and many parents considered membership a mark of distinction.

Each social club was directed to file with the principal of the school a list of its membership and officers, including the name of its adult sponsor. But rigid enforcement of restrictive rules had not been totally successful in eliminating the undesirable activities of the social clubs, and had been known to drive them underground.

In 1941 the evening daily paper of Pacific City had carried a red-ink banner headline: "West High School Boy Dies Following Fraternity Initiation." The boy had attended West High School for only a few weeks, having come from another state. The day following his hazing he had been found dead in his bed. An autopsy had revealed that he had suffered from a dangerously weak heart; so weak, in fact, that excitement or over-exertion of any kind could easily have been fatal. The social club had disbanded voluntarily. The public reaction had been to hold the schools responsible.

Prior to 1944 West High School had followed the practice of electing a popular girl as Campus Day Queen. Customarily, at a sports-clothes dance held on a Friday evening, the five finalists had been honored and the queen crowned, the other finalists becoming princesses. But in 1944, as the 10:00 p.m. coronation hour had drawn near, the five finalists were nowhere to be found.

About 9:55, as the dance committee waited in consternation, the queen candidates—dressed in their finest formals and each accompanied by a retinue of boys in formal attire—entered the ballroom.

They swept through the crowd and onto the stage to accept their crowns, after which they left the hall and returned to the social club dance they had all been attending. Investigation indicated that all of the candidates had been members of social clubs and were honored guests that evening at a ball sponsored by the boys' social clubs. Parent reaction was strong, and queen or princess contests were thenceforth banned at West High School.

After the initiation episode in May, 1957, the Principal of West High wrote to the Superintedent of Pacific City Schools as follows:

> On the night of May 22nd, the K.R.'s and the Baronetts initiated eight boys at Silver Beach. The boys were stripped of all their clothes, paddled, and painted on the body with some severe irritant which blistered their skin. They were then turned loose unclothed to hitchhike home. One boy was burned so severely that he stopped at a house and asked for help. He was given a shower and the householder telephoned his mother. The boys initiated had their hair cut with a conspicuous "X" mark. One parent so far has protested. She is the mother of Ronald Jones. The boys arrived home about 2:30 in the morning.
>
> We have a listing of the K.R.'s membership but none for the Baronetts. It is an indication of the type of boys in the K.R.'s to read this information:
>
> Member I and Member II were involved in drinking and in the beating of two junior high school boys in November. This was a juvenile court case.
>
> Member III was involved in drinking beer in a car at noon.
>
> Member IV was recently fined $25 and two days in jail for negligent driving.
>
> Member V was involved in beer drinking with Member III.
>
> Member VI has been suspended three times for truancy.
>
> Member VII drove his car on a new lawn in order to get even with a girl's father.
>
> Member VIII has a record of fighting, truancy, dishonesty, forgery and suspension from school.
>
> Member IX has had two truancy suspensions.
>
> Here are some questions we need to consider:
> 1. Does action of this kind outside of school call for school action?
> 2. Does the fact that probably most of the school is aware of the episode because of the hair clippings have any bearing?
> 3. Will action now reduce boldness another time?
> 4. What action is needed to achieve more for these boys than merely an early vacation?

While the roster of members of the K.R.'s included a number of boys with delinquent backgrounds, the Baronetts were later described as being almost to a man the "better type of student."

Because, as the Principal explained it to his colleagues, the incident had taken place so near to the closing of school and graduation, and because it appeared impossible to ascertain which of the members had taken part in the hazing and which had not, the only action taken at the time was to call together the officers of both clubs, the parents of all who were known to have been present at the hazing, and the officers of all other social clubs, and to give them a severe warning that their clubs must disband if any further embarrassment were caused to the school. Without exception school officials said they felt this was insufficient punishment, but they said privately that they did not wish to make any difficulties for students on the roster of the Baronetts not directly involved in the hazing, a group which included many school leaders.

Within six months the K.R.'s were in trouble again. On Saturday, November 16th, they held a dance at the Westbrook Country Club, across the county line from West High School. Several couples in their early 20's acted as chaperons, but supervision was ineffective. The manager of the Country Club stated that continuous drinking took place in cars, and that when the dance was over he collected more than 100 beer and whiskey bottles on the grounds. One member of the K.R. Club was escorted from the dance floor intoxicated. On two separate occasions during the evening the manager called the county sheriff for help in controlling the crowd.

Five days later a repetition of the earlier incident took place: eight initiates of the K.R. Club appeared at West High School with their heads shaved. The shaving had taken place on the previous evening at a K.R. Club meeting at the home of one of the members. No adult sponsor had been present.

On November 23rd the Baronett Club held a pajama dance at the Westbrook Country Club without parents or authorized adult sponsors being present. While many of the dancers reportedly behaved themselves well, the costumes of some of the girls were described by the manager as highly provocative. Much drinking took place in cars. Damage to shrubbery and to a window, amounting to $15.00, was later paid for by the student club.

After consultation with the Principal and others, the Superintendent of Pacific City Schools wrote to the parents of each member of the K.R. Club as follows:

> Because of their hazardous character, secret organizations are banned unequivocally from the high schools by state and local regula-

tions. Non-secret clubs tend at times to assume attributes of secret organizations. They have a tendency to become more and more secret in character and then eventually to develop activities leading to excesses. Often they interfere with school work on the part of their members.

It has come to our attention that the K.R. Club of which your son is a member has not been operating within the limits outlined by the School Board and has violated them in the following respects:

1. Meetings have been held without an authorized adult sponsor being present throughout the entire period.
2. The K.R. Club held a dance at the Westbrook Country Club on Saturday, November 16, 1957. While it is reported that several young couples acted as chaperones, the supervision was ineffective. The manager of the Westbrook Country Club states that a great deal of drinking took place in cars, that he collected more than 100 liquor containers on the grounds. One initiate was escorted from the dance in an intoxicated condition. Twice during the evening the manager became alarmed with his inability to control the crowd and sent for additional deputies.
3. On November 21, eight initiates of the K.R. Club returned to school with their heads shaved. The shaving took place in a K.R. meeting at the home of one of the members on Wednesday evening. They, of course, attracted a good deal of attention around school and disturbed the school program.
4. The K.R. members were warned last spring after participating with another club in an initiation stunt at Silver Beach where initiates were stripped of all clothing and with painted bodies turned loose on the street to find their way home.

It is the decision of this office that the K.R. Club must disband for the remainder of this year and engage in no activities whatever. If at the end of this school year the members of the club can produce evidence that they have in no way violated school rules, this office will consider reinstating the club. Failure of any student to abide by this rule disbanding the club will result in suspension and will seriously damage a student's chances for graduation. The school administration has been particularly long-suffering in its dealings with the K.R. Club and hopes that you as a parent of a member of the club will understand that this action is taken in the interests of better education for all the students at West High School.

A similar letter was sent to parents of members of the Baronetts Club, which was likewise ordered disbanded for the rest of the school year. On December 17, 1957, George Murphy, student president of the Baronetts Club, wrote as follows to the Superintendent of Pacific City Schools:

> Your recent letter directed to myself as well as to all other members of the Baronetts Club has been read and studied carefully. We respectfully appreciate your opinion and wish to advise that we have acted upon your request for temporary disbandment of the club for the period mentioned.
>
> Our reason for promptly acting in this matter is because of our genuine concern over the allegations set out in your letter against us. We, in fact, feel that if such statements were true and factual as outlined there would be no desire on our part to ask for reinstatement. Therefore, we fully subscribe to your feelings in this matter unless it is within our power to prove otherwise. We feel that in all fairness you will allow us this opportunity.
>
> May we have the pleasure of meeting with both you and the principal of West High School at your earliest convenience. We would like to be represented by a small committee composed of a parent, our officers, and a Baronett's Club sponsor. We will attempt to review all issues in question with you to your complete satisfaction and very much hope that our Baronett Club will prove to be a credit to our school and our community in the days to come.

On the grounds that the evidence of misconduct was clear and that further discussion could not change the fact, the Superintendent declined to meet with the student committee. The principal of West High School talked privately with the president of the Baronett Club and explained that at the end of the year, if the club members had shown themselves worthy, a discussion might be arranged.

Parents reacted in two ways: some resented the school's interference in their children's social life; others expressed appreciation for the prompt action taken by the school. One wrote as follows to the Superintendent of Schools:

> We surely appreciate the letter we received about the K.R. Club at West High School and we are sorry that our boy was connected with the group that has embarrassed the school.
>
> We were not aware of course that this club was under probation or that any such behavior had gone on in the club before. Having taken and picked up our son at the dance at the Westbrook Club we know *we* had control of that situation *in his case.*
>
> We are encouraging other activities and he spent Saturdays for

two years at Confirmation, belongs to a church league, and a youth choir. We are taking him skiing and hope that he can join the ski club.

He is working for high grades and better things, honor society, scholarship, etc., and thinks seriously about a career in science, engineering, or architecture.

We are grateful for a watchful school administration to assist us in guiding our son in his choice of values. He will discontinue this activity.

The Superintendent replied:

I very much appreciate your letter regarding our action involving social clubs. Certainly it should not be taken as reflection on your son personally. With parents like you to guide him I am certain he has every opportunity for reaching goals he has set.

May I wish him every success in his high school and college career.

As the year closed, the school administration in Pacific City agreed that the problem of social clubs remained unsolved. These were the questions about the matter put down in writing by one school official:

1. Can the menace of social clubs be eliminated by meeting the needs of teen-agers in some other way?
2. How can the activities of those high school clubs which are sponsored neither by the school nor by responsible community youth-serving agencies be held in check?
3. How can the school which is in no way involved with the sponsorship of social clubs protect itself from the bad publicity resulting from delinquent behavior of the clubs?
4. How can parents and students be made aware of the risks involved in social club membership?

SELECTED READINGS

Bloch, Herbert, and Arthur Niederhoffen, *The Gang: A Study in Adolescent Behavior.* New York: Philosophical Library, 1958.
Hollingshead, August B., *Elmtown's Youth: The Impact of Social Classes on Adolescents.* New York: John Wiley and Sons, 1949.
Packard, Vance, *The Status Seekers.* New York: David McKay Company, 1959.
Remmers, H. H., and D. H. Radler, *The American Teenager.* Indianapolis: The Bobbs-Merrill Company, 1957.

CASE 7

Grenade

On June 1, 1956, at approximately 11:40 a.m., a tear gas grenade exploded in the basement of the Grove City High School. The gas spread quickly through the building, and a fire alarm was sounded. Classrooms and offices were vacated. There was great excitement, but no panic. No personal injuries were reported. The students milled around outside until the Principal dismissed classes for the day.

Meanwhile, the Mayor, Police Chief, Fire Chief, Fire Marshal, Superintendent of Schools, Assistant Superintendent of Schools, Fire Commission Chairman, firemen from three engine companies, fifteen uniformed policemen, and a number of reporters arrived on the school grounds, to view the damage and take action. Firemen wearing gas masks entered the building and found the grenade among rubbish barrels in a basement stairwell. They set up fans and opened windows. The Police Chief assigned two detectives to the case. The Mayor ordered a full investigation, stating that he regarded the incident "most seriously." He added, "It is not a mere prank. It could have had far more serious consequences."

The inquiries of the detectives led them on the same day to George Rankin and Peter Tajoles, sixteen-year-old sophomores at the high school. They were taken into custody on technical charges of idleness. When questioned, they admitted responsibility for the explosion. This was their story:

104

On May 31, during the lunch period, Rankin was in the high school yard, discharging cherry bombs. Tajoles approached, and they began to talk. Tajoles informed Rankin that he had a tear gas grenade at home. Rankin told him to bring it to school the next day.

On June 1, the day of the incident, Tajoles came to school with the grenade, and gave it to Rankin. Rankin carried the grenade around all morning. When he came into the school cafeteria for the lunch period, he met Tajoles and some other students. They all ate lunch together, then left the cafeteria and walked along the hallway of the basement until they reached the stairway leading to the first floor. Rankin held up the grenade. He pulled the pin and threw the grenade under the stairway. The group then ran from the building.

Rankin and Tajoles stated that the others in the group had no part in the incident. They said that the latter knew about the grenade and the plans to explode it, but had come along just "to see what would happen."

The two boys were asked by police why they had done it. They said they had done it as a prank, just "for fun."

Tajoles said that he had bought the grenade a month before the incident, from an unidentified youth. He had paid one dollar for it.

Released under bond of $500, the boys were suspended from school pending future hearings.

On June 4th the local Director of Environmental Sanitation announced that all exposed foods in the school cafeteria had been ordered destroyed because of possible contamination by tear gas fumes.

The court hearing was held on June 19th. Rankin was accompanied by his mother, Tajoles by both parents. The boys pleaded *nolo contendere* (no contest) to breach of peace charges. Tajoles said that he "didn't think the bomb would go off," that its label called for use before 1936. Rankin stated that he had not expected the grenade to make so much noise and cause so much smoke. They maintained that they had not at the time realized the seriousness of the act, or they would not have committed it. Defense attorneys told the judge that, in their opinion, the boys had been punished enough, that they were "upset and sorry."

It was brought out that Rankin had been president of his grammar school graduation class, and a Catholic priest, testifying on his behalf, reported that he attended mass regularly.

The court established that Tajoles had purchased two grenades from juveniles who had stolen them from the Grove City Fire Department training school in January. One had been discarded in a nearby river, the other used in the Grove City High explosion.

Before sentence was passed, the judge said that he had "mixed emotions" about his decision in the case. He observed that "a panic could have ensued" after the explosion, and that "nation-wide notoriety" had resulted.

In placing the boys on probation (with *nisi* continuances), the judge left the way open for readmission to Grove City High. He asked the boys what they thought the attitude of the Board of Education was toward them. Tajoles said that the Board was probably "resentful," and Rankin expressed the belief that it was "pretty mad at us." The judge then said that an unidentified Board member had contacted him and recommended leniency. It was the hope of the member, disclosed the judge, that the boys would be permitted to continue their education without animosity. Under the terms of the *nisi* continuances, the boys would be released and put in the care of the court probation officer until July 1, 1958. Hence, the boys would be free to attend school, if readmitted, and would complete their term of court probation on the first of the month following their scheduled graduation.

The judge said that, in arriving at his decision, he had been obliged to consider not only the welfare of the boys but the impact of the incident on the community. "This case," he stated, "has brought about the condemnation and indignation of the entire community." He pointed out that students could have been hurt if panic had developed, and that policemen and firemen could have been injured in hurrying to the school grounds. He told the boys that it was within his power to send them to the county jail or to a nearby reformatory: but, he said, "you have to gamble with young persons."

On June 20th an informal meeting of Grove City High School teachers was reported in the local afternoon newspaper. A summary of the story follows:

> The reactions of the teachers to the court hearing were extremely adverse. The anonymous recommendation for leniency announced by the judge was criticized. Consensus was that the boys should not be readmitted, and in their comments teachers expressed anxiety that

the anonymous recommendation meant a lack of support for their position by the Board of Education. They "promised" a written petition to the Board if action against readmission were not taken before the opening of school the following September. "All over the country," said a teacher, "boards of education are backing teachers 100% to control juvenile delinquency, and what do they do here? Practically condone it. And don't think the kids don't know it! I don't know what this place will be like next semester." School discipline was described as "remarkably good" since the grenade incident. "Now, however," a teacher observed, "it is hard to evaluate what it will do to the morale of the staff. We want the Board to stand behind us." Another warned, "If a child can set off a bomb and get away unscathed, there's no limit to how far the kids can go."

School officials later maintained that the "meeting" was essentially the invention of an overzealous reporter who based his story on remarks solicited from individual teachers. However, a top school official who had had an opportunity to hear teachers express their opinions conceded privately that the majority appeared to be opposed to readmission of the boys.

The President of the Board of Education declared that the recommendation for leniency had come from one who spoke "as an individual and without the authorization of the Board." He said that he did not know who had made the recommendation, but that, in his opinion, the person was acting within his rights as an individual citizen.

On June 21st the judge who had presided in the case reported that the controversial recommendation had been submitted by "a member of the educational system." He stated that his earlier reference to the source of the recommendation as a member of the Board itself had been inadvertent. He added that he had, in fact, received two recommendations: while the one had advocated leniency, the other had urged appropriate punishment of the boys if found guilty.

On June 25th the Board of Education convened to consider the case. After reports on the previous school records of the boys were read, the Assistant Superintendent of Schools and the Director of Pupil Services both recommended that the school psychiatrist be consulted before the Board took any final action. The Board accordingly voted unanimously to solicit a report from the school psychiatrist, and following receipt of the report to hold another meeting. At that time the Board would decide, on the basis of available evidence, whether or not to readmit the boys to school.

*   *   *   *   *

The incident occurred in a New England city. Grove City was large, with a population in the 125–175,000 class. It was old, with roots extending to the first half of the seventeenth century. It was economically complex, with more than 600 industrial, 500 wholesale, and 5500 retail establishments. It had eleven banks and trust companies, two airports (one municipal), seven golf courses, twenty-three movie houses and one legitimate theater, seventeen hotels, four hospitals, two newspapers, four radio stations, and its own symphony orchestra. In the extent and diversification of such facilities Grove City conformed to the pattern characteristic of contemporary urban industrial centers in this country.

The population of Grove City was also diverse. The latest national census report showed that, of employed persons over fourteen years of age, 11% were professional and semi-professional workers; 9% proprietors, managers, and officials; 22% sales, clerical and kindred workers; 14% craftsmen, foremen and kindred workers; 27% operatives and kindred workers; 10% domestic and service workers; and 6% laborers. Approximately 32% of the dwelling units in the city were owner-occupied, and 68% tenant-occupied.

The religious composition of the population was indicated by a special census which, while twenty years old, corresponded generally to more recent estimates. Of the Grove City church members, 57% were classified as Roman Catholic, 22% Protestant, and 19% Jewish. (2% were classified as "other.")

The predominance of Roman Catholics reflected the ethnic composition of Grove City. According to the latest population census, 78% of the residents were native-born whites, 16% foreign-born whites, 6% Negroes, and less than ⅔₀ths of 1% members of "other races." Of the total population of the city, 53% were of foreign white stock: of these, 30% were foreign-born, and 70% native-born of foreign or mixed parentage. Of the foreign white stock, 42% had origins in Italy, 13% in the Irish Free State, 13% in Russia, 8% in Poland, and 5% in Germany. These five stocks composed over 80% of the total foreign white stock and almost half the total population of Grove City.

The educational profile of the community showed the following features. Of persons over twenty-five years of age at the time of the last census, 4% had completed no schooling; 14% grades 1–6; 29% grades 7–8; 15% 1–3 years of high school; 21% four years of high school; 6% 1–3 years of college; and 7½% four or more years of college. (The remainder did not report years of schooling.) The median number of school years completed was 9.1. The educational facilities of Grove City included thirty-eight public grade schools; two senior and four junior high schools; thirteen parochial schools; four non-parochial private schools; a state teachers college; a professional art school; a college of pharmacy; a junior college of commerce; a Roman Catholic college for girls; a YMCA junior college; a junior college of physical therapy; several business and vocational schools; and a prominent independent university. Grove City was not only a manufacturing but an educational center, a circumstance reflected in the relatively high proportion (7½%) of residents with four or more years of college completed. The university in particular attracted a substantial number of persons with advanced degrees to fill faculty and administrative posts.

The Grove City Board of Education at the time of the grenade incident comprised eight members, appointed by and including the Mayor. While explicitly nonpartisan, the Board was selected intentionally to reflect the religious composition and occupational diversity of the community. Thus there were four Roman Catholics, among them the Board President and the Mayor; two Protestants; and two Jews. The President was an insurance executive; the other members included a physician, a housewife, a CIO executive, a former teacher in Grove City High, an architect-engineer, and a university professor. Under the statutes of the state the Board had broad discretionary powers in the areas of school management, studies, classification, and discipline: disposition of the grenade case was clearly within its province. Board policies and decisions were implemented by a variety of local educational officials. Current reports of somewhat strained relations among the Board, the Office of the Superintendent, and the school principals were typically expressed in this way:

> You may have heard that the Principal of Grove City High doesn't get along too well with the Board and the Superintendent's office. Now a lot of people will say: "After all, what can you expect? The Board President, the Superintendent, and the Assistant Superinten-

dent are Irish Catholic, and the Principal is Jewish." But that's only part of it, and it doesn't mean the Board and the Superintendent's office are on the best of terms. The fact is, there's lack of confidence all around. The principals complain that the Superintendent's office interferes when it shouldn't and fails to act when it should. At the same time, you hear complaints from the Superintendent's office that the principals take it on themselves to decide on matters that belong downtown, and pass the buck downtown when it comes to the matters they ought to take care of themselves. The Board doesn't work closely with either the Superintendent's office or the principals, and there isn't enough trust from one to the other. There's nothing especially unusual or surprising about it: they don't particularly want to get out on a limb, but they don't want anyone else to do anything that might make their own position seem less important. It's a familiar enough story.

The public high school in which the grenade incident took place had originated a century earlier and had occupied its present site adjacent to the university since 1903. It had 62 home rooms and 34 rooms devoted to library, study hall, and shop activities, with a total seating capacity of 3729. It had an auditorium seating 1404, a boys' and a girls' gymnasium, and a cafeteria said to "feed more people in seventy minutes than any restaurant in the state." It had an enrollment of 1916 (approximately 1500 were reported in attendance when the grenade was thrown), drawn from all socio-economic levels of the city; a staff of 116 teachers, administrators, and librarians; and a high academic rating.

In summary, Grove City was no cottage community. It was neither rural village nor small town. It was a large, very old, and highly diversified industrial and educational center.

*   *   *   *   *

George Rankin and Peter Tajoles, born forty-one days apart in the fall of 1939, came from relatively large families. Rankin, the older of the two, was the youngest of eight children. He had one older brother and six older sisters. Tajoles was the second oldest of five children. He had one older and one younger brother, and two younger sisters.

Both were native-born whites. Rankin had blue eyes and brown hair, and was 5 feet 10½ inches tall. Tajoles had brown eyes and brown hair, and was 5 feet 4 inches tall.

Rankin's parents were native-born. His father was a machinist in a local factory, and his mother a housewife with no outside occupation. Tajoles' father was born in Turkey, of Greek derivation, and his mother was native-born. His father was a retired dealer in second-hand furniture of such dubious aspect that a top school official associated him with "the junk business." Mrs. Tajoles, who assisted her husband in the store before it was sold, had no occupation other than house-wife at the time of the incident.

The home neighborhoods of the boys were comparatively depressed areas. Rankin lived in a district full of old houses which had been fashionable thirty to forty years earlier, but which had become seedy and shabby over the years.

Business enterprises had gradually moved into the area as its attractiveness as a residential site diminished. Tajoles lived in a slum district, liberally stocked with saloons interspersed among rickety and cluttered houses, and generously strewn with litter. According to ratings based on Davie's [1] six-class residential scale, Rankin lived in a class IV area, Tajoles in a class V area. These areas had the following characteristics:

	Class IV (Rankin)	Class V (Tajoles)
(a) Percentage of city's householders in area:	13.2%	37.2%
(b) Predominant type of structure:	two-family houses	two-family houses of low valuation
(c) Nativity:	mixed [a]	mixed [a]
(d) Predominant religion:	Roman Catholicism	Roman Catholicism
(e) Major occupations:	artisans and laborers	laborers and artisans
(f) Proportion of families with income above or below $1500:	2/3 below	75%–90% below

[1] Davie, J. S. *Education and Social Stratification*, unpublished doctoral dissertation, Yale University, 1951.

	Class IV (*Rankin*)	*Class V* (*Tajoles*)
(g) Number of residents in social register (city total: 1002):	13 [b]	7 [b]
(h) Number of residents belonging to graduates' Club, a leading gentlemen's organization (city total: 349):	2 [c]	1 [c]
(i) Delinquency rate:	average	high
(j) Dependency rate	average	high
(k) Number of residents in Who's Who in America (city total: 179):	1 [d]	1 [d]
(l) Number of institutional (penal and abnormal) cases among sixteen-and seventeen-year-olds (city total for age group: 51):	penal: 2 [e] abnormal: 4	penal: 13 [e] abnormal: 10
(m) Percentage of non-institutional sixteen- and seventeen-year-olds attending school:	74.1% [f]	70.7% [f]
(n) Public/private school attendance among sixteen- and seventeen-year-old students:	public: 86.9% [g] private: 13.1%	public: 90.4% [g] private: 9.6%

---

[a] Native-born of native parents, native-born of foreign mother and/or father, and foreign-born.

[b] Compared to 715 in class I, 233 in class II.

[c] Compared to 279 in class I, 59 in class II.

[d] Compared to 141 in class I, 32 in class II.

[e] Compared to 0 penal and 1 abnormal case in class I; 1 penal and 3 abnormal cases in class II.

[f] Compared to 98.2% in class I, 88.9% in class II.

[g] Compared to 57% public and 43% private school attendance in class I; 78.6% public and 21.4% private school attendance in class II.

Both boys had been formally, if casually, affiliated with "good citizenship" programs: Rankin as a member of the Junior Police, Tajoles as a member of the Boy Scouts. Both joined while in elementary school. The Head of the Youth Division of the City Police Department recalled Rankin's enlistment in the Junior Police: "As part of my job, I go into the various schools, tell them about our program, and sign up anyone who wants to join. On one of my visits Rankin joined. He was eleven years old then. He was a quiet little round-faced boy. Seemed nice enough. He came to the first meeting, and that was all. After three years we stopped looking for him, and took him off our rolls. I guess he wasn't much for organizations." Tajoles held onto his troop membership, but was hardly a dedicated scout: he was said to be a "small, nervous, overactive" fellow who liked "belonging" but not responsibility.

Although Rankin's connection with the Junior Police was fleeting, he at least managed to stay on the good side of the law until the grenade-throwing incident. Tajoles was not so successful. At the age of thirteen he was taken into custody on a pre-delinquency charge: he and a companion had been shooting matches with clothespins, and one of the matches had started a fire in some rubbish piled on a truck. There had been no damage, and he was released with a warning. Subsequently he was taken into custody several times on delinquency charges: in the summer of 1953, for setting fire to a mail box; in the spring of 1954, for possessing and carrying a dangerous weapon (a 32 caliber revolver); in the spring of 1955, for implication in the traffic of obscene literature and pornographic photographs. Though evidently penitent on these occasions, he remained a "troublemaker."

While IQ ratings were not available for Rankin and Tajoles, the Iowa tests were administered locally to eighth-grade pupils as a standard achievement measure. On these tests, taken by the boys in 1953, Rankin was a year and a half ahead of his grade in reading vocabulary; a year behind in reading comprehension; a year behind in arithmetic skills; a year and a half behind in language skills; and two years behind in work study skills. Tajoles was at par for his grade in reading vocabulary and comprehension; a year behind in work study skills; two years behind in arithmetic skills; and three years behind in language skills. A guidance official, commenting on the significance of the last score, observed, "He is not articulate."

For the elementary grades, Rankin attended a parochial school,

Tajoles a public school in a building cited by a 1947 survey as one of twelve "that definitely should be scheduled for immediate or early abandonment." They attended the same junior high school during the ninth grade, then enrolled in Grove City High. Rankin was an indifferent student in elementary and junior high school. Although he obtained a C rating in English, art, and music while in junior high, he was generally a D-F student. At Grove City High he was also a D-F student, and showed great academic instability from quarter to quarter. In English, for example, he compiled a C-F-B-D (final mark: D) sequence. In both junior and senior high school his attendance record was extremely poor. In the ninth grade he was absent thirty-five times and tardy nine. In the tenth grade, at Grove City High, he was absent thirty-one times and tardy ten. Tajoles was an average student in elementary school, and a C+ student in junior and senior high school. In junior high he received as his best marks an A in shop and B in music and art. His course work at Grove City High was generally consistent in quality; one of his better marks (B) was in English. He was fairly regular in his attendance. Of the two boys, Tajoles was definitely the more effective student.

Neither, however, had college plans. They were enrolled in the General course at Grove City High. This was largely a terminal course, and one which made relatively light scholarship demands on those who took it.

The health of the boys was generally normal. Physical examinations of Rankin were largely negative, showing no significant disabilities or aberrations except thickened ear drums, notably in the right ear, and chronic mouth breathing. Three years before the grenade incident he suffered a mild concussion, which was followed by tonsillitis. Subsequently he was advised that he needed more sleep (ten hours a night were recommended) and milk: his customary beverage was tea. Tajoles was reported normal except in nutrition. He had occasional colds, and was a nail-biter.

In terms of dynamic or energy potential, Rankin was characterized as listless and apathetic in comparison to the more active Tajoles. Both boys were relatively restricted in the scope of their extra-curricular interests, Rankin more than Tajoles. Rankin's extra-curricular interests were so limited that an acquaintance was led to observe, "He has none to speak of." In the fifth grade he reported airplanes as his hobby. The only extra-curricular interest he expressed in junior high school was home-room baseball; in high school he reported none. These extra-curricular interests were recorded for Tajoles: the Boy Scouts, automobiles, and general mechanical "tinkering."

Both boys had job experience. While enrolled in junior high school, Rankin worked as a grocery clerk after classes and on Saturdays. In the summer of 1955 he worked as an usher in a downtown movie theater. In 1956, from January to March, he worked after high school hours as a car-greaser in a Grove City garage. He said that he left this last job because it did not pay enough money. Tajoles worked off and on as an automotive mechanic, assisting his brother afternoons in a local garage (other than the one in which Rankin worked). Unlike Rankin, Tajoles expressed a vocational goal: he wanted to be a mechanic, truck driver, or construction worker.

In their behavior at Grove City High prior to the grenade-throwing, Rankin and Tajoles qualified as problem students. Rankin not only "escaped" schoolwork by cutting classes excessively, but tended to be insolent and surly toward teachers. He was rated "below average" in industry and reliability. His school citizenship rating on entering Grove City High was F, and he maintained his poor citizenship record during his brief high school career. On one occasion, he requested permission from the Assistant Principal to leave school in order to take a drivers' examination; when refused, he left anyway. On another occasion, he was removed from a class by the head of the department for insolence to the teacher. Although in junior high school he was criticized for incessant talking in class, he was generally regarded as a fairly quiet, withdrawn boy who balked at class routine and teachers' orders. In staff appraisals, he was described as "lackadaisical," "lacking effort," "sly and untrustworthy," "a sulker." In some classes, where he could sit more or less passively, he caused no trouble; in others, he met teachers' directives with resistance and hostility. Although he "got along well enough" with other students, he did not extend himself for their sake. He dressed like other students, made casual conversation with them, but was reported to have "no close friends" in or out of school. He was rather solitary and aloof with his fellows and superiors alike, and resented opposition. He was defensive about his troubles, and inclined to blame them on others. In this he was supported by his mother.

His mother was called repeatedly by school officials, advised of his poor attendance, conduct, and achievement, and asked to come to school to discuss the problem. She refused, and indicated that as far as she was concerned the deficiency was in the school and not in her boy. As one teacher observed, "It was always the school that was at fault." According to a psychological appraisal, Mrs. Rankin showed a psychotic reluctance to entertain the possibility of error or inadequacy in her son. When her attention was called to his frequent absences, she protested that there must be something wrong with the school, since the previous year, in junior high school, he had gone to classes regularly. When it was pointed out that his absences in junior high school had been even more numerous, she continued to protest and refused to cooperate with the school in considering what might be done about the situation. Granted that like most mothers she wished to protect her son, and that he did not tell her all the things he did or failed to do, she was pictured as extreme in her protectiveness and persistent defiance of appeals from school officials.

Tajoles was a more energetic and enterprising "troublemaker" than Rankin. On one occasion he forged a slip which excused him from English class. On another occasion, he used a skeleton key to gain entry into a locked schoolroom during recess. On still another, he exploded a large firecracker in the boys' lavatory. He was once caught throwing books out a window, and four months before the grenade incident was put out of school for a week for a misdemeanor. Although two teachers said that he was polite and respectful in their classes, and did his work, he was said by others to be "troublesome," "discourteous," and "aggressive." He was "mean" to a substitute teacher who asked him if he had a nickname. Like Rankin, he tended "to sulk," and was said "to do things behind your back." Psychological workers found him a weak, nervous, frightened boy who wanted to persuade himself and others that he had "a lot of guts" by pseudo-desperado behavior; he could not understand why his aggressive acts did not bring him the approval he desired. It was suggested that conventional distinctions between right and wrong were blurred for him by his need to show that he was "somebody" regardless of legal precept. As he himself indicated to others, he wanted to be a "good guy" and belong to a "gang" that would respect him. It was made clear that he did not want to be considered just a "small, scared Greek" from the slums. Although Rankin threw the grenade, Tajoles was reputed to have "put him up to it." In the estimation of others,

Tajoles was "not a leader" but sought to attach himself to potential allies, "egg them on," and try to impress them with his daring.

Like Rankin, Tajoles was not unpopular, yet not adept at making friends. Whereas would-be acquaintances were put off by Rankin's aloofness and inattentiveness, they were wary of Tajoles' active and aggressive quest for acceptance. Like Rankin, Tajoles was not set apart by dress; but unlike Rankin, he was set apart by short stature. If he could not be *big*, he could, and did, try to "act big." While neither boy had any great talent for verbal expression, Rankin seemed to prefer a "strong, silent" role; Tajoles, on the other hand, was more actively interested in expressing himself and at the same time more handicapped in language skills. If he could not communicate effectively in words, he could, and did, try to "put himself across" by eloquent if illegal actions.

Unlike Mrs. Rankin, Mrs. Tajoles came willingly to school when called about her son's conduct. She was a "cooperative" and "sensible" woman who was concerned about the situation and wanted to help. She said that Peter was a problem at home as well as in school, and that she and her husband could not seem to manage him. While George was the only one of the Rankin children still living at home, Mr. and Mrs. Tajoles had to look after not only Peter but the other children, and they found it difficult to keep track of him. Nevertheless school and home collaborated in giving Peter a talking to, and thereafter his behavior would improve temporarily. Between lapses he showed a capacity for application and tractability. Despite his troubles, he kept up his attendance and grades. A comment made by one of his teachers is instructive. After noting that he and Peter had had their differences, the teacher said: "But you know, he sure used to warm up when I spoke to him as a friend."

*   *   *   *   *

There were essentially two positions taken in the case: one, that the boys should be readmitted to school; the other, that they should not. The basic arguments and interpretation supporting each position may be summarized as follows.

(1) The boys should not be readmitted. The teachers are opposed to their return, and since they are primarily responsible for maintain-

ing school discipline, their stand should be supported. Staff morale should not be undermined for the sake of two problem students. The principal is behind the teachers; he has said that he will not readmit the boys unless ordered to do so by the Board of Education. If the Board does not back up its school officials in this case, not only will the status and authority of the officials be seriously damaged, but the mutual confidence so necessary to effective relations between school and Board will be jeopardized. Nor would readmission of the offenders be fair to the other students. Those who so irresponsibly endanger their fellows should not by design be kept among them. Rankin and Tajoles are not innocents abruptly fallen. If this had been their first offense against the school, it might be argued that they deserved another chance. But they have offended again and again, and have had chance after chance. Their records show persistent misconduct, and it would be wrong to sacrifice the safety of the school to the possibility that trends so clearly marked will reverse themselves. One may wonder if it would not be a disservice to the boys themselves to teach them, in effect, that they can get away with delinquency and vandalism. This is a dangerous lesson, and one easily spread. The incident has attracted widespread attention in a time of national concern with this very problem, and the Board should show its readiness to support the teacher, back up the administrator, protect the student body, and reaffirm the precept that no one has the right to set aside the mores that safeguard all.

(2) The boys should be readmitted. It is not the job of high school officials to anticipate a decision which can only come from the Board of Education. They may, of course, express their personal feelings, but if these feelings were allowed to determine policy, the Board would be deprived of its legitimate function. There are, moreover, teachers who would like to help the boys, and if these are less vociferous than the rest, they are no less entitled to consideration. To say that the Principal will not readmit the boys unless ordered to do so by the Board is simply to recognize that the power of decision belongs not to him but to the Board. Yet all this is secondary. Students do not exist for the sake of schools and their officials, but schools and officials for the sake of students. The welfare of the latter is the crucial issue in the case. It is wrong, first of all, for the opposition to suggest that the offending students are condemned by their records. The purpose of such records, after all, is not to condemn but to show when and where help is needed. To refuse to help George Rankin and Peter Tajoles would show all those who have been following the case that

there is really no hope of solution. Surely we can do better than to maintain that we should try to cure delinquency, but not delinquents. And there can be no cure in turning the boys away. The most powerful reformative force at our disposal is education. This is particularly true for boys who come from relatively depressed neighborhoods, where opportunities for constructive growth are limited. The real danger lies in sending them back to these neighborhoods, not in reopening the school doors for them.

Their records not only show that they need help, but indicate the areas in which each may be approached. We can build on Rankin's tendency to be quiet and well-behaved in the absence of coercion. The unevenness of his quarterly grades shows that he is capable of good work when motivated. We should not give up on him without trying seriously to improve motivation through less restrictive, more sympathetic treatment. One need not be a genial go-getter to have social promise. His selection as president of his elementary school graduating class two years ago testifies to his promise; he certainly is worth saving. Similarly, we can build on Tajoles' energy and strong desire for acceptance and approval. Sound counseling can show him the advantages of implementing this deire through socially constructive action. There is no question of his ability to keep up on his school work. In dealing with a young offender as responsive and active as Tajoles, the goal should be not to squelch those qualities but to turn them to good purposes.

If readmitted, Rankin and Tajoles would not endanger the other students. We need not offer the generalization that peer groups can handle their own. We point out, in the first place, that they are not boys who seek to hurt their associates. Rankin has a policy of live and let live, and Tajoles one of "good guy" fellowship. In a very real sense, they just want to "get along." In the second place, the grenade incident, serious though it was, has been exaggerated. It should be remembered that they threw the grenade while in the company of other curious students, into an empty stairwell, and that no one was injured. Without condoning their use of it, we can recognize that tear gas, after all, has largely nuisance value. If the incident was a shock to the public, it was, together with the commotion and trouble it entailed, certainly a shock to the boys. It may well have been, as the court indicated, the very shock they needed. They are repentant, and they well realize that they can ill afford another lapse. With so many watching, they are in a postion to redeem themselves: we should let them try.

*   *   *   *   *

The boys were not readmitted. A committee of the Board convened in August, shortly before the fall term was to begin, and voted to suspend them indefinitely. Two conditions were attached: (1) that damages resulting from the incident were to be paid by the boys' parents; and (2) that the boys were to submit themselves to school medical services. Compliance with these conditions would open the case to further review, and the progress reports made by the school psychiatrist to the Superintendent would indicate if and when the boys were ready for readmission. The feeling evidently was that the boys were guilty and that a suspension ruling was appropriate to the offense, but that the boys should not be deprived of opportunity to show their willingness to improve and to work toward future reinstatement. The decision was in a sense responsive to both positions noted. On the one hand, readmission was withheld; on the other, the boys were not expelled, and the way was opened not only for future readmission but for the preparatory guidance designed to help them take more constructive school and community roles.

Mrs. Tajoles agreed with the committee that her son deserved to be suspended, but asked that he be permitted to attend night school. The committee held that the suspension applied also to night school. Peter said that he was reluctant to go back to school anyway and have everybody pointing at him.

The damages were set at $194, half to be paid by each family. The parents objected to the imposition of such "fines" and declined to pay. They expressed misgivings about the "medical services" provision; they were wary of the stigma which, they felt, was associated with psychiatric treatment. Nevertheless, Mr. Rankin said that he would be willing to have George try it. Mrs. Rankin, however, said that he did not have to if he did not want to. Mr. and Mrs. Tajoles, despite their doubts, agreed to let Peter begin talks with the school psychiatrist.

The psychiatrist had been unable to enlighten the Board earlier, since the boys had not been available for consultation. The Board ruling paved the way for such consultation. Rankin, however, did not appear at all for "medical services," and Tajoles came only once.

The psychiatrist found Tajoles an emotionally immature boy who tended to be highly dependent in situations calling for independence. He was ambivalent about his own welfare. Before the grenade incident he had wanted to graduate; now he wanted employment requiring no further schooling. He aspired to a normal life, but could not understand how his aggressive actions interfered with this objective. He wanted acceptance, but lacked the maturity to make effective use of socially acceptable behavior. He rejected the attempts of the psychiatrist to explain such features and to show how they led him into trouble; yet he wanted to stay out of trouble, particularly in view of his probationary legal status. The psychiatrist noted that he possessed fair resources capable of development, and recommended that the school take him back on the stipulation that he submit to additional treatment and to the guidance of the school social worker.

But the onus of psychiatric treatment was too great for Tajoles, and after the first visit he expressed his uneasiness to his parents. His mother shared his anxiety. Despite her desire to cooperate with school officials, she could not surmount her feeling that such treatment stigmatized him. He asked his father what he should do, and his father, concurring in the apprehensions of wife and son, advised against further visits. The advice was readily taken.

Since the conditions set by the Board were not met, Rankin and Tajoles lost their eligibility for reconsideration. Rankin proceeded to enroll in a parochial secondary school in the suburbs, and Tajoles prepared to go to work.

SELECTED READINGS

Barron, Milton L., *The Juvenile in Delinquent Society*. New York: Alfred A. Knopf, 1954.

Glueck, Sheldon, ed., *The Problem of Delinquency*. New York: Houghton Mifflin Company, 1959.

Nye, F. Ivan, *Family Relationships and Delinquent Behavior*. New York: John Wiley and Sons, 1958.

Warner, W. Lloyd, et al., *Who Should Be Educated?* New York: Harper and Brothers, 1944.

Weinberg, Samuel Kirson, *Social Problems in Our Times*. Englewood Cliffs: Prentice-Hall, 1960.

A Model
Is Broken

CASE 8

Lakewater High School had been in session for two months. It was the major high school in a community of the same name, which formed part of a mid-western city of some 200,000 population. The building was a well-kept, three-story structure that was in better condition than the other buildings in the community. Along the streets large shade trees were beginning to turn golden and rust-colored.

For approximately ten years since the end of World War Two, the social structure of Lakewater had been undergoing rapid changes, so that it was now in many ways a very different community. Several large industries had been developed and were prospering. The once very adequate residential neighborhood of Lakewater was becoming a center for apartment houses which were actually reconstructed large homes. The business centers were expanding, and shopping centers were appearing along the main streets. With the changes in the residential areas and business sections, there were shifts in population composition. Since the rents were lower in Lakewater than in any other part of the city, the minority groups and low-income groups tended to settle there. The streets directly adjacent to the business center contained long rows of tenements and apartment or rooming houses, although the trees did seem to lend relief to the monotony. Toward the outskirts the homes were better in appearance. Here and there were little enclaves of slum-like homes in which large families of Negroes lived.

122

Most of the students who attended Lakewater High School were in the lower middle and low income groups. Some people in the community said the erection of the school's new building had been an attempt on the part of the county school board to make up for the very stormy past the school had experienced. The name Lakewater High seemed to call to mind a school attended by less privileged students. Many newspaper items had been written in the past about the high rates of delinquency that prevailed in the area, and generally negative and often sensational reports had been written about the poor discipline of the students and the high drop-out rates. The curriculum was generally directed toward the General courses. A few of the students took the college preparatory program, but most seemed to be interested only in getting some employment on leaving school and seemed to feel that their chances were best if they followed the General courses. The drop-out rate among the boys was far in excess of that for the girls.

As the students came to school each day, most of them walked in small groups with very little mixture across racial or ethnic lines. Some of the older boys had early model cars which were reassembled into hot-rods and jalopies of one type or another. They were often packed with students who evidently banded together. In the winter, more than at any other time, the students were frequently tardy or absent.

Fall weather had been unusually warm until this particular Wednesday in late October. The day began with very overcast skies, and a strong wind from the north swept the littered streets into whirls of dust and paper. Most of the students who walked to school appeared to walk faster because the wind was cold and their clothing did not seem to be appropriate for such weather. The bell had already rung for the tenth grade beginning class in social science. Bill Downing, a frequently tardy Negro of 16, strolled at a leisurely pace across the street toward Lakewater High School. The wind had already swept a good deal of refuse against the bicycle racks that held a few rather dilapidated vehicles. The door was difficult to open because of the wind and Bill's hesitancy. He had cut classes three days in the preceding week. He had told his mother that he was sick with the flu but had gone with his buddies to listen to music and sit around and talk and sleep.

The other students were seated by the time the teacher came into the classroom. Mr. Rutherford was always scrupulously prompt. He

had been at Lakewater High School for three years and had a reputation among the students as an interested man "who was fair and
square with the students." He had attended a university in a large
eastern city and had worked his way through school with various
night jobs and scholarships. In his school days he had belonged to
clubs that were considered socially-minded, and he generally prepared
projects for his classes which dealt with social problems. His personal
life had been different, for the most part, from those of his present students; his father had owned his own business and had encouraged his
son to seek a profession. On his first day at school that year Mr.
Rutherford's class had given him a round of applause, which he described to a friend as a mark of friendliness.

Mr. Johnson, the social science teacher who had preceded Mr.
Rutherford, had resigned after one year. In his resignation letter to
the Principal, Mr. Johnson expressed some strong feelings about the
poor attitude of the students toward their work and about their un-
ruliness. Another teacher had had his car vandalized after a series of
incidents with some of the Negro students in his class. He too resigned
and wrote a letter to the school board indicating that he felt the vandalism was a reprisal against his attempt to bring order and strictness
to the classroom. The board did not answer his letter or that of Mr.
Johnson. Mr. Johnson's predecessor had resigned after only six weeks
in the class.

On this late fall day Mr. Rutherford was dressed in a dark suit that
made him look larger than he was. He was rather lean, with a strong
voice and a good command of the language. The project for the week
was housing in an urban area near industrial and commercial zones.
The teacher had noticed the changing structure of Lakewater in the
three years he had been there and had discussed the changes with
people who had lived in the community for the past twenty years.
The basic plan of the project was to indicate the forces behind the
changes and the impact of the changes on the people in various areas.
Observing that businesses were expanding toward the peripheral areas
of the city and that formerly residential zones were taking on a new
complexion, the students were to be encouraged to analyze their own
residential streets.

Mr. Rutherford had made model displays of streets and buildings
for the class project. The displays indicated the historical changes in

the city plan and included a structural layout similar to that of Lakewater. Mr. Rutherford had described the rates of delinquency and of other types of personal and social problems, such as alcoholism, suicide, and unemployment, in the city. A large number of Negroes from the southern states had settled in the city, and Mr. Rutherford had made available to the students booklets on social relations and rates of movement to the city and within the city.

The students in this class came from Lakewater, and there were mixed feelings about handling such an acute and intimate problem in a work project in social science. One model that Mr. Rutherford had designed was general and did not have the distinctive features of Lakewater, and the students were told that an ideal type was being used.

Although there was a majority of white students in the class, there was a strong and vocal minority of approximately one fourth who were Negroes. On the first day of the project, Monday, the students had left the classroom in small groups, discussing the issues of public housing and the problems of minority rights. A group had stopped at Mr. Rutherford's desk and sought to get the teacher's personal views on these major issues. Mr. Rutherford had told them that he could not make any comments because he wanted them to come to their own conclusions. On Tuesday a white boy and a colored boy had discussed minority rights. Both boys had begun to raise their voices, started to push each other, and talked about settling their differences after school.

This Wednesday morning, when Bill Downing opened the door of the classroom, Joe Ford and Harry Williams, Bill's best friends in the class, looked up from their books and started laughing in a hushed manner. Joe and Harry, both Negroes, were frequently seen together with Bill both in the hallways and outside the school. They had been Bill's companions when he had cut classes three days the previous week. The three had stayed at Joe's house to listen to records. They had been sent to the office on many occasions for disturbing the class with loud noise, for being tardy, and for generally recalcitrant behavior in the classroom. The teacher in first-year algebra had written a report to the guidance teacher, saying that she felt that the two boys were led by Bill and that he encouraged them to follow his example. Mr. Rutherford had sent the three to the office during the first three weeks of school to have them disciplined for pouring ink on the text pages. Bill Downing was the instigator of this misbehavior, Mr. Rutherford had told the Principal.

Mr. Rutherford had been concerned about the persistent tardiness of some pupils, and in his announcement of rules at the beginning of the year he had stressed punctuality as a major demand he made of his students. When Bill opened the door, and Joe and Harry laughed, Mr. Rutherford looked at them hurriedly before his glance fell on Bill, who was smiling at his two friends. The teacher stiffened and looked sternly at Bill and then back toward the section of the room in which Harry and Joe were seated.

Bill Downing was physically well-developed with a weight of 145 and a height of 5 feet, 8 inches. He was a dark-complexioned Negro youth with irregular teeth and several scars on his arms. During his first year at Lakewater High School he had been sent to the office for disciplinary matters on ten occasions. His major infractions of the rules were fighting and tardiness. He was expelled on one occasion for hitting a smaller white boy with a rock. Among some of the students he had a reputation as a bully and a hot-head.

When Bill was three years of age his father had deserted the family, and his mother had taken Bill to live with her mother. The three had lived in Alabama for five years, and then Mrs. Downing had taken her son and moved to the mid-west.

Joe Ford, too, had lived in the south for the first three years of his life; he had moved with his parents to this town when his father had sought to get a job in one of the flour mills that were the principal source of income for many residents. His father had been killed in an accident in the mill four years after his employment, and Joe and his mother were living together on the pension money they received.

Harry was an illegitimate child. His mother had married an alcoholic. Harry had been seen in the school infirmary on occasion, and there was a medical report that he had been abused physically by someone. Harry had told his guidance teacher that his step-father had been drunk one night and had beaten him. The court records showed a number of arrests of Harry's stepfather for disturbance and abuse of his wife and children.

The three boys had often remarked to each other that they were all "in the same boat." Joe and Harry always took Bill's side in any issue that arose. Their families were known to welfare agencies in the city.

The Downings had been on Aid to Dependent Children Welfare for years and according to welfare authorities had shown little desire to change their situation. The characteristics of the Downings, the Fords, and the Williamses were similar to those of many of the Negro families in the community.

Bill's footsteps echoed in the room in a slow, noisy tread. The tenseness in Mr. Rutherford's stance relaxed, and he continued to talk to his class, as he arranged the scale models on the tables in the center of the room. The last one, which he had completed the night before, demonstrated how the rooming houses had once been large homes in upper class residential areas. He glanced up and noticed particularly three white boys, Frank Jones, Paul Lafleur, and Larry Baker. This trio had been at odds with the three Negroes, Bill, Joe, and Harry during the entire school year. He noticed that the exchange of looks between the boys was not friendly. He surmised that they resented Bill's seemingly intentional disruption of the class and his selfish behavior. They had tried in the past to control the decisions of the class. At the beginning, when Mr. Rutherford had suggested that the class select projects and issues of interest, the three white leaders had teamed up in an attempt to have the class discuss baseball and recreation and delinquency. They had received a good deal of support from other members of the class, but Mr. Rutherford had eliminated any study of baseball and recreation, explaining that he felt these issues were not as vital as certain social issues. Lunch hour comments from other teachers had indicated that a struggle was going on in the school between these groups of boys. The six boys were reportedly trying to be the big shots in the school.

The tension was high as Bill moved across the room. The teacher glanced toward the door and gave Bill what he later described as a very grave and disapproving look. He was on the verge of reprimanding the boy when he was distracted by the whispers of the students. A chair scraped across the floor, and Mr. Rutherford asked, "Who pushed that chair?"

For a brief moment the room was in a state of mild disorder. Bill, with a show of hostility, swaggered noisily across the room, knocking the scale model of the urban slum area from the table. The model fell to the floor and broke into a number of pieces. Bill moved on to his desk and glanced about as if to see if his behavior was being noticed by his friends. Mr. Rutherford became enraged. He ran across the room and met the student as he reached his desk. He reached out, took Bill by the collar of his shirt, and shook him as he yelled at him.

These, as accurately as they could be reconstructed, were his words and the events that followed.

"I've taken all I am going to from you, Bill. You've had a smart aleck attitude all along, and I won't stand for it any longer. You broke that scale model on purpose, and you know you did. Come with me, Bill. This is the last straw. We're going to the office now!"

The young Negro took Mr. Rutherford's arm and tried to free himself. He then yelled back, "Let go of me!"

The room was in a state of confusion. Harry and Joe were tense and upright in their seats.

"Let him go! He didn't mean to do nothing," Harry protested to Mr. Rutherford.

"You ought to be able to lick a young kid," Joe Ford called out, as he stood erect and shook his fists.

Just as the friends of Bill came to his support in the crisis, the rival trio of white boys expressed their feelings about the matter.

Larry Baker cried, "That Bill is always messing up. It's about time somebody got to him."

Paul was flushed and shaking as he yelled, "That nigger is no good. Throw him out of this class before he ruins it!"

By this time, Mr. Rutherford had tightened his grip on the young Negro student and was leading him forcibly toward the door. He was outwardly shaking with anger.

"Let go, you damned bully. You white bastard. Cut it, man," yelled Bill as he tried to free his shirt, tearing it as he struggled with his teacher.

The room appeared to be divided into two camps, and the whole scene was charged with emotion.

Mr. Rutherford demanded quiet, as he yelled, "I am going to settle this insubordination once and for all. I don't want any interference from anyone. I've taken enough from you, Bill. This time is the last for you and your surly attitude. The rest of you take your seats and be quiet!"

Bill continued to resist Mr. Rutherford, as they went through the door of the classroom quarreling and entangled.

Joe and Harry jumped from their seats and ran toward the pair but stopped short as they reached the door.

The trio of white leaders jumped to their feet and shouted to the Negro supporters. "You guys had better stay out of this if you know what's good for you." "You take one more step and we'll knock you on your asses." These threats were given simultaneously by Paul and Larry.

"Bill has always been a damned mess-up. He has raised hell with this class ever since he has been here." Frank spoke toward the entire class.

Bill's two friends were standing belligerently by the door.

Joe yelled, "Mr. Rutherford has always had it in for the Negro students."

Paul replied, "That's a lie. Shut up or I'll let you have it in the mouth."

Frank added, "It's about time that Mr. Rutherford got rid of that trouble-maker."

Larry shouted at the Negro students: "If you want to make something of this, we'll meet you after school."

Some of the students tried to busy themselves with other things, apparently so that they would not have to participate. Some of the girls shook their heads and looked harshly at both groups of boys.

"I've never seen Mr. Rutherford get so angry before. I don't think a teacher ought to let his temper get so wild. But these boys are enough to do anything," one girl said to her friend.

"Well, I guess he was pretty angry because that Bill knocked over the model. I don't think it was just because he's clumsy," her friend replied.

Similar statements were made throughout the room. As several students later reported, there seemed to be general agreement that the problem was pretty serious, and that everyone would have to take a stand one way or another.

As the teacher and Bill entered the office, Mr. Brown, the principal, looked up from his desk. He could gather from the obvious strain between the two and the quick breathing and mumbled words, that their tempers were high. He motioned for Mr. Rutherford to bring Bill into his private room.

During the year, Mr. Rutherford had usually been able to handle his problems without taking the children to the office. Mr. Brown had previously spoken of him as a good disciplinarian. On the other hand, he had spoken of Bill as a boy who had come to the school with a reputation for being a constant source of trouble, and as a difficult boy who seemed to let his anger flow fairly freely. Some teachers had talked about this problem with him recently while discussing the fact that Bill was able to get good grades in school on the infrequent occasions when he tried. During the two months of this school year Bill had been brought to the office on four different occasions. He had been brought there for insubordination in the gym class, for fighting on the playground with another boy, for strong-arming a smaller child to get some school supplies, and for dropping books from the second story window—after he had covered the pages with ink. Twice, Joe and Harry had accompanied him to the office.

Mr. Rutherford tried to tell the Principal about the preceding incident with calmness, but he kept losing track of the chronology. Mr. Brown stopped him once to ask a question about the incident, and at that point Mr. Rutherford was able to gain more control over himself. Bill did not say a word, as Mr. Rutherford recounted the story of the quarrel and struggle in the room following the breaking of the model.

The Principal said, "Bill, this is the last straw. I haven't anything else to do except to expel you from school. You will have to stay out of school until you can convince us that you will obey the rules and regulations. When you prove to us that you can live within the rules and with the other students, without any further disrespect and violence, then we will consider whether to permit you to return to this school."

Bill replied, as his voice quivered, "Mr. Rutherford was always taking it out on me, because he doesn't like the Negro students in the class. He's always talking about how the Negroes live in poor homes and don't have much money, and that they are always getting into trouble. Just yesterday he said that the Negroes always live in slums and don't know any better."

Mr. Rutherford explained to the Principal, "We're having a project in public housing problems. Bill has misunderstood the entire project. I never said anything of the sort."

Three teachers were standing in the outer office at the time. Since they were largely unfamiliar with the situation, they began to talk about what must have happened. They had seen the white teacher forcibly taking a Negro boy to see the Principal, and they had heard the verbal abuse that each was giving the other—the teacher in a commanding but firm way, and Bill Downing in a vindictive and name-calling fashion. One of the teachers was a young Negro woman. She stood back, apparently attempting to avoid any conversation about the incident.

Another of the three was Mrs. Rondo, a middle-aged white woman who taught algebra. She had always been the sponsor of the Senior Class. She had a reputation for being a crusader in some social issues. Her efforts were usually considered sincere by most people, but she had been known in the past to become upset about any altercation in race relations in the school. It had been reported that she and Mr. Rutherford were not on friendly terms because he had never consulted her about any of his projects in social science, and she had discussed with others his neglect to include her. She began talking with the other teacher, Mr. Simms, who taught manual training. Mr. Simms, also white, said that he felt the whole situation was an inevitable result of the behavior problems in the school, and he expressed sympathy with the social science teacher's decision to bring the boy to see the Principal, even though he had had to use force to do so. Mrs. Rondo said that she disapproved of the man-handling that the Negro children often received and that she never had felt Mr. Rutherford was qualified personally to handle these issues in his class, because he did not truly understand the problems of racial conflict.

The expelled Bill left the office, walking with a heavy and scraping pace, clicking his taps against the marble floor. He was talking to himself in a very low and unintelligible manner. As he met various students in the halls, he told them his version of the incident, saying that he had been unduly punished and that everyone was against him. He appealed for support in his struggle with the administration. After he had gathered up his belongings, he slammed the door of his locker. He walked out of the main entrance to the school and headed for the local drug store on the corner. He told his version to many of the members of the community, apparently trying to win sympathy and support for himself in this "discrimination," as he called it.

Mr. Rutherford talked with the Principal for a few moments after Bill had stormed out of the office. He said, "I'm sorry that I lost my temper, but I felt I had to take action. There has been a mounting conflict over a long period of time in the class between some of the

Negroes and some of the whites. I felt that I had to bring Bill here forcibly in order to have any semblance of control and order and effectiveness in the classroom."

Mr. Jones reassured him, "I'm going to support you in this action, and I feel confident that the students will realize that what you did was right."

After Mr. Rutherford left the office, he met a good friend of his on the faculty. He told him what had happened and then said, "Ted, I probably was a little hasty and maybe too harsh. I've always tried to be fair in dealing with these troubles in the classroom. Maybe I did create a scene. I'm really disturbed about this."

As he returned to his own classroom he thought he heard a remark by one teacher to another that in her opinion the social science teacher was probably just prejudiced against Negroes. He later reported that he had been amazed at the thought that such a statement could have been made by a faculty member. He said that he had dismissed it as probably a result of failing to hear the conversation accurately.

When he entered his room, the students were still talking and muttering. The broken model still lay in the middle of the room. He asked two of the students to put the pieces back on the table. There was a moment of hesitancy, and then his request was carried out by the two young white boys, Frank and Paul. He looked over a group of students who were paying very little attention to him, but were eyeing each other warily and seemed to be readying themselves for a fight. As he later recounted this situation, he said that the class seemed to drag on for another fifteen minutes, during which time he felt considerable resistance toward the things he said on the part of one faction of the students and acceptance of what he said on the part of another group; the students seemed to be divided into two opposing groups. The bell rang, and the students began to file out.

Joe and Harry were close together as they passed the seats of Frank and Paul and Larry. The two groups spoke harshly toward each other and threatened to fight there in the room. Mr. Rutherford appeared in time to tell them to break it up and leave at once. Reluctantly the two groups did leave the room, continuing to exchange threats.

Frank seemed particularly vindictive as he said, "You niggers are scared, now that your big shot has gotten booted out of school. We'll see who are the big shots now." The attitude of the group led by Joe and Harry seemed to be one of wishing for revenge and retribution toward both the teacher and the group led by Frank, Paul and Larry.

Mr. Rutherford stood in the door watching with concern the two groups of angry boys go down the hallway to the other classrooms.

During the lunch period there were several minor fracases among the students, as they waited in line in the cafeteria. The number of children who left the school to go home for their lunch hour was noticeably smaller than in the past, and some of the teachers commented about this occurrence, surmising that some of the students were getting ready to fight this battle out.

As the subject was discussed among the teachers at the next lunch period, a mounting polarity of feelings developed. Mrs. Rondo said that the "abuse" of Bill Downing had been unnecessary. Other teachers said that the scene had not been especially unusual, and that there had been adequate cause for the disciplinary action taken.

That afternoon the Principal sent notices to Mr. Rutherford, to Mrs. Lehi, the school social worker, and to Mr. Ramsay, the boys' counselor, asking the three to meet with him to discuss the incident. The matter was analyzed by the members of this committee. Each person talked about the need for some positive and effective action immediately. They decided that the stronger boys among the Negroes and the whites should be called in separately, by the social worker and by the counselor, to sessions in which they might express their views.

The members of the committee decided that the solutions to the problems manifested in the incident that morning would indeed be complex. They agreed that the problems had existed for a long time in the community and within the school. The counselor commented on the disruption of the balance of power and the status groupings in the classroom. He pointed out that it was an acute situation that needed strategic handling. Mr. Rutherford talked about the very obvious display of friction between the two leading groups of students who had participated in the struggle that morning, and he added that, looking back over the year's work, he realized now that the tension between the groups had frequently been high. The Principal said that it was going to be difficult to talk about the incident with these children because of the high tension level and the deep hatred that appeared to exist below the surface, even in the more perfunctory meetings of these groups in the school and in the larger community.

Mrs. Lehi said that to attempt to ignore the incident would be dangerous. She added that the committee should be ready to understand and cope with the problems they were likely to face if the two groups became polarized and entrenched in feelings they felt they must express, possibly through physical force or persistent misbehavior in the school. She said an unsettled issue such as this one could be a constant worry and sore spot with teachers and students in general, as well as with those students who were quarreling among themselves.

Mr. Rutherford said that, looking at the problem more closely, he realized that Frank and Larry and Paul were probably happy that the Negroes were weakened by the expulsion of Bill Downing. Now they would have a chance to take over more control of the room with less opposition from Joe and Harry, who had always seemed to depend on Bill for leadership. He said that if the trouble continued, he would predict that little incidents of revenge and retribution would occur and would likely grow into major issues and cleavages throughout the school session. He pointed out that his position in this class would be in jeopardy.

Mr. Ramsay indicated that he thought that sessions with the two racial groups would be good, because they would give the boys a chance to air their feelings, gain insights into the actual incidents and their effects, and release some of their tensions. He thought that all the boys involved should be consulted, and he strongly expressed a feeling that sides should not be taken, and that great caution should be taken to insure that the groups were aware of the objectivity of the administration.

The committee decided to have the groups meet with the counselor and the social worker. Mr. Rutherford said that if he met with the boys he could perhaps create the feeling that the administration did not feel that adults were always right and invincible and might thus give the boys a feeling that they were understood.

That afternoon after school several fights took place in the yard and on the streets. At one point several teachers discussed calling the police to get the students to move on peacefully. The boys were warned that if any reprisals occurred in the neighborhood that night the police would be warned. The students then broke up into their usual groups and started toward their homes.

The school social worker, Mrs. Lehi, went to the home of Bill Downing that evening to talk with Bill and his mother about the problem in school and Bill's expulsion. When she arrived, Bill was not at home. His mother said she knew nothing of the incident and expressed deep concern over the fact that her boy had been expelled. She told the worker that Bill was generally easy to manage around the house and that she thought his troubles were caused by the fact that he ran around with lots of older and tougher boys. She named Harry Williams and Joe Ford. She said that she thought that everything would be all right in time and that she would give Bill a good talking-to when he came home that night.

Mrs. Lehi told Mrs. Downing, "The school rules have been broken, and we feel that the best thing to do now is to attempt to have Bill see the seriousness of his action. He is a good student when he applies himself, but he frequently seems to care little about school work."

"He gets awful nervous when he has to sit around all closed up like that. I think he really wants to get out and get a job," Mrs. Downing replied.

"Do you feel that the school has been fair, Mrs. Downing?"

"I suppose."

"We can re-admit Bill when we feel that he can return and abide by the rules. Can you help him attempt to understand our policy?"

Mrs. Downing said that she would discuss these matters with her son and let the worker know as soon as possible.

Just as Mrs. Lehi was ready to leave the house, Bill came walking toward the door. He hesitated for a moment and came into the room when his mother called out to him.

"Hello, Bill. I have come to talk with you and your mother about the things that happened today and about getting you back into school," Mrs. Lehi said as she looked closely at Bill, who was shifting from one foot to another.

"Yes, ma'am," Bill said tersely.

"I wonder if you feel like talking about things now, or should I return later?" the worker inquired.

"I want to go to my room now. I guess you have already told my mom about things," Bill said.

"Your mother and I did discuss your being expelled. I shall return tomorrow when you feel more relaxed. Good night, Bill." The worker turned to the mother and said that she had enjoyed being able to meet her and hoped they could work out the conflicts. She left the house and walked to her car. Bill and his mother began to talk.

Mrs. Lehi later reported that on her way home she thought to herself that getting Bill back into school was going to be a very serious project, because of the past anxieties and hostilities which now were emphasized more than ever. She hoped they would not grow into more serious problems. She knew that Bill would be on the defensive because of the dispute with Mr. Rutherford. She hoped that her talking with Bill might have a cushioning effect for him when he returned to school. She knew that prior preparation through timely group work with the other boys and individual talks would help to clear the air of bitterness.

The next day the counselor met with the two groups of boys, and Mr. Rutherford also talked with them. The counselor stressed the importance of the members of each group trying to understand the attitudes of the other group. He pointed out that if they understood each other, and themselves, they would tend not to be so emotional, and there would probably be fewer fights between the groups. Mr. Rutherford told the boys that adults make mistakes, too, and that the administrators and teachers were going to make every effort to understand the boys even more. He pointed out that representatives of both groups would have frequent opportunities to talk to the administrators and give their points of view on important matters.

Mr. Rutherford did not hold his class that day, but instead the visual aids department showed a film about the dynamics of prejudice. After the class had seen the film, a short discussion was permitted, with students having a limited time to speak. Some invidious remarks were made during the picture, but the mood seemed less tense than on the previous day. When the students filed out of the classroom, there were some exchanges of name-calling and threats of revenge.

The committee met again at the lunch hour and discussed the progress that had been made. They decided that it was difficult to predict the effects of planning in such a situation. The timing in the handling of the program was most important. The attitudes of the people who were involved must be understood, Mrs. Lehi concluded in her discussion with the group. The Principal stated that the success of the solution of this entire problem was dependent in large part on the ability of the adults to be accepting and strong people, able to handle their own emotions and create good relationships with the people who had been the instigators in this conflict in the classroom. Mr. Rutherford stressed that everyone had to try to express himself fully and truthfully, so that each could communicate with the others and not be isolated from them, failing to understand their goals and objectives. He did not want people to be angry and unable to talk with one another.

On the following day Harry and Joe were taken to Juvenile Hall, a detention home, for questioning about loitering in front of a store. There had been a burglary there the night before. The two boys were cleared of any implication and were released that same night. The worker, Mrs. Lehi, returned to the home of the Downings and found Bill freer and easier in his manner. He inquired about the events of the day.

Three days after his suspension Bill Downing was readmitted to Lakewater High. He remained there for another month and then, after the Christmas vacation, found a part-time job and did not return. When he was seventeen he entered the armed forces.

SELECTED READINGS

Allport, Gordon W., *The Nature of Prejudice.* Cambridge, Massachusetts: The Addison-Wesley Publishing Company, 1954.

American Council on Education, Intergroup Education in Cooperating Schools, *Intergroup Education in Public Schools: Experimental Programs Sponsored by the Project in Intergroup Education in Cooperating Schools: Theory, Practice, and In-Service Education.* Washington: the Council, 1952.

Cohen, Albert K., *Delinquent Boys: The Culture of the Gang.* Glencoe: The Free Press, 1955.

Glueck, Sheldon, and Eleanor Glueck, *Unraveling Juvenile Delinquency.* New York: The Commonwealth Fund, 1950.

Gordon, Calvin Wayne, *The Social System of the High School: A Study in the Sociology of Adolescence.* Glencoe: The Free Press, 1957.

Kvaraceus, William C., *Juvenile Delinquency and the School.* New York: World Book Company, 1945.

Nye, F. Ivan, *Family Relationships and Delinquent Behavior.* New York: John Wiley and Sons, 1958.

Redl, Fritz, and William W. Wattenberg, *Mental Hygiene in Teaching,* rev. ed. New York: Harcourt, Brace and Company, 1959.

Sherif, Muzafer, and Carolyn W. Sherif, *Groups in Harmony and Tension: An Integration of Studies on Intergroup Relations.* New York: Harper and Brothers, 1953.

Mutiny in the Gymnasium

CASE 9

On Wednesday, February 16th, 1956, twelve freshman and sophomore girls, members of a physical education class at Asbury High School, attempted to induce the entire class to refuse to take part in the planned activity for that period, and subsequently disobeyed instructions to go to the dressing room to change into gym clothes.

The class in physical education for freshmen and sophomores at Asbury High School was taught by Mrs. Greta Fairfax. It met from 2:30 to 3:25 on Mondays, Wednesdays, and Fridays. On this particular day four girls, Judy Camp, Carol Jones, Barbara Farris, and Mary Frank, who were on their way to the gym, met Mr. Monroe, the principal, in the hall. They asked him if ". . . it would be all right if the gym class went for a hike today instead of playing basketball." Mr. Monroe replied that they had his permission if Mrs. Fairfax thought it was a good idea and if the entire class wanted to go. Continuing on their way to class, the girls met Doris Wheat and Winnie Grant, two other members of their friendship clique, and told them that they were going to try to persuade Mrs. Fairfax to let the class go on a hike.

Before the class changed into gym clothes and proceeded with the activity for the day, it usually met first in the gym, for roll-taking and to plan and discuss the day's activity. On this day, after roll had

138

been taken, Barbara Farris asked Mrs. Fairfax if the class could go on a hike that afternoon. This request was supported by enthusistic comments from her friends. Mrs. Fairfax replied that she did not think it was a very good idea. The plan that she followed for the class provided for basketball that day, and while it was flexible and could be revised, the weather outside was raw and chilly and the ground was quite muddy. Other students indicated a preference for staying indoors. After several students expressed their views, the matter was put to a vote, and the majority voted to have the hike at some later date when the weather was more pleasant. The original plan to play basketball was adopted.

Before sending the girls to the dressing rooms to change, Mrs. Fairfax left the gym to go to one of the dressing rooms to see if the maintenance men who had been repairing the hot water heater there had finished and left. Finding that they had gone, she returned to the gym and told the class that they could go to change. The entire class of 60 girls remained clustered at one end of the gym, no one making a move or speaking. After a moment, without responding to this insubordination or to the tension in the faces and postures of the girls, Mrs. Fairfax turned and walked into the corridor leading to the dressing rooms. She stopped there for a few seconds, then returned with a smile on her face, as if to give the impression that she was unaware of any difficulty. She repeated her instructions. Immediately, Martha Hanks pulled away from the group and went toward the dressing rooms. Martha was a freshman, who had a reputation for being quiet and conforming, and who recently had undergone a religious conversion at a revival meeting conducted by Billy Graham at a nearby town. Martha was followed by Audrey Slack, a freshman who enjoyed great peer approval and had many friends at school. In spite of the fact that some of the girls were obviously holding on to others to prevent them from leaving the group, most of the class followed Audrey to the dressing room, leaving twelve girls who still refused to move.

Mrs. Fairfax went to the sophomore dressing room, leaving the twelve recalcitrant girls in the gym. While they were changing, some of the more outspoken sophomores told Mrs. Fairfax that they were afraid to go back out onto the gym floor because the others would "jeer at them." Mrs. Fairfax also heard some of the girls express the feeling that they probably should not have changed because the others would make life miserable for them afterwards. Mrs. Fairfax asked some of the girls why they had changed, and they replied that ". . . it was the right thing to do." Mrs. Fairfax told this group that it was best that they do their own thinking and not let others think for them, adding that they did not have to worry about being jeered at when they went back to the gym.

As soon as the girls had changed, Mrs. Fairfax led them back to the gym in a group. She walked directly up to the twelve girls who had not changed. They stopped talking among themselves and waited in silence until the entire class had gathered around Mrs. Fairfax. Then the basketball activities were planned, teams decided upon, time-keeping arranged, and so forth. The twelve non-dressers were left out of the plan. The rest of the class began the basketball, and Mrs. Fairfax told the twelve to come with her.

Ordinarily such a discipline problem would have been taken directly to the Principal, Mr. Monroe. However, he was not in his office, since at that time of the day he always went to check the school buses. Mrs. Fairfax placed the girls in the study hall conducted by her friend, Mrs. Alexander, for the remainder of the period. She explained later that she decided on this action in order to avoid the hasty and incomplete handling of the problem likely to ensue when there was so little time left in the school day and Mr. Monroe was occupied with other matters. Girls from this class had been placed in the study hall before, when they had become minor disciplinary problems, or when they had been unable to participate in an activity for reasons of health.

After school Mrs. Fairfax went to Mr. Monroe and told him about the incident and how she had handled it. She said that until some action was taken the twelve girls would be excluded from the gym class. Mr. Monroe's initial reaction was one of considerable anger. He said that he felt they should be expelled from the class for the remainder of the year, losing credit for physical education for the semester. Mrs. Fairfax said that she felt this was too severe and might preclude positive or constructive action to help the girls.

Mr. Monroe said he would talk to each of the girls separately and then discuss the problem further with Mrs. Fairfax before final disciplinary acion was taken. He also decided to notify each girl's parents about the incident and to request written statements from them acknowledging the notification. It took the remainder of that week and most of the following one to talk with the girls and notify the parents. In the meantime the girls were temporarily excluded from the physical education class. On Thursday of the following week, Mr. Monroe left for a national convention of school administrators in Atlantic City; he would be away for seven days. He deferred taking final action until he returned.

Asbury High School was one of two high schools serving Westford County. The county, with an area of 150 square miles, comprised five townships. On its eastern edge, about twenty miles from Asbury, was Minton City, an industrial and transportation center with a population of about 30,000, dominating the economy of the county. More than a third of the fathers of school age children in the county drove there for their jobs, chiefly in manufacturing and transportation firms. Recently the federal government had started developing a large project there which was bringing in workers from adjoining states. Minton City's large high school served all of the county except Red Creek and Asbury townships, whose children attended Asbury High School.

Red Creek lay on the major state highway between Minton City and Asbury. The fathers of a majority of the students from Red Creek township worked in Minton City, of which Red Creek was rapidly becoming a bedroom suburb. Red Creek provided no important community services for its residents. The average length of residence of students' parents was considerably lower for Red Creek than it was for Asbury.

Asbury had a population of 452. There were two small grocery stores, several filling stations, and seven small churches. There were no recreation centers of any kind. Most of the students from Asbury township came from homes whose providers were engaged either entirely in farming or in other occupations that kept them within the township.

Asbury High School was a part of Asbury School, which included grades 1–12. The high school was composed of grades 9–12. The first eight constituted the elementary school for Asbury township, with most of the pupils coming from farm homes outside the town itself. The upper four grades, with an enrolment of 170, consisted of students from both Asbury township and Red Creek township. The school occupied two buildings. The main and older building housed the first six grades and most of the classrooms for grades 7–12. The library doubled as a study hall. The newer building consisted of a gymnasium, a cafeteria, the home economics room, the commerce room and three other classrooms. There were no science laboratories or facilities for shopwork.

The curriculum at Asbury High School consisted of three courses of study: academic or college preparatory, commercial, and vocational home economics. There was no organized guidance or counseling program. Mr. Monroe, the principal of the entire school, handled all disciplinary problems referred by teachers.

Generally speaking, Asbury School was considered to be overcrowded and understaffed. Special services and specialized personnel were lacking.

·The county school nurse was able to visit Asbury School only about once every three weeks.

Physical education was handled by three teachers. Mrs. Fairfax was in charge of all girls' physical education, with freshmen and sophomores together and juniors and seniors together constituting her two physical education classes. The girls from Asbury township who had attended grades 7 and 8 at Asbury had had two years of physical education prior to entering ninth grade. The girls from Red Creek township had not previously had any physical education. Mrs. Fairfax was the first teacher to have handled physical education for girls in ten years who had been trained and licensed for the subject. Equipment for physical education was sparse.

Extracurricular activities at Asbury School were few. In addition to the varsity boys' athletic program, several plays were put on—Mrs. Fairfax coached the junior and senior class plays—and there were two band groups, "Beginning Band" and "Regular Band." Because most pupils came to school by bus, there was little in the way of extracurricular activity taking place under school auspices after the end of the school day at 3:30.

Mr. Monroe, age 50, had been principal of Asbury School for nine years. He was born in Asbury and, prior to becoming principal, was the varsity coach at Asbury High. He was reportedly well-liked and respected in his community and was considered to be one of the best administrators in the county. He had a reputation for being a good executive and organizer in his school, but Mrs. Fairfax later said she had felt soon after coming to Asbury that he had a tendency to allow students to talk him into reversing decisions on small matters. Students appeared to perceive him as a friendly and warm person. Several other of the older teachers were considered to be much firmer disciplinarians. However, he was quite insistent on handling himself important disciplinary functions at all grade levels. He was described by teachers as not disposed to delegate authority or responsibility and as tending to try to deal personally with all matters coming before him. As well as administering the school, he taught one class.

Mrs. Fairfax taught high school English and physical education. She had been in public school work for nineteen years, having taught in the elementary grades as well as in senior high school. She considered her major specialization to be language arts in the junior high school. However, she had taught only physical education for seven years in Chicago. She and her husband had moved to Minton City the summer before, when her husband's firm had transferred him from Chicago. The only teaching position she had been able to secure was the one in Asbury. While the salary was low and it involved a twenty-mile drive each way, she explained that she enjoyed teaching, and that the situation at Asbury was one which, because of her experience, afforded her some status and an opportunity to make more than a routine contribution.

The twelve pupils who refused to change into gym uniforms comprised three freshmen and nine sophomores. They were all Asbury girls who had attended Asbury School in the elementary grades. These girls, particularly Barbara Farris, Judy Camp, and Mary Frank, were reported to be popular not only with girls in their classes but with leaders in the junior and senior classes. They tended to have leading roles in the social activities of their age group in the community and in the school. They were popular among the boys. Most came from middle income homes. There was considerable rivalry and mutual hostility between girls from Asbury and those from Red Creek; those from Asbury showed signs of feeling superior to those from Red Creek.

During the week following the incident Mrs. Fairfax asked each of the girls in her physical education class to write her a letter telling her why she thought the difficulty had arisen and what she thought should be done about it. While quite a few girls indicated they did not want to write such notes, Mrs. Fairfax assured them that their remarks would be kept confidential and insisted that each submit a note or letter to her. The following are sample letters from members of each group.

Sample statements from those who did not dress for gym.

1. Mrs. Fairfax,

   First of all I would like to say I'm sorry for everything I've done wrong in Physical Education. I know that has been a lot, but seriously I'm very sorry. You would like to know what's wrong with that class. On Monday we have volley ball, which I don't mind so much, Wednesday we have girls' basketball which they don't play anymore, Friday mostly square dancing which isn't as popular as it used to be, besides they don't square dance like we are being taught in Physical Ed. You're the teacher and I'm not telling you how to run your class, but this is my opinion.

   One reason why I didn't dress, is because I wanted to go on a hike, because it was a pretty day and on that certain day I never felt like playing (if you know what I mean). I could have walked out of Mr. Monroe's office on Wednesday and said I was sick, which was right, but I didn't because I didn't want to play girls' basketball anyway.

   If you think I didn't walk out of there just because I would think somebody would call me chicken, square, brown-noser and other things, you're wrong. Nobody runs my life for me, they used to, but not anymore. I've learned a lot about that from General Business. We have to figure out things for ourselves someday, so it might as well be now. Mrs. Fairfax, I know I do things in physical education to make you mad and I know if I was the teacher I would get mad, too. But I don't do all of these things just to be mean or to show off, believe me. I can honestly say I have learned a dog-gone good lesson from this. I know the teachers have a hard time trying to teach us something, from now on I'll pay attention to them.

   I think in Physical Education we are more free than in most classes, maybe that's the reason we try these things. I rightly don't know myself.

   There are some kids who try to boss and everything in that class, I know I'm no angel. I get sort of out of hands a lot of times. Maybe that's what's wrong with the class. I think if we could have some kind of games we would like to play once in a while we would get along better, of course we have our jitterbugging at times, but then we have about 3 or 4 square dances, and by that time we have time for one jitterbug. I know you said we've got to learn 3 square dances, so I tried even if I don't like them. I think we should have tumbling and exercises, I thought that was what Physical Education was really when I first started taking it. But you're the teacher. I hope you're not real angry with me. This is the way I feel right now. I'm as much to blame as the rest.

                                                        Judy Camp

2. Mrs. Fairfax,

   I think our gym class has been a poor one because we have not been cooperating. Now that we have been out we know we really miss gym. If we get back in I think we will cooperate wonderfully and really have a lot of fun in gym. We really haven't been appreciating gym, but I'm sure we do now. I am not trying to polish the apple, I am just telling the truth. You say the class has done well since our departure, but if we get back in we will be so glad to get back in we will do anything you say. I will be very benignant if I get back in. We will do as edified. Our reason for doing this foolish thing was just to be smartelics.

Doris

3. Mrs. Fairfax,

    I don't know what exactly is wrong. The one thing that I hate is playing volleyball and games we play over and over. And I think everybody agrees that they are tired of volleyball too. I think we ought to have more to do. I think also that we ought to be able to go on a hike. On days that we play basketball the ones that don't play always get in trouble. We should be able to play ping pong and tumble while the others play.

    Another thing wrong is everybody tries to boss and get mad when they can't tell the class what to play. I think everybody has learned their lesson. All the girls has said they would behave if they were back in. We need our credit very bad and realize we made a mistake by not dressing. It will never happen again. I don't know any more things thats wrong except you don't try hard enough to make us behave like we should. One other thing. Everybody could learn to square dance if they wanted to but they don't want to. Simply because square dancing is out of style. Nobody goes square dancing any more.

Carol Jones

4. Mrs. Fairfax,

    I think that the whole trouble is that us twelve girls are the ones in your gym class that are full of meanness. By that I mean that we, well think we can tell you what to do and get by with it.

    That day that we pulled that little stunt, while it was happening we really thought we were cute. But then when it resulted into all this I don't think that there is one out of the twelve girls that wouldn't give anything to get back in.

    Myself I'm dying to get back in, but it's up to you and Mr. Monroe and I'll just have to take my medicine.

Barbara Farris

5. Mrs. Fairfax,

    I think our class didn't get along because we didn't cooperate. I realize now that people have to do a lot of things they don't want to. I have to get my credit so now I realize that I shouldn't have got myself kicked out. I know that you're supposed to do what the teacher tells you whether you want to or not. I would like very much to get back into Phy. Ed. I would be more than glad to do what you say from now on. For one thing, I thought we should go on a hike, but it doesn't really matter now, because I know that I shouldn't expect to get everything I want. I guess you might say that we were taking advantage of the teacher, I think maybe that time. Now, I can see how dumb that was because, it doesn't pay. If you decide to let us come back, me for one, won't make one wrong move. I think that I was just mostly acting a fool, or else, I would not have set there. I should've got dressed, no matter what anyone said, I guess from now on I'd better think for myself. I always like to play basketball and volleyball, but it seems like we don't get to play very long, and we have too much idle time. I think when we're not playing we should have something else to do. It's not that I wanted to get into trouble, because, really I didn't think that you'd kick me out. I wish that you would let me in and let me try to prove that I could be a good student. Just as good as the very best. Last year I got practically straight A's in your class.

I think that we should get to go on a hike every now and then. I also think it would be fun to have other activities a lot of times, girls don't feel like running and stuff like that. It would be nice to have different things to do. All I can say is that I'm terribly sorry, I acted like a child instead of my age. I understand a lot of things now then I did. I hope I get back into class this year though. I'll really try a lot harder if I do.

Mary Frank

6. Mrs. Fairfax,
    A lot of our trouble is that to many try to run the class. Some of our new students do not know how to play the games that we play and the rules and we do not have enough patients with them. Some of the students do not like the games that we play. I think we should have more races. A few hikes would help. I think our class will be O.K. when we teach the others the rules to the games.

Winnie Grant

Sample statements from those who did dress for gym.

1. Mrs. Fairfax,
    Those girls were kicked out of gym class because, they wanted to take school activities into their own hands. I believe the reason they will not co-operate is because, they have not had the proper training at home. The teacher's are too liberal with them at school. They try to gain popularity at the cost of other students. They do not respect their teacher's for example; when Barbara was kicked out of gym class the last time, she told Mrs. Fairfax she was sorry to get back in class, then later, she laughed about it. The teacher's could help bring about cooperation with these students by, contacting their parents. When students are kicked out of class their parents know nothing about it. If these difficulties had not been allowed to prevail they would not have insisted on taking a hike instead of doing as the teacher asked. Also, I might add that I think we have had a more cooperative group without these girls.

Fran

2. Mrs. Fairfax,

I think a lot of trouble in the gym class is caused from the kids who will not follow instructions. They liked to act smart and show-off to make everybody laugh or look up to them.

If we don't follow a certain few, they talk about us, leave you out of things, so much that you feel miserable for a long time of afterwards.

The gym class has been well organized since a few are out, who were always starting trouble.

I have not thought too much about whether they should get back in class or not, but they deserve some sort of punishment to teach them a lesson.

Patti Ames

3. Mrs. Fairfax,

I think the trouble is that some of the girls are trying to run over us girls. And trying to criticize us just because we don't know how to play basketball, volleyball and dancing as well as they do.

Fay Murrow

4. Mrs. Fairfax,

Since you have asked the opinion of the remaining students of your phy. ed. class on the departure of several of the more troublesome students of our class, I feel it is my duty as a upholder and citizen of Asbury to express my convictions about this situation.

These troublesome students have been causing a lot of trouble lately and I think they should be kept out of class for a while longer at least.

I think Carol Jones, Doris, Mary Frank, Judy Camp, and Barbara Farris were causing the most trouble.

I know it's up to you and Mr. Monroe to decide if they should come back to class, but I think they have had to many chances already, and the more they have, the more things they'll try to get by with. I know, I've gone to school with them all my life.

I have had more fun in phy. ed. since they left, and I think everyone else has too. And I think you've had a lot less trouble.

(unsigned)

5. Mrs. Fairfax,

I think the girls should not be allowed to come back. If you let them come back they might not define you, but they will still do the same things to us. I would like to give you some reasons why I think they shouldn't be allowed to come back. I think that if we make a mistake you could correct us, but Barbara Farris (and the others, she is the head of it so I will refer to her) yells at you herself. She made fun of me and many others you do not know how to play as well as she does. I'll always remember the time that I swung at the ball and she made fun of me. But the thing that gets me is that if she misses it, it is a big joke, or if one of her friends miss it it's just all right. One time when you had us in rellay races I was in her group and she said

"Oh get Audrey out, we'll lose for sure if she is in our team," and carried on. Several girls who claim to be my friends joined in because they wanted to be popular with Barbara Farris. She (and some others that you kicked out) think that their little Gods and that they can't do anything wrong. That is why and other girls I know hate to come to the class, cause we know that whether we try or not we would be yelled at. Those kids are probably thinking right now, well Mrs. Fairfax will let us back in, and in a little while they will start yelling at you again. But if you make them stay out they will know that you mean business when you say something. You said that you would prefer us to sign our name, well I am proud of the way I feel and I don't care who reads this, but some are scared to really voice their opinion because Barbara Farris wouldn't like them any more. But if any fuss ever came over this I wouldn't be ashamed to read this because I am proud of the way I feel and I am not scared of Barbara Farris or any of those popular girls. And in closing I want to say that since you have kicked them out I have never enjoyed myself more these days than all the three years that I have been taking this Physical Education.

I will be moving pretty soon over to Greenville and if I don't get to thank you before I leave I want to say thank you for all the times you have put up with things that I have done in all your classes. And thanks for everything.

Audrey Slack
9th grade

6. Mrs. Fairfax,
I don't think those girls should be let back in class for many reasons.

They have been kicked out quite a few times now and they have always gotten back in. If they get back in they will try more stunts just in spite of you. They almost know they will get back in this time.

The reason they do these things is just to get you upset and attract attention. Teachers aren't any different than anyone else. Teachers are human beings as well as we are and I think they should be treated that way. I like every teacher down here and you can have more fun and friends if you get along with the teachers.

We have had a lot of fun and it has been peaceful with them out of class this week and I hope it will remain that way.

I like nearly everyone that got kicked out but they seem to take advantage of everything.

(unsigned)

7. Mrs. Fairfax,
The trouble started before you came over to the gym. The kids (some of them) wanted to go on a hike and, if you wouldn't let them they wouldn't do anything.

As for myself I don't want them back this year or ever! Our class has had a lot more fun without the following: Judy Camp, Carol J., Barbara F., Mary Frank, Doris, and Winnie Grant. They think they are too good for us! They try to tell us what to do and what not to do. If we couldn't do something they'd make fun of us. For the sake of our class and you, *please* don't let them in. I think you noticed how much better class we have had since they've gone. You've already given them a lot of chances, and the more you give them the more they want.

Trudy Klass

8. Mrs. Fairfax,

I think the reason the girls in physical education acted the way they did was because they are at a rebelious age. There is a time in everyone's life when they want to be the boss and won't pay any attention to what anyone says. I imagine you have felt the same way at one time while you was a teenager.

I don't know what I would do if I was in your shoes. It would be a pretty hard decision. If they are kicked out of class for the year they are going to have extra subjects to carry, but if they get back in they will think they can get away with it again if they were able to once.

All I can say is I hope you are a better judge than me.

Donna T.

9. Mrs. Fairfax,

I don't think it was right for them to disobey a teacher. Most of them are the ones who get in all the trouble. It doesn't matter to me whether they come back or not. Only I will say that some of the girls who were kicked out have tried to boss some of us Red Creek girls around. I think there's just to many in our class.

(unsigned)

10. Mrs. Fairfax,

The trouble started when some of the girls wanted to go on a hike. They said Mr. Monroe said it would be alright by him if it was alright by Mrs. Fairfax. Of course they thought they would get to go since Mr. Monroe said he didn't care. They forgot it was your decision whether we could go or not. Myself I did not want to go. They thought it was warm enough to go, but actually it was not that warm. Before you came into the gym they had decided that they were going on a hike. When you did come into the gym you said a man was in the dressing room and that we would have to wait a minute. Before the man came out of the dressing room they asked about the hike and Mrs. Fairfax said "no." That was when the trouble started. They said, "When the man comes out just sit here." And that is just what they did. When the man came out they just set there. The first one to go to the dressing room was Martha. The next person was Audrey Slack. They clapped for them. When the other went they called us "chickens." After that Mrs. Fairfax took them to study hall. I must say we have had a better class. When those others were in class you could not have any fun at all. Every time Mrs. Fairfax would say we were going to play a certain game they would start arguing with her and everything. Since those kids have been out I have had the most fun in gym class that I have ever had. Every time you make a mistake somebody laughs at you or bawls you out, you cannot have any fun. Also I have noticed that Mrs. Fairfax has been in a better humor. I know with those kids carrying on like they did, it was sure to make her upset. As far as I am concerned I don't think they should be let back in. They do nothing but upset the class, cause trouble and make fun of people. The ones that cause the most trouble are the following:

Judy Camp
Carol Jones
Barbara Farris
Doris Wheat
Mary Frank
Winnie Grant

These girls try to boss or run the whole class just because they think they are better than anyone else. Sometimes they do not use nice language either. We get along better without them. We have had a much better gym class since they have gone.

Lois Milner

The following comments on the twelve girls who disobeyed were later written by Mrs. Fairfax herself.

1. Judy Camp

Middle class. Nice country home. One younger sister, one younger brother. Both parents work. Judy has and takes care of many responsibilities at home. She is only allowed to date and to attend school activities on weekends. Must be in at a definite time. (She feels that her parents haven't given her the privileges that other girls have in this matter.) Parents very cooperative in school matters. Came out for Cheer Leader competition this year. Was defeated and cried for two days over it.

Commercial Course
Grades:—above average—A in English if she tried but often doesn't try for her best grades.
Behavior records:—Never in serious trouble.
Class offices:—Sec. of Booster Club this year.
Ambition:—Wants to be a secretary.

2. Doris Wheat

Middle-class. Father is an "independent contractor"—sometimes does very well financially—other times no work. Mr. W. is very dependable and honest in his work. Respected and well liked. Beautiful home—mortgaged since the older boy has gone to college. Neither mother or father has any more than H.S. education. Mother and father graduated from Asbury High School. (Mother tried to operate a grocery store last year but no one would trade there and it failed.) . . .

Commercial course

Grades:—Good English student—Never makes the honor roll however.

Class offices:—Pres. of Soph. class.—Pres. of F.H.A. (Home Ec. Club) in freshman year. Pres. of Future Teacher's Club this year.

Came out for Cheer Leader 3 years—never came near making it.

Ambitions:—Thought that she might like to be a teacher but is taking the commercial course.

Behavior record:—Not too bad. Drives to school when she lives only 3 blocks away. Isn't supposed to, but gets by with it.

3. Carol Jones

I have no information on the father—He was never around Asbury—mother works in a factory. Carol has an older sister, Nancy, who is a senior this year. The home is never supervised. It's one block from school and a number of the girls go down for lunch and their cigarette. Boys hang around from after school until mother comes in about 6:30. Carol has responsibilities at home. She has done good work in Band. There's one older brother— went to college and was sent home because of poor grades.

Course of study:—Home Ec.

Grades:—fair to poor.

Behavior record:—Poor—cutting classes—leaving school in cars without permission, etc.

Ambitions:—None.

4. Barbara Farris

Barbara is second youngest of nine children. All of them have gone to Asbury. Three of the girls have been forced to quit before graduation. One since I've been in the school, at the end of her Soph. year. She came back in Jr. Year and attempted to finish, but had her second child before the first was a year old.—The father is a self employed plumber. He makes good money, but the home doesn't have a bathroom or hot water. However, the children have always come out of the home clean and extremely well-dressed.—Parents disagree in all situations involving the children. If father says "No", mother allows them to deceive him and do what they want.—Split religion—mother Catholic, father no church affiliation but trying to have his children attend the Methodist Sunday schools. Some do and some don't. They must go far to attend the Catholic church and are not regular in attendance.

Barbara is a pretty, attractive girl—excellent athlete. Pres. of 8th grade class. Caused serious trouble on an F.H.A. trip to Indianapolis—put out of the club and then influenced six other girls to quit. She is popular with the boys. She dates the "better boys" (basketball kids).

> Commercial course:—Since she "got mad" and was thrown out of F.H.A. club, when she changed from Home Ec.
>
> Grades:—Above average.
>
> Ambitions:—None of the teachers I know have had her express ambitions. She did well on an aptitude test this year given by Employment Service.

5. Mary Frank

Background—middle class—stepfather truck driver—mother works some as a waitress. Mary has many responsibilities at home. At one time they were taking care of 3 welfare children—age 8, 10, 12—the mother was working and Mary cared for them and cooked both noon and evening meals (in summer). She has a brother of her own age 13 and a step-sister age 12—both in 7th grade now.

> Academic course
>
> Grades always A's & B's
>
> Ambition:—Mother would like her to go to college and she has thought she'd like to be a Phy. Ed. teacher but says—young people are too hard to handle. Works in Sunday school work.

6. Winnie Grant

Nice home—one older sister and four brothers—one in Grade 7. Winnie was the "pick of the family"—sensible, assumes responsibilities but not too popular. Very likeable and extremely truthful in little things that come up. Her younger brother is in trouble all the time, which embarrasses Winnie very much.

> Academic course

Grades:—B—but she has to work for everything she gets.

Ambitions:—Has never considered college—Maybe Beauty Operator training.

7. Dorothy Driscoll

The family with four Jr. High and Sr. High daughters have always lived in a trailer. Father used to be with a side show at circus. Mother very nice. Both parents have always worked.—The oldest daughter was forced to leave school in October.—Dorothy is the stable one of the three. A very attractive girl—popular. Usually likeable and trustworthy.

Commercial course and also Home Ec.:—Switched to commercial this year.

Grades:—Excellent

Ambition:—Stenographer.

8. Catherine Hart

Very poor home—children unsupervised in weiner [sic] roast and outdoor parties held there. Just anyone may "crash" the party so I've been told. She is allowed to date boys from other schools and was in attendance at a questionable dance hall—"road house" on several occasions—at one of which there was serious trouble with boys who came from Minton City. Catherine comes to school ungroomed, unclean, not like the majority of our girls. I have never called in the home and have never met either father or mother.

She has a younger brother repeating the 7th grade—has the highest I.Q. in H.S.—143—but caused so much trouble that his English teacher failed him because she wouldn't keep him in class enough of the time that he accomplish enough to go on.

Commercial course

Grades:—very poor

Behavior:—Bad

Ambitions:—None, that I know of.

9. Greta Moore

Excellent home. Well-educated parents. Mother worked in an office, but was away from home only while the two girls were in school. Didn't work when they were young. Father good executive job. Younger sister in Grade 5.

Greta likes to join all clubs—musically inclined—excellent artist—
quite emotional—quick temper but very reasonable and easily
talked to. Greta's mother has told me many times that Greta is
just like her and has much to overcome. She belongs to the
young group at the Country Club and youth organization of
Eastern Star in Minton City. (I never could figure Greta getting
in this group and trouble. Her mother called me the night it happened and Greta had gone home and told her immediately that
she had got involved in trouble at school. Her mother asked for
disciplinary measures that might help Greta to realize her mistake.) The younger daughter is very nice in school—not as emotional as Greta.
Academic course
Grades:—above average
Ambitions:—Art college.

10. Eve Hardwick

I don't know a thing about the parents or home. I've never even
seen from the outside where they live. There's been a number of
them in school. All very poor students and antagonistic to whatever the group wants to do. Eve is known in dramatic club just
to vote opposite to be different.
Home Ec. course
Grades:—very poor
Behavior:—bad
Ambitions:—none

11. Charlotte Lackey

Mother died when she was in 6th grade. Father a farmer. An older
sister was in the home one year after mother died. I've never
called in or seen the home. Carolyn is neat and clean but not
popular. She has a decided speech defect.
Home Ec. course
Grades:—fair to poor
Ambitions:—House wife

12. Sandra Coss

I've called in the home—very poor, fairly clean—good mother—
father with very little education came from Georgia 3 years ago.
Mother would like the best for her children but does not have
the necessary means. The younger brother in 6th grade.

Home Ec. course
Grades:—average
Ambitions—to get married
Behavior—nothing of consequence

After Mr. Monroe had returned from Atlantic City, he discussed the problem further with Mrs. Fairfax. Mrs. Wheat, Doris' mother, had written Mr. Monroe saying, "George, get that 'brat' back in Gym Class, we want her to graduate."

Mr. Monroe and Mrs. Fairfax decided that the following steps should be taken:

1. The girls' conduct grades for the term would be "F." (In each subject students were given letter conduct grades in addition to "course grades.")

2. Each girl was required to write a theme on the subject, "Right and Wrong Attitudes in High School Classes."

3. A girl would not be allowed to return to the gym class until the theme had been submitted and her parents had acknowledged notification by the school of the incident and penalties.

4. For each day that a girl was not in gym class, 3% would be deducted from the final grade. (Letter grades had "percentage equivalents." Thus her absences alone would cause a student with an "A" (90–100%) who missed eight classes before the theme was handed in and the parents had contacted the school, to receive a grade of "C" (76%) or lower. As a result most of the girls would have received a failing grade in gym.)

5. The girls to be ineligible for all hikes for the rest of the year.

6. Any infraction of rules in gym would be punished by expulsion for the remainder of the year.

The plan was carried out. However, several parents objected to the reduction of course grades to "F" as too drastic. Mrs. Wheat said she thought Doris was going to college and she didn't want an "F" on the girl's record. After Mrs. Fairfax had put the course grades on the students' cards, Mr. Monroe asked her to change them all to "C," leaving only the conduct grades at "F." The other girls in the class all received "A's" and "B's."

During the remainder of the year three hikes were taken; each time the twelve girls were placed in study hall for the period. There were no further incidents.

SELECTED READINGS

Anderson, Vivienne, and Daniel R. Davies, *Patterns of Educational Leadership*. Englewood Cliffs: Prentice-Hall, 1956.
Coyle, Grace L., *Group Work with American Youth*. New York: Harper and Brothers, 1948.
National Society for the Study of Education, *The Dynamics of Instructional Groups: Sociopsychological Aspects of Teaching and Learning*. Fifty-ninth Yearbook. Chicago: University of Chicago Press, 1960.
Seidman, Jerome M., ed., *The Adolescent: A Book of Readings*. New York: The Dryden Press, 1953.

CASE **10**

A Nice, Quiet Boy

By October, 1953, it was clear to
members of the Grove City High School staff that Joseph Manners, a
junior, was preparing to drop out of school. His attendance had become so irregular that he made only token appearances in class, and
he was far behind in his schoolwork. The usual school warnings and
offers of guidance had brought no positive response. The problem
now confronting school officials was whether to take special action to
try to keep him in school, on the grounds that his record justified it;
or to let him drop out of school as a matter of course, on the grounds
that any further action would, on the basis of his record, be unwar-
ranted and unavailing.

Joseph Manners was born in Grove City [1] in June, 1936, of native
white parents. His mother was described by social workers as an
unstable, immature, tense woman of limited intelligence. She had had
a miscarriage before Joseph was conceived, and reportedly had not
wanted children. His father—described by Mrs. Manners as an abu-
sive, threatening man who drank heavily—noted that she was such a
reluctant mother that she did not want to nurse Joseph or his younger
(by seven years) brother James. According to Mr. Manners, Joseph

---

[1] Grove City is described in case no. 7.

did not seem particularly unhappy as a child, although he occasionally appeared upset and nervous, and had nightmares. Mr. Manners recalled that Joseph used to bite his nails, and was jealous when James was born. He remembered also that Joseph played regularly with little girls: there was a shortage of boys his own age in the neighborhood.

The family religion could be characterized as casual Catholicism. The home atmosphere was strongly secular. Commenting on the home environment, Mr. Manners observed that it was a "poor" one for his young sons. He pointed out that he and his wife fought constantly. Since the family occupied only two rooms, the children were persistently exposed to parental bickering. Mr. Manners said that his wife frequently went out and left him with the children, and that the arrangement did not work out well. He said that Joseph did not like being left with him, that the boy seemed afraid of him. Mr. Manners remarked that Joseph was more attached to his mother, and expressed the belief that she turned Joseph against him. He said that they changed their residence about twice a year, and that he did not try seriously to find and settle down in a "real" home, since he did not expect the marriage to last.

The neighborhoods in which the Mannerses lived were relatively depressed socioeconomically. The addresses given were in a class V area, according to Davie's six-class residential scale.[2]

The instability of the parental marriage was reflected in a 1940 visit by Mr. Manners to the office of the city prosecuting attorney. On that occasion he voiced his suspicion that his wife was carrying on with other men, and said that he often caught her in lies. He said that he and his wife argued constantly, and that they wanted a separation. At the time he was employed in a sports goods and munitions factory and earned about twenty-five dollars a week.

According to Mrs. Manners, the unhappy home life was not all her fault. She indicated that her husband often became drunk, and beat her. She said that he was "a liar and a sneak," and that she hoped Joseph would not grow up to be like him. She suggested that Joseph's quietness could be traced to the times when her husband was drunk and Joseph, consequently, frightened. She noted that her husband was so menacing while intoxicated that she frequently had to call the police.

---

[2] For explanations of this and later references to social class characteristics, see case no. 7.

If Joseph had troubles at home, he also had them at school. In October, 1944, while Joseph was in the fourth grade, the principal, concerned over his irregular attendance and spotty academic performance, sent a school social worker to his home. The worker observed that home conditions were scarcely conducive to the production of scholars, and informed the mother that Joseph's schoolwork was so poor that he might not be promoted unless something were done. Joseph was home during the visit, and the social worker noted that he seemed unusually pale. Mrs. Manners said she had been unable to give Joseph much care since the birth of his brother, and that she was not satisfied with his physical condition. She indicated that poor health was holding him back in school.

Five days after the visit, Joseph was assigned to the school Health Room. His new teacher had a relatively small number of pupils, and he received more individual attention than before. He seemed happier.

His teacher suggested that a standard estimate of his mental ability would be helpful, and early in November he was given a Revised Stanford-Binet, Form L Test. The results were: chronological age, eight years, five months; mental age, six years, four months; intelligence quotient (IQ), 75. The findings were, however, qualified by the observation that Joseph was "extremely shy and withdrawing," and that the test may not have provided a true picture of his ability. This observation, to be supported by later intelligence ratings, was based partly on his less restricted performance on one section (Gray Oral Paragraph) of the test. It was recommended that he be reexamined in the future.

Joseph continued to be lax in his school attendance. In December the visiting teacher called on Mrs. Manners, who said that she could do nothing with him, that he just sat and moped. Later in the month another home call was made. Mrs. Manners reported that he did not eat or sleep well. She said that her husband complained that he could not afford the fees of private doctors. She mentioned plans to take Joseph to a clinic during the Christmas vacation period.

After the holidays, Joseph was absent from the second week in January to the first week in March. According to Mrs. Manners, he seemed to lack the desire to get ready for school, and she was kept so busy with little James that she was unable to help him. She appeared to resent the responsibility of caring for James. The doctor who had checked Joseph at the clinic reported to school officials that his physical condition was poor and that his school activities should be restricted on his return. The doctor told Mrs. Manners that she should see to it that Joseph got enough sleep and nourishing food.

During the month following his return Joseph was absent about once a week. On April 2, 1945, the school social worker revisited his home. Mrs. Manners said that he was so slow that some days she simply could not get him ready for school on time. The worker suggested that she might try getting him out of bed somewhat earlier, since he would probably not be promoted unless his attendance improved. Mrs. Manners said that she wondered if any of the children were molesting him. The worker promised to make inquiries.

The worker then talked to several children who lived in the area, and they contended that Joseph bothered them. The worker asked one of the boys, who occasionally associated with Joseph, to show greater friendliness toward him, and to stop by his home on the way to school. The boy said he would do this.

On April 10th the school social worker learned that Joseph had improved his attendance, was deriving some satisfaction from the companionship of other children on the way to and from classes, and seemed happier in the classroom. Nevertheless his work was described as still poor.

In June the principal reported that Joseph appeared to be happy in school, and that his teacher in the Health Room believed he was working as well as he could under the circumstances.

The circumstances, however, changed. The relations between his parents became more and more strained. Mrs. Manners refused to permit the school social worker to try to help, on the grounds that her husband was too ignorant and would resent the intervention. The following year Mr. and Mrs. Manners separated. Divorce proceedings were apparently initiated by Mrs. Manners but not completed. Although no legal arrangement was made for the custody of Joseph and his brother, the parents agreed verbally that Mrs. Manners would have custody. Joseph wanted to remain with his mother, but he and James were placed in an unlicensed foster home in a somewhat "better" neighborhood (with a Class IV rating). James soon returned to his mother, but Joseph stayed, now by preference, in the foster home. His foster parents, Mr. and Mrs. Carmen Rotanni, were reportedly elderly, "limited" people who received him with kindness and affection. Their two married daughters and grandchildren, who lived nearby, also took a friendly interest in him, and he got along well with a feeble-minded stepdaughter who lived with the Rotannis. The over-all atmosphere was characterized as warm and happy. His father paid a weekly sum to the Rotannis for his support.

Joseph transferred to the elementary school in the neighborhood of his foster parents. He seemed quite content with his new surroundings. In 1947, for example, inquiries from the Family Society brought the information that he appeared to be happy in his foster home, and that he was adjusting well in school and was not a classroom problem. His IQ rating was slowly improving: in March, 1948, he was retested on the Stanford-Binet, Form L, and obtained a score of CA 11–9; MA 9–6; IQ 81. Although he had repeated grades 4–5, he was regularly promoted after he entered grade 6 in 1948. In January, 1949, he took the Iowa Every Pupil Basic Skills Test. The results were: [3] Reading 5–8; Work Study Skills 5–2; Language Skills 5–6; Arithmetic Skills 5–0. In October, 1950, while in grade 8, he again took the Iowa test, obtaining these scores: Reading 6–7; Work Study Skills 6–5; Language Skills 5–8; Arithmetic Skills 6–3. Although his Iowa ratings were low, he appeared able to keep up with the classwork. He became very fond of his foster family, and consistently expressed the wish that he be allowed to remain with them.

His mother, however, began to intefere with the relationship between Joseph and the Rotannis. She displayed jealousy of his affection for them, criticized their handling of him, belittled them in conversations with other people, and threatened to take him back.

At intervals his physical condition was checked. An April, 1948 physical examination showed that, although he was otherwise normal, he was 13% underweight and, like his father, had a heart murmur (rheumatic). The major findings of a June, 1950 examination were posture fatigue, circles under his eyes, scarred tonsils and reddened throat, slow-moving nervous system, rheumatic heart with slight murmur at apex and rough murmur at base. The examination report also noted that he was under the care of the pediatric clinic for his heart condition. In October, 1950, he was examined at a cardiac clinic: the diagnosis was patent ductus arteriosis. The recommendations were (a) that he continue in school with no restrictions, and (b) that he

---

[3] Scores indicate the achievement grade level. Thus Joseph, while in the sixth grade, did as well on the Reading section of the test as the average fifth-year eighth-month pupil.

return to the clinic in six months. It was decided to operate within a year, and his name was placed on the surgical list. It is interesting that, according to the medical record, his mother had been told that he had a heart murmur at birth but had not contacted a doctor about it.

Meanwhile his family situation grew still more complicated. His mother was now living on a commonlaw basis with another man and that year had a baby by him. The man, Frank Zhulki, indicated his willingness to support Joseph, and Mrs. Manners persisted in her threats to take Joseph from the Rotannis. Mr. Zhulki, who worked as a building superintendent in a nearby school, had plans to acquire a farm, on which he might "train" Joseph. The prospect did not please Joseph, who told the Rotannis that if he ever had to leave them, he would run away and return to them. Mr. Manners, who was living with his own mother and sister, held that neither he nor his mother could look after Joseph, and that the boy ought to stay with the Rotannis. But his satisfaction with the existing arrangement was not shared by Mrs. Manners. She indicated that she suspected the Rotannis of turning Joseph against her, and that she was best qualified to care for him. She was described by the school social worker as a highly made-up woman whose appearance suggested loose living.

Joseph was admitted to Grove City Hospital in the middle of January, 1951. He was described by the medical social worker as a slight, pale, fair boy with large brown eyes, a wide mouth, and a small mannerism of moving tongue against lips. The cardiac (patent ductus arteriosis) operation was successful, and it was decided to permit him to return to school the following month with no restrictions except on competitive sports. Before his discharge from the hospital, the play nurse supervisor noted that he had changed his behavior pattern from marked withdrawal to "silliness" designed to elicit laughs. He had difficulty relating to boys his own age, and his preferred playmate in the ward was a girl six years old. He said he did not want to go home, and a nurse observed that he became quiet and seemed depressed after the date for discharge was set. He expressed anxiety that after his discharge he might be prevented from returning to the Rotannis. His mother and father visited him, without evident positive effect. His mother nagged him, and seemed to observers to be more concerned with her own health than his welfare: she complained at length to members of the hospital staff about her minor ailments. When notified of his pending discharge, she showed little interest in making the arrangements. She criticized the Rotannis and spoke of moving him elsewhere. When advised by the medical social worker that moving probably was upsetting for him, and that the doctors thought he should remain with the Rotannis, she said vaguely that if it ever appeared necessary she would move him, perhaps to a place where there were no children. She seemed more interested in complaining than in taking action. Near the time of discharge, Mr. Zhulki came to the hospital for Joseph, who refused to go with him. The following day Mrs. Rotanni came with a signed authorization from Mrs. Manners, who did not feel like coming to the hospital. Joseph returned with Mrs. Rotanni to his foster home.

He went back to school in February. The school guidance counselor observed that his health seemed vastly improved. He continued to keep up his schoolwork, and obtained average marks. He was pictured by his teachers as a shy, quiet, withdrawn boy who rarely volunteered an answer but was likely, when called on, to have the correct one. If attention was directed to him in class, he seemed disturbed and blushed readily. He was depicted as generally serious, but inclined to show great amusement over humorous class remarks or incidents. He had a reputation for being self-conscious and timid and did not associate with his classmates. He was usually the first to arrive in the classroom, and moved from class to class alone. According to his foster mother and one of her daughters, he was called "sissy" and teased by the other boys. Mrs. Rotanni had a grandson about his age, who accompanied him to school and sometimes fought on his behalf.

Mrs. Rotanni and her daughter showed much concern about his "quietness." They observed that, although he was "good" and "obedient," he seemed afraid to be otherwise. He appeared to be greatly worried that his mother and Mr. Zhulki would take him away. When his mother telephoned, he sometimes cried and refused to talk to her, or answered in monosyllables. He suffered from nightmares. He rarely began a conversation with the adults in his foster family. He often flushed if they spoke to him suddenly, and about once a day appeared so withdrawn that he did not seem to hear when they addressed him. He did, however, enjoy playing with the younger grandchildren.

He visited his mother about once a week. She persistently berated him, even in the presence of others. She called him "dumb," and criticized him for not coming more often. When he stayed away for awhile, she complained to social service workers and even to the principal of his school. Yet when he did come she did not make him welcome. He also made a weekly visit to his father. Mr. Manners described him as very "close-mouthed" during these visits. Mr. Manners' mother tended to become angry at Joseph because he would not answer questions. Mr. Manners tried to assure Joseph that he did not have to say anything if he did not want to, and that he should not worry about the threats of Mrs. Manners to remove him from his foster home. Nevertheless Mr. Manners could not himself refrain from quizzing Joseph and reminding him of the potential agent of removal by talking about Mrs. Manners. Despite his reputation as a heavy drinker, Mr. Manners worked regularly in the same factory and kept up his weekly contributions to the Rotannis. Social workers noted that, however ineffectual he was as a father, he seemed well-intentioned and sincerely interested in Joseph's welfare.

In June, 1951, shortly before his fifteenth birthday, Joseph graduated from elementary school. At that time a conference on his problems and welfare was held at Grove City Hospital. Participants were the director of social work at the hospital, the medical social worker, the school social worker, a pediatric clinician, and a guidance clinic's psychiatrist and social worker. The psychiatrist observed that an area of particular conflict for Joseph appeared to be his relationship with his mother, and that this conflict was especially significant in view of his fear that she would take him from his foster home. The psychiatrist felt, however, that there was no particular evidence that Joseph was schizophrenic; he pointed out that there were many withdrawn children who were not and never would be schizophrenic. He emphasized that before anything could be done for Joseph, his environment had to be stabilized. The school social worker noted that Joseph had been withdrawn ever since she had first known him in 1944. She expressed the belief that his mother seriously rejected him, and remarked that even when he was a small boy his mother seemed to expect a lot of him and complained constantly in his presence. According to the pediatric clinician, there was no justification for associating his past health difficulties with his heart, since he had a congenital cardiac lesion with no heart enlargement. The clinician noted that the surgery had been essentially prophylactic and that Joseph had made a good recovery. His intelligence was now rated as low average and potentially higher.

In short, it appeared that his physical and mental equipment was generally adequate, and that the key problem was the insecurity of his family situation. Possible ways of stabilizing it were considered, and the reluctance of the principals to take constructive action was discussed. His mother could not be depended on either to leave him where he was or to take him back and give him the affection he needed. Mr. Manners was not a strong or vigorous father figure to Joseph, and since he had agreed that his wife would have custody, probably would be unwilling to act. Mr. and Mrs. Rotanni, while fond of Joseph, were not prepared to secure a foster home license. Nevertheless the conferees agreed that he should stay with the Rotannis, that the type of stability desired was some assurance that he could do so, and that if Mrs. Manners should move to take him away they would request the State Humane Society to intervene. They also decided to send notice of the existing situation to the guidance counselor at the junior high school which Joseph was scheduled to attend in the fall.

During the summer the medical social worker visited the Rotanni home and discovered that the relationship between Joseph and his mother seemed to be getting worse, although no attempt had yet been made to remove him. Mrs. Rotanni said that Joseph stayed close to the foster home and cried when she encouraged him, unsuccessfully, to go to the beach with the other children.

Joseph entered junior high school and the ninth grade in September, 1951. The following month the school social worker contacted the school guidance counselor, who reported that she had informed his teachers of the need for establishing a friendly relationship with him and for trying as well as they could to make schoolwork a satisfying experience for him. The teachers, for their part, showed a willingness to cooperate and to endeavor to be friendly and helpful. When the school social worker talked with Joseph, he said that he was getting along in his classes and liked his teachers. He was still largely a recluse among his schoolmates, however. He reaffirmed his desire to remain in his foster home and expressed the fear that the reason his mother wanted him back was his potential usefulness as a baby-sitter for his half-brother.

During the school year 1951–2 he seemed to be making some progress. He was taking a business course and said he might later enroll in a trade school to learn printing. Though generally a poor student, he showed promise in art, music, and woodwork. Despite his recluse role, he managed to attend a CYO dance. He did not, however, engage in any other activities of this type. He appeared to be somewhat less hesitant to talk about his problems. For example, on his own initiative he contacted the school nurse, told her he did not feel too well, and in the discussion that followed apprised her of his concern over his family situation. He also began to talk more freely with the school guidance counselor about his feelings.

While the possiblity of leaving the Rotannis still disturbed him, he seemed to be worrying increasingly about money. He wanted money of his own, to buy such items as clothing. Since his father contributed only eleven dollars a week to the Rotannis, he felt that in his present situation he could not expect to secure what he believed he needed. Clothing was a favorite theme, and he expressed a great disappointment that he lacked an Easter outfit. The school social worker and guidance counselor observed that he did not look shabby or neglected.

At the suggestion of the school social worker and guidance counselor, he took a psychological examination at a community guidance clinic early in May, 1952.

According to the final summary offered by the psychologist the tests showed that Joseph was a shy, retiring boy who was currently operating at an average intelligence level (IQ 95 on the Wechsler-Bellevue Intelligence Scale). His intellectual potential, however, appeared much higher, but he was hampered by a low motivation level and a lack of facility in applying past learning, especially in a social context, to his present situation. Although he tended to deal with most problems by active withdrawal, he was pictured as potentially able to behave in a less constricted manner. Despite a proclivity toward impulsive and unconsidered actions, notably in situations calling for the expression of his personal feelings, his present behavior was appraised as probably adequate. His social difficulties apparently centered in his perception of a hostile world, featuring rejection by mother figures.

In June, 1952, Joseph completed grade 9, with passing if undistinguished marks. The school guidance counselor reported that she believed Joseph had made considerable progress during the year. He seemed friendlier and was occasionally seen with another boy. He would take a general course at Grove City High in the fall.

In the summer of 1952 Joseph took a job in a restaurant to earn some spending money before entering Grove City High. His employer was a friend of his foster mother. After he had worked a few days, his employer complained to Mrs. Rotanni that he was spreading stories about the restaurant, and that her business would suffer if she employed him any longer. Mrs. Rotanni was disappointed, and had an argument with Joseph. As an additional point of dissension, she charged him with failure to help with the household chores. A serious rift developed, and finally she asked him to leave.

First he went to the home of his father, who told him he could not stay there but would have to return to his mother. He did so.

In the fall Joseph went to Grove City High School. By November 18th he had been absent about thirty times and tardy six, and his work was headed for failure. A recurrence of difficulties with his health was reported. Sometimes these difficulties were given as reasons for the absences: among the complaints were headache, cold, toothache, virus, sinus, sore throat, pain in side. Sometimes no reasons for absences were given.

The school guidance counselor tried repeatedly to contact Mrs. Manners, by telephone and letter. Mrs. Manners responded only once, she made an appointment to come to school for a conference but failed to keep it. Meanwhile Joseph told the guidance counselor that Mr. Zhulki and he could not get along, and that Mr. Zhulki wanted him to leave. He complied, and from November to March lived with the Rotannis. Mrs. Rotanni received him willingly at first, but they could not close the old rift. She could no longer accept his secretiveness and unresponsiveness, and he could no longer depend on her for affection and forbearance. Again she asked him to leave; he returned to his mother. His mother took him back reluctantly: she now knew that Mrs. Rotanni did not want him and Mr. Manners could not keep him, and she did not profess as before a desire to have him. Joseph himself was not happy about returning, but he now had no other home.

While Joseph was going from family to family, he was going from job to job. He worked awhile in a bowling alley, between six and eleven P.M. When advised by school officials to take an afternoon instead of night job, he tried to obtain a position in a local department store. He was not hired; the management felt he would not "fit in" successfully among the store employees. He then found a job in a laundromat. For a time he worked afternoons in the laundromat and nights in the bowling alley. Then he left these jobs for a succession of other minor positions. He banked some of his wages, but when his pocket funds were exhausted on clothes and petty spending sprees, he often borrowed, from his real and foster mother and associates however casual, small sums which he neglected to repay.

Joseph moved not only from family to family and job to job, but also from classmate to classmate, seeking a friend. He could not communicate adequately, however, and was rebuffed. He apparently tried to conceal his shyness in silly behavior, which did not appeal to his contemporaries. Girls complained that his attentions were unwelcome.

In his classes he was a D–F borderline student, although he salvaged a "B" in world history. His intelligence rating, which had climbed consistently before his break with the Rotannis, dropped sharply. On the Primary Mental Abilities Test, taken in January, 1953, his IQ was 71. His relations with his teachers did not appear to be outstanding, in either a positive or negative sense. He was not a discipline problem, he was treated considerately and permitted to make up missed examinations, but his teachers found him somewhat difficult to reach, particularly since he was absent so frequently.

His record indicated that he was capable of better work, and had in fact made definite gains in school performance and attendance, IQ ratings, health and even sociability, before his falling out with the Rotannis. Because of this, school officials were reluctant to have him drop out of school. On the other hand, they were confronted by a real question concerning the extent to which the school should or could involve itself in efforts to stabilize Joseph's home environment, however important such stability was to his progress.

On October 7, 1953, the school social worker and school guidance counselor briefly discussed the situation with Joseph. They pointed out that the school was still open to him and that all resources were available to help him, but did not exert pressure on him to remain. Basically the message was that he was welcome to stay in school if he wished to do so. No commitment was asked, and none was given.

Two weeks later Joseph withdrew from school.

Subsequently his job difficulties became more serious than ever. His employers regularly discharged him a week or two after hiring him. The reasons consistently given were that he indulged in petty pilfering, requested small loans from customers, and made silly remarks to female workers.

At home his troubles continued. By the end of 1953 relations with his mother and Mr. Zhulki had become so strained that he made a familiar but no longer effective move. He returned for the last time to the Rotannis . . . and for the last time was sent back.

SELECTED READINGS

Bloch, Herbert A., *Disorganization: Personal and Social*. New York: Alfred A. Knopf, 1952.

Havighurst, Robert J., and Bernice L. Neugarten, *Society and Education*. Boston: Allyn and Bacon, 1957.

Stanley, William O., et al., eds., *Social Foundations of Education*. New York: The Dryden Press, 1956. Esp. chs. 22–25, 37–38.

Wood, Margaret Mary, *Paths of Loneliness*. New York: Columbia University Press, 1953.

Off
the
Cuff

As the home-room period began in Old City High School one morning in May, 1954, teachers discovered that few pupils were listening to the daily announcements. Instead, they were reading and chuckling over a thirty-one page, mimeographed booklet, entitled "Off the Cuff." When teachers asked about the source of the publication, pupils reported they had been purchased that morning for twenty-five cents from two boys stationed across from the school. Glancing through the publication, among innocuous-sounding titles teachers found some which merited examination.

The first item in the publication, labeled as "Editorial Page," was entitled "Let's Free Sacco and Vanzetti, or What This World Needs Is a Return to Absolute Monarchy." "News Items of Interest" contained a report of a purported interview with "Senator Joseph McLarky." On the second page, listed among such special editors as Lavrenti Beria, Mickey Spillane, Farouk II, Joseph DiMaggio, Joseph Anastasia, Bishop Fulton J. Sheen, Father Divine, Whittaker Chambers, Alger Hiss, and others, were the names of the two student editors: David Stevens and Jerry Raleigh.

On the third page in the "Letters to the Editors Dept." teachers found one which caused them concern. It read thus:

Sirs:

I have read an advance copy of your magazine and I think that the aspersions you have cast on your journalism department are mean and unfair. How dare you suggest I swear in class. Why dammit, you lying sons-of-bitches, I have never used a profane word in public in my life, and I demand that you print an immediate retraction.

(signed)
Journalism teacher who
prefers to remain anonymous

Teachers who had taken time to examine the publication began sending copies to the principal of the school. In the meantime, one boy had taken his copy to the senior boys' counselor, claiming he had been embarrassed by the publication. The counselor had sent for David Stevens and Jerry Raleigh. When asked whether they were responsible for the publication, the boys quickly admitted they were. The counselor took a serious view of the publication and informed the boys they were undoubtedly facing serious charges because of the improper language used and because of certain biased criticisms of departments of the school, particularly the journalism, R. O. T. C., and social studies departments. Then the boys were sent on to their classes.

The Principal did not summon the boys to his office until shortly before lunch. He had conferred with their counselor and had read the complete publication. By the time the boys entered his office, he was, they reported later to their parents, "in a rage bordering on the apoplectic." He began his interview by reading passages from the publication, at times somewhat incoherently because of real or simulated anger. He read first the "Letter to the Editor" which had earlier caught the attention of the home-room teachers. Then he read from the article, "Colonel Had's Report," which had the following line in it:

I was greeted by a wild-eyed crone, who greeted me with a 'god-damn' and heaved an inkwell at my head . . . This seemed to call for a new outburst by the woman in charge, who had begun to throw books at me with the precision of a howitzer. This attack was accompanied by a barrage of profanity (That woman's vocabulary would make a camel driver envious) and I hid behind a desk for protection.

The Principal informed the boys that they were in serious trouble. They ventured the statement that they had anticipated trouble. The Principal told them that he would urge the journalism teacher to file a suit for libel. The boys replied that the "Letters to the Editor" did not misrepresent the journalism teacher's action. They doubted she would be able to establish a case, since other journalism pupils would testify that on several occasions Mrs. Gary did use profanity to pupils and had thrown books at them.

The Principal dropped that tactic and asked the boys whether copies of the publication had been sold in school. The boys said that all copies had been sold off school property. Then he wanted to know whether any other students, faculty members, or parents had helped with the publication. The boys replied that the publication was their own idea and work, although they had asked and been given permission by members of their creative-writing class to reproduce some of the stories, essays, and poems which helped to fill the publication.

The Principal then told the boys that, although they were seniors and due to graduate at the end of two weeks, he could see no reason now why they should be graduated with their class. He hinted that there might be no diploma for them—that he might decide to expel them. He shook his head and lamented that boys of their ability should allow themselves to become involved in so questionable a situation when graduation was in sight. Cautioning them that they were not to sell any more copies, he allowed them to return to their classes temporarily.

In the meantime he sent word to teachers to pick up and send to his office any copies of "Off the Cuff" which they saw in their classes.

The Principal then called the parents of David Stevens to tell them of the publication. Although he read passages from the booklet to the mother, she did not seem especially disturbed; she did apologize for her son's lack of judgment and taste. The father, when reached, was less indulgent. He assured the Principal that he took a less tolerant view of his son's publication than did the mother, and he promised to stop further sale of it and to discipline the young man. When the Principal reached the grandmother of Jerry Raleigh, with whom Jerry made his home, the grandmother could not understand what the Principal was discussing. Knowing the boy took a great interest in science-fiction, she presumed he had written such a story and said

the Principal had no right to be so concerned about it. She terminated the incoherent conversation by saying, "Well, after all, they
sell them in magazines at all newsstands. I don't think it is anything
to get upset about."

During the afternoon of the same day the Principal called a meeting in his office of those in charge of the departments which had been
attacked in "Off the Cuff," the boys' counselor, and the head of the
English department, who taught the creative-writing class from
which many of the articles had been obtained. All were present with
the exception of Mrs. Gary, the journalism teacher, who thought it
"unwise to leave my class unattended."

The Principal opened the meeting by saying he wanted advice as to
how to discipline the boys. He also said he wanted the others involved
to express the attitudes they took toward the publication and the
boys responsible for it. Before giving the others an opportunity to
speak, he pointed out that many of the articles were good pieces of
writing done by other seniors who did not know they were to be included in a publication with questionable articles. He went on to
imply that the creative-writing teacher could not be altogether innocent of the plan to publish the questionable articles with the bonafide
ones. The teacher of creative writing had this to say:

> I infer that you think I am responsible for this unsponsored publi-
> cation. It is true that the boys may have had their original idea from
> a remark I made two or three weeks ago. Then I said that since so
> much good writing had been done in the class it was too bad we
> didn't have time to select the best pieces and mimeograph a collec-
> tion to be sold to other students. Several in the class, including David
> Stevens and Jerry Raleigh, were enthusiastic about the idea and
> wanted to carry it out. I told them that it was too late in the year
> to do it. I mentioned that all the articles would have to be read by
> all members of the class and a vote taken of those to be included. I
> also mentioned that laying out the publication, cutting and proof-
> reading stencils, and finally organizing the sale of the booklet would
> take more time than we had left in the year. I also said that I would
> be too greatly involved in my department duties attendant to the
> completion of the school year to help with such an undertaking.
> Two days later David and Jerry came to ask me if I would permit
> them to carry out the projects themselves. I told them I could not per-
> mit them to do the job without my supervision, and that I did not have

time to supervise it. They suggested that they might go ahead with the project without permission. I cautioned them that if they did they could not represent the booklet as either a school or a class project. I allowed them to solicit materials from other pupils in the class, believing that they would soon discover that the work to be done in so short a time would be impossible and that they would then abandon the project. I was as surprised as everyone else this morning when "Off the Cuff" appeared.

The creative-writing teacher then identified the following selections as having been written for his creative-writing class: "The Man Who Lost Saturday," a stream-of-consciousness type of revelation of a man's rather sordid life and death, written by Jerry Raleigh; "Momentary Idol," a short story of a girl who changed her mind about leaving school to get married; "Of Real Estate and Terror," a short story of an elementary-school teacher who accepted a ride downtown with a man she thought was the father of one of her pupils; "The Sidewalk," a short, surprise-ending story told from the viewpoint of an ant; "Night Walk," an innocent lyric poem; "Sir Walter Raleigh instead of a Treatment," an amusing light essay whimsically treating Sir Walter Raleigh and contemporary tobacco advertising; and "No More Nickels," a serious, mature short story written by David Stevens.

The Principal said that these selections were inoffensive, perhaps a credit to the class, but that the other articles were another matter. He said he had already talked to Mrs. Gary about the castigations against her and her department since she could not leave her class to attend the meeting. He explained that she was not of a vindictive nature. She had ventured the opinion that the boys had a certain facility in writing but had always shown poor judgment and bad taste in their articles. It had been for these reasons that she had not continued them on the newspaper staff after the first semester. The Principal reported that Mrs. Gary was not worried about how the publication might reflect upon her and hoped that it would not reflect badly upon the school. She had no desire to have the boys punished.

Then the Principal asked the sergeant in charge of R.O.T.C. at Old City High School how he felt about the attacks in "Colonel Had's Report." He said that he did not think the boys were malicious. He thought the article had been written in a spirit of fun.

He laughed when the Principal read the following excerpts from the articles:

> Arriving at the ROTC room, I was informed by one of the fellows (a company sergeant I discovered) that the instructors were out. There was something in his tone which suggested to me that it would be indiscreet to [ask] any more questions. Here, I thought, was an excellent opportunity to ask the students themselves what their opinions of ROTC were. The questioning ran something like this:
>
> Myself: What kind of system of promotions is used?
> Him: The merit system.
> Myself: Explain, please.
> Him: (a guttural, questioning noise.)
> Myself: What do you mean by merit system?
> Him: Well, if you make the rifle team you merit a promotion, and if you make the crack squad you merit a promotion
>   . . .
>
> Seeing that I could get no more information out of him, I turned to another non-com, who was staring dejectedly at a typewriter.
>
> Myself: Tell me, my good man, how do you like ROTC?
> Him: I like ROTC fine. Say, mister, I'm having a hard time finding the w on this typewriter. Could you help me?
>
> I pressed the necessary key, and he gave me a look of sheep dog devotion.
>
> Him: Gosh, thanks.
> Myself: Tell me, how did you become a non-com?
> Him: I was on crack squad.
>
> The crack squad, it seems, is a group who do juggling tricks with rifles. They can't be very talented, for they only juggle one rifle at a time.
>
> Just at that moment a student officer swaggered in, his chest be-weighted with more medals than a general of the armies usually possesses. "He's on the rifle team," my conversant explained. The fellow halted, gave me an amused glance, and I was informed he had given me two checks for improper uniform.
>
> Still standing, no one had yet offered me a chair, I walked over to another non-com, and gathering my courage, asked him if he knew where the instructors were. "Over at the Legion club," he replied. [The American Legion Club is across the street from Old City High. Because smoking is not permitted on school property, the instructors go to the Club to smoke during free periods.] When I asked what

they were doing over there, he answered that they were "having an orange ade." There was a snicker on his face which I didn't understand.

Following this selection in "Off the Cuff" appeared the following letter:

Gentlemen:
Keep slugging fellows. Its sure good to know that someone else has it in for the Army. After present difficulties clear up in Washington, I plan to investigate the ROTC, and you can bet Old City will be one of the spots where my committee will hold sessions. As plans run now, the hearings will be held in the bar of the Athletic Club. In case any of you need Summer jobs, there has been a recent opening on my staff, and I would be glad to [word omitted] any or all of you. Enclose find one gross of McLarkey for President buttons.
                                    Yours subversively,
                                    Senator Joe McLarkey

The sergeant proffered the information that Jerry Raleigh had been in the R.O.T.C. regiment since the ninth grade, that he had been a private first class, then a sergeant, and finally in his senior year a second lieutenant. He also stated that David Stevens had been a member of the band company during his freshman year but had not re-enrolled after the first year. He reported that neither boy had been a trouble-maker. Although Raleigh had not shown very much enthusiasm in the regiment, the sergeant said he had dispatched his duties as an officer in an acceptable fashion.

The sergeant said that he did not think the article was to be taken seriously nor that it would embarrass the corps, the school, or himself and fellow officers personally.

When the Principal asked the head of the social studies department to comment, she stated firmly that she thought the boys should be severely penalized. She mentioned that the head football coach shared her view and had gone so far as to suggest that the boys be arrested for their offense. She did not think there was a basis for having them arrested, but she did want to see them chastised, although she did not venture an opinion of the method to be used. She called attention first to a letter in the "Letters to the Editors Dept."

Sirs:

I just want you to know that I like your magazine so much that I have given up reading my favorites, TRUE CONFESSIONS and KRIME KOMICS. As a matter of fact, I have stopped watching my favorite TV program, "Life isn't worth living," by Rabbi Fulton J. Sheen(y). Please send me a five year subscription and good luck.

(signed)
Leon Trotsky
Shadyside rest for the mentally
ill. Ratoons, North Africa

Disregarding the context in which the name was used, the head of the social studies department dwelt on the use of the name "Fulton J. Sheen(y)." She said its coinage and use were more than an exhibition of poor taste; they were an attack upon two minority groups. Then she stated that she found the following article equally distasteful:

Our Social Studies Dept. and Why We Love It . . .
(Because certain radicals about school have been so wild as to suggest that certain aspects of our social studies dept. are as outmoded as the iron maiden, we have here undertaken to attempt to show that such heresy is simply untrue. Since outlines, these wonderful inventions first introduced in the middle ages, are most heavily fired upon, we are here reprinting a social studies outline so that all may recognize its obvious merit . . . Hold on kiddies.)
Section 8¼—Political and cultural aspects of the Lower Anglo-Saxon Sudan . . .

I. Geography—Country is mostly under water all the peasants being good swimmers. Chief exports are:
1. Wombat droppings
2. Square bottle caps
3. Adulterated Chylorophyll
A: Natives haul produce to markets on square-wheeled carts.
B: Most popular religion . . . Nepotism
C: Largest city still undiscovered: . . .
II. Rise and fall of Dictator
A: In 1459, Ahmed Al Baldi, a fugitive from the village of JUstice, shot and killed the king and his advisers and since there were no other inhabitants except for a Norwegian nepotist, he automatically became dictator. In 1460 he died suddenly of Cholera, and thus fell from power.

III. Reasons for studying—Wentworth Clarke [a popular and bald-
ing teacher of history at Old City High] is a direct descendant
of Ahmed Al Baldi . . .

Source: Oxman—*Nepotism: A Faith for our time.*
Unpius XII—The Index of Nepotism
Clarke—Ahmed Al Baldi: Patriot, Gentleman, Scholar
Wormsley—The rise of the lower Anglo-Saxon Sudan Em-
pire from Elmer the Elongated to Oman the Inebriate, with
Autobiography of Peter the Impotent.

It should be obvious to everyone, that making out and handing in
outlines is of tremendous value to everyone. Far, far better to copy
from dusty volumes than to read and understand. Now let's have
no more silly criticisms, huh?

The Principal listened to the head of the social studies department
who said the authors of such an obscene and unfair attack upon an
important teaching device should be made "examples of" to the rest
of the school. He did not comment. He then concluded the meeting
by saying that he would consider the comments made by the several
persons present, confer with the parents and grandparent again, and
then decide upon the nature of the punishment to be administered.

Before school was dismissed that day, the Principal summoned the
two boys to his office again. On this occasion he appeared less angry
and more objective. First, he asked them where they had secured the
materials and facilities with which to produce the booklet. David
Stevens said they had used materials and equipment in his father's
office. Had his father known the nature of what was being mimeographed? David had told his father only that they were going to reproduce the best writing done in their creative-writing class. His
father had then given them permission to use materials and equipment. They had worked at the office alone the preceding Saturday
afternoon and all of Sunday. They had done all the work themselves.
David admitted that his father was displeased when he found how
many stencils and how much paper had been used and said that he
would have to reimburse his company for them. When he had given
the boys permission, he had had no idea they were planning to have
so many pages or more than just enough copies for the members of
their class.

When the Principal asked the boys how many copies they had sold that day, they told him approximately three hundred. He asked them how many copies they still held. They admitted to a dozen or so, which they brought from their lockers at his request. He made them promise that they would destroy the stencils and any other copies they might still have.

Although David Stevens had been selected the previous week on the basis of competitive try-outs to deliver the senior commencement address, the Principal did not comment on the fact. Instead, he told the boys that for the time being he would allow them to continue attending their classes. He assured them the case was not closed, that he was going to give further thought to it, and that he would confer with the parents again. He warned them that ultimately they would be punished, but he did not say in what manner. Then he dismissed them from his office.

The public high school in which this incident occurred was on the western edge of the city's business district. The building contained sixty-three home rooms and ten rooms devoted to libraries, study halls, shop, music, art, military drill, and visual-education activities and had facilities to accommodate approximately 2500 pupils. It had an auditorium seating 1500, a combined girls and boys' gymnasium, and a cafeteria which served the enrollment of 2150 pupils in three twenty-five minute shifts.

The pupils of Old City High were drawn from all socio-economic levels of the city and from widely diversified neighborhoods: from the American-Italian section to the southeast, the Negro district to the near north, the small-apartment section surrounding the business section and occupied by transients, the middle-class areas lying mainly to the near west, and the wealthy suburbs lying farther west and south. The religious composition of the community was approximately 46% Roman Catholic, 46% Protestant, 6% Jewish, and 2% classified as "Other." Although Old City was only one hundred years old, it was a highly diversified, cosmopolitan, and well-established city.

Old City High School had a high academic rating; between 75% and 80% of its graduates continued their education in college. It had been named by various national organizations as one of the twenty-five to one hundred best high schools in the country. Its curriculum was heavily traditional, providing four-year courses in English, history, mathematics, science, Latin, and modern languages; yet it also offered general courses for terminal students. Its college-bound graduates qualified for admission to all the Ivy League colleges for men and their counterparts for women, as well as other private colleges, universities, and the great technical schools. Approximately one-fourth to one-third of its graduates qualified for scholarships.

                                *   *   *   *   *

David Stevens was born on December 14, 1936, the second in a family of three. He had a sister two years older and a brother eight years younger than he.

David had light brown hair, blue eyes, a fair complexion, and was of stocky build. He was five feet, eight inches tall. Although he had an intelligent appearance, his face did not reflect the mobility of expression usually associated with a high intellect.

David's parents were native born, originating in the state to the east of Old City. His father was in personnel work with a local utilities company; and his mother, a housekeeper, had no outside employment. The father was of Scotch-Irish descent; the mother, Pennsylvania Dutch. They were members of a local Presbyterian church. Both were graduates of the state university of their birth-place, and both earned their expenses while in college. Both parents were wide, if not discriminating, readers.

The family seemed to be in good circumstances financially. They resided in a neighborhood which, twenty years earlier, had been occupied by the wealthy. It was still a substantial neighborhood, inhabited by upper middle-class families. The Presbyterian church attended by the family and only a few blocks from their home was still the fashionable church of the city. One of the best elementary schools, the one which David attended, was also nearby. Not far away were two large municipal parks with recreational facilities. Also within a mile was a shopping district where most necessities could be obtained. In addition an expensive gift shop, a custom furniture store, three first class restaurants, two decorators' studios, music and art studios, and a motion picture house that showed foreign and art films were found in the center. There were two commercial swimming pools within two miles. The municipal university was nearby, and its library was accessible to the family.

David traveled by bus to Old City High School three miles away.

During his elementary-school years David Stevens made two attempts to align himself with youth groups, but he stayed with neither long. As a member of the Boy Scouts, his scoutmaster recalled, David seemed to enjoy the camp-outs, but he was not much of a mixer. Whenever he was expected to perform with a large group, he stood apart, and he often became unruly. He seemed to get along well with one or two boys in the troop. When asked, after a considerable absence from troop meetings, why he did not attend, he said he did not believe that scouts are "loyal, trustworthy, kind, obedient, clean in mind and body, etc." For a short period he was a member of the local Y.M.C.A. and participated in the swimming and sports programs. He dropped that activity because, as he said at the time, "the boys disgust me."

David was born with a web of flesh between the thumb and index finger of his right hand. An operation at birth left the thumb shortened and the index finger crooked. During the time his hand was immobilized, David developed a left-handedness which persisted. As a child he seemed to have no ability as an athlete, the deficient right hand keeping him from becoming skilled in games involving throwing or catching a ball.

David's elementary-school teachers remembered him as a small boy who always tried to avoid the sports program of the school. Among the other boys he was not popular mainly because he was unable to participate creditably. From the fifth through seventh grades David appeared to be the lowest on the social scale of his peers, since his inability in sports, the criterion of popularity for his group, was markedly evident.

During his first four or five years of elementary school, David's teachers recalled he was exceedingly quiet but a superior pupil scholastically. He learned to read early, and reading became his main interest. The subjects which require better-than-average ability to read were the ones in which David excelled. In fact, during his fourth- and fifth-grade years he was nearly always at the top of his class. He liked to "doodle" and draw cartoons. He also showed some talent as an actor. When he was allowed to direct his classmates in a school program, he participated and did very well. He was uncooperative, however, when he was denied the privilege of taking charge.

In the sixth grade, David encountered a teacher whom he did not like, and his academic standing fell. He went from top pupil in his class down to average and showed less and less interest in classwork and other activities. During an interview with his high-school counselor, David said he began to hate discipline, regimentation, and the demand to conform which for him characterized the upper elementary grades. He said that he had hoped to escape these restrictive matters when he reached high school but was greatly discouraged when he found them evident there too. Both his upper-elementary-grade teachers and his high-school teachers mentioned in evaluation of David that he was not working up to his capacity.

At the age of eleven David had some work experience as a newspaper carrier. He kept this job until he was fourteen, when he went to work after school and during vacations in a grocery store, carrying customers' purchases to their automobiles. The paper-route work brought David into contact with boys from poorer environments. He told his counselor that it was with these boys that he first tried smoking, did some petty stealing, and learned about salacious literature. Caught stealing in a neighborhood store, David said that the manager gave him a severe lecture and warning but released him without informing his parents or calling the police. His fright on this occasion deterred him from further exploits involving theft. In conjunction with his paper route, which lay along a railroad, David learned to "hop" freight trains simply to save himself a few blocks of walking. He said he never thought of running away from home, even though he learned to hate school during his seventh- and eighth-grade years.

David was regular in his attendance at Sunday School until his senior year in high school, when he attended only when his parents compelled him to. When he was younger, David had shown an unusual interest in and devotion toward religion, and his family thought that he might become a minister. During his last years of elementary school he began to show less enthusiasm for religious matters and often was downright apathetic or unruly in Sunday School. His church teachers of these years reported him as being a trouble-maker and often insolent toward them.

In December of his senior year in high school David passed his driver's test and was granted a license to drive. Shortly thereafter, while driving the family automobile home from school one night, he was involved in what first appeared to be a minor accident. A young university student, jaywalking, emerged suddenly from between two parked automobiles in mid-block. He was struck by David's car, which was traveling at a slow rate of speed, and which David had almost stopped when it nudged the student. The young man fell, struck his head on the pavement, but did not lose consciousness. After being examined by a doctor, he was reported uninjured and sent home. David was required to go to the police station while the outcome of the accident was in question. There his father was summoned; and, after routine matters were concluded, David was allowed to go home. He had been exonerated of blame. However, about thirty days later, the victim developed severe headaches and within a few days died. A *post mortem* revealed that the bump he had suffered in the accident was the cause of death.

About this incident David told his counselor the following story:

> When I was told that Jack had been taken to the hospital because of his headaches, I began to pray to God not to let any further harm come to him. It had been a shock to me, that accident. I would see him lying on the pavement again and again, the crowd gathering and looking at me as if I were a criminal. Then the ambulance would arrive, and I would go to the police station. Then I heard that Jack was in the hospital, seriously ill, and then that he had gone into a coma. I prayed even harder and made many promises to God if he would only let Jack get well. Then Jack died. Suddenly I no longer believed in God. All religion seemed a big hoax to me. I no longer wanted to go to Sunday School or church because it did not mean anything. God had let me down; therefore God did not exist. I lost my faith completely.

Before discussing David's high-school record, let us become acquainted with Jerry Raleigh, the second boy of the incident.

Jerry Raleigh was a handsome young man. Standing almost six feet tall, physically well proportioned, his dark brown hair carefully groomed, his mouth finely chiseled and usually smiling, Jerry gave the impression of being alert, well-adjusted, and poised, the son of stable and well-to-do parents. In his R.O.T.C. officer's uniform he carried an air of competence and authority.

Jerry attended several elementary schools in two towns, as well as in Old City. In his creative-writing class, in an unrestricted atmosphere, Jerry wrote an autobiography. From it we can gain some understanding of his early years.

Jerry's grandmother was a divorcee in the days when such a status, especially in a small farming community, was thought sinful. His mother was reared by her grandmother, since the divorced mother had to work. When her grandmother died, Jerry's mother returned to live with her mother. There was ill feeling between them and while still in her teens, she married an itinerant, small-league baseball player. Two years later, in 1935, Jerry was born. Before Jerry's birth, his father, Floyd Hugh Raleigh, had managed to squander in ill-advised business ventures the inheritance which Jerry's great-grandmother had left his mother. During the first two years of his life, the baby lived a nomadic existence as his father went from job to job in a succession of small towns in the state.

When Jerry was two, his father and mother separated. In his autobiography Jerry wrote:

> I have not seen my father since I was two years old. I have only a jumbled image of him. In all the years since my parents' separation, I have received nothing from my father in the way of support. About every two years I receive a letter from my father, filled with maudlin sentiment and pleas for forgiveness. He has become a financial success, so the letters run, and is now prepared to help me materially. Nothing concrete ever comes from these letters.

After the separation Jerry and his mother went to live with his grandmother. For the next three years the three of them subsisted on the small old-age pension check which his grandmother received.

> When I was five, my mother obtained a job with the WPA as a recreation worker. For a year or more she worked at this boondoggling job. My grandmother kept house for the three of us. With the return of prosperity, the WPA folded, and my mother lost her job. My mother had a nervous breakdown, which apparently amounted to moments of uncontrollable anxiety. I remember vividly one Chrstmas Eve when my mother became completely unnerved, dashing out into the night without hat or coat. Finally my mother was placed in the mental ward of a large hospital in a nearby town.
>
> In those days provincial minds classed mental illness in the same dark niche with murders and unexplained noises in the night. The ensuing scandal forced my grandmother and me to leave town.

Jerry and his grandmother went to the town where his mother was a mental patient. There the county welfare agent moved them into a rundown house and entered their names on relief rolls. Shortly after they were settled, Jerry's mother was released. She was given "aid for dependent children" for Jerry, and the three decided to stay where they were. However, the two women began to quarrel violently. The daughter blamed her mother for ruining her life by living with her during her marriage. (The grandmother had contributed her share of the living expenses and even more.) "The quarrels," Jerry wrote, "were the most frequent terror of my childhood."

Then a new complication entered their lives:

> When I was about seven, my mother started dating a local, re-tired engineer, a married man with two half-grown sons. There was some fumbling effort at divorce. One day my mother left town. Several months later she gave birth to a baby boy in a hospital in Old City. She chose to keep the baby, and, with support from its father, settled down in Old City. It was during this folderol that my grandmother gained legal custody of me.

For the next two years Jerry and his grandmother continued to live in the "outraged community."

> My classmates and even some of the more addled adults asked me knowing questions about my new baby brother. More often than not I was forced to fight my way out of school. My grandmother, feeling that she had contributed nothing to her daughter's downfall, stayed on as a living refutation to any stories that she had.
>
> These two years as the central figure in a public scandal had an unavoidable effect upon my personality. Although I had been some-thing of a lone wolf before, now I became completely isolated from my age mates. All my life I have been accused of being a physical coward. I do not deny this. But how does one learn the art of self-defense with a mob chasing him? I remember one school Valentine's Day party when I did not get a single card. Even my efforts to join the Cub Scouts were frustrated. Apparently the den mother did not want a little *cause celebre* among her clean-cut American boys.
>
> My religious education was terminated the day the Sunday school superintendent slapped me for looking at a book in the adult section of the church library.

Despite all these baleful occurrences, I never really felt sorry for myself. Instead, I developed a kind of haughty independence that would stay with me until adolescent giddiness took its toll. I served as a sort of undersized majordomo for my grandmother at this time. I went to the grocery store, paid the utility bills, and did sundry other errands. The scandal subsided into a sort of local tradition. My nightly race with the school bullies had also become a tradition.

Once more Jerry was to have his tenuous roots disturbed when his grandmother decided to join her daughter in Old City.

My mother had an apartment in one of those community eyesores which mayors' committees are constantly deriding. The landlord allowed us to share my mother's apartment provided that I did not make childish noises, play baseball in the backyard, or invite friends over. I was also told to make my exits and entrances as quietly as possible. He need not have had any fear on the last part. My new domicile embarrassed me so much that I was constantly devising ways of entering it unnoticed by the passersby.

The reunion in Old City was not to be a happy one.

My grandmother and mother spent a great deal of their time fighting. Often I would return from school to hear them shouting at each other. I would sit out in the hall, waiting for the shouting to subside. Recent events had given them new and ample material for mutual harassment. My mother resented the legal control my grandmother had over me. In rebuttal, my grandmother would go through a detailed account of my mother's recent licentious behavior.

My little half brother and I did not strike it off either. He violently resented me and demonstrated the fact by those explosive means open to a two-year old.

As for things financial, my mother received an ample allowance from my half-brother's father. My grandmother, on the other hand, received an ADC check for me plus an Army allotment check from her son.

The big city terrified my grandmother. She was convinced the youthful population of Old City was made up of crazed hoodlums. I was made to come home immediately after school. . . . I didn't have much to stay at school for. I think my whole childhood could be summed up in the words, "No, kid, you can't play with us." Where once I had been refused access to the playground because of my scandal-tinted name, now I was refused because of simple ineptitude. I couldn't catch a cold, or so the joke went. Only at supervised gym periods did I ever get a chance to engage in sports.

Later in my grade-school career I developed some proficiency in soccer. This did not improve my status one iota. Nobody likes Cinderellas.

For some reason I was summarily stricken from the list of county mendicants. This forced my mother to go to work in support of a child she had no legal control over. This situation, of course, led to more violent quarreling.

Shortly after my graduation from eighth grade, my mother remarried. Her second spouse also had had an unsuccessful first marriage, the sole fruit of this unhappy union being a daughter who was later institutionalized for feeblemindedness.

My grandmother and I moved to another apartment in the Victorian brick pile which continued to house all of us. My uncle married, thus making my grandmother ineligible for her Army allotment. With no financial aid from my mother, this made us quite destitute. My grandmother eventually found work as a practical nurse.

Some insight into the manner by which Jerry learned in elementary school may be gained from his autobiography:

I was never taught to read; I picked it up by a sort of osmosis. During those years when most children are struggling with the primary grade readers, I was often at home with illness, real or simulated. Comic books were my only entertainment during those long hours of enforced idleness. Who can remember when they first learned to read? It seemed that one day I could only look at the colored panels; the next day I could read and fully understand the balloon-encased type. Perhaps this explains some of my half-conscious scorn for formal education. I learned to read independently of these frilly education machines mass produced by the state teachers college. Since the pedagogues failed to teach me the primary instrument of learning, I felt anything else they had to offer would be of dubious quality.

Jerry was fifteen before he entered high school, one year beyond the age of the average entrant. Of this time he wrote:

I entered Old City High School in September, 1950. Right off I cannot think of one happy memory involved during my stay here.

The self-centered confidence that I had carefully built up was laid waste by adolescent anxieties. I was scared to death all the time. During my whole high school career I have never been invited to a party, attended a dance, or had a date. (I did escort a girl to the Military Ball this year, but I had no choice in the matter.)

Much of my social ineptitude may be blamed on a lack of money. Although my grandmother could supply me with only carfare and lunch money, she refused to let me get a part-time job. I took ROTC not because I was interested in it but because it supplied me with most of my wardrobe for these four years. In my junior year and against my grandmother's wishes I did get a part-time job.

During my childhood I was able to obliterate partly my loneliness with technicolored imaginings, but the adolescent ego longs for concrete accomplishments. The few friends I have are peripheral figures like myself, from poor homes and with bleak futures. I have hated my classmates for their nice clothes, their cars, and their infernal chatterings about social doings. I used to daydream of lining them up before a firing squad in full evening dress. Now I realize they are all as frightened and uncertain as I am.

I read a great deal, spending much of my time haunting the public library. Generally speaking I have ignored my studies. My semester grades usually run the gamut from 1 to failing.[1]

Although they had been in some of the same classes, David Stevens and Jerry Raleigh did not become friendly with each other until they were both dropped from the school newspaper staff at the end of the first semester of their senior year. This seemed to be a bond to bring them together.

Both Stevens and Raleigh were above average in intelligence; the Terman McNemar Test of Mental Ability administered to them during their freshman year, 1951, revealed intelligence quotients for Stevens of 147 and for Raleigh of 125. During the same year the California Coöperative Reading Test, Advanced, Form AA, was administered to them. Stevens showed achievement at the 14.7 grade level and Raleigh at the 13.5 level, the two boys being in advance of their actual grade placement by 5.7 and 4.5 years respectively. In the senior class at the time of the incident Stevens ranked 84th and Raleigh 139th in a class of 313, scores which placed them in the sec-

---

[1] The grading system used at Old City High School was as follows: 1—93 to 100%, 2—85 to 92%, 3—78 to 84%, 4—70 to 77%, and 5—below 70%, failing.

ond quartile of their class. Stevens' grade average was 3.03 and Raleigh's 2.34.

Both Stevens and Raleigh were enrolled in the college-preparatory course in high school and planned to attend college. The charts on this page show the grades each earned in the several areas of study.

English	S.	R.	Mathematics	S.	R.	Social Studies	S.	R.
I	2	2	General Math. I		4	World Geog.	2	2
II	2	3	II		3	World Hist. I	2	2
III	2	3	Algebra I	2	5	II	2	1
IV	1	4	II	3		Civics	2	2
V	2	2	Geometry I	2		Mod. Probs.	2	
VI	2	3	II	3		Economics	2	2
VII	1	2				Am. Hist. I	1	1
VIII		2				II	2	1
Cr. Wrtg.	1	1				Eng. Hist.		2
Journal'm I	2	2						
II	2	2						

Science	S.	R.	Languages	S.	R.	Speech	S.	R.
Biology I	1	4–	German I		5	Debate I	2	1
II	1	4	Latin I	2		II	1	2
Physics I	3		II	2		III	2	
II	4		III	2		IV	1	
			IV	2		Express'n I	1	1
						II	2	2
						Pub. Spkg.		2

Phys. Ed.	S.	R.	R.O.T.C.	S.	R.	Type	S.	R.
Phys. Ed. I		1	Band I	2		Typewriting I		5,5,
			Band II	2				3
			Mil. Drill I		1			
			II		3			
			III		4			
			IV		4			
			V		4			
			VI		4			
			VII		1			
			VIII		3			

Both Stevens and Raleigh took four years of English with considerable success. Both boys showed a marked preference for electives in speech. Furthermore, both boys took four years of social studies, although the college-preparatory course required only three. Stevens took two years of Latin, but Raleigh failed his first semester of German and took no more foreign language work. In mathematics Stevens completed a year each of algebra and geometry; Raleigh failed his first semester of algebra and qualified for graduation with one year of general mathematics with below-average grades. Stevens completed a year each of biology and physics; Raleigh completed only one year of biology. It is interesting to notice that Raleigh, who did not try a second time to master a foreign language or algebra, persisted for three semesters until he had mastered basic typewriting.

Both boys participated in a variety of extracurricular activities. School records show the following: [2]

Stevens	Raleigh
Register [school paper] Staff 1	Senior Committee
Concert Band 1	ROTC 1, 2, 3, 4—2nd Lieut.
Debate 2, 3, 4	Non-Com. Officers Club 3
Pep Squad 4	Com. Officers Club 4
National Forensic League 2, 3, 4—President 4	Debate 2
Road Show [all-school variety show] 1	Fall Play Committee 3
Old City High Players 3—Sgt.-at-Arms 4	Old City High Players 2, 3, 4
Latin Club 2	Chess Club 2, 4
Journalism Award 4	Science-Fiction Club 1, 2, 3, 4
	Secretary 3
	President 4
	Science-Math. Club
	Teacher's Helper 3

A comparison of the two boys' attendance records and cumulative number of credits earned follows:

Attendance	Absence		Tardiness		Credits earned [3]	
	S.	R.	S.	R.	S.	R.
1950–51	8	16	3	0	9½	9
1951–52	11	12	2	0	20	16½
1952–53	6	1	2	1	29	25
1953–54	7	5	3	3	37½	35

On the basis of their senior-year teachers' and counselor's judgment, Stevens and Raleigh had been rated before the incident of the publication as follows:

	Poor		Fair		Good		Excellent		Superior	
	S.	R.	S.	R.	S.	R.	S.	R.	S.	R.
Reliability					X		X			
Industry					X		X			
Initiative					X		X			
Personal appearance							X		X	
Cooperation					X	X				
Conduct					X				X	

[2] Numerals indicate the year of participation, 1 being freshman year, etc.
[3] Thirty-two credits are required for graduation.

Although Stevens' intelligence was higher, and his grades better than Raleigh's, Raleigh made the better impression upon his teachers and counselor.

Before graduation both boys applied to colleges for admission and scholarship aid. Neither boy qualified for aid; Stevens because his family's financial circumstances were good, and Raleigh because his academic record was low. College admission had been assured before the incident. Stevens had applied for admission to the University of Chicago, his first choice, but decided to attend Carleton College when it accepted him. Although Raleigh had hoped to get scholarship aid to attend Drake University, he decided he would have to attend the Municipal University of Old City.

*   *   *   *   *

Shortly after the boys published their booklet, the head of the English department at Old City High called them in for a conference. He told them they had not been fair to their classmates when they had solicited their articles without telling them that they would appear in the context of a scurrilous publication. As a result, some members of the class had been embarrassed because they had been associated with the project. The boys were apologetic.

When asked why they had written articles attacking personalities and departments of the school and included them with the others, the boys said that the idea had occurred to them in a moment of levity. They thought there should be some spice—something controversial and shocking—in the publication if it were to sell well. "We just decided to jazz it up," they commented.

Then the teacher took up each of the questionable articles. Although the editorial, "Let's Free Sacco and Vanzetti," had some offensive statements in it, it was, according to Stevens and Raleigh, intended only to be humorous. The teacher dismissed this article to take up those which had aroused the faculty. When asked why they had used such a name as *Fulton J. Sheen(y)* in the publication, the boys said they had no intention of showing dislike of Roman Catholic or Jew. The name had come out in such a form only because they were attempting to disguise slightly the name of a well-known lecturer and writer whose ideas they could not respect.

Asked why they had written the article attacking the use of outlines in history courses, the boys said they thought having to make such outlines was a waste of time. They thought they might be of value "only to the morons" in the class. For them, having to write outlines took valuable time which might be spent better in wider reading. When told that the head of the social studies department had been deeply offended by the article, David Stevens, who acknowledged authorship, was surprised that she had found it more than mildly offensive. When asked whether he had any ill feelings toward Miss Burke, he replied, "None at all. In fact, I think she is a very bright woman, and she conducts an interesting class." He volunteered to apologize to Miss Burke. David was later somewhat surprised when Miss Burke failed to take his apology as made in good faith.

When asked why they had attacked the R. O. T. C. department, Jerry Raleigh, who was the author of "Colonel Had's Report," said that he had no personal feeling of animosity toward the sergeant in charge, but that he thought all the "rigamarole and hocus-pocus" of military organization and the system of promotion were silly. He said that he was an individualist and as such could not support whole-heartedly any system which gave older pupils the authority to "boss" the younger ones or to make them "work off penalties" by physical exercise. The teacher then read to him the following excerpt from his autobiography written earlier in the semester:

> I dutifully signed up year after year for ROTC more to save on my small wardrobe than anything else. The promotion system, as everyone knows, is a farce. A friend of mine, Robert Focht, through great personal effort, managed to become a first sergeant during our junior year. He saw to it that I was promoted to Master Sergeant, although my previous rank had been that of PFC.
>
> Eventually he was forced out by the powers that be. Focht quarreled constantly with Dick Shapiro, a sort of a Ivy League Sammy Glick type, who became lieutenant-colonel this year. Just how they managed to eliminate Focht I can't find out, for he never does more than swear about the incident. It seems to me that ROTC is good training for future junior executives in the art of infighting.

After hearing his account read to him, Jerry said that he thought most promotions went to the boys of influential families and not to those whose soldierly conduct merited promotions. When asked whether he was from an influential family, he admitted he was not.

(He was wearing his second lieutenant's uniform during the interview.) He then said the article merely expressed his views in an objective way toward a system of which he disapproved but from which he was too lazy to detach himself. He said that the whole activity had palled on him in his junior year, but that he had continued with R.O.T.C. in order to get the promotion he had earned. He said that the sergeant had treated him fairly, and that he had no personal motive in putting him in a bad light. He said he just wanted other boys to see how "stupid" the system was; furthermore, he admitted he could not resist "putting in a little sensationalism" for effect.

David said he had been unable to engender any interest in military drill as a freshman, even though he was with the marching band, and had not reënrolled. He thought that Jerry's accusation against the system of promotion was accurate.

When asked about the personal and somewhat vicious attack upon the journalism teacher, they admitted they both had personal grudges against her. They charged that she was in the habit of using foul language to her pupils and that, at times of anger, she threw erasers, books, and other objects at pupils. They said that any journalism pupil would testify to the truth of this charge.

They said they had enrolled in journalism with very serious intentions, but that almost all their contributions had been rejected because they were too controversial or too mature to be published in a high-school paper. They admitted that after finding none of their articles was being accepted for publication they had begun to waste their time and ultimately became discipline problems. At the end of the first semester of this year they had been dropped from the staff. They felt they had been mistreated, that they wrote better than most of the staff, and that they should have been retained and allowed a freer hand. When the creative-writing teacher pointed out that such freedom might have given rise to articles as vicious as theirs in "Off the Cuff," they admitted that the journalism teacher may have had a valid reason for dropping them. However, they said that their taste was higher than hers, and she was not the kind of person who should be permitted to teach.

When asked why they had not gone to the Principal with their charges against the teacher instead of publishing them, they replied they did not believe in "making trouble for a teacher." Furthermore, they said they did not respect the Principal and felt he would not treat their charge seriously, that "he would get back at us for it." They said that he often "shouted at kids in the hall" and "lost his temper when you tried to talk to him." When asked if they did not feel the article attacking the teacher was even worse than reporting her to the Principal, they admitted it might be. They thought "she had it coming to her" but agreed that it had been underhanded to attack a teacher, especially a woman teacher, in such a way.

In Jerry Raleigh's autobiography there was an account of his relationships with the journalism teacher that seems to illuminate the statements made in the interview:

> For as long as I can remember, up to my senior year in high school, my only ambition in life was to be a journalist. Many times I would stand staring into the first-floor news room of one of the local radio stations. There, I thought in my youthful rapture, was the world sputtering out its trouble over Western Union teletype machines. My journalistic ambition was throttled by Mrs. Gary. Good old Mrs. Gary.
>
> Her employment of the more vigorous profanities common in Anglo-Saxon usage is the lady's most outstanding feature. Woe unto the hapless student, male or female, who crosses Mrs. Gary's path during her more wrathful moments. If a victim shows any fight, he may have McDougall's *Modern Newspaper Reporting* heaved at him from a short distance. Mrs. Gary had no tolerance for my journalistic ambitions. As a rule she ignored them. When I pointed out my vocational aims, she informed me that I wrote like *shit*. It was disconcerting to say the least.
>
> The school paper is, by standards of any sociological textbook an *in* group activity. An overwhelming majority of the staff are members either of the most exclusive Jewish fraternity or sorority or one of the not-so-secret clubs, organized along the pattern of college Greek societies. The Jewish social clubs lead an unhampered existence due to their supposed religious character. Secret clubs, unable to use this enviable pious front, are more harried. These two groups make up a sort of unofficial power elite that many students are blissfully unaware of.
>
> Although I was receiving a one-half credit for working on the paper, none of the editors gave me a story assignment. For a while I tried writing feature stories, which were thrown into the wastebasket without being read. The ideas for a couple of these were later picked up by the *Old City Daily News'* writers.

The humor section of the school paper last semester was edited by an anemic little girl who thought "I Love Lucy" the ultimate in humor. One day she returned a number of stories I had submitted informing me I was not working for the *Daily Worker*.

This had reference to my articulate support of Adlai Stevenson and my weekly perusal of the *New Republic*. This convinced a large number of the Old City High's suburbanite Tories that I was a card-carrying communist. Actually I am the last of the Norman Thomas' Socialists, which makes them close by their standards.

Finally I began to devote my enforced hour in the journalism room by shaping up its library. This was a large, jumbled collection of books which defied Dewey's Decimal System. I had worked my way up to the 500's when Mrs. Gary decided to eliminate some "dead wood." I was among the decapitated brands. After I had voiced some protest, Mrs. Gary hurled a thesaurus at me.

Certain signs suggested, by the way, that Jerry Raleigh's feelings against Mrs. Gary were shared by some of her colleagues. Some teachers spoke of her as badly groomed. They claimed to have heard that she patronized bars excessively. Some who had been invited to her home told of being embarrassed by her quarrels with her husband in their presence, and criticised the order and cleanliness of her home. Some of them had privately said that she should not be retained on the faculty.

Following the interview with the two boys, the head of the English department informed the Principal of the boys' explanations for their actions. The parents of David and the grandmother of Jerry said they felt the boys had committed only a misdemeanor and believed their grilling and scolding by the Principal and others constituted sufficient punishment.

The R.O.T.C. department refused to take the publication seriously and expressed no desire to penalize either boy. Mrs. Gary did not ask that they be punished.

Three general views were expressed among the rest of the faculty.

The one most widely held was that on the basis of their past records as students and citizens, after being well scolded they should be forgiven. Among most of the faculty there seemed to be no strong feeling against them. With minor exceptions, it was pointed out, they had been good students; they had acquitted themselves well in their extracurricular responsibilities; and they had shown a reasonable degree of respect for most of their teachers and subjects. Many seemed to feel that the students' speaking out against aspects of personnel and activities of which they disapproved was not a serious offense. A few teachers spoke secretly of admiring their ability to write and to carry through such an undertaking.

Although some copies of "Off the Cuff" were still circulating and being read by parents and pupils, the boys had destroyed the stencils and given the Principal their unsold copies. They had voluntarily apologized to the head of the social studies department, to the R.O.T.C. sergeant, to the teacher of creative writing, and to the pupils whose writing they had reproduced. They had admitted the publication was lacking in good taste and judgment. They had convinced the Principal and some of the teachers that they had not intended to belittle any minority group. They had apoligized for the profanities and minor obscenities in the publication. They did not act like martyrs or heroes. Most teachers indicated that they were favorably impressed by their attempts to make amends.

A few teachers held that David Stevens should not be allowed to represent his class and deliver the commencement address. They argued that allowing him to escape any penalty might give rise to further publications attacking school personnel. They also wanted Jerry Raleigh to be demoted to private in the R.O.T.C. Allowing him to wear his officer's uniform, they said, was an invitation to the young cadets to become insubordinate. A number of other teachers favored denying the boys the right to graduate. Miss Burke urged their expulsion. The Principal and the Superintendent of Schools, however, seemed reluctant to punish the boys severely.

When by the end of the week no action had been taken against the boys, Miss Burke voiced a strong protest to the Principal. She urged that the boys be dropped from school immediately and forced to take a full semester of work the next fall before being given their diplomas. The Principal suggested that she was being too harsh, that the boys' publication was insufficiently serious to merit such treatment. When the Principal refused to honor her request, she wrote a letter to the Superintendent. In it she asked him to make an example of the boys and threatened, if the boys were not punished, to write to the local representative of the Anti-Defamation League and call his attention to the name, *Fulton J. Sheen(y)*. The Principal discovered in an interview with her that she thought the term *iron maiden*, in the article concerning her department, was a personal reference to her. The boys denied having such an intention.

After the Superintendent had conferred with the Principal, they conferred together with Miss Burke. A Roman Catholic, she had objected strongly to two references: the use of the name *Fulton J. Sheen(y)* and *Unpius XII—The Index of Nepotism*. The Superintendent told her that her insistence upon punishment of the boys seemed to be a personal matter and, as such, unbecoming to her usual equanimity; in her relationship with pupils and teachers she had never shown any religious bias. She withdrew her complaint and her demand that the boys be punished.

No further action was taken against the boys. Although the Principal did not tell them that they were not to be punished, they seemed to understand that nothing would be done. Ultimately David Stevens gave the commencement address to lukewarm applause. Jerry Raleigh kept his commission.

The rush of closing school and the many activities coming during the last two weeks drew attention away from the publishing incident. Parents, pupils, and teachers became interested in other matters; and there was little reference to the incident. No copies of "Off the Cuff" were to be seen in the school, although there were rumors to the effect that those who still had copies valued them as collectors' items, and, in some instances, sold the privilege of reading them.

Summer vacation came, pupils scattered, teachers took up new activities, and interest in the case came to an end. In the fall both boys entered college.

SELECTED READINGS

Ehlers, Henry, and Gordon C. Lee, eds., *Crucial Issues in Education: An Anthology*. New York: Henry Holt and Company, rev. ed., 1959. Part I.

Friedrich, Carl J., *Constitutional Government and Democracy: Theory and Practice in Europe and America*, rev. ed. Boston: Ginn and Company, 1950. Chs. 1–2, 19.

Hamilton, Robert R., and Paul R. Mort, *The Law and Public Education; with Cases*. Chicago: The Foundation Press, 1941.

Kalven, Harry, Jr., "Law and Education," *The School Review*, Vol. LXV, Number 3 (Autumn, 1957), pp. 287–303.

Lindner, Robert, *Must You Conform?* New York: Rinehart and Company, 1956.

MacIver, Robert M., *Academic Freedom in Our Time.* New York: Columbia University Press, 1955. Ch. 12.

Redl, Fritz, and David Wineman, *Controls From Within: Techniques for the Treatment of the Aggressive Child.* Glencoe: The Free Press, 1952.

Strike-Out

On the afternoon of December 9, 1946, about twenty-four students from Center School visited a picket line of striking employees at the local salesroom and executive offices of a large automobile company, some distance from the school.

At first, they simply observed the picket line, which was originally a small demonstration; but as the afternoon progressed, they joined it. Union organizers augmented the line with striking office workers, workers from a subsidiary plant in an adjoining state, and other sympathizers. As a result the line soon extended for over a city block and even impeded traffic at a busy intersection. As had been anticipated, the picketing was peaceful throughout.

Late in the afternoon the students were joined by one of the faculty members of their school, Mr. Jamison. He was a teacher of history and social science, and the instructor of most of the students involved in this incident. The students, with their teacher, marched enthusiastically, despite falling rain and the early dusk of a winter's afternoon. Then, about seven or eight o'clock, they dispersed to their homes.

The sequence of events on December 9th, the day in question, was as follows:

Class 9-1 as usual had met with its teacher, Mr. Jamison, during the first period. The class was one in social science, and Mr. Jamison in-

199

formed his students that a sympathy strike was to be held that afternoon at the salesroom and offices of the Standard Automobile Company. When asked by his students if he was planning to go down to
the scene of the strike, and if they could accompany him, he informed
them that he was going and that the line would be made up of
strikers and lay people who wished to express their protest too. Hence,
"whoever else wants to come is welcome." He did add that he did not
feel it was particularly their place to go, considering their youth and
their student status.

In recent sessions the class had been discussing Greek culture and
influence. But Mr. Jamison was never one to limit the subject areas
with which his classes dealt. Rather, it was his custom to cut across
topics and chronological periods in order to show interrelationships
among ideas, thoughts, and the patterns and sequences of history.
Constant parallels were drawn between ancient and modern history
and culture, and the facts and lessons of the past were used to illuminate the issues and problems of the present. Consequently, when
timely matters of current concern were raised, attention was given to
them by the teacher and class cooperatively. Two class sessions per
week were devoted quite specifically to current events.

There is some indication that the whole matter of strikes, their
function, union-management relationships, and attempts at "breaking
the unions" had been discussed in previous classes.

There is also some evidence that mention of the strike and its im-
plications had been made the preceding week in the Discussion
Group, an extracurricular activity whose faculty adviser was Mr.
Jamison.

Considerable enthusiasm was generated among the students about
this issue. Mr. Johnson explained that this particular strike was being
organized by workers in the local area to express their general accord
with the striking workers of the main automotive plant of Standard
Auto Company in another state, who were currently engaged in a
lively labor dispute with their employers.

Neither the Principal nor the other teachers were consulted by
Mr. Jamison about a possible student visit to the strike.

For the second period the students in class 9-1 went to their next
classroom. There they organized themselves to visit the strike. A few
indicated that they did not care to participate. The others cut their
morning classes, went to the Arts and Crafts room—without permis-

sion—and made posters and signs to carry as they participated in the picket line. The signs carried such mottoes as: "Center Supports Standard Auto's Strikers."

They went to lunch with some of their friends from other classes, and after lunch some of them requested permission of their afternoon teachers to be dismissed from afternoon classes. This permission was denied them. Nevertheless, soon after lunch, at about one o'clock, a large body of students left the school. Small groups of friends traveled together to the picket line using public transportation. Not all of the boys and girls involved were in class 9-1.

It was at about four o'clock that Mr. Jamison joined the group. According to some reports, two or three other teachers from Center also marched on the picket line, but there was no verification of this.

One of the students involved described the trip later as a "fantastic educational experience." Another said, "We really learned by doing that day." A third concluded that this was "the most vivid, memorable and significant learning experience" of his high school or college days.

The parents of some of those involved did not know where their children were from the time of the school's usual dismissal until eight o'clock when they returned home. Other students had informed their parents previously about the projected trip or telephoned them during the day.

As a result of this incident there was considerable discussion on the part of parents and teachers. Protests from parents were directed towards Mr. Jamison and towards the principal of the school and the administration.

No Parent-Teacher Association meeting was called specifically for the purpose of discussing this matter, but it was discussed at the next regularly scheduled class parents' meeting.[1]

At the meeting, the parents were able to air their views. The question reiterated most often was this, "Are these children old enough to know what they are doing?" One mother said, "I didn't allow my daughter to go because I didn't want to foist adult political opinions on so young a child. Personally, I was in sympathy with the

---

[1] The parents of the students in group 9-1, chiefly from middle class homes, were a particularly cohesive group. On their own initiative they had organized a special class parents' organization, to supplement the very active general PTA; its purpose was to discuss and consider any problems or needs encountered by this class.

strikers." Another remarked, "Jane's friends were angry with me for not allowing her to go." Several parents who had known of the plan ahead of time and had allowed their children to go were sorry later that they had. One father announced, "If I had thought about all of the implications of the trip in advance and realized how it was to be carried out, I would never have given my permission to Sammy." Another mother said,

> The whole thing has annoyed me considerably. The children were too young; the thing was not adequately supervised throughout. But I grant you the experience was probably a valuable one for the kids.

On the part of a small segment there were some expressions of distress about the partial view that they felt the students got of the labor-management picture as a result of this trip. "Why not show the children big business functioning smoothly, or let them hear some of the employers' grievances against the union?" one of the advocates of this point of view—an irate father—insisted.

Some parents said that they had allowed their children to go only because of their confidence in Mr. Jamison, although they themselves had had some doubts as to the wisdom of the excursion. Several parents protested that they had not even known that such an expedition was to take place. One mother exclaimed, "I had no idea where Laura was all afternoon, and when she didn't get home in time for dinner, I really began to worry."

Repeatedly voices were heard in unqualified support of Mr. Jamison. Typical of these comments was the following: "I approve of virtually everything Mr. Jamison does. He's an outstanding teacher, and he *knows* what he is doing." Another added,

> I have no intention of relegating the duties and responsibilities of the home to the school, but I do say this. If we entrust our students to a school and a staff of whom we approve, then we must leave their teaching procedures and devices up to them. We, after all, are lay people, not educators.

No specific decisions or recommendations were made at this class parents' group meeting.

The matter was, of course, discussed informally by the other teachers of the school. There were those who expressed hearty approval, saying that they "would have done the same thing," and that it was "in the tradition of the school"; others said they were quite peeved and incensed by the entire incident. In this latter group were those teachers who objected in principle, those who objected to having classes disrupted, and those who opposed having a small group of students bearing banners proclaiming school support for a specific cause and participating in a dispute outside of the concern of the school as "representatives" of the school. Some applauded Mr. Jamison; others condemned him. None opposed his stand on the issues of the strike; all called themselves "New Dealers." The objections they pressed were not to peaceful picketing per se—only to the involvement of their students in it. Some of the teachers did, however, show signs of resentment of the students' unusual loyalty and devotion to Mr. Jamison.

The subsequent effects of the incident on the students were also considerable. The next day and for days following, the matter was discussed. Some of the students who had participated in the strike said they had done so because they approved of the principle involved. Some said they had participated out of a desire to emulate Mr. Jamison. Some said they had been carried along by the challenge of the classroom discussion, their own enthusiasm, and the excitement of the events which ensued. There was some ostracizing of the boys who had not participated in the outing by their peers in class 9-1. The excuses of the girls were apparently more readily accepted.

* * * * *

The incident occurred in Hamilton, a large urban community with a population of over one million.

The national origins of the inhabitants of Hamilton were extremely diverse. The population of Keansville, the area in which Center School was located, was also extremely heterogeneous. Native-born whites of European extraction constituted more than 50%: the chief nationality groups included Irish, Germans, and Russians. Smaller groups of Poles, Mexicans, Central and South Americans, Austrians, and British, and a scattering of Filipinos, Chinese, and Japanese lived in Keansville. A substantial Jewish population inhabited the area; the very high percentage was evidenced by the number of synagogues and temples. The statistics in Table I are indicative of the situation near the time of this case.

Table I

Cultural Group	Approximate Per cent of Total Population in Keansville
Native-born whites of European extraction	58.6
Foreign born white	30.6
Puerto Rican	6.9
Negro	3.0
Other non-whites	.9

The Jewish population in the area represented the stable element; most of their families had lived there for a period of thirty-five to forty years or longer. Many of them were professional people, and a larger number maintained their offices or businesses in the area. Although some of the children of this group attended public schools, many attended private or parochial schools. The same was true, to a lesser extent, of the Irish and Germans. These groups, except for the financially less able, were tending to move away from the area, however—especially families with young children. There were proportionately fewer children of school age belonging to the white groups, both gentile and Jewish, than to the non-white groups in the area.

Increasingly the children of Keansville were Negro and Puerto Rican, a fact reflected in the enrollments of the nine public elementary and junior high schools that served the area. There was only one high school located in the vicinity; many students traveled to another part of the city for the upper grades.

The Negroes' and Puerto Ricans' economic status, in general, was depressed; and their living areas, contiguous to the upper and middle class areas, reflected poverty and crowded slum conditions.

The median income in Keansville in 1949 varied with the district, ranging from $2,729 in one district with a large housing project to $5,384 in another.

Dwellings erected before 1919, and considered "old," accounted for from 46% to 65% of the living quarters, depending upon the section. Of these, 15% to 23% were designated as dilapidated, while 7% to 11% were considered overcrowded. The average monthly rent in Keansville was about $60.00.

The average educational level reached by residents of Keansville was 11.4 years, but again this varied with geographic location and race.

The area's delinquency rate was as low as 19.2 and 20.2 per 1,000 in certain sections, but rose to 43.1, 43.4, and 46.2 per 1,000 in sections where there had been an influx of new groups.

The social agencies in the area included nineteen day nurseries, nursery schools, and kindergartens, thirty-eight group work and recreational centers and other volunteer agencies, three public libraries, no mental health hospital clinics but two related services, five child health centers, and two non-hospital clinics. Outside the area but serving it were three hospitals, three health centers, and numerous other city agencies.

There were some forty-one Protestant and Orthodox churches in Keansville, five Roman Catholic churches, and eighteen synagogues and temples.

In addition to the public schools there were seven Roman Catholic schools, one institute, one junior college, and one professional school located in the community.

It was in this heterogeneous and complex area that Center School was located. It was not the only private school in Keansville (there were eighteen others), but it was fairly well known because of its interesting origins, its varied programs, and its fair degree of success in getting its graduates placed in top-rated colleges. Its graduates attended such institutions as Harvard, Yale, Columbia, Rockford College, the University of Michigan, the University of Chicago, the University of California, Ohio State University, and the big seven women's colleges among others.

Center was a small, private day school of under 500 enrollment with approximately equal numbers of boys and girls. It admitted students from the age of three, but entrance could be effected on any grade level. The school consisted of nursery and kindergarten grades and grades one through eight—the lower school—and a four-year high school which formed the upper school. The secondary course was a college preparatory program, but art, music, shop, and crafts courses were also offered. Approximately 97% of each graduating class went on to college.

The school's faculty consisted of thirty-five teachers, representative of quite varied racial, religious, and cultural backgrounds, who worked together effectively. It included some distinguished educators, writers, and contributors to art fields. They were an active group in civic affairs. Their professional preparation, in general, was of excellent calibre.

The school's library included more than 6,000 volumes, but students made use of the resources of the city's libraries also.

The school plant was located in one of the more attractive sections of Keansville, in an area where property values were high. It was easily accessible to public transportation. Its students were drawn from the entire city of Hamilton, but the majority of them lived in Keansville within walking distance of the school.

The school regularly offered a number of partial scholarships to qualified students unable to meet the tuition fee—in 1946, approximately $900 yearly. About 20% of the school's population received some scholarship aid. School policy aimed to secure a cross-section, geographically and ethnically, of the metropolitan populace. Substantial scholarships had been offered to able Negro or Oriental students, for example, in order to establish a broader ethnic base for the school. But, despite the school's efforts to obtain students of such extraction, at the time of the strike incident there were few in attendance.

At this time most of the student body belonged to middle-class upward-mobile families. The new entrants represented a somewhat wealthier element than their predecessors. This was reflected in the make-up of the school's very active PTA. Generally speaking, the parents maintained homes in which cultural interests played a part; most of them had fairly extensive home libraries. Many, but by no means all, of the parents of students in class 9-1 were liberal and progressive politically.

The children themselves were precocious, if not exceptionally mature. They had an incisive kind of intelligence, were decided in their views, and were ever ready with words and reasons—good ones. Although the girls were a fairly timid group, somewhat tongue-tied, and considerably less aggressive than the boys, they were equally as bright. Among the boys were at least two exceptionally rugged individualists. One, Kenneth, had made unsatisfactory adjustments at several previous schools but adored Center despite feeling himself something of a misfit because of his clumsy relations with his classmates, his different attitude toward life, and the fact that he was much older than the others. Another, Danny, was a young rebel— always in some kind of difficulty; but a leader, nonetheless, of one faction in the class.

Several cliques existed in this class, as in any class, but they were not significantly disruptive elements. Some division existed on the basis of relative social status, or on the basis of intelligence (or rather academic achievement). Another minor source of disunity lay in the fact that some students in 9-1 had attended Center since kindergarten, whereas others were relative newcomers who had to face problems of adjustment to a new situation. There was no observable pattern, however, determining which students went to the picket line and which did not.

The school's establishment and growth had paralleled closely the development of progressive education in America. Center School had been established in 1914 in the tradition of pragmatic progressivism, or, perhaps more accurately, in the tradition of experimentation; new ideas and teaching techniques were explored and utilized. New findings in the fields of psychology and psychoanalytic theory were applied to education, the psychological growth of the child was emphasized, and individual guidance and the provision of favorable conditions for development were stressed. Education here did not proceed through repetition and drill. It proceeded instead through pupils' participation in direct experiences, through learning by doing, in which thought was stimulated and knowledge absorbed by finding solutions to "real" problems presumably significant to the individual. In such an environment experimentation flourished.

The founders of Center School had dispensed with rigid discipline in favor of a more permissive type of atmosphere in which, they said, the individual exercised control from within in performing his tasks and undertaking his responsibilities. Although an atmosphere of free inquiry and individual initiative had prevailed at Center since the founding of the institution, by the time of the strike incident it had been somewhat modified, so that the general school approach was a more conservative one. The older teachers, who still adhered to the earlier Progressive tradition, for the most part taught students in the lower grades. Most of the newer and more conservative staff members taught in the upper school. The principal of the school had been appointed only a few years before the strike incident; in many particulars she clashed strongly with the old position.

The students in the high school maintained their own governmental machinery. Classes elected representatives to a Student Council, and the entire school elected the Council's officers and representatives to the Inter-School Congress. Fourteen Voluntary Committees enabled students to enrich their programs through extracurricular activities. These included a dramatic workshop, a stage crew, a discussion group, as well as newspaper, art, literary, music, social exhibition, and drives' committees. In addition, some intermural and intramural sports were played; these included football, baseball, basketball, tennis, and hockey.

The chief sources of the school's funds were contributions from foundations and individuals, and tuition fees.

Mr. Jamison was described by those who had known him best as a remarkable and complex individual—imaginative, reflective, creative, outspoken. He was reputed to be energetic and resourceful, patient, practical—yet visionary. Born in the Middle West, he had been educated in the East at an Ivy League college and at the graduate school of Harvard University. Prior to teaching at Center he had been a social worker at a settlement house in New England, and served for a year as coordinator between public and private social agencies in a large city on the eastern seaboard. He had taught at Center for almost twenty years prior to the incident in question. In the early days he had been one of a "devoted, earnest, almost missionary group of teachers who believed strongly enough in the Center idea to work for the unbelievably low wages which were sometimes paid." Mr. Jamison himself once said,

> In consequence, by right, we taught as we pleased. However, this teacher never did so arrogantly, but sought ever, as a committeeman, to function only with his con-freres, and in a cross-creating entity of great delight.

He was always responsive to change, and to the "hows" and "whys" of things. As a result, his former pupils described his teaching as invariably stimulating and dynamic.

Mr. Jamison was also an innovator. It was he who had instituted at Center the practice of taking children—after much advance preparation and cooperative planning—on overnight trips, lasting from a few days to several weeks.

Mr. Jamison taught three classes in the upper school and was also adviser to the Discussion Group and the Dramatic Workshop. His methods in extracurricular activities, as in the classroom, were progressive and experimental. For example, the workshop—endeavoring to write and produce a play about juvenile delinquency—visited settlements and community centers in order to obtain background information.

In the classroom Mr. Jamison taught history; a graduate of the school later called it "history as experience, history as life." A student was permitted to bring up anything germane, but as Mr. Jamison had said, "We made short shrift of him were he riding a hobby, a horse, or propaganda only."

Mr. Jamison described his own courses in history and social science as "a synthesis of several subjects: history, civics, English, literature, dramatics, and others." His students were asked to produce as well as to absorb—and they did produce, individually, creatively, and in group activities. He once said in writing:

> Teaching is personal—and must be ceaselessly reciprocal through the personal; in fact the child, being emulative, often moves forward through his transferred attention to the personal interest of the teacher.

He saw it as his aim to "elicit orderly thought," and "to encourage liveliness, humor, free-thinking."

He could maintain the discipline necessary in his classes while allowing them, at the same time, considerable freedom.

Mr. Jamison showed good insight into people and an uncanny understanding of human nature. At times, however, he would employ a "shock approach" in dealing with the problems of a shy or a recalcitrant child. This, according to one parent, helped many children, including her niece, but made her own daughter retreat even further into her shell. Nevertheless, the same mother often described Mr. Jamison as "an outstanding and rare personality who had a great deal to offer children."

Mr. Jamison was immensely popular with most of his students and commanded great respect and loyalty from them. His personality was such, however, that he aroused strong likes and antagonisms. Few spoke in neutral terms about him. A significant number reportedly found him "their most inspiring teacher of high school or college days."

Despite their disagreements, the principal of the school showed deep respect for Mr. Jamison. Soon after her appointment she had said, in introducing old faculty members to new, "If you want the truth, go to Mr. Jamison. But don't expect sugar and cream. . . ."

Some faculty members on occasion expressed personal antagonisms toward Mr. Jamison. Others indicated agreement with the position taken by the principal against the "old tradition of full force experimentation." Mr. Jamison's own relationship to the others on the staff was a most cordial and friendly one, and he did not engage in internal school politics.

*   *   *   *   *

The faculty met to discuss formally the issues arising out of the incident. Several questions were formulated and various views were presented. Three main issues seemed to emerge upon which there was disagreement among the faculty.

The first was the question of what was to be done about the behavior of the students involved. Some argued in favor of punishing them for going beyond established limits in invading the Arts and Crafts room, hijacking supplies, cutting classes, leaving school without permission, and participating in a community activity not sanctioned by school authorities—especially since such participation had been mildly discouraged even by the teacher involved. They agreed that although discipline and order should be imposed from within by each individual, according to the progressive precepts of the school, still in this instance "order" had broken down, and freedom had become license.

Those opposing this position argued that the students had undertaken this adventure as a genuine learning experience from which they had undoubtedly derived much profit. The disturbance to the school's regimen, they insisted, had not been shattering; besides, part of the institution's tradition was to alter the regular schedule whenever necessary in order to provide other meaningful experiences. The school urged interaction between the students and the community and favored students' being aware of social problems. According to all reports, the students had conducted themselves creditably while on public transportation and at the scene of the picket line. Should they, this group questioned, be penalized for their initiative in undertaking an experience outside of the classroom, when the school recognized the value of such experiences? Granted, they should have obtained permission, but even so, should they be called to account for this deed?

The second major issue raised was what censure, if any, Mr. Jamison merited for his part in the event. Should he be subject to official censure, unofficial censure, or no rebuke at all?

One group held Mr. Jamison responsible for the defection of the students from the school on the day in question. After all, he had mentioned the subject in his classroom and earlier in the Discussion Group. He knew that his students would want to participate, and that anyway they were likely to do what he did, unless he specifically forbade it; he, of course, did not. Mr. Jamison, in effect, had encouraged their going. His own enthusiasm had been communicated to his students. In addition, there was no quelling the natural exuberance of these particular youngsters.

Mr. Jamison also, this group averred, was not present to supervise the children during the entire time that they were participating in the picket line. There had been considerable unexpected disruption of school affairs, with inconvenience and annoyance resulting for his colleagues. Then, too, the trip had been a source of concern to those parents who had not known where their children were that afternoon. Finally, Mr. Jamison might have been imposing his own bias in favor of union action on his students.

Those who supported Mr. Jamison countered these arguments with the statement that "the proof of the pudding is in the eating." The experience, they felt, had been tremendously valuable and significant to the children. Trip taking and experimentation were part of the tradition of the school. In actual fact, Mr. Jamison had not urged the students to participate; rather he had indicated that it would be better for them not to go. It would be unthinkable for a dynamic and creative teacher, or any teacher for that matter, not to refer to a matter in class simply because students might be moved to action by the discussion of it. The matter was timely and of concern to a class discussing social attitudes and problems of past and present ages. Must a teacher, they inquired, be accused of bias simply because of the implications of current events? Were not the students practicing "democracy in action" when they expressed their feelings by peaceful picketing? Was that so different from casting a peaceful vote in a voting machine to show where one stood on an issue?

The third important issue that was repeatedly discussed by school personnel was whether the school pattern should be altered in any particulars. This apparently referred to whether or not the more conservative trend at Center should be accelerated.

The three issues had the following outcomes.

Most of the staff agreed that the students' need for adventure corresponded to a stage in their adolescent development and that they would outgrow it. They decided that the students in class 9-1 and those in other classes who went to the picket-line would not be censured or accused of insubordination for cutting classes; nor punished for actually participating in the strike. Their part in the incident was ignored.

Mr. Jamison's part in the incident was discussed at a staff meeting. Teachers took stands for and against his conduct. According to Mr. Jamison, many of those he had expected to support him did not, and the reverse was also true. The upshot was that the Principal suggested that he take a sabbatical leave during the next school year. He returned the year following, but students observed that his total teaching approach became somewhat more cautious.

With regard to school policy in general, increased conservatism became the rule of the day. Observers of the school describe it as remaining basically independent, democratic, and innovating. Nevertheless, while the school still held to its tenets of progressivism in education, experimentation was modified. Shortly thereafter there was serious dissension between faculty and administration, involving considerable upheaval; it was not directly related to the sequence of events detailed here.

Another subsequent occurrence which can be traced to the picket-line incident was the severe curtailing of previously existing student rights, with increasing control by the faculty of student activities and affiliations. The autonomy of the student council was decreased, and strong faculty pressure was placed on individual students to discourage them from joining "too liberal" groups. The proposed organization of a student political body, linking several student groups, was vetoed by the staff.

SELECTED READINGS

Benedict, Ruth, "Continuities and Discontinuities in Cultural Conditioning." In Clyde Kluckhohn and Henry A. Murray, eds., Personality in Nature, Society, and Culture. New York: Alfred A. Knopf, 1948, pp. 414–423.
Chamberlain, Ernest Barrett, Our Independent Schools: The Private School in American Education. New York: American Book Company, 1944.

Dewey, John, *Experience and Education*. New York: The Macmillan Company, 1938.

Fromm, Erich, *Escape From Freedom*. New York: Rinehart and Company, 1941. Chs. 1, 2, 4, 7.

Gerth, H. H., and C. Wright Mills, trs. and eds., *From Max Weber: Essays in Sociology*. New York: Oxford University Press, 1946. Chs. 8–10.

Mercer, Blaine E., and Edwin R. Carr, eds., *Education and the Social Order*. New York: Rinehart and Company, 1957. Ch. 6.

National Council for the Social Studies, *Bulletin* No. 12, "Developing Citizenship Through School Activities," edited by Laura M. Shufelt. Washington: the Council, 1949.

Pigors, Paul, *Leadership or Domination*. Boston: Houghton Mifflin Company, 1935.

Riesman, David, et al., *The Lonely Crowd: A Study of the Changing American Character*. New Haven: Yale University Press, 1950. Ch. 2.

CASE **13**

A Nongraded School Emerges

For several years, scores on the Metropolitan Readiness Tests had indicated that a large percentage of the children about to enter the first grade at the John Conley School were poor risks for the first grade. (See Table I.) Many of the children failed and then repeated the grade, but there was evidence that most of them gained little from repeating. Even after two years in the first grade most of the repeaters had not successfully completed a reading program built around one of the state-adopted basic reading series.

Four of the primary teachers said they felt that many of the entering children would benefit if a prolonged "reading readiness" period came before the formal teaching of reading.

After some discussion of the problem, Mrs. Jones, the principal, raised the question with the superintendent for the area of the city in which the school lay. He had previously expressed concern about the number of failures in the primary grades at the school. The Area Superintendent's office assigned to the school Mrs. Conrad, a former kindergarten teacher, to take charge of a pilot study for the school year 1957–1958. The purpose of the study was to determine whether a prolonged reading readiness program would better prepare children to read. In September, 1957, children who scored low normal

214

or below—i.e., were rated "D" or "E"—on Form R of the Metropolitan Readiness Tests were placed in Mrs. Conrad's readiness group. For four months she deferred the formal teaching of reading in favor of reading readiness activities.

The scores which members of this group obtained on reading readiness tests given in January are shown in Table II.

Table I

Letter Ratings and Statuses Corresponding to Scores in Total Readiness [1]

Scores Tests 1–6 Total Readiness	Letter Rating	Readiness Status	Significance
90–100	A	Superior	Excellent risk for first-grade work.
80–89	B	High Normal	Good risk for first-grade work provided other indications, such as health, emotional, etc., are consistent.
65–79	C	Average	Likely to succeed in first-grade work.
40–64	D	Low Normal	Likely to have difficulty in first-grade work.
0–39	E	Poor Risk	Chances of failure high under ordinary instructional conditions.

Table II

Comparison of September 1957 and January 1958 Ratings of Children in Mrs. Conrad's Readiness Group
(Comparable Tests)

1. Children Rated in September as "D" (N=11)
   Number receiving a January rating of A 1
   Number receiving a January rating of B 4
   Number receiving a January rating of C 6
   Number receiving a January rating of D 0
   Number receiving a January rating of E 0
2. Children Rated in September as "E'" (N=8)
   Number receiving a January rating of A 0
   Number receiving a January rating of B 0
   Number receiving a January rating of C 2
   Number receiving a January rating of D 5
   Number receiving a January rating of E 1

September average: About half-way between F and D
January average: Slightly under C
Average improvement: 2.2 points

---

[1] *Metropolitan Readiness Tests,* Form R. Yonkers: World Book Company, 1949.

During the second half of the school year Mrs. Conrad started her group on reading. However, in June none of them had completed the prescribed first-grade curriculum.

At the end of the school year Miss Evans, another first grade teacher, who had not given her class a prolonged reading readiness program, reported that there was such a range of differences in her class that she had to divide them into four reading groups. The most immature group was still at the readiness stage, and even the most advanced had not completed the prescribed first grade curriculum. If school policy were followed none of these children would be promoted to second grade.

Both teachers were faced with deciding whether or not these children should repeat the first grade. They agreed that branding them this early in life as failures should be avoided and decided that a change was worth trying.

In the spring of 1957 Mrs. Conrad, while attending a meeting of primary grade teachers at a conference of the Association for Childhood Education International, had heard about a nongraded school. The primary supervisor of a school system which had had a "nongraded primary school" in operation since 1942 had described the operations of this school. Mrs. Conrad suggested that she and Miss Evans investigate the possibility of making John Conley into such a school. Miss Evans concurred.

During the summer of 1958 Mrs. Conrad corresponded with the speaker she had heard and secured literature explaining the plan. She also secured material from another school system where a similar arrangement had been introduced for grades one through six. In the fall Mrs. Conrad, with Mrs. Jones' permission, circulated these materials among the primary teachers of the John Conley School. There was general agreement among the primary teachers and the Principal that they would like to try out the plan.

The following spring, at the request of the primary teachers, Mrs. Conrad and Mrs. Jones went to see Dr. White, the Area Superintendent, and presented their problem to him. He seemed very interested in the plan and gave them his "blessing" and the "go ahead" signal. They reported this to their colleagues the following day. The entire staff agreed that they wanted to try out the plan.

Before the close of school in June, 1959, the first, second, and third grade teachers of the John Conley School made a record card for each child, on which were entered his chronological age, his first grade readiness score, and his reading achievement score as of that month. On the basis of these data they tentatively grouped the children for September, 1959. They disregarded ordinary grade assignments and put no more than two reading groups into one class. At the same time they arranged it so that in each class there would be an age span of no more than two years.

In August, at the suggestion of Mrs. Conrad, she and Mrs. Jones had a conference with Miss Hamilton, a visiting instructor at a nearby university. During the school year Miss Hamilton served as vice-principal of a nongraded primary school. They also talked with Professor Seward, a regular faculty member at the university, who was a specialist in elementary education and had had eight years' experience in such a school. They explained their situation and their plan and asked for advice.

Professor Seward told them not to expect continuity in children's learning to result from the mechanical application of an administrative device. She said that the nongraded school was not a method of teaching and that it involved no procedures of instruction which departed from those long used by good teachers. She said it would not solve the problems of teachers "who have limited conceptions of child growth and learning" and "who are determined to teach each child the same material in the same way." She characterized the nongraded primary school as simply an organizational arrangement permitting more flexible grouping and providing longer blocks of time for a child to learn skills and knowledge without the stigma of "failing a grade."

Mrs. Conrad, Mrs. Jones, Miss Hamilton, and Professor Seward discussed the preparations the staff had made before deciding to try out the plan. Mrs. Conrad said the primary teachers had expressed a strong interest and desire to make the change because of their concern about pupil retentions and their inability to meet grade standards. They had made a careful study of the materials from the two systems which Mrs. Conrad had contacted. They were particularly concerned about getting help in grouping their children, breaking the news to their parents, developing a reading record, revising their system of reporting progress to parents, and orienting two new staff members to the plan.

Miss Hamilton and Professor Seward recommended that Mrs. Conrad, Mrs. Jones, and her staff examine a new book [2] by two educators dedicated to the plan. Then they both said that their own experience in nongraded primary schools made them feel it was important that not only the teachers who were directly involved should desire to make the change but also the rest of the staff. They indicated that perhaps this was one of the reasons that the schools where they themselves had taught had been successful in making the change. They emphasized that the parents and children, too, needed to be prepared for the change.

The two consultants raised the question of the relative merits of starting the nongraded plan by instituting it with the first year pupils only as against abolishing all existing grade levels in the first three grades at once. In the systems with which they had been associated, the approach had been gradual. Each year the parents of children entering the first grade had met with the staff, which had explained the organizational arrangement to them. Mrs. Conrad and Mrs. Jones said their staff had already decided to abolish existing grade levels over the entire span of grades one through three. They asked Professor Seward if she would work with their staff during the preschool planning period. They wanted help in explaining the organizational change to the total staff, in grouping their children, and in planning a meeting with parents. She agreed to meet with them during the pre-planning week.

On Tuesday, August 25, 1959, Professor Seward met with the whole staff of the John Conley School, before meeting separately with the teachers who would be directly involved in the nongraded primary unit. Her notes for the talk were as follows:

> When Mrs. Jones told me that you were planning to establish a nongraded primary school I agreed to describe the possibilities of the nongraded school for facilitating continuity in learning.
>
> What is an "Ungraded Plan?" At the outset, it seems appropriate to state what an "Ungraded Plan" is not and some of the things which it does not pretend to do. First, it is *not* a method of teaching. Second, it does *not* include procedures of instruction that are a departure from those long used by good teachers. Third, it does *not* solve the problems of teachers who have limited conceptions of child growth and learning and who are determined to teach each child the

---

2 John I. Goodlad and Robert H. Anderson, *The Nongraded Elementary School* (New York: Harcourt, Brace and Company), 1959.

same material in the same way. It is an administrative tool whereby a child is not asked to repeat a grade, but is given an opportunity to use more time to learn the skills and knowledge which he needs without the stigma of 'failing a grade.' It is an organizational arrangement within an elementary school to permit more flexible groupings and to provide longer blocks of time. It may embrace the first three traditional grades, the last three traditional grades, or all six grades of a six-year program. During any or all of these three periods of time, children are grouped without any designation of grade other than "Primary School," "Intermediate School," or perhaps "Miss Brown's Group."

At the end of three years beyond kindergarten in the Primary School, most children move on to the fourth grade or the Intermediate School. Other children stretch out their programs another semester or year. Some children whose patterns of growth are faster complete the program in a shorter length of time. Likewise, the Intermediate School may embrace the span of three or four years beyond the Primary School, depending upon the individual child. Thus, several grades are replaced by a single unit of three or four years. Within this longer period of time, without the pressure of artificial preconceived grade level expectations, some think that it is possible to eliminate many unnecessary gaps and overlaps that fail to recognize each child's lags and spurts in his individual pattern of development. Thereby, opportunities are afforded for each child, in the company of children similar in chronological age, to move along as smoothly and as rapidly as possible in all areas of development and learning. Usually each pupil's progress is recorded by levels of academic achievement. Other aspects of growth are also used to measure readiness and progress.

Where can ungraded plans be found? Systems where pupils are classified by divisions rather than by grades are scattered throughout the United States. Surveys reveal that there are various forms of the ungraded plans located in such widely scattered places as Milwaukee, Wisconsin; the Tampa, Florida area; Park Forest, Illinois; East Orange, New Jersey; Dearborn, Michigan; the Los Angeles area; Trenton, New Jersey; Wichita, Kansas; Provo, Utah; Marblehead, Massachusetts; Caribou County, Idaho; Richmond, Indiana; International Falls, Minnesota; Cabool, Missouri; Billings, Montana; Reno, Nevada; Orange, Texas; Springfield, Vermont; Richmond, Virginia; and Rochester, New York. This is by no means a complete list of places where school systems are trying to solve their organization problems by the elimination of grade lines. . . .

Perhaps a brief explanation of an ungraded plan will give a better picture of its potentialities for developing continuity in the educative process.

In the Smithton Public Schools, where I taught for 17 years, the Primary School organization has been in operation since 1942, when the plan was initiated in one school. Gradually all of the Smithton schools have established the ungraded plan in their primary grades. The Primary School covers the span of a unit of six, seven, or eight semesters above the kindergarten. On leaving kindergarten, a child becomes a P-1. At the end of the first semester, he becomes a P-2. In the third semester, he is labeled P-3, and so on, through P-6, P-7, or P-8, depending on his need to stretch out his primary program.

Careful records are kept of his academic progress and his personal and social development. His progress card, which he takes home, gives information about his growth and learning. It indicates whether he is making progress or needs improvement in personal and social growth as well as in growth in learning and skills. . . .

Behavioral evidence of growth or absence of growth in the areas of reading, language, and arithmetic is indicated. Areas in which a child shows special interest such as arts and crafts, music, science, social studies, stories, poetry, and physical activities are noted. On the back of the card is a record of the dates a child advanced from one reading level to another. In each child's cumulative folder is a complete record of every book he has read and the semester in which he read it. The individual reading record sheet lists twelve reading levels: (1) Prereading or readiness, (2) Experience chart reading, (3) Pre-primers, (4) Easy Primers, (5) Hard Primer, (6) Easy First Readers, (7) Hard First Readers, (8) Easy Second Readers, (9) Hard Second Readers, (10) Easy Third Readers, (11) Hard Third Readers, and (12) Independent Reading. The approximate date on which a child advances from one reading level to another is noted.

These individual records, together with other records of academic, social, and physical growth give a picture of what each child's growth is and enables his teacher to select challenging new experiences for him and his classmates.

At the close of each semester the primary teachers and the principal have a planning conference to study the problem of regrouping. With records of academic progress and social development before them, they try to make desirable changes. If it is possible, a group stays with the same teacher for a year. Groups are organized so that no child is more than one year younger or older than the other children in his room. Through careful regrouping, there is a gradual shifting of slow learners and accelerated learners so that the length of their programs is stretched out or shortened and enriched to meet their particular patterns of growth and learning.

Parents become partners in the Primary School Plan by becoming acquainted with its philosophy and operation before their children begin the Primary School. Throughout the child's stay in the Primary School, frequent parent-teacher conferences are arranged so that parents will have an understanding of their child's placement and progress. They are prepared for the possibility of their child's staying in the Primary School three, three and one-half, or four years.

Does the ungraded plan solve problems? Do these attempts to break down grade lines solve problems of continuity? The answer to this question is obviously "no." Continuity in learning cannot be achieved by mechanically applying an administrative device. However, schools where grade-to-grade barriers are removed do offer teachers opportunities to implement a continuous instructional program through which children can progress as normally and as rapidly as possible. The ungraded plan does have the potentialities for flexible grouping of children with provision for individual variations of differences. A longer span of years may provide greater opportunity for pacing learning to the readiness of the learners. If individual records of all areas of progress are used to guide children in their learning, each child can have experiences for which he is ready and gaps and overlaps in his learning can be avoided as much as possible. The slow learner and the child whose school attendance has been interrupted by illness, moving, or vacations are not asked to "repeat." Instead, it is possible to offer these children experiences which build on their previous experiences. The rapid learner is not "skipped" or forced to move along without available experiences for which he is ready. The removal of stratified subject matter organized around graded materials to be hurdled grade by grade frees teachers to use centers of attention such as problems and ideas which have valid extensions in understandings and in educational use.

Schools where grade-to-grade barriers are removed do offer teachers opportunities for knowing each child well, living with him over a period of time, and helping him work on problems that are of importance to him. When these opportunities are used chances are greater for helping each child to perceive continuities and to relate his learning for himself.

The question-and-answer session after Professor Seward's talk proceeded approximately as follows:

Miss Brown: What do you feel contributed most to the successful development of the nongraded program where you taught?

Professor Seward: The teachers engaged in serious and continued study of the plan before and after they adopted it. It was tried out in one school first for three years, and then other schools asked that they might try it too. It was a matter of the choice of a staff. Parents' understanding of the plan was critically important.

Miss Smith: What would you recommend to any school contemplating the introduction of a nongraded plan?

Professor Seward: On the basis of my own experience and the research done by Robert Anderson and John Goodlad, who sent questionnaires to 35 nongraded schools, I would recommend that you take time to get full parental understanding and consent; that you have the cooperation of your entire staff; that you move slowly and evaluate every move; that you work closely with your PTA and keep them informed on your progress; that you introduce the plan in one grade at a time over a period of years; that you have a sound program of testing and evaluation; and that you report carefully to parents and use the parent-teacher conference method of reporting pupil progress, as well as a report card that evaluates a child's individual pattern of progress.

At this point Professor Seward circulated brochures, reading records, and report cards from five school systems and talked with individual teachers about these materials. The two new staff members had done their student teaching in a nongraded school in another state and expressed great enthusiasm about making the change, telling Professor Seward about their experience.

After the staff had taken a break, the primary teachers met again. They retained their plan to "nongrade" grades one through three immediately. Under Mrs. Conrad's leadership they spent the rest of the morning reexamining the record cards of children and consulting with the children's previous teachers concerning appropriate placements for them on the basis of age, social adjustment, and academic achievement.

During the afternoon the primary teachers discussed other matters, the possibility of keeping all of their reading materials in a central place, plans for keeping reading records, the need for a new report card, the characteristics of a good parent-teacher conference, and the way they would go about informing the parents and children about their plans to "nongrade." They copied a leaflet sent home by another school to inform parents about the change. They also made plans to invite the parents to a special PTA meeting the week after the "nongrading" had taken place, in order to tell them what had happened. Professor Seward agreed to come to their meeting to help break the news.

Monday, August 31st, was the first day of school. When the children came to the assembly that morning, Mrs. Jones told all of those who would have been in grades one, two, and three that they would no longer have signs on their classroom doors saying what grade they were in, but would be grouped in classes with boys and girls with whom they could work best. She told them that they would do as much work as they could in one year and continue from that point the next fall. She also told them that they might be in classes with children who had been in other grades the previous year. They were assigned to Mrs. Conrad's group, Miss Evans' group, Miss Miller's group, Miss Dunn's group, Miss Brown's group, and Miss Sullivan's group. Mrs. Jones had some difficulty convincing several children that they had not failed even though they were placed with the teacher they had had the previous year. Several others seemed disturbed by the fact that the children they were grouped with were children who had been in a grade below them the previous year.

That afternoon a notice of the PTA meeting to be held on the afternoon of September 9th was sent home with each child. With the notice went the leaflet which had been copied and reproduced. (See Figure 1.)

Early on the morning of the second day of school, Mary Thomas' mother came to see Mrs. Jones to find out "just what the score was." She said Mary had come home very upset because she had been separated from Priscilla Bowen, her best friend, with whom she had started kindergarten. Mrs. Jones attempted to explain the operations of a nongraded primary school as best she could. Mrs. Thomas left threatening to go to the central office to have Mary transferred to the school in the next district.

On the afternoon of September 9, 1959, the special meeting of the PTA was held in the school auditorium. Mrs. Jones said that, considering that many of the mothers worked, she was pleased with the attendance. Privately she estimated that the people in her school

FIGURE 1.

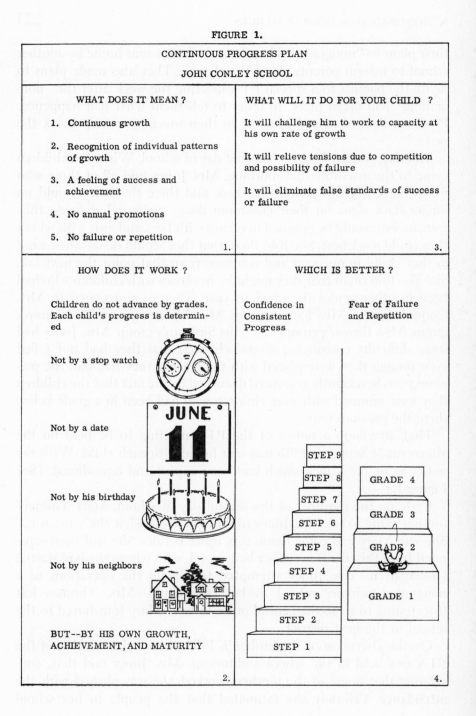

CONTINUOUS PROGRESS PLAN

JOHN CONLEY SCHOOL

WHAT DOES IT MEAN ?

1. Continuous growth

2. Recognition of individual patterns of growth

3. A feeling of success and achievement

4. No annual promotions

5. No failure or repetition

1.

WHAT WILL IT DO FOR YOUR CHILD ?

It will challenge him to work to capacity at his own rate of growth

It will relieve tensions due to competition and possibility of failure

It will eliminate false standards of success or failure

3.

HOW DOES IT WORK ?

Children do not advance by grades. Each child's progress is determined

Not by a stop watch

Not by a date

JUNE 11

Not by his birthday

Not by his neighbors

BUT--BY HIS OWN GROWTH, ACHIEVEMENT, AND MATURITY

2.

WHICH IS BETTER ?

Confidence in Consistent Progress

Fear of Failure and Repetition

STEP 9
STEP 8
STEP 7
STEP 6
STEP 5
STEP 4
STEP 3
STEP 2
STEP 1

GRADE 4
GRADE 3
GRADE 2
GRADE 1

4.

community fell in categories 5, 6, and 7 on Warner's seven-point parental occupation scale.[3] (See Table III.)

Table III

Representative Occupations from Warner's Scale

Rating	Occupation
1	Lawyers, doctors, dentists, high school superintendents, engineers, architects, chemists, regional managers of large industries
2	High school teachers, trained nurses, chiropractors, accountants, insurance salesmen, newspaper editors, postmasters, large farm owners
3	Grade school teachers, optometrists, auto salesmen, contractors, bank clerks, secretaries to executives, social workers, postal clerks
4	Stenographers, bookkeepers, rural mail clerks, railroad ticket agents, sales people in stores, dry cleaners, factory foremen, watchmakers who own business
5	Beauty operators, dime store clerks, carpenters, plumbers, barbers, firemen, policemen, tenant farmers
6	Moulders, semi-skilled workers, baggage men, taxi or truck drivers, gas station attendants, waitresses, small tenant farmers
7	Heavy laborers, migrant workers, odd-job men, miners, janitors, scrub-women, newsboys, migrant farm laborers

The president of the PTA turned the meeting over to Mrs. Jones, who in turn introduced Professor Seward. The notes for Professor Seward's talk follow:

Mrs. Jones has asked me to talk to you about the nongraded school because I taught in one for eight years. The nongraded school is not a new idea. The system where I taught began its first nongraded school in 1942 because we were becoming more and more aware of the part a child's maturity plays in his learning and living. We found that the nongraded primary school was a means of making functional a philosophy of child growth and development that we had had for some time. It was a way of adjusting our teaching and administrative procedures to meet the differing social, mental, physical, and emotional growth of children.

We knew that children differ widely in their ability to learn. We also knew that no two children develop abilities at the same time or at the same rate. The nongraded school made it possible for teachers to guide each child along the learning road at a time and rate best suited to him. Our basic philosophy was that we accept each child

---

[3] W. Lloyd Warner, *et al.*, *Social Class in America* (New York: American Book Company, Stratford Press, 1949), pp. 140–141.

where he was and move him along as fast as his capacity to learn would permit. In the nongraded school each teacher tried to begin where each child was and endeavored to take him as far as he was able to go in one year's time. Teaching was adjusted to the individual growth pattern of each child. When competing with his own ability, the child had a feeling of satisfaction and achievement rather than one of frustation because of a so-called poor performance. Each child proceeded according to his own ability. All his movement was forward. He was never failed or made to repeat a grade. However, some children did require more than three years to complete the nongraded primary grades if their rate of learning was slower or their school attendance had been interrupted by illness or by moving from school to school.

The nongraded school accepted and respected all children—tall and short, fat and thin, shy and aggressive, flighty and well adjusted. It recognized individual patterns of growth. It provided for academic, physical, social and emotional differences. It had no annual promotion—only from kindergarten to primary school and from primary school to fourth grade. Each child's progress was determined not by a stop watch, not by a date, not by a birthdate, not by a neighbor, but by his own growth, achievement, and maturity. It was often advisable to shift some children for social or academic reasons at the close of a semester so that the learning range within a class would not become too wide. Growth in learning and in social and personal development was noted on a progress card. Parents were able through these records and conferences with teachers to follow the achievement of their child.

At this point Mrs. Thomas interrupted Professor Seward, calling out, "But what happens at the end of three years? I can't see the difference between failing a grade and staying in the nongraded school four years."

Professor Seward used the blackboard as she tried to answer the question. She said that when a child repeated a grade he would have an overlapping in his program. In the nongraded plan a child's program might be prolonged, but there were greater possibilities of avoiding unnecessary gaps and overlaps.

Before Mrs. Thomas reacted to Professor Seward's explanation, another mother interjected, "I'd like to ask a question, too. What if we move to Greenfield School which still follows the graded plan?"

"A complete record of your child's progress would accompany him to Greenfield School. Mrs. Jones would write a letter recommending what would be the most appropriate placement."

"Well," Mrs. Thomas said, "I don't think we should let our children become guinea pigs for some 'progressive' experiment."

Mrs. Jones took over the meeting and recognized other mothers from the floor. Six mothers rose to express their opinions and commended the staff for their effort to establish a plan that they felt would benefit their children. Then Miss Sullivan, one of the primary teachers, expressed her gratitude and the gratitude of the other staff members for the mothers' expression of confidence in the staff's attempt to plan for improving the educational program of their children.

Mrs. Jones reported that during the following week, much to her surprise, Mrs. Thomas came to her office and said that she had been talking about this nongraded plan with her husband, and that maybe it was not a bad idea. Mary liked her new teacher, she said, and they had decided that she should stay at Conley.

Since the beginning of the school year the enrollment at John Conley had warranted the addition of another teacher. In the middle of October Miss Hayes was added to the staff. She was given a class made up of the least advanced of one group and the most advanced of another.

At the beginning of November Mrs. Conrad asked Mrs. Jones' permission to invite Professor Seward to meet with the group, for the purpose of developing a reading record form. With the consultant's help the teachers examined samples from ten other schools and developed their own form. It included a check list of every book in use in the nongraded block, listed by publisher and by reading level. Books from fourteen publishers were included, classified at ten reading levels, from preprimers to hard third readers and books for independent reading.

Before the first parent conferences in November, the primary staff had developed a report card which met with the approval of Mrs. Jones and of Mr. White, the Area Superintendent. A copy is given in Figure 2. This report card was used as the basis for the conferences. On the day of the conferences children were dismissed 50 minutes early. Each conference lasted one half hour.

The agenda of the conferences included examination of samples of work and discussion of work habits and attitudes, social development,

FIGURE 2

PRIMARY SCHOOL PROGRESS REPORT
JOHN CONLEY SCHOOL, AREA 10

To the Parents:

This report is our evaluation of the progress of your child in his school subjects and in the development of those traits and qualities that make good citizens.

We suggest that you examine it carefully so that you may be aware of the growth and development of your child as he continues his work throughout the year.

Individual growth is the principal basis for evaluating the work of your child rather than a comparison with the achievement of other members of the class. Your concern should be "Is my child doing the best that he can?"

The principal and teacher will be pleased to confer with you concerning the progress of your child. If you desire a conference with the teacher, it should be scheduled after school to avoid interruption of class work.

Dr. Wm. S. White
Area 10
Superintendent

	REPORT PERIOD			
	2		4	

HEALTH HABITS
Adequate sleep
Good posture
Practices habits of cleanliness
Practices good safety habits

PERSONAL DEVELOPMENT
Plays well with others
Respects rights of others
Observes rules and regulations
Shows growth in self-control
Accepts responsibility

WORK HABITS AND ATTITUDES
Follows directions
Completes work begun
Works well independently
Works well with others
Uses material carefully

SCHOOL ATTENDANCE

Absence or tardiness, for however short a time, interferes with school progress.

REPORT PERIOD	1	2	3	4	TOTAL
Days Present					
Days Absent					
Times Tardy					

FIGURE 2 (Continued)

NAME _____

Year above Kindergarten

1   2   3   4

TEACHER'S COMMENTS

1. Parent-Teacher Conferences

2. _____

3. Parent-Teacher Conferences

4. _____

Parents', Comments or Suggestions

First Report - Conference

Second Report

Signature of Parent

Third Report - Conference

Fourth Report

Date _____

Next year, 19___, 19___,

will be in _____

Teacher's Signature _____

Principal _____

229

FIGURE 2 (Continued)

READING PROGRESS RECORD

LEVEL   BEGINNING DATE

1. Reading Readiness _____
2. Chart Reading _____
3. Pre-Primer _____
4. Primer _____
5. Supplementary Primer _____
6. First Reader _____
7. Supplementary First _____
8. Second Reader _____
9. Supplementary Second _____
10. Third Reader _____
11. Supplementary Third Reader _____
12. Independent Reading _____

YOUR CHILD CAN BE COMMENDED FOR:

2. _____
4. _____

GROWTH IN LEARNING AND SKILLS

REPORT PERIOD   2   4

Explanation of marks

A-Outstanding
B-Satisfactory
C-Needs to improve
D-Unsatisfactory

ORAL EXPRESSION
Takes part in conversation
Is a good listener
Expresses ideas clearly

SPELLING
Spells correctly words presented in the lesson
Spells correctly words in written work

HANDWRITING
Forms letters correctly
Spaces well

READING
Shows readiness for reading
Reads with understanding
Is acquiring needed reading skills
Reads independently for pleasure
Reads independently for information

ARITHMETIC
Understands the meaning of numbers
Is learning number facts
Solves simple problems

230

and progress in skills. The seven teachers in the nongraded primary block reported that during the first conference period no parent expressed regret because the school had been "nongraded." One expressed preference for a conference. "I find out so much more about John's progress than when I get a report card." All parents who conferred with Mrs. Conrad seemed interested in the books being used, and she reported that they asked questions indicating keen interest in the success of the nongraded school.

Twice a month during the year the teachers in the nongraded primary unit met with Mrs. Jones to discuss current grouping and ways to improve it. The room in which the children read was considered their homeroom. But, agreeing that slow progress in one area of the curriculum did not necessarily mean slow progress in other areas, for arithmetic the staff shifted children from room to room, so that they could work with comparable groups.

Before the second series of parent-teacher conferences at the end of March, the nongraded primary teachers had a special meeting to discuss these conferences. Mrs. Conrad had borrowed materials from the central curriculum library, including books, bulletins, pamphlets, and magazines. She acted as chairman and led the discussion. She listed the teachers' suggestions on the board. The group agreed that it was important to have the physical setup "just right." If the conference was to supplement or take the place of a report card, they would have to evaluate pupil progress using the same categories as the report card. If the child's work had not been as good as it could be, it was important to conclude the conference on a hopeful note with practical suggestions as to how the child could be helped.

By April the teachers were beginning to talk about the grouping of pupils for the fall of 1960. They expressed dread of parental repercussions likely to follow when the programs of at least a dozen of the children were extended over four years rather than three. They seemed distressed that Mrs. Jones so seldom came to their meetings and left most of the responsibility of reorganization to Mrs. Conrad, especially since Mrs. Conrad was going to have a child and would not be returning in the fall. On the other hand, they expressed pleasure at the absence of pressure for the promotion of children who under their graded system would have failed because they had not completed a reading program based on a state-adopted series. In general, they expressed satisfaction with the experiment. Indeed, they had told friends on other school staffs about their nongraded school, who in turn had expressed a desire to try it out. Three such interested people had telephoned Professor Seward about it.

Before school opened in September, 1960, Mrs. Jones enlisted the assistance of Miss Fox, a former kindergarten teacher who had recently been appointed supervisor for the area. She asked Miss Fox to help the primary teachers to group the primary children for the fall. Miss Fox borrowed Mrs. Jones' materials about the nongraded school. She worked with the staff the week before school opened and expressed a great deal of interest in continuing the plan and initiating it in other schools in the area.

Plans were laid for introducing the nongraded scheme in grades four to six, starting immediately with all those pupils who had just left the nongraded primary school.

Mrs. Jones had many telephone calls from other school officials in the city, inquiring about the success of the nongraded plan. On September 22, 1960, at the request of five schools in her area and with the permission of her Area Superintendent, Mrs. Howard, an Area Supervisor, made plans for "nongrading" the primary grades in five schools beginning in September, 1961. Some observers attributed the growing interest in the scheme to a public announcement that state funds were to be made available to assist schools in moving in this direction.

SELECTED READINGS

Benne, Kenneth D., and Bozidar Muntyan, eds., *Human Relations in Curriculum Change: Selected Readings with Especial Emphasis on Group Development*. New York: The Dryden Press, 1951.

Davis, Allison, *Social-Class Influences Upon Learning*, the Inglis Lecture for 1948, Harvard University. Cambridge, Massachusetts: Harvard University Press, 1948.

Goodlad, John I., and Robert H. Anderson, *The Nongraded Elementary School*. New York: Harcourt, Brace and Company, 1959.

Mackenzie, Gordon N., and Stephen M. Corey, *Instructional Leadership*. New York: Teachers College, Columbia University, Bureau of Publications, 1954.

Stendler, Celia Burns, *Children of Brasstown*. Urbana: Bureau of Research and Service of the College of Education, University of Illinois, 1949.

A Decade
of Peaceful
Change

CASE 14

In September, 1946, Mr. Swiller, Assistant Principal of the Burgoyne Junior-Senior High School, asked Mrs. Edith Polls to develop a course outline for seventh grade social studies.

Burgoyne Junior-Senior High School was situated in a predominantly residential area which was socio-economically above average. There were no industries in the school district. Financial support for the schools came largely through property taxes from home owners. The majority of the taxpayers were college graduates engaged in business or professional pursuits in a nearby city. They had taken great pride and interest in their schools, and most were able to provide, and apparently desired, college education for their children. The excellent reputation of the schools had been prominent among reasons given by newcomers for moving into the area. Up until 1954 the taxpayers had never defeated a bond issue. In that year a bond issue for a new school was defeated. However, the opposition had questioned not the need for the building, but only its proposed size. A few months later, with some modification in the proposed size of the new school, the plans and the bond issue were approved by a two-to-one majority.

Two unincorporated communities, Faysville and Northrup, maintained their own six-year elementary schools. In 1931 the communities

233

had formed a consolidated high school district for grades seven through twelve and erected a high school building near the common border of the two elementary school districts. Additions had been constructed in 1937, and again in 1951. Voters in each community elected a three-member board of education for the elementary schools. The two boards together formed a six-member consolidated high school board of education.

There had been little friction in school board affairs. Although it might be expected that when the two boards united to form the consolidated high school board, local pride and jealousy would have affected school matters adversely, such was not the case. This can probably be attributed to the fact that the two districts were in unincorporated villages that already looked to the township for street and sewer facilities, police service, and other aspects of government. Because of the size of the communities and their homogeneity no factions had arisen—no town group versus a rural group, or old residents versus new residents. (There were few old residents in comparison to the more recent settlers.) The men and women who served on the board had no political axes to grind. Interested in good schools, most served long tenures on the board. That there were minor irritations and rumblings no one would deny, but these never reached the stage of upsetting the entire community or disrupting the educational program.

The Supervising Principal always exercised his leadership role. The members of the school board seemed to respect him; they consulted with him rather than dictating to him. Since 1931 the school district, its board, and the Principal had, in a sense, grown up together. At annual district meetings it was not uncommon for taxpayers to propose budget increases. As of 1958, although tax burdens had grown, new residents had moved into the district, and teachers' salaries had lagged, still there had been little friction.

Burgoyne prided itself on being a community school long before that term gained popularity in educational circles. Parents visited the schools, attended the school activities, and were well informed. As the school district population increased, every attempt was made to keep newcomers informed about the schools through brochures, the PTA, and so on. The Consolidated High School Parent Teachers Association was active, and its meetings were well attended. Husband and wife teams served as officers, thus assuring male attendance and leadership. It is significant that the Supervising Principal, the President of the Board of Education, and a past PTA president had held high state offices in their respective groups.

There were slightly over 900 students enrolled in the six grades of Burgoyne Junior-Senior High School in 1945. There were thirty-eight teachers who—working in a wealthy community—were better paid than the teachers in neighboring districts. The Board of Education required of applicants for teaching positions a minimum of three years of previous successful teaching.

PERSONNEL INVOLVED

Edith Polls. Mrs. Polls had a Bachelor of Science degree from a teachers college. She was certified by the State Department of Education to teach junior high school English, social studies, and elementary grades. Before joining the faculty of Burgoyne in 1931, she had taught self-contained elementary grades for nine years. Mrs. Polls had been at Faysville's elementary school when the consolidated high school district was organized, and had elected to join its faculty as a seventh grade social studies teacher. She married in 1938 and, because of a board ruling against the employment of married women teachers, was compelled to resign her position. In 1944, when the Board rescinded the regulation, Mrs. Polls returned to Burgoyne Junior-Senior High School. While not choosing to take graduate courses, she managed to keep abreast of education curriculum and methods through wide professional reading.

Mrs. Polls was regarded as a good teacher and was highly respected by parents, faculty, administration, and the Board of Education. While shunning the limelight, she was forceful in following her convictions. She was one of the few teachers remaining who, together with the Supervising Principal, had opened the doors of Burgoyne Junior-Senior High School in 1931.

Peter Wickar. Peter Wickar had been the first principal of Burgoyne. He had previously taught English and been a high school principal in another state. He had received his Bachelor of Arts degree with a major in English from a liberal arts college and his Master of Arts degree in school administration from a university. When the school enrollment increased following World War II, a Junior High

School Principal was named, Mr. Swiller was named Senior High School Principal, and Peter Wickar was promoted to Supervising Principal.

Jerome Swiller. The Assistant Principal of Burgoyne at the time the curriculum change was instituted was Mr. Jerome Swiller. He had received his Bachelor of Arts degree with a major in history from a liberal arts college. He had later attended a university and earned an M. S. degree in school administration. After three years of teaching history in a city school system, Mr. Swiller had joined the Burgoyne faculty in 1931. A few years later he had been made head of the social studies department, and in 1942 he was promoted to Assistant Principal.

Evans Maxer. Evans Maxer, head of the social studies department, was designated Junior High School Principal by the Board of Education in 1951. He held a Bachelor of Science degree with a major in junior high school social studies and a minor in English. Later, he earned a Master of Arts degree with a major in history from a university. Mr. Maxer had taught a self-contained classroom in a small, semi-rural community for two years, and then taught departmentalized social studies in a junior high school. Joining the Burgoyne staff in 1936, he taught junior high school social studies. In 1939, he began teaching American history in the senior high school grades at Burgoyne, and in 1942, upon the promotion of Mr. Swiller to Assistant Principal, he became department head.

Evart Roose. The fifth person who had a major role in the later stages of the curriculum change was Evart Roose. Mr. Roose had received his Bachelor of Arts degree from a liberal arts college and his Master of Arts degree from a teachers college. His major fields had been English and Speech, with a minor in history. After five years' experience as a core teacher in a neighboring state, he came to Burgoyne Junior-Senior High School in 1953.

*   *   *   *   *

In 1946 Mrs. Polls was given the task of preparing a course of study for seventh grade social studies at Burgoyne. Mr. Wickar and Mr. Swiller requested that the course of study be completed within one year and be based upon the State Education Department's recommended content of state history, government, and geography. Mrs.

Polls was to adapt the State Education Department's suggested syllabi to the Burgoyne community and students, but she was to go beyond the State Department's suggestions and provide an enriched course of study. Projected enrollments indicated there would be additional sections of seventh graders in the near future, and a basic outline was deemed essential for all teachers.

Mrs. Polls reported that she was having difficulty in finding sufficient time to cover the literature relating to the state, and she requested that she be given one seventh grade English class during the year she would be developing the course outline. Permission was granted; she was given the same section for English and social studies, though not in consecutive periods. Although strict subject departmentalization was the school's curriculum pattern, she endeavored, as the year went on, to achieve some continuity between her pupils' work in English and their work in social studies. She said that she had little success because of the separation of the two periods.

During this year Mrs. Polls wrote a course outline which included units on the following topics:

> Indians
> Exploration and colonization by Europeans
> The state during the revolution
> Transportation
> Regions of the state
> State government
> The local community

At the same time, she searched libraries and book company publications for literature related to these units. From her own ideas and interests she developed an outline for correlation between social studies and literature. When she found a wealth of short stories, poems, and novels dealing with various phases of state history, she found it impossible to use these materials within the departmentalized social studies curriculum. Therefore, for the following year she asked Mr. Wickar for a two-period block of time, during which she would be responsible for teaching English and social studies to one group of students. The administration agreed to her petition, and during the school year 1947–48 she was scheduled for English and social studies in consecutive periods.

To reiterate, the ideas for the new program were her own. They had grown out of her interest in relating literature to social studies and her concern about the lack of continuity when other classes intervened between the time she met her group for social studies and the time she met them for English. Coincidentally, through her professional reading, she became aware of developments along similar lines in other states, particularly Michigan, where Unified Studies programs were coming into their own.

In September, 1947, when Mrs. Polls started the school's first block-of-time class, her pilot group consisted of thirty-four seventh-grade boys and girls. All other seventh graders in the school were scheduled for departmentalized classes.

No attempt was made to test the experiment. During the year neither Mr. Wickar nor Mr. Swiller visited the classroom to observe the program. Direct supervision at Burgoyne was considered unnecessary, since only experienced teachers of proven mettle were employed. The course outline was in the hands of the administrators and was scrutinized by them. They had talked with Mrs. Polls at different times and questioned her concerning the program.

Yet because the group took the same departmental examinations as the rest of the seventh graders, some comparison could be made. The children in Mrs. Polls' group did "better" on both the social studies and the English tests. The same was true at mid-year in 1947–48, the second year of the arrangement.

Mr. Wickar expressed great faith in his teachers. When Mrs. Polls stated she liked having the same group of children for seventh grade social studies and English, he seemed to accept the plan without reservation. Through his attendance at professional meetings and through literature in the field of education, he kept abreast of curriculum trends. Sensing a similarity between Mrs. Polls' efforts and the national movement in core curriculum, he indicated that he saw this as another pioneer venture in his school, which already was earning a reputation as a leader in new developments and scholarship. He also indicated that he believed the program to be beneficial.

For the school year 1948–49 Mr. Wickar decided upon the extension of the block-of-time program to all three seventh-grade classes and all three eighth-grade classes.

Presenting the new program to the school board posed no problem. The members were well aware of Mrs. Polls' ability as a teacher and her reputation among the parents. Most of them had known her personally for several years. The program was mentioned as an innovation which might well serve to ease the transition from the elementary school to the junior high school. With stress on the richer program in literature of the state, time for research by the children, and the possibility of improved spelling as well as greater opportunity for writing, the Board viewed the block-of-time program as educationally sound. They approved Mr. Wickar's recommendation that the program be extended to all seventh and eighth grades.

While taking courses at a midwestern university, Mr. Swiller had come to know a Professor Johnson, who had helped several schools in Michigan develop Unified Studies programs. Mrs. Polls knew of Johnson through some of the articles he had written concerning the programs. Mrs. Polls and Mr. Swiller approached Mr. Wickar with the suggestion that Johnson be invited to visit Burgoyne to assist the staff in planning their program. Some of the faculty had indicated doubts about the new curriculum plan, which they would have to follow next fall. Mr. Wickar promptly agreed. At its regular meeting in January, 1948, the Board of Education unanimously approved the expenditure of seven hundred dollars for the purpose and the plan which accompanied it.

Professor Johnson agreed to spend the week of February 16 at Burgoyne Junior-Senior High School. Two seventh-grade teachers and three eighth-grade teachers were released from classes during the entire week, and substitutes were hired to conduct their classes. One member of the Board of Education and representatives of the PTA and the community met with the teachers and the professor. In addition, Mr. Swiller attended most of the sessions, while Mr. Wickar attended when his busy schedule permitted. In all, twenty persons met in a kind of seminar to question, debate, propose, and compromise. According to Mr. Swiller, the week's workshop was one of the most stimulating educational experiences he had ever had. On Monday several of the teachers were doubtful about the program. By Friday they were anxious to begin the program the following week. "The only bad feature of the workshop," according to Mr. Swiller, "was its timing. We should have held it in September just before the opening of school. Then our teachers could have gone directly into the classroom and tried their ideas."

To compensate for the time-lag, the Board of Education approved the use of funds from "administrative travel" to finance a three-day trip to observe Unified Studies classes in Middletown, Michigan. Mrs. Polls, Mr. Maxer, and two eighth-grade teachers visited Middletown in late September, 1948. Each of the teachers observed several seventh- and eighth-grade Unified Studies classes in different schools. They talked with many teachers and attended a Unified Studies faculty meeting. In addition, they met with the curriculum co-ordinator. The group discovered a strong resemblance between Mrs. Polls' program and the Unified Studies program in Middletown. It was agreed, however, that Michigan was doing more with resource units, whereas Burgoyne was primarily following a course of study.

Before returning to Burgoyne, the group stopped by at Professor Johnson's institution for further discussion of programs with him.

By September the six teachers at Burgoyne who were scheduled to take part in the new program were reported "in agreement about the advantages of the new approach." They also agreed, because of the basic similarity between their plan and the Michigan one, to follow Mrs. Polls' suggestion that they give the block-of-time classes at Burgoyne the name "Unified Program."

The community was informed about the new program through many channels. The PTA and community leaders who attended the February workshop were resource people for various lay groups. At "parent-go-to-school nights" the Unified Program teachers outlined the new curriculum, explained its advantages, and answered questions raised by parents. Similarly, sixth-grade parents meeting in their elementary schools were given the opportunity to discuss the program and ask questions. During the spring term, sixth-grade classes visited Burgoyne and attended classes as an orientation to the school and curriculum.

From one teacher's experiment, to the administrative decision to adopt throughout the seventh and eighth grades, to the Board approval and the parents' acceptance, the change came about smoothly with no uproars or heat of controversy.

In 1951–52 the junior high school faculty devoted many meetings to the development of a statement of a common philosophy and goals for the whole school and for the various curricular offerings. This statement had a threefold use. First, it helped to crystalize the thinking of the faculty and resulted in some basic agreements. Second, it served to communicate to the Board of Education the feelings of the faculty concerning junior high school education at Burgoyne. (The document was well received by the Board.) Third, the report, in synopsis form, was distributed to parents and helped to explain the program at Burgoyne. It was further used as the basis for parent meetings.

* * * * *

In 1951 a second phase of curriculum change began. In that year a principal for grades seven, eight, and nine was appointed, Mr. Maxer becoming the first junior high school principal at Burgoyne.

Mr. Maxer was an enthusiastic supporter of the Unified Program. He now gave much-needed leadership to the program, and he succeeded in getting one English teacher to experiment with a Unified Program in a ninth-grade class. On the basis of the enthusiasm of this teacher, another section was added in 1953.

The year 1953 also marked the addition of Mr. Roose to the faculty. Mr. Roose had been a core teacher in a neighboring state, and Mr. Maxer explained his appointment by saying that new blood would benefit the now well-established Unified Program. Mr. Roose's experience had been largely with the form of core defined by Grace Wright as "Type C." [1] In this type of core, teachers working together develop "resource units" whose content is chiefly built around problems of youth and of society. Each core class makes selections from among these pre-planned units and plans the further development of these units with its teacher.

Mr. Roose followed the Unified Program outline developed by Mrs. Polls for the seventh grade. As he became familiar with the school, the community, and his students, he experimented with teacher-pupil-planned units which seemed to be of interest to his classes even though the units were not part of the Unified Program. Through conversations with other seventh-grade Unified Program teachers, he kept them informed concerning progress of his classes. Some of them accepted his friendly offer to have teachers visit his classes to observe the program in action. Students from his classes wrote to other Unified Program classes to invite them to visit. Through such inter-class visitation ideas were exchanged, and one other teacher and his classes experimented with interest units.

At faculty meetings Mr. Roose challenged the Unified Program at

---

[1] Grace S. Wright, *Core Curriculum Development: Problems and Practice.* United States Office of Education, Bulletin 1952, No. 5, p. 8.

Burgoyne. He did this in what colleagues described as "a professional way," by asking relevant questions and making suggestions. One of these suggestions concerned attendance at a Michigan State Core Conference. Mr. Maxer seemed to like the suggestion and secured financial support from the Board for such a venture. It was a policy of the school board to encourage attendance at conferences, and there was no opposition to the trip.

In the fall of 1953 three seventh-grade Unified Program teachers, including Mr. Roose, attended the Michigan State Core Conference. Once again Michigan made a contribution to the Unified Program at Burgoyne. This time it was the informal atmosphere at the conference as well as the program which made the contribution. The three Burgoyne teachers recognized the diversity of programs represented at the Michigan conference. The majority of teachers were working with Unified Studies programs, but a few represented schools where more advanced forms of the core were in operation. The three out-of-state visitors were also impressed by the stress which the teachers in Michigan placed on resource units.

Returning to Burgoyne, the three teachers reported to the junior high school faculty. Mr. Roose suggested that Burgoyne's faculty begin to develop resource units. Mr. Maxer agreed and further suggested a conference with neighboring schools where block-of-time programs also existed. In March, 1954, eighteen teachers from several schools in the area assembled at a YMCA camp to spend the weekend discussing the future development of the Unified Program.

After much discussion led by Maxer, Roose, and the two other Burgoyne teachers who had attended the Michigan conference, the representatives of three schools agreed that the programs in their schools should now progress toward a "Type C" core. Each of them agreed to develop one resource unit with his respective faculty group. The resource units were then to be exchanged. It was further agreed that such an informal conference was a definite aid in getting to know teachers from other schools. The sharing of common problems had proved stimulating, they said, and they enthusiastically voted for a similar conference the following year, to be on a larger scale and with a planned program.

While the representatives from Burgoyne were at the Michigan conference, they had learned of the first national core conference, which had been held at Morgantown, West Virginia. The second national core conference was to be held in Michigan in the fall of 1954. The

Board of Education of Burgoyne Junior-Senior High School voted the necessary money to send a group of teachers to this meeting. Mr. Maxer, Mr. Roose, and two seventh-grade teachers who had attended the Michigan conference, one eighth-grade teacher, and one ninth-grade teacher constituted the Burgoyne delegation to the second national core conference. There were evidences that Burgoyne was coming to be recognized nationally.

In subsequent years few changes were made in Burgoyne's Unified Program, except that in 1955 it was extended to all ninth grades.

Meanwhile, the rapid growth of the suburbs of Faysville and Northrup necessitated a new building. Voters of the Consolidated High School district approved a 1200-pupil junior high school building in 1954. During 1954–55 Mr. Maxer and the faculty were occupied in making plans for the new school. The Unified Program teachers were requested to submit their ideas for the type of classroom best suited for core. Most of their major suggestions were included in the final plans. In November, 1955, grades seven, eight, and nine moved from Burgoyne Junior-Senior High School into the new junior high building, leaving the older building for grades ten, eleven, and twelve.

The practice was adopted of having an informal evaluation mailed to parents twice a year. These evaluations were planned each semester by the students and teachers in the Unified Program classes. The aim was to have pupils evaluate their own progress in achieving the yearly goals established by their classes.

To prepare students and parents for the Unified Program, various procedures were used. Brochures prepared by Mrs. Polls and her first classes were duplicated and sent to parents to help explain the Unified Program.

Regional core conferences continued. Within three years there was a chairman of the Unified Program at Burgoyne Junior High School, which now had twenty Unified Studies teachers. However, no formal inservice education program existed. Parent-school relations continued to be "most cooperative." As part of the adult education program of parent education, a team of faculty members regularly visited each of the four elementary schools to orient parents of sixth-graders to the junior high school. Another facet of this program was a series of meetings for parents of seventh-graders, parents of eighth-graders, and parents of ninth-graders. These were in addition to the regular "parent-go-to-school nights."

The practice was adopted of having every sixth-grade class, on a rotating basis, spend one day in the spring at the junior high school. Each sixth-grader was assigned a guide and followed him through a schedule of classes. The guide was a seventh-grader who had attended the same elementary school as the visitor. These tours were timed to occur just prior to the sixth-grade parent meetings, so that there would be "dinner-table correlation."

A monthly report was sent to all parents of junior high school students. This report contained a calendar of events, news items of school interest, and a feature article. The latter might be a report of some significant occurrences in a classroom, a discussion of reading, or a discussion of any of the curricular and co-curricular offerings of the school.

During the school year 1956–57, the Board of Education of the Central High School District examined all curricular areas in the junior and senior divisions. Among other things the Board reported that it was favorably impressed with the Unified Program.

SELECTED READINGS

Beene, Kenneth D., and Bozidar Muntyan, *Human Relations in Curriculum Change: Selected Readings with Especial Emphasis on Group Development*. New York: The Dryden Press, 1951.

Caswell, Hollis L., and Associates, *Curriculum Improvement in Public School Systems*. New York: Teachers College, Columbia University, Bureau of Publications, 1950.

Coch, Lester, and John R. P. French, Jr., "Overcoming Resistance to Change" in Eleanor E. Maccoby et al., eds., *Readings in Social Psychology*, rev. ed. New York: Henry Holt and Company, 1958. Pp. 233–250.

Lewin, Kurt, "Group Decision and Social Change" in Eleanor E. Maccoby et al., eds., *Readings in Social Psychology*, rev. ed. New York: Henry Holt and Company, 1958. Pp. 197–211.

Seeley, John R., et al., *Crestwood Heights: A Study of the Culture of Suburban Life*. New York: Basic Books, 1956.

Sharp, George, *Curriculum Development as Re-education of the Teacher*. New York: Teachers College, Columbia University, Bureau of Publications, 1951.

United States Department of Health, Education, and Welfare, United States Office of Education, *Bulletin* 1952, No. 5, "Core Curriculum Development: Problems and Practices," by Grace S. Wright.

Whyte, William H., Jr., *The Organization Man*. New York: Simon and Schuster, 1956. Ch. 28.

Plato Comes and Goes in Lochton

CASE 15

For fifteen years there had been little change in the program of studies at Lochton High School. Although sections had been added to certain courses, and the facilities of the school had been expanded, no new courses had been offered in that time. The enrollment at the school had slowly been expanding. In the course of the school year 1953–1954, therefore, the faculty of Lochton High School and a number of interested parents separately began informal discussions about the possibility of expanding the curriculum.

In the fall of 1953 such discussion usually took the form of statements that "something ought to be done." Few concrete proposals were made. However, by the spring of 1954 a few of the more interested faculty members had developed specific proposals for new courses. One of the English teachers, who also sponsored the school newspaper, outlined a journalism course for the 11th and 12th grades, with the production of the newspaper to be a continuing laboratory project. The industrial arts teacher proposed an automobile shop course, with a prerequisite of one year of general shop. The science teacher proposed a general, non-vocational course in agriculture, to be open to all students. By April, 1954, these courses had been submitted to and approved by the Principal for inclusion in the curriculum during the next school year.

245

In order to make possible these additions to the curriculum, the schedules of the teachers involved were readjusted, and those afternoon sections of other courses which had had small enrollments during the years were dropped. For example, an afternoon general shop class with an enrollment of six was replaced by the automobile shop class.

The student enrollment in the new courses that fall averaged twenty. No sooner had these courses become part of the operating curriculum in the fall of 1954 than it appeared that, however badly needed they had been, there was a place for still another course or other courses. Attention was directed, for example, to the case of a 9th grade girl who had received a score of grade 15.5 on a total achievement test battery. (She was to achieve similarly highly over a 3-year period, although, interestingly enough, over the same period her IQ as measured by the California Test of Mental Maturity would deviate very little from 108.) For some time this situation had been commented upon by the social studies teacher, the journalism teacher, and the industrial arts teacher. It was reported that a number of parents, too, had made some private comments about it to the teachers and to the Principal.

At a fall faculty meeting the situation was discussed, but no action was taken. Shortly afterward, however, the social studies teacher proposed to the Principal that an introductory course in philosophy be offered the following year. The Principal, withholding comment at the time, suggested that the proposal be discussed in November at the next faculty meeting. This was done.

The reactions of the faculty and the administration were at first mixed. Although indicating that he was fascinated with the idea, the mathematics teacher noted that because of the small size of most of the classes in the school, and because of the intimate association which the teachers had with their students, it was very likely that the needs of the able students were already being met. Others raised the question whether a philosophy course was needed in a community such as Lochton. One teacher said, "Lochton is a small town, a rural town. Wouldn't a course that was practical be of greater value here?"

The main concerns of the Principal seemed to be administrative. He did not know, he said, whether State University would accept such a course for college entrance credit. Not only college admissions but also continued state accreditation for the school would depend upon such approval. He also wondered, he said, who would teach the course, and when in the day it would be taught.

Nonetheless, in March, 1955, he asked the social studies teacher to submit a prospectus for the course, indicating the time when it might be given, the proposed teacher, the kind of students who might take the course, and the materials and methods to be used. In April the teacher made the following suggestions:

1. The proposed philosophy course could be given daily during the fourth period, the one which was now devoted entirely to such non-academic courses as physical education, shop, and band. This would avoid any possible conflict with those regularly scheduled subjects which were required for graduation.

2. The social studies teacher himself would teach the course because of his stated interest in it and because he had the fourth period free.

3. Students would be selected from the senior class. From those who indicated interest, no more than ten would be chosen on the basis of aptitude and achievement test scores.

4. Two text books would be used in the course. The first would be Will Durant's *The Story of Philosophy*, which the students would be required to buy in a paper-back edition. The second text, to be provided by the district, would be a book of essays edited by Lawrence and Weinberg, *Readings for Today*.

5. The method of the course would be primarily conversational. The class was to be small, and this method would give each student maximum participation.

Lochton, the seat of government for Jones County, was a small town in a West Coast state.[1] It was a little more than 100 miles from a large metropolitan center. The town was bounded on the east by a large lake and was surrounded by mountains. The community was relatively isolated, except in the tourist season and the harvest season, which overlapped in the summer months. One bus a day entered and left town. The only other method of entry was by private car over mountain roads which, until recently, the casual visitor had not been willing to travel during most of the year. Only one third of Jones County was settled. The other two thirds was wilderness.

Lochton and the two agricultural valleys which it served had been settled in 1850 by English and German settlers. Many of their descendants still lived in the region. The early history of the area was woven

---

[1] See the author's "The Ecological Organization of Lochton," *Sociology and Social Research*, 41 (May–June, 1957), pp. 366–369.

with the romantic threads of Indian legends, an uprising of Indians, followed by their massacre at the hands of the cavalry (who took after them in boats across the lake), and stage coach robberies.

The religious composition of Lochton was diverse. There were twelve churches of various Protestant denominations and one Roman Catholic church. Of these thirteen churches, the Roman Catholic, Episcopal, Methodist, and Baptist had the largest congregations.

Lochton was the service community for the area around it and, as noted, the county seat. Here were to be found the county courthouse and the offices of government, the sheriff's office, the county headquarters of the state highway patrol, and the largest library in the county. There was one bank, the only motion picture house for thirty miles, and sixty retail stores and eating places.[2] There were two hospitals, two hotels, and two weekly newspapers. Many residents subscribed to one or more of the metropolitan daily newspapers. There were no wholesale outlets, nor was there any industry. In fact, industrial growth had been thwarted. Both a wood-processing mill, to have been built a few miles north of town, and a minimum security prison for juvenile first offenders had been discouraged by groups in Lochton.

The wealth of Lochton was derived from pears, walnuts, and tourists. In pear-growing, Jones County was the eighth ranking county in the United States. The bulk of the pear-growing was in the two agricultural valleys served by Lochton. The county ranked sixty-seventh in the nation in the growing of nuts and berries. Within the city limits of Lochton there were twelve motels to serve the tourists, an estimated eighty per cent of whom came from the metropolitan center. There were more motels on the lake shore north of town, and a large resort area about twelve miles south. Although the tourists represented a sizeable portion of Lochton's wealth, there was great social distance between them and the people of the town. As one resident put it, "During the summer we lock our doors."

The population of Lochton, the largest town in Jones County, was 1,983 in 1950. There were perhaps another 2,500 people living in the two agricultural valleys. The total population of the county was 11,481—75.4 per cent of whom were classified as rural nonfarm residents, and 24.6 per cent of whom were classified as rural farm residents. The population of Lochton was to all intents and purposes

---

[2] Compared with 233 stores in the county in 1952.

homogeneous. In 1950 it included only six Indians and one Negro. There were, however, two Indian reservations in the two agricultural valleys. Because of the lack of industry and the concentration of the community's economy upon services, the occupational composition of the population, too, was homogeneous. To judge by a 20 per cent sample studied in 1954, 69 per cent of the members of the work force in Lochton were in the occupational categories of professional persons, managers and proprietors, and sales, clerical, and kindred workers. The great bulk of unskilled labor functioning in Lochton's economy was seasonal and migratory.

The age composition of Lochton's population was as follows: 29.1 per cent of the population was under 21 years of age; 25.4 per cent was over 55; and, taken as a separate category, 15.4 per cent was over 65.

If a stranger had questioned the residents of Lochton regarding the existence of social classes in the community, the answer would probably have been that there were none. Investigation of the twenty per cent sample revealed that on the Warner Index of Status Characteristics [3] there were four. (See Table I.)

The lack of industry, the ownership of business by individuals, the stability—perhaps even the static quality—of business life, all presented a general lack of economic opportunity. Social mobility *within* the community was almost an impossibility, and most adults in Lochton looked beyond the mountains for opportunities, not for themselves—many of them had already been there—but rather for their children.

Table I

Social Class Membership in Lochton
1954

	Per Cent
Upper Upper	0.
Lower Upper	0.
Upper Middle	7.0
Lower Middle	49.5
Upper Lower	38.5
Lower Lower	5.0
Total	100.0

[3] W. Lloyd Warner, Marchia Meeker, and Kenneth Eells, *Social Class in America: A Manual of Procedure for the Measurement of Social Status.* Chicago: Science Research Associates. 1949.

The educational facilities of the town consisted of one elementary school and one high school. The elementary school had a kindergarten and eight grades, the high school grades nine through twelve. Because of overcrowding in the elementary school a new campus had been built in 1955 for grades six, seven, and eight on a site at the north end of town, creating an unofficial junior high (or intermediate) school.

Lochton High School had been built in 1905 to replace the Lochton Academy, which had burned down. It occupied a site on the shore at the north end of town. There had been four additions made to the main building: a gymnasium built in 1936 by the W.P.A.; a band house built in 1939; a large home economics room built in 1950; and a new shop building constructed in 1955 from two large Quonset buildings put end-to-end. There was also a new football field. The school had twelve classrooms (exclusive of the shop and the gymnasium), a chemistry laboratory, a library, and a cafeteria. The enrollment of the high school was just over 200 students.

In 1954 the faculty was composed of twelve teachers. Three had bachelor's degrees from private colleges and universities; the others from public institutions. Three also had earned the degree of master of arts. Ten were fully certified by the State; two possessed provisional teaching credentials.

There was a high rate of teacher turn-over at Lochton High School. Six teachers had left in 1952, five in 1953, three in 1954, three in 1955, and seven in 1956. The most frequently stated reason for leaving was that Lochton High School was in a non-tenure district. According to state law in districts whose enrollments were below 850 pupils in average daily attendance, tenure was not automatic unless explicitly granted by the district's board of education. At Lochton High tenure had not been granted to either the teachers or the Principal.

The administration of the high school consisted of the Principal alone. During his occasional absence one of the senior teachers was assigned to make any necessary decisions, these being mostly in the area of student personnel. The Principal had come to Lochton High School in the early 1930's. After a decade as the science teacher and athletic coach he had become Principal. Quite active in professional circles, he was president of the State Small Schools Association, chairman of the regional finance committee of the State Teachers Association, and area chairman of the State Association of Secondary School Administrators.

The college nearest to Lochton High School was a two-year junior

college some sixty miles south. The nearest state colleges were in the
metropolitan center, as were State University and a number of private
colleges and universities. Most of the students who attended college
from Lochton High School went to the junior college, with the intention of transferring after two years as juniors to a state college or to
State University. A few students attended private colleges and universities.

Lochton High School had an undifferentiated curriculum, i.e., all
courses in the school were open to anyone who wished to take them
and had the necessary prerequisites. No distinction was made between
academic, general, and vocational programs of study. An outline of the
curriculum as of June, 1955, follows. (All courses were offered for one
year unless otherwise noted.)

ARTS:
    Art (4 years offered)
    Band (4 years offered)
COMMERCIAL SUBJECTS:
    Bookkeeping
    Shorthand
    Typing (3 years offered)
INDUSTRIAL ARTS:
    Architectural Drawing
    Auto Shop
    General Shop (4 years offered)
    Mechanical Drawing (4 years offered)
LANGUAGES:
    English (4 years offered)
    Journalism
    Spanish (2 years offered)
MATHEMATICS:
    Algebra (2 years offered)
    Consumer Mathematics
    General (High School) Arithmetic
    Plane Geometry
    Solid Geometry (one semester offered)
    Trigonometry (one semester offered)
PHYSICAL EDUCATION: (4 years offered)
SCIENCE:
    General Science
    Biology
    Chemistry
    Physics
SOCIAL STUDIES:
    9th Grade Social Studies
    World History
    United States History
    Civics and Social Problems

OTHER COURSES:
Home Economics (3 years offered)
General Agriculture

Every high school in the state was required by law to offer all those courses which were required for entrance to State University. Lochton High School offered little beyond what was required and offered no courses which could be considered truly vocational.

The high school curriculum was most often criticized for not being academic enough and for not adequately preparing students for college. One parent, a teacher at the elementary school, said bluntly, "This high school program does not give my son adequate enough background to go to college."

And the people of Lochton did send their children to college. Of the 163 students who composed the four graduating classes 1953–1956, 80 attended college. Table II indicates the relationship between college attendance of graduates and the occupational class of their parents.

In sum, Lochton was a small white collar community. Its social system—demographic, economic, and class—was homogeneous. The interest in the high school, exhibited by the residents, tended to center about the quest for more academic courses by which to prepare their children for college.

Table II

*Classification of Graduates of Lochton High School
by Occupational Class of Parents, 1953 to 1956*

Occupational Class of Parent	Total Number Graduates	Number Attending College	Number Not Attending College	Per Cent Attending College
Professional	5	5	0	100
Business Owners and Managers	36	25	11	69
Sales, Clerical, and Kindred	24	10	14	43
Skilled	10	4	6	40
Semi-Skilled	19	6	13	32
Farm Owners and Managers	63	28	35	44
Farm Laborers	1	0	1	0
Unskilled Laborers	5	2	3	40
	163	80	83	

During the spring semester of 1955 much of the discussion of the curriculum centered about whether or not the philosophy course should be given and the problems attendant to giving it.

In the discussions—primarily between the social studies teacher and the Principal—two major points were agreed upon. The first was that such a course would be accepted by the community and would be compatible with its stated interest in sending more students to college. That interest was found to be high not only among the college-educated parents,[4] but as well among those parents who had not gone to college. One faculty member cited an incident as illustrative. The Principal reported that the parents of a 10th grade girl had sought his assistance in having a teacher change the grade of a book report from a D to a B and that the mother's appeal was supported solely by the statement, ". . . my daughter must go to college."

The second point of agreement was that a course in the introduction to philosophy would give the opportunity for a number of the more able students to become familiar both with college level work and with many of the basic ideas of Western European and American thought.

The following points were also worked out between the social studies teacher and the Principal. That the social studies teacher should teach the course was logical, not only for the practical reason that he was free during the proposed hour, but also because his preparation included teaching minors in philosophy and English. The books which were chosen for use in the course were judged to be stimulating and broad enough in scope to meet the requirements of such a course, and flexible enough to allow for individual differences among the students. The Durant volume had the necessary historical perspective. The book of readings was used in college freshman composition and literature courses; its span of authors, from Plato and St. Augustine to Margaret Mead and James Thurber, would add the perspective of depth.

For this experimental venture the class would be kept small. It was also agreed that the students would be selected from the senior class. Not only would they have greater maturity for grasping the material of the course, but their motivation to learn would probably be high.

As the discussions progressed, three issues continuously arose. The first had been mentioned in the faculty meeting of November, 1954. Many of the faculty had pointed out that they were already seeking

---

[4] Of those individual adults who had children in the high school in May, 1954, 18.4 per cent had themselves attended college.

to stimulate individual students of ability. In a high school as small as this one, and with the degree of intimacy which characterized student-teacher relations, would the new plan burden the curriculum with a course one of the chief aims of which was already being realized daily?

A second issue was that of teacher load. The teachers of the so-called "solid" subjects taught six hours a day, five days a week. One hour a day was free for conferences and preparation—the fourth period in the case of the social studies teacher. The social studies teacher was already scheduled for a load requiring three preparations a day. With his open hour taken up by the philosophy course, his teaching load would become abnormally heavy if one of his other classes were not transferred to another teacher or discontinued. But that would further complicate scheduling problems and might stretch the school day beyond its capacity to operate efficiently.

A third issue arose over whether other courses could be added to the curriculum which might reach not just a few selected students, but all the seniors intending to enter college, or which might be of more immediate and practical value to other seniors. The teacher of the senior English classes had already told the Principal that a special English course ought to be added. It had been common practice among the high schools of the state to offer, in addition to the regular English IV, a course in grammar and composition designed specifically to aid students in passing the English examinations required by most colleges and universities in the state. Such a course at Lochton High School, the argument ran, even though it would tend toward a differentiated curriculum, would certainly help all concerned.

Two years of a foreign language were required for admission to State University. At Lochton High School this requirement was fulfilled by Spanish. More than a few parents and students had indicated that not enough foreign language was being given. Many of the parents wanted more than two years of Spanish given, a few saying that the teaching of it should begin in the elementary school. Some students indicated a desire to have the school offer another foreign language in order that they could exercise a choice.

Consultation by the Principal with the commercial teacher revealed that a second year of shorthand and a course in office practice might be offered.

*   *   *   *   *

In June, 1955, the Principal decided that beginning that fall the philosophy course would be given. He explained that his decision was based on several factors.

He had inquired and had found that the course would be accepted by State University as an elective. The philosophy course, he said, would bring together history, social philosophy, and aesthetics in a kind of synthesis of the social studies and the humanities, which would be an important addition to the curriculum. The study of philosophy would also, he said, provide the curriculum with an advanced course in the social studies and humanities, paralleling the advanced studies in the natural sciences and mathematics already in the program of the high school.

The Principal said he did not feel that the other courses that had been suggested could be offered at the time. The recent additions to the curriculum had been possible because classes with smaller enrollment could be shifted. But the school had reached its limit in that direction. The addition of other courses would necessitate hiring new teachers without, however, providing a full teaching load. Because the philosophy course was to be given as a voluntary and experimental venture within the structure of the existing curriculum, these problems were avoidable.

The Principal also referred to the policy agreement that Lochton High School should maintain its emphasis on general education. He had often indicated that Lochton High School was not a vocational school, and the shop teacher frequently said that he taught industrial arts, not manual training. "We do not train students to step into jobs," the Principal said. "Our task is that of general education—giving them a broad background."

The Principal announced that although the philosophy course would likely enroll students who were college-bound, this was not to be considered a prerequisite for enrollment.

The philosophy course was given by the social studies teacher during the school year 1955–56. Two boys and five girls were enrolled. Six of these students were seniors, and one a junior. Six other students had indicated interest in the course. Three were rejected by the teacher because their achievement test scores were below the norm for seniors. The other three found that other interests conflicted with the course; one girl, for example, decided to enroll in the third year of home economics, because it was her proposed major in college.

The IQ scores for the students enrolled in the course ranged from 104 to 128, compared with a range of 82 to 128 for the senior class. Their achievement test scores were above average; for example, scores on reading comprehension ranged from grade 13.9 to grade 15.5.

The students were all from the lower middle class. The occupations of their parents were as follows: three small farm owners; two small motel owners; an owner and operator of a wrecking company; and a field supervisor for a public utilities company.

From the beginning of the course the students showed a great deal of enthusiasm for it. All indicated that the unaccustomed level of reading and the abstractness of thought involved made it a challenge to their abilities. The nature of the required readings, the wide choice of supplemental readings possible, and the variety of topics covered seemed to contribute to the continuing interest of the class.

The reactions of the faculty to the course were, in general, favorable. Nearly all agreed that it was a valuable experiment and a valuable addition to the curriculum. The one dissenter was the music teacher, who indicated some concern because he had lost three members of the school band to the course.

The course had not been announced to the public. No such announcement had been made when other courses had been added to the curriculum, and the Principal had said that this course should not be an exception. News of the course had filtered into the community via the students enrolled and their friends. With one exception all those parents who made their opinions known to the Principal and to the teacher indicated they were favorably disposed toward the course. The one voice of doubt was that of the mother of one of the boys enrolled in the course, who wondered if the course would lead her son away from his religion. Her fears calmed, she enthusiastically supported the course.

The following year five of the students went to college. Two attended State University; two entered state colleges; one, who also got married, attended the nearby junior college. The remaining two students married shortly after graduation.

Also the following year the social studies teacher who had introduced the course left the school. The reasons he gave were familiar ones to the Principal: lack of tenure and the unwillingness of the school board to vote it, together with the offer by another district of a substantial increase in salary. The teacher who replaced him was inexperienced and did not feel qualified to assume the responsibilities involved. Nor did the Principal, with seven new teachers to orient to the school, seem anxious to push on with any sweeping change in the curriculum.

The philosophy course was discontinued.

SELECTED READINGS

Benne, Kenneth D., and Bozidar Muntyan, eds., *Human Relations in Curriculum Change: Selected Readings with Especial Emphasis on Group Development*. New York: The Dryden Press, 1951.

Butterworth, Julian E., and Howard A. Dawson, *The Modern Rural School*. New York: McGraw-Hill Book Company, 1952.

Hollingshead, August B., *Elmtown's Youth: The Impact of Social Classes on Adolescents*. New York: John Wiley and Sons, 1949.

Lynd, Robert S., and Helen Merrell Lynd, *Middletown in Transition: A Study in Cultural Conflicts*. New York: Harcourt, Brace and Company, 1937. Chs. 6, 12.

Warner, W. Lloyd, et al., *Who Shall Be Educated?* New York: Harper and Brothers, 1944.

The Innovator

In February, 1949, by authorization of the Director of Public Education for the Department of Cauca, Colombia, the Zonal School Inspector paid an official visit to the village of Lora. His specific purpose was to investigate a complaint, received by the Director from a group of purported fathers of village schoolchildren, that the teaching provided by the incumbent schoolmaster was unsatisfactory, that his pupils were being passed "when they had done nothing but play," and that a replacement was accordingly in order.

The Inspector consequently prepared to look into the community-school situation and the charges brought against the schoolmaster. He would then decide whether to recommend that the schoolmaster be recalled or that he be permitted to remain.

Lora was a small (pop. 400) Colombian community situated between the central and coastal ranges of the Andes in the Department of Cauca highlands. It was in the temperate zone, had a mean annual temperature of approximately 19° Centigrade, and was about 1745 meters above sea level. There were two main seasons: winter (the rainy or wet season) extended from September to June, and summer (the sunny or dry season) from June to September. The terrain was hilly and covered by a wide variety of vegetation which was put to dietary, handicraft, and medicinal use. Wild life in the area was fairly abundant, but little utilized. Lora lacked electricity, paving, and plumbing.

Lora was typical of a common type of Latin American community, the rural "Mestizo" pueblo, in that its population was racially and culturally mixed, with indigenous and Hispanic elements predominant in the mixture. It was founded in 1737 by a group of erstwhile impressed laborers assigned to the estates of a Spanish nobleman and freed by his widow. Until the second quarter of the twentieth century it was known as a community of Indians, but by 1930 the key symbols of Indian status (native language and dress; communal land tenure) had been abandoned, and Lora had joined the non-Indian "Mestizo" ranks.[1]

Lora was an agricultural community. Its most important crops were corn, yuca, beans, sugar cane, platano, arracacha, cabbage, potatoes, and coffee. Although the people were basically farmers, there were such part-time occupational statuses as barber, cobbler, carpenter, tailor, dressmaker, curer, midwife, policeman, welldigger, and merchant.

The people lived in small, single-storied houses with mud, adobe, bamboo, or brick walls and tile or straw roofs. Common household articles included simple wooden chairs, tables and benches; wooden slat beds; brick, adobe, or cement stoves; holy pictures and small altars; candles; cheap earthenware and metalware; log water troughs; grass mats; leather bags; grass brooms; stone implements for grinding corn and coffee; gourd containers; fiber and cane strip baskets. There was little ornamentation: items which were not utilitarian were considered more appropriate for "rich city people."

There were no social classes in Lora, but there were individual differences in social status. These differences were based on such factors as material affluence, knowledge, community interest and service, industry, and conformity. Teachers customarily enjoyed a relatively high status, since they earned more than most of the local residents, were recognized as people "who know much," and were professionally dedicated to an important public service. There were no social clubs or formal social organizations in the community. The most important social ties an individual had were with his family and his godparent affiliates. Only esteemed persons were selected as godparents, and

---

[1] The extent of these ranks is indicated by John Gillin in "Mestizo America," in *Most of the World*, edited by Ralph Linton, New York, 1949, pp. 156–211.

teachers who spent more than a trial year in the community were considered likely choices.

The people of Lora were nominally Roman Catholics, but their Catholicism was mixed with indigenous nature-spirit elements. Lora had a church, a sexton, a church council, and two church societies, but no resident priest. Although the parish priest came to conduct mass only on important Catholic holidays, the church was open every Sunday morning for prayers. Schoolchildren were required to attend these weekly prayer sessions, and each Sunday they assembled at their respective schools and were led to church by the teachers. Teachers had a recognized ecclesiastic responsibility, especially since religion (Roman Catholic doctrine) was taught in school.

The civil government of Lora was run by a police inspector, his deputies, and a secretary. These were technically appointed by the alcalde of the *municipio*,[2] but the selection was ultimately responsive to public opinion. Local civic associations were the self-perpetuating Council for Public Improvements and the all-inclusive Men's and Women's Councils. The officials and councils had little real power except through the organization and formal expression of public opinion: leaders whose actions were not generally approved and supported were soon replaced. Teachers were often consulted on civic issues and were expected to contribute time and money to civic projects. The people of Lora were predominantly affiliated with the Liberal Party and tended to associate the opposing Conservative Party with "the rich" of the city and large country estates. Although the people were not well-informed politically, they took their politics, however vague, seriously. Expressions of dissension were regarded with suspicion and hostility, and it was considered advisable for teachers whose political loyalties did not coincide with those of the community to keep their views to themselves.

A key value in Lora, as in much of Latin America, was *respeto*: respect. "*Siempre es necesario tener el respeto* (It is always necessary to have respect)." One should respect one's associates, oneself, one's work, one's gods; respect was an all-pervasive virtue. Practically every act that called for social condemnation could be construed as "*una falta de respeto* (a lack of respect)." The teacher was definitely a personage to be respected; at the same time he was expected to be sensitive to, and to respect, local opinion.

---

[2] Comparable to a U.S. county, as a Department is comparable to a U.S. state.

In the course of his investigation of the charges against the school-master, the Zonal Inspector looked into the school program, which had the following characteristics:

Segregation

A formal school program had existed locally since the middle of the nineteenth century. The *escuela alternada* system had prevailed until 1924. The *escuela alternada* had been a single elementary school attended by the boys one day and the girls the next. In 1924 the present system of separate schools for boys and girls had been instituted. Since in those years no buildings had been designed and constructed expressly as schoolhouses, classes had been held in such places as the police office and the parsonage of the visiting priest. The Boys' School had been built in 1933–4, the Girl's School in 1941. Coeducation had never been practiced in Lora.

Duration

Two grades were regularly taught in each school. In some years a third and fourth grade had been offered to outstanding second-year graduates, but two grades were the norm. All children who were neither infirm nor urgently needed at home were expected to attend school two years. The duration of school training was accepted locally as a satisfactory compromise between the widespread desire for literacy and the recognized demands of farm life. There was a general agreement that a little book-knowledge went a long way for a country farmer.

Administration

The educational officials of Lora were:

1. *The Maestro and Maestra.* The *Maestro* was the schoolmaster, the *Maestra* the schoolmistress. The *Maestro* taught the boys of the community, the *Maestra* the girls. Both were employees of the Department. Departmental pay for teachers ranged from approximately $35 to $50 U.S. per month. Rent-free living quarters were also provided. A teacher assigned by the Department to a particular community could request a transfer at any time. A transfer request was normally granted, if an opening was available. A teacher who wished to remain in his current assignment would be permitted to do so as long as his work was satisfactory. The incumbent schoolmaster had not requested

a transfer. If people were dissatisfied with a teacher in their community, they could petition the Department for a replacement, as they had done in the present case. There were four school zones in the Department. Each zone was supervised by a School Inspector, who periodically visited the schools, dispensing study materials and checking the work of the teachers.

2. *The Local Inspector.* Unlike the teachers and the Zonal School Inspector, the Local Inspector was by design a native of the community. He served as an intermediary between the teachers and the local residents and might be characterized as a neighborly truant officer. He contacted parents when their children reached school age and pointed out that the youngsters were now ready to become pupils. If children were withheld from school, he discussed the situation with the parents, and if he believed that their excuses were unsound, he tried to persuade them to reconsider. Should diplomacy fail, he might appeal to the community Police Inspector, who could exert a direct if nebulous pressure on the reluctant family. The authority of the Police Inspector was limited by the vagueness of the requirements for school attendance. Theoretically school was compulsory for all children, but age limits and exemptions were not clearly defined. The Police Inspector and Local Inspector had to rely mainly on their persuasive powers and public opinion.

After children began their school careers, the Local Inspector was concerned with the regularity of their attendance and investigated all prolonged or habitual absences. Tact was again essential, since collusion between parent and truant child could result in an illness plea difficult to disprove. Actually he expected, and was given, little trouble. Parental cooperation with the Local Inspector was the rule.

The Local Inspector was selected by a committee consisting of the *Maestro*, the *Maestra*, the Police Inspector, the outgoing Local Inspector, and a few prominent members of the community. The committee nominee, if he agreed to accept the position, was confirmed in office by the alcalde of the *municipio*. He was chosen for an indefinite term but was expected to serve at least a year. The usual reason for a change was the voluntary request of the incumbent that he be relieved of his duties, but the teachers and leading citizens of the community could move to replace him if they became dissatisfied with his work. The Local Inspector and members of the organizations described below performed their duties largely as a service to the community, and the moderate prestige associated with their offices was not matched by financial rewards.

In the present case no break was reported between the incumbent Local Inspector and the schoolmaster, and the school organizations were not formally opposed to the schoolmaster. However, no strong support for the schoolmaster was in evidence from either source, and individual members of the organizations were reported to be aligned against him.

3. *The School Council.* The School Council was an intermittently functioning organization expected to "take an active interest in school affairs" and to make whatever recommendations it wished. Its members were elected at a meeting of the teachers, the Police Inspector, the Local Inspector, and interested fathers of schoolchildren. The elected members then chose their president, secretary, and treasurer.

4. *The School Examination Board.* An Examination Board was appointed annually by the *Maestra* for the Girls' School, and another by the *Maestro* for the Boys' School. Four or five members were customarily named to each Board. The more literate adults of the community were preferred as appointees. The *Maestro* was regularly named to the Examination Board for girls, and the *Maestra* to the Examination Board for boys. The *Maestra* was usually the only woman on either Board. The procedure might be varied in any given year by the designation of a single Board to examine all pupils; in that case, by custom the *Maestro* selected its members, and the *Maestra* was chosen first.

The examinations, given to pupils at the close of each academic year, were authorized by the Departmental Board of Education and the Zonal School Inspection Board. The teachers familiarized Examination Board members with test schedules and supplied them with test materials. One member of each Board was selected as president, to supervise the test sessions.

5. *The School Repair Board.* An irregularly functioning organization concerned with school maintenance was the School Repair Board. Whenever school repairs were urgently needed, the Board could be activated to collect the funds and solicit the labor required. The most recent Board had effected repairs on the Boys' School, four years previous to the present case. Its members had been elected by the School Council. Board officers had been a president, vice-president, secretary, and treasurer.

Enrollment and Tuition

New and returning pupils were registered at the beginning of the school year; name, grade, sex, age, height, date of enrollment, birthplace and birthdate were recorded. First-grade pupils regularly outnumbered second-grade pupils, who in turn outnumbered "advanced" pupils. The average annual enrollment, according to records on hand, was thirty-six pupils per school. The customary age range for pupils was seven to twelve years.

Local children did not normally enroll in schools outside Lora. Although there was no intermediate or secondary school in Lora, no local "graduates" were reported to have continued their education by enrolling in such schools elsewhere.

The local schools were public institutions supported by the government, and pupils paid no tuition.

Facilities

The school facilities of Lora were considered adequate for the region.

1. *Buildings and Furnishings.* The Boys' School was a single-storied, tile-roofed structure with adobe and brick walls, cement and brick floors, wooden doors, and open windows fitted with wooden bars and shutters. The Girls' School was a single-storied, tile-roofed structure with brick walls, cement and wooden floors, wooden doors, and glass windows. Each school had an antechamber, a classroom, a kitchen, and a bedroom. The kitchen and bedroom were the teacher's quarters. Each school was furnished with a national flag, student work tables and benches, a table-desk for the teacher, straight chairs for the teacher and visitors, a picture of Jesus, portraits of national heroes, a blackboard, a wall map of Colombia, a wall calendar, and an abacus.

2. *Grounds.* Each school plot served as a combination playground and garden. The two plots were at opposite ends of the pueblo, and their aggregate area was less than an acre. They were used and tended exclusively by the pupils and teachers. On each plot were outhouses and a well.

3. *School Supplies.* Study and teaching materials, in addition to such "furnishings" as blackboards and benches, included notebooks, lined and unlined paper, small slates, slate pencils, plain and colored lead pencils, dip pens, white and colored chalk, small stick counters, word cards and matching pictures, and textbooks. The major text-

books were *Alegría de Leer* (a general reader representing a miscellany of information drawn from such fields as history, natural science, and hygiene), *Catecismo Mayor* (the Roman Catholic catechism), *Catecismo de la Doctrina Cristiana* (a simplified catechism), *Aprendamos Nuestra Historia* (a primer on world and national history), and *Compendio de la Historia de Colombia* (a more detailed primer on national history). Every pupil was required to own a copy of the simplified catechism. Pupils did not own copies of the other texts.

The Zonal School Inspector, during his annual visits to Lora, dispensed small quantities of such items as notebooks, chalk, pens, and ink. Most school materials, however, had to be purchased by the teachers and pupils. The general rule was that teachers provided their instructional materials and pupils their personal study materials.

4. *Funds.* There were no funds specifically available for school use. No school "expense account" was maintained by special benefactors, and government aid to the local schools was customarily limited to the provision of teachers and the supplies distributed by the Zonal School Inspector. School expenses, such as renovation costs, were met as they arose by contributions solicited from community residents. Those who felt they could spare no money could donate labor.

5. *Library.* The local "library," situated in the Boys' School, consisted of approximately thirty brief volumes dealing largely with mythology, biblical doctrine, and outstanding figures and events in world and national history. The collection was designed for relatively unskilled readers and served essentially as a highly simplified compendium of worldly and other-worldly information.

The *Maestro* supervised circulation of the books. The collection was stored in a wooden cabinet with various school supplies, and volumes were loaned without rental fee to local residents. Nevertheless, borrowers were few and far between; reading was not regarded locally as a particularly appropriate activity for semi-literate country farmers.

Activities

The school year began in mid-September and ended in mid-July. The school week was Monday through Friday, exclusive of Church and national holidays. Daily school hours were 8–11 a.m. and 1–4 p.m. The schoolmaster followed for the most part a conventional course of activities.

1. *Classes.* The school day opened regularly with collective recital

of the catechism; the teacher then checked the attendance and made study assignments. One grade was typically directed to copy sentences or pictures into notebooks, while the other was put through oral drills.

Such "subjects" as social studies (including history and geography) and language (Spanish vocabulary and grammar) were designed to provide varied practice in reading and writing. The basic objective of the program was literacy, coupled with the promotion of national and local pride and loyalty. Accordingly materials tended to stress Colombian and Departmental achievements and resources.

Other "subjects," less oriented toward literacy, included mathematics, religion, speech, music, art (drawing), physical education, crafts, and deportment. The mathematics taught might be characterized as marketplace arithmetic. With the aid of stick counters, blackboard diagrams, and an abacus, pupils were instructed in simple addition, subtraction, multiplication, and division. Religious training centered in Roman Catholic doctrine. From time to time pupils were asked to prepare and deliver short speeches on various topics, and the more proficient speakers were chosen by the teacher to present addresses on special occasions. The addresses were largely concerned with, and served to reinforce, religious and patriotic values; they carried such titles as "To My Flag," "My Christ," "The Hands of My Mother," and "What Is Love?" A similar tendency was reflected in music and art studies. Pupils were taught such songs as "Colombia" and "The Soldiers' Hymn," and a student chorus was selected to sing appropriate pieces on important holidays. Student art work included pencil and crayon drawings of patriots and other inspirational figures, the national flag, the country itself (in simple maps), and such points of collective pride as the local church.

Physical education comprised the various recess activities. These were largely informal and spontaneous games and gambolings, but the teacher was expected to suggest play forms when pupil inspiration was exhausted or divided, and on occasion to serve as coach or referee. On fiesta days, basketball or soccer contests were sometimes scheduled between teams from the Boys' School.

An example of the training in crafts was the instruction in sewing and embroidery offered by the *Maestra* to interested girls after regular class hours. Lessons in deportment were basically explicit endorsements of the values sanctioned more indirectly and implicitly in other studies; pupils were enjoined to be patriotic, pious, industrious, courteous, and respectful. The teacher gave special holiday talks extolling the virtues of the dignitaries being honored and urging the children to follow their example.

The notebooks kept by the pupils served as cumulative progress records, to be checked periodically by the teacher and admired generally by the parents. A pupil could include in his notebook not only the written exercises and illustrations assigned to all, but also materials reflecting his special interests. Thus a boy with a penchant for guitar music might, after he finished transcribing historical data from a text or multiplication tables from the blackboard, enter diagrams showing the basic finger positions for guitar chords.

2. *Examinations*. Although the over-all class performance of a pupil during the school year was taken into consideration, by custom the annual examinations largely determined whether or not he passed. A representative test timetable showed an allocation of thirty-five minutes each for the examinations in mathematics and language and twenty-five minutes each for examinations in other subjects. Pupils who quickly demonstrated their competence might, however, be released before expiration of the allotted time. Pupils appeared individually before the School Examination Board, and according to the material under review might be directed, for example, to answer questions orally, solve problems on the blackboard, read text paragraphs aloud, or write phrases and sentences dictated by Board members. Every pupil was awarded a point score ranging from one to five in each of the subjects covered by the Board; these were usually religion, language (coupled with speech, pertaining to oral skills), mathematics, social studies, art, crafts, music, and physical education. Higher scores indicated greater proficiency; since the top score per pupil per subject was five, the highest possible total score per pupil for the eight subjects was forty. The relative difficulty of examining pupils directly in art, crafts, music, and physical education was reflected in the tendency to base ratings in these subjects to a greater extent on past performance than in the other subjects. Assessments of past performance were accordingly provided by the teacher. Following the examination sessions, the teacher discussed with Board members the scores made by his or her pupils, and a pass-fail line was established. According to sample statistics, approximately two-thirds of the pupils passed annually.

3. *Gardening*. The pupils of each school maintained a small garden

and devoted one to four days a month—depending on the current crop phase—to its care. They typically raised flowers, corn, and coffee. According to a Departmental directive, the produce had to be used exclusively "for the benefit of the pupils." The edibles harvested were commonly prepared in the school kitchen and consumed on the school premises. Flowers and left-over edibles might be taken home. Whether at school or home, pupils regularly made direct use of the produce: it was not customary to sell it and divide the money among them. The school gardening activities in Lora, as in other rural areas, were designed to help prepare pupils for the farming life.

4. *Programs and Processions.* In addition to special pupil contributions (including participation in processions) on important fiesta days, school programs were regularly scheduled on Mother's Day and at the end of the academic year. These programs gave pupils an opportunity to display their respective talents (the relatively untalented might join in class songs) before parental assemblages, and served as occasions on which prevailing values were formally sanctioned in a school setting.

*   *   *   *   *

In his investigation the Inspector found that the schoolmaster "followed the official program" and used the regulation texts. Turning from formal organization to results, he proceeded to examine the pupils. He found that they were learning at a normal rate; their progress compared quite favorably with that of other groups whose teachers had not been criticized, and it was evident that he could not hope to understand the grievance without looking elsewhere. So far he could find no support for the charges.

Irregularities did, however, appear in teaching methodology. One clue was the accusation that pupils were being passed "when they had done nothing but play."

As the Inspector knew from visits to other pueblos, and to Lora before the present schoolmaster came, recitation was characteristically a group activity. Timid or tentative responses were lost in the common clamor, and pupils who shouted wrong answers too loudly were apt to be corrected swiftly and derisively by their fellows. There was a feeling among local residents that a good school should sound not unlike a beehive, and the din emanating from the classroom tended to assure them that the teacher was on the job and that education was taking place.

Moreover, group recitations had considerable appeal to the pupils. Like children elsewhere, they welcomed the opportunity to vocalize energetically in concert with their contemporaries. Recitation sessions were typically sparked with an enthusiasm comparable to that attending school pep rallies in the United States.

In the customary approach, although the emphasis was on group response, individual pupils were not ignored in oral drills. Those who appeared to require special attention were questioned and coached singly at the discretion of the teacher.

However, the incumbent schoolmaster appeared to be less taken than his predecessors with established teaching methods. The people of Lora could no longer depend on hearing regularly the accustomed hum of group recitations. To a greater extent than his predecessors the schoolmaster tended to be a counselor of individuals rather than a group director or drillmaster. Pupils were given more leeway than before, and their activities were less strictly supervised. The new informality and apparent relaxation of controls readily suggested that schoolwork was becoming more like play. "You don't hear them reciting the way you used to, and as far as you can tell everybody's up to something different, so you have the feeling they're just playing around over there," was a representative comment. The schoolmaster—himself a middle-aged man of unremarkable appearance and conventional background—was using a conventional format and conventional materials, but in an unconventional way. The results did not matter; it was a violation of custom, and "people here don't like it when a stranger takes liberties with the ways they're used to."

As part of the new informality, a development occurred which severely strained schoolmaster-community relations. The pronoun customarily used in the area by a teacher in addressing a pupil was the formal *Usted*. According to community codes it was important to maintain between them the social distance indicated by the term. So vital, moreover, were the "respect" connotations of the term that local use of the familiar *tu* was normally restricted to contexts of marked intimacy, jest, or derogation. The incumbent schoolmaster, however, regularly used *tu* in addressing his pupils. He did so not only because in other areas *tu* was not infrequently applied to children, but because it seemed especially appropriate to the informal, personal teacher-pupil relationship he was working to foster. Yet to the people of Lora such usage was objectionable—"It's a lack of respect all around."

In the first place, the schoolmaster, striving to be something of a *tu* companion to his pupils, appeared to be demeaning himself. By community standards he was bringing himself down to their level. The judgment was typically expressed in this way: "If one would become a child among children, one cannot at the same time expect to be regarded as a man among men." There was a saying in Lora that reflected an important precept: "Let men talk with men, and children with children." The schoolmaster did not by any means openly advocate a complete bridging of the teacher-pupil social gap. But in seeking to close it even partially and using *tu* in the process, he seriously lowered himself in the estimation of the community.

In the second place, the actions of the schoolmaster were viewed as derogatory to the pupils and their parents. "Such behavior is insulting to the families the school serves." He appeared to be taking undue liberties with his pupils in treating them so informally. "The pupils cannot safely presume to call *him* 'tu', and familiarity that goes only one way degrades. We do not want our children to be objects of condescension." The schoolmaster seemed to be showing a lack of respect toward the pupils and, by extension, their parents. In effect he appeared to be taking advantage of the pupils' lower status and reminding them of it, by doing what could not have been done by them. His familiarity was unsolicited and, under the circumstances, offensive.

The schoolmaster had been in Lora a comparatively short time. Any appearance of condescension from an outsider was apt to be particularly resented as an insult to the entire community. The people of Lora, as poor farmers, were openly aware of their vulnerability to patronizing attitudes, and acutely sensitive to them. "We need no reminders from outsiders that we are peasants." Although from the vantage point of the schoolmaster, no condescension may have been intended, this could not be proved. The people of Lora evidently found it easier to interpret his actions in terms of a slight they could understand than a compliment for which they had no precedent.

While the pupils themselves were first to respond with a rather vague and confused hostility, their parents had been largely responsible for crystallizing, reinforcing, and promulgating it. While local organizations did not formally oppose the schoolmaster, as important agencies of communication they facilitated the spreading of the hostility.

The charges against the schoolmaster did not include open criticism of his religious or political conduct. However, there were signs that the public hostility evoked by the new "methods" would presently extend explicitly into such spheres. It had already gone far beyond a school context, and the stage of pertinent hints was being reached. Although the schoolmaster appeared to be conventional in his religious and political behavior, his seeming lack of respect toward community codes in one area made him suspect in others. However diligent his outward observance of religious and political prescriptions, like others who for one reason or another had incurred public disfavor he was subject to insinuations of underlying insincerity, hypocrisy, and disrespect. If such insinuations could not be proved, neither could they effectively be disproved. What in the narrow sense could be construed as a controversy over "methods" was clearly spreading to the point of general alienation of the teacher from the community.

After he had had an opportunity to assess the situation, the School Inspector notified the schoolmaster of the complaint against him and showed him the list of signers. The schoolmaster was evidently surprised at the complaint, if not at the disapprobation it expressed. A joint examination of the list of signers, however, revealed that a number of the purported fathers did not, after all, have children in school. A further examination disclosed that some of the signatures were not authentic, that the names of various persons had appeared on the list without their authorization. Hence the School Inspector could conclude that the complaint, while reflecting a genuine dissatisfaction with the schoolmaster, was not itself genuine technically.

In summary, the School Inspector found that in terms of the program followed, texts used, and results obtained, the charges against the schoolmaster did not appear substantiated. He found, moreover, that the complaint could be rejected on technical grounds. (The schoolmaster himself made no special defense, but stressed the relevance of these considerations.) However, the complaint was significant in that it reflected a real and widespread disaffection toward the schoolmaster. Opposition prompted by his use of informal, personalized methods which violated community codes had developed into a serious and extensive impairment of teacher-community relations.

Confronting the School Inspector were two basic alternatives. He had to decide, on the basis of the evidence, whether to recommend that the schoolmaster be recalled, or that he be permitted to remain. The considerations and interpretations supporting each position could be summarized as follows:

1. The schoolmaster should be recalled. In a community like Lora public cooperation and support are essential to the ultimate success of a teacher. Since public opposition to the incumbent is strong and increasing, he should be recalled for his sake as well as that of the community. It is true that he has followed the official program, used the regulation texts, and achieved some positive scholastic results, but in the process he has so antagonized the community that he is doing more harm than good to the cause of education. As a Departmental representative, a teacher has to be especially circumspect. He must be careful to show respect for community codes, as long as they are within the law. By heedlessly violating local custom the incumbent has shown his unsuitability as a representative. Where good will is needed, he has created ill will. Education cannot be truly effective in an atmosphere so hostile. Whatever pupils learn in school can soon be unlearned at home, and as parental hostility toward the source of the lessons is communicated increasingly to the pupils, they will be less and less likely to learn them in the first place. Regardless of his competence in other respects, a teacher should not be retained in a community whose members he has so alienated that his efforts, however laudable in intent, are not only virtually wasted but potentially prejudicial to the larger work. There are other teachers who can accomplish as much scholastically as the incumbent, and at the same time get along with the members of a community like Lora. One of these should accordingly be sent to Lora, and the incumbent transferred to another community, perhaps in a less restrictive urbanized area, where his work would be better received and hence more effective.

2. The schoolmaster should be permitted to remain. The complaint is, after all, specifically concerned with his teaching, and this cannot in all fairness be judged unsatisfactory as long as he produces results with officially approved materials within an authorized program. The

government can prescribe format and materials and require results, but should not dictate methods. Teachers are not, of course, all alike: each has his own approach, and methods suited to one may not be suited to another. If the methods of the incumbent have met with community opposition, it is unfortunate, but he is not thereby obliged to abandon them or deserving of recall. He does not tell his neighbors how to do their work, and they should not tell him how to do his. He is an educational specialist, and entitled to take the lead in his field and in his assigned community. A good teacher is not necessarily a popular one. It is well known that innovators are commonly subjected to public opposition and hostility, since every change threatens one or more established precepts. But if innovators were dissuaded by disapproval, progress would be retarded, and public officials would in time become far too responsive to Loras and afraid to suggest reforms and improvements. It is true that progress has brought ills, but its benefits are needed, and it is said that death begins where growth stops. To transfer the schoolmaster would simply be evading the issue. The Department should not begrudge him the right to experiment and should not withdraw support when he needs it most.

Moreover, although the opposition and hostility to the schoolmaster appear to be increasing, it is entirely possible that a decrease may follow, since acceptance of change commonly follows initial resistance. A decrease is especially likely if he receives Departmental backing. Those who hire a teacher and send him into a community have a responsibility not only toward the community but toward the teacher. They should uphold him against charges of dubious accuracy and admissibility. However inauspicious his community relations, the charges against the incumbent are directed not to these but to his teaching, and from the standpoint of the Department his teaching has been satisfactory. Furthermore, the charges are not, strictly speaking, admissible at all, since the complainants have misrepresented themselves. This may be a technicality, but it is an important one in a case so serious, and if other considerations do not prevail he is certainly entitled to its protection.

＊   ＊   ＊   ＊   ＊

After considering the case, the School Inspector officially cleared the schoolmaster of the charges against him. While note was taken of the misrepresentation involved in the authorship of the complaint, the complaint itself was adjudicated on the basis of its specific concern with the teaching provided and was in that respect held invalid.

In the months immediately following the decision, the schoolmaster and the community appeared to be at an impasse. This was broken in May by an attempted appropriation of the Boys' School coffee crop by a few local "leaders." The schoolmaster was not intimidated, but openly issued a strong protest to the Departmental Director of Public Education. Those responsible, now on the defensive, had some explaining to do, but the schoolmaster did not press the matter. Thereafter they were somewhat subdued. Two of them were duly named to the School Examination Board, and as the term ended, relations between schoolmaster and community seemed at least temporarily improved. Indeed, at the closing school exercises one of those involved in the coffee affair, "on behalf of the people of Lora," expressed "general satisfaction" with his work.

The schoolmaster was subsequently given a routine transfer. He indicated he was well aware that his differences with the community may, however indirectly and inadvertently, have prompted it. But in view of the substantial vindication received he did not consider that resistance was now necessary.

SELECTED READINGS

Benne, Kenneth D., and Bozidar Muntyan, eds., *Human Relations in Curriculum Change*. New York: The Dryden Press, 1951.

Mercer, Blaine E., and Edwin R. Carr, *Education and the Social Order*. New York: Rinehart and Company, 1957.

Nordskog, John Eric, ed., *Social Change*. New York: McGraw-Hill Book Company, 1960.

Spindler, George D., ed., *Education and Anthropology*. Stanford: Stanford University Press, 1955.

Windsor High: An Inadequate School

CASE 17

On April 4, 1958, the State Board of Education took action that changed the high school at Windsor from an "Approved" to a "Non-approved" school. This, in effect, forced the closing of the only high school in the community. The decision was the culmination of a three-year controversy between the State Board and the residents of Windsor concerning the adequacy of the educational program provided by the local school district.

Like that of many mid-western states, the cultural setting of the state in which Windsor was situated had been greatly influenced by its dependence on the soil as the principal means of its livelihood. The state had a population density of nineteen persons per square mile, and agriculture had long played a dominant role in the state's economy. The most important sources of the state's revenue were farm products, principally livestock, hay, wheat, corn, alfalfa, and sugar beets. Because of limited mineral resources, the state had not been favored with a large amount of industrial activity except in its two metropolitan areas and one oil-producing section.

The population of the state had remained fairly static in the past forty years. In 1920 1,296,372 lived in the state, and in 1950 1,325,510. Within the United States, it ranked thirty-first in population in 1920 and thirty-third in 1950. During the decade 1940–1950, 46.9 per cent of the people resided in urban areas, and 53.1 per cent lived in a rural environment. This compared with 23.7 per cent and 76.3 per cent respectively in 1900. In these last ten years, approximately 80 per cent of the increase in population had been in the thirty-four larger urban areas. The shift in areas of residence had been accompanied by a decrease in the number of farms from 124,417 in 1920 to 107,103 in 1950. Approximately 44 per cent of these farms were 240 acres or more in size.

The growth of population in the urban areas and the decrease in the number of farms had implications for the structure of the state's school system. Although there had been a constant decrease in the number of school districts, there still remained a large number of smaller high schools which served a declining rural population.

In 1957–58 the state had a greater number of independent school districts than any other state. An emphasis upon school district reorganization had resulted in the dissolution of 2,292 districts since 1949. In spite of this, there still remained 4,069 elementary schools which enrolled fewer than fifty pupils. The secondary school situation was similar; the state had 449 high schools. Table I shows their distribution by size of enrollment.

Table I

Size of High Schools

No. of pupils	No. of schools
1 – 49	171
50 – 99	146
100–199	76
200 or more	56
Total	449

The thirty-four larger school systems in the state provided education for approximately 46 per cent of all students. Some 107 high schools were staffed by three or fewer teachers each; 174 schools had fewer than six teachers.

The financial support of schools was borne principally by the local school districts, with approximately 92 per cent of school revenue coming from them. The state contributed about 2 per cent to the total cost of school operation. The tax base in the state rested almost entirely upon real and personal property valuation, with no state sales or income tax. Recent attempts upon the part of some groups to broaden the tax base and to provide for increased state support for schools had not been successful. Professional school groups in the state generally favored both of these proposals.

Although the formal control of education lay with the local school district, certain functions had been given to the state administrative agency. In 1953 the people of the state voted to create a State Board of Education, an elected body of six lay citizens, who were in turn to appoint a State Superintendent of Schools to act as Executive Officer of the Board.

The State Board was given the authority to

> . . . establish standards and procedures for classifying, approving, and accrediting schools, including the establishment of minimum standards and procedures for approving the opening of new schools, the continued legal operation of all schools, and for the approval of high schools for the collection of free high school tuition money.

Within this framework the State Board of Education was specifically charged with the responsibility of establishing

> . . . a procedure for accrediting the elementary and secondary schools of the state, both public and private. The major purposes of such procedure shall be to maintain adequate school programs, and to encourage and assist schools in their purpose of increasing better instructional opportunities for the boys and girls of the state.

Working under the jurisdiction of the State Board of Education in implementing these provisions was the Department of Education, headed by a Superintendent of Schools. The latter was appointed by the State Board for an indefinite term. The Department of Education was composed of four principal divisions: Administration, Supervision, Vocational Education, and Rehabilitation Services, each under the direction of an Assistant Superintendent. In addition there were approximately fifty professional people who composed the State Department staff.

The Division of Supervision had the primary responsibility for accrediting high schools in the state in accordance with standards formulated by the Department. Using these standards, the State Department classified high schools into four categories: "Accredited AA";

"Accredited A"; "Minor Accreditation"; and "Non-accredited" or merely "Approved." Table II shows the distribution of accredited and approved high schools.

Table II

Accredited and Approved High Schools, 1958

Accredited AA	6
Accredited A	234
Minor Accreditation	72
Non-accredited (Approved)	121
Total	433

Those systems which did not meet any of the prescribed standards were listed by the State Department of Education as "non-approved." A non-approved school was permitted to continue in operation but not to accept tuition students; that is, students from other districts in the same county which did not have their own high schools. In accordance with state regulations, districts with high schools whose accreditation permitted them to accept tuition students received $12.50 per week for each such student. This fee was financed by a mill levy on the taxpayers of all the districts in the county.

Prior to 1953 the State Superintendent of Schools was elected by the people of the state. With the establishment of the State Board of Education, the Superintendency became an appointive office. After the creation of the State Board of Education, there were attempts to change the Superintendent's post back to an elective position. One of these attempts was undertaken by an organization known as the State School Improvement Association. This group sponsored a petition for a proposed constitutional amendment to this end, but the drive failed because of the lack of necessary signatures. In addition to favoring the election of the State Superintendent, this association generally opposed school redistricting and was a vocal supporter of the small high school.

Before a school system was "non-approved" by the State Department of Education, it was issued a warning that placed it on probation for the ensuing year. This was to allow it to correct deficiencies in its education program.

The high school at Windsor was issued such a warning and duly placed on probation for the school year 1956–57. On January 16, 1957, the Coordinator of School Visitation of the State Department of Education informed the School Board at Windsor that the school was likely to be put on the non-approved list for the next year. Early in February, however, the patrons of the school received a letter from the Department of Education saying that the school would be approved until July, 1958. But then four days later another communication was received from the State Department of Education. It stated that the first letter had been in error, and gave notice that the school would not be approved after July, 1957. (The supporters of the school maintained that the Assistant State Superintendent of Schools had made a verbal promise to keep the school open one more year, and that the notice of non-approval had violated that promise.)

To the supporters of the school this was indeed a serious blow. The leader of the group indicated the future tenor of the controversy by stating, "I'll fight it. I'll keep on fighting it. That is not fair—to promise one thing and then not to hold their promise."

Upon receiving the notification of non-approval, the patrons and the school board members held a meeting to discuss what action should be taken. About eighty persons attended this meeting. After much discussion of the problems facing the school, a committee was selected to go to the capital to see what might be done to retain approval. Before adjourning, the Chairman called for a standing vote to see how many wished to retain the local high school. The vote was unanimous to take the steps necessary to meet the requirements of the State Department.

The next week the school committee met with officials of the Department of Education and pleaded for an extension of time. The committee indicated that they were fully aware of the inadequacy of the physical facilities of the school, but wished to have the school approved for another year in order to survey the possibilities of joining with additional districts to ensure a sounder financial base which would permit them to correct these deficiencies. They also pointed out that the junior class was larger than it had been in several years and that they were concerned with the difficulties which might be encountered in transferring students at that time to another school.

The representatives of the Department of Education pointed out that very little progress had been made to correct the local school situation during the year of probation; they consequently recommended to the State Board that the extension not be granted. The

State Board met on March 26, 1957, and voted to approve the recommendation of the State Department, and the school received official notice of non-approval on April 4. As in the case of all non-approved schools, the State Board granted Windsor an opportunity to appear before it and to show cause why such action should not be instituted. This hearing was scheduled for April 23, 1957.

A delegation of citizens from Windsor appeared before the State Board and requested a delay in non-approving the Windsor High School. They wanted time to continue their efforts to form a consolidated high school district, with an estimated total assessed valuation of $5,000,000 and with an estimated high school enrollment of forty to fifty pupils. The Board praised the community's efforts to solve the problem of the local high school and voted to grant a one-year extension to Windsor to work on the program of redistricting. On April 28, 1957, the State Commissioner of Education formally notified the secretary of the local school board that Windsor would be continued on an approved basis for the 1957–1958 school year subject to the following conditions:

> 1. Prior to this next school year you correct inadequacies of your school program that were stated in the letter from the State Supervisor who visited your school this past year;
> 2. That you bring to successful completion the proposed redistricting program mentioned in our meeting with you yesterday;
> 3. That you provide the State Board of Education with a progress report indicating the steps you have taken to comply with the above mentioned changes.

One year later, in April 1958, the State Board of Education voted to non-approve the Windsor High school because of its failure to comply with the conditions previously established. No appeal was made by the residents of that community for an extension. After the decision was announced, the citizens of Windsor held several school meetings to consider what action to take with respect to their local high school.

The village of Windsor was in an agricultural area, forty miles from the nearest city. It was in Bard County, whose county seat, Holden, a town of 3,500 population, was just nine miles distant. The high school at Holden was an Accredited A high school, with an enrollment in 1957–58 of 300. The villages of Spencer and Easton, each with a population of approximately 350, were six and eight miles respectively from Windsor. Each of these towns had a high school, both Approved schools. In all, there were nine high schools in the county, five of these being Accredited A, two having Minor Accreditation, and two being Non-Accredited or Approved schools.

Windsor served as a commercial and trade center for a small agricultural area surrounding the town. It had the usual service facilities of a small farm town, with a bank, grocery stores, implement dealers, and several smaller businesses. The principal economic enterprises of the community were the grain elevators which serviced the surrounding area.

The school district at Windsor encompassed some six and one-quarter sections of land, and thus the village and the district were not coterminous. Farms in the Windsor school district averaged about 200 acres with an average value in 1954 of $27,228. Almost two out of every five farms in this area were operated by tenants. About 48 per cent of all people living in the county resided on farms, another 32 per cent in rural non-farm settings, with 18 per cent of the population listed as living in Holden. The county was 756 square miles in area, with a population density of 22.4 persons per square mile.

The county population consisted almost entirely of members of the white race, with only six non-whites in a total population of 16,923. About 95 per cent of the people in the county were native-born whites of European backgrounds. The median year of education completed by the residents of the county was 8.9.

Windsor had characteristics similar to those of the county. At the time of these events it had a population of 151, compared with 167 in 1940, and 259 in 1900. It was an all-white community with almost all of the citizens being of European ancestry. The Lutheran church had the largest congregation in the community, with the Roman Catholic and the Presbyterian churches next in size.

In 1958 the school district had an assessed valuation of $478,243, with village real estate representing $98,070 of that total; farm real estate amounted to $233,800; automobiles to $24,195; personal property to $81,650; and public utilities to $40,528. The district had a school levy of 28.58 mills; a township levy of 3.82 mills; a county levy of 7.836; a state levy of 9.744; and a fire district levy of one mill. The district had no school bond indebtedness.

THE LOCAL HIGH SCHOOL DISTRICT

The high school at Windsor was in a two-story frame building which served as both an elementary and a secondary school. The elementary grades occupied the first floor, with the high school facilities in the basement and on the second floor. The State Department of Education had constantly stressed the need to improve the school plant, a need also recognized by the committee of Windsor citizens urging the retention of the school. One supervisor's report rated the school plant as very poor and noted that "The cloak room is connected to the typing room, a small room behind the furnace has been set aside for a shop, and the science facilities are completely inadequate." There was no gymnasium or auditorium.

There were two teachers in the Windsor High School. Mr. Meyer served as Superintendent, and in addition taught classes in English III, English I, Typing I, Typing II, and Physical Education. Mr. Webster had the title of Principal, and in 1957–1958 had responsibility for the following courses: General Math, American History, Bookkeeping, Shop, General Science, and Vocal Music. The curriculum was operated on an alternate-year plan, with the freshmen and sophomores taking the same courses together, as did the juniors and seniors. In 1957–1958 the juniors and seniors were enrolled in English, American History, Business, and Shop, with the freshmen and sophomores taking English, Mathematics, General Science and Shop. The state supervisor reported:

> Students are limited to an academic program of four years of English, two years each of social studies, mathematics, and science. There is no social studies for grade nine, no math for eleven and twelve, no science for eleven and twelve, and only vocal music.

Superintendent Meyer was forty-four years of age, a graduate of an accredited college, and held an initial administrative certificate. His undergraduate preparation included thirty-three semester hours of English, eighteen hours of social sciences, eight hours of mathematics, eight hours of chemistry, seventeen of German, eight of fine arts, and eight of physical education. He had completed twelve graduate hours in the field of education. Mr. Meyer had been Superintendent at Windsor for three years.

Mr. Webster was fifty-six years of age, held a permanent high school certificate issued in 1934, and had been at Windsor for one year. His undergraduate record showed he had completed sixteen semester hours of English, forty-eight hours in the social sciences, eleven hours of mathematics, fifteen hours of sciences, eight of Spanish, eight of accounting, three of shop, five of general agriculture, and five of physical education, in addition to his professional training. He had completed nine graduate hours in the field of school administration. Both men had held several different positions in smaller schools in the state over the preceding few years.

In the 1957–1958 school year the high school at Windsor enrolled twenty students in grades nine through twelve. Twelve of these pupils resided in the school district; the other eight were non-residents, for which the school received tuition. Of the twenty students, five were enrolled in the ninth grade, four in the tenth, three in the eleventh, and eight in the twelfth. The current school census showed seventy-eight individuals residing in the school district who were under twenty years of age. Twenty of these were under five years of age; ten in the five- and six-year old age category; thirty-three from seven to fifteen years old, and fifteen between sixteen and twenty.

Although no specific record had been kept regarding the occupations or further education of Windsor High School graduates, there was some indication that the preponderant majority did not continue their education beyond grade twelve. Most of the boys continued to reside on farms in the area, while a large number of girls sought employment in neighboring farms and towns.

The K-12 school budget for 1957–1958 was $17,675, including revenue from free high school tuition, with slightly over $11,000 of this allotted to the secondary school, and about $6,000 for the elementary school.

The expenditures for school support in Windsor had increased in the previous few years. However, the school district had no bonded indebtedness from school building construction. State law limited the amount of the building levy for any district by specifying that such levy "shall not exceed five mills on the dollar upon the assessed value of all taxable property."

THE CASE AGAINST RETENTION OF
WINDSOR SCHOOL

Under the state law each county was required to form a reorganization committee to study the possibilities of reorganizing school
districts. At the invitation of the Bard County Reorganization Committee the state university in 1956 completed a survey of the high
schools in Bard County. As part of this survey the university personnel
listed a minimum of forty-nine areas of the curriculum believed to
characterize an adequate secondary school. Of these forty-nine the
high school at Windsor offered fourteen. Art, instrumental music,
advanced science and mathematics, foreign languages, speech, and advanced commercial courses were among the areas which were not
found in the Windsor High School. The survey report also took note
of the inadequacy of the library facilities in the school system.

The university survey rated the school plant facilities at Windsor
as 200 on a 1,000 point scale. On this scale 1,000 points were supposed
to represent an ideal situation; 750 points were regarded as adequate.
The university personnel recommended that the school plant at
Windsor "should be abandoned in any case. It is inadequate either as
an elementary or a secondary school." The school plant at Windsor
rated the lowest of the high schools in the county on the survey
team's evaluation scale.

State officials maintained that an adequate high school program
could not be developed for a high school the size of Windsor; according to the school census there was no reason to expect that the enrollment would materially increase in the next few years. As one member
of the State Board of Education commented,

> The matter boiled down to whether local communities can be al-
> lowed to determine the quality of their schools or does the state have
> an obligation to insure that all communities have adequate education
> facilities.

According to state officials the caliber of the teaching staff was far
from desirable. One state supervisor's report claimed that Mr. Webster was teaching general mathematics with a background of eight col-

lege hours of study in the field, shop with no college hours, American history with no specific college preparation, bookkeeping with eight hours, music with no college hours.

The survey team proposed that the county be reorganized and that the number of school districts in the county be reduced from 111 to 6. Under this reorganization plan the high school at Windsor would be incorporated into a school district which would have an assessed valuation of $22,834,000 with an elementary school population of 950 and a single high school of 550 pupils. The survey committee proposed that the high school be located at Holden, the county seat, nine miles from Windsor. The recommendations of this report were not adopted by the residents of the county, partly because the proposed location of the new high school met with some opposition. Although between 1956 and 1958 the number of districts in the county was reduced from 111 to 100, most of the reduction came about through the abolition of rural elementary districts. No action was taken to reduce the number of high school districts.

THE CASE FOR THE WINDSOR SCHOOL

Not all of the residents of the community of Windsor favored continuation of the school. Generally, parents who had children in school favored some action which would ensure a better educational program. As one parent expressed it, "All I want is to make sure that my kid gets an education equal to that of any other person's child in the state."

However, a small, influential group of citizens led the opposition to the action by the State Board. The leaders of this group were the president of the local bank and the owner of a grain elevator, the latter being the largest business enterprise in the town. These individuals consistently maintained that the quality of education provided in a small school was equal or superior to that in a larger school. The bank president in a letter to the State Superintendent wrote as follows:

> . . . In my experience, and that stretches over a period of more than twenty-five years, as a teacher, parent, school board member, and now as a bank executive for many years, together with a close association with rural youth, 4-H, etc., I have found that the students who

have graduated from the smaller high schools have measured up to and in many instances have far excelled those who have graduated from top systems. Certainly we know that the one room school house must go in order to have better, smaller high schools. However, we definitely need these smaller systems in order to have a balanced, democratic, and sound way of thinking. The colleges need these students as much as they need the colleges.

He pointed out further that in the preceding several years two of the graduates of Windsor High School had, as a result of their performance on statewide competitive examinations, received state university scholarships. In 1956 a Windsor representative received the second highest score on a test on local, state, and national government which was administered to approximately 300 boys from high schools all over the state. This seemed to be further evidence that the high school at Windsor was doing a creditable job of promoting education.

Several residents of Windsor cited, as a statement of their own views, the following editorial which appeared at about this time in a farm journal with statewide circulation:

> There are two sides to every question—the right side and the other fellow's side. Here is the other side of rural school redistricting. Many rural people believe the present plan of redistricting is not right.
>
> I don't deny that there is a big problem in keeping our small high school and rural schools operating effectively. However, I believe the proposed plan will not meet the needs. . . .
>
> One reason for redistricting is that in the larger schools the increase in tax money will allow the schools to have better teachers. True, for more money a teacher with more college training can be hired. However, there is more to teaching than holding an A.B. degree. Such a degree should make a good teacher better but there is a natural ability for teaching not found in books. Then there is this to think about; the time between a teacher's own grade experience and that of teaching. The longer this span of time after maturity, the harder for the teacher to adjust herself to the pupils. There also may be too long a span of time between the studying of elementary subjects and the teaching of them. There is little in high school or college of factual elementary subject content, thereby letting the college graduate forget much of the material to be taught in the grade school.
>
> The advantage of larger classes with more competition is offset by the fact that in the smaller group each student receives more indi-

vidual help on things that trouble him. So, until the school gets extremely small, say less than four or five, it is doubtful that the size of the school has much effect on the scholarship of the students.

Many argue that there is more social development in the larger group. Here, too, the advantage is not as one-sided as at first it seems. In the small group, all must join to make it go, thereby making it less likely that cliques will be formed leaving the (some) student "out in the cold." In the little group the small student must "stretch" to play the big kids' games and vice versa—the larger children must shrink sometimes as they play kid games again. Thus the student in the little group learns to make bigger adjustments than those in the larger group who run with their own cliques.

Another argument is that redistricting will mean better equipped schools. Good equipment is necessary, but it is possible to over-equip a school and kill initiative. For example, our rural school had no basketball court. The teacher and larger boys made backboards from discarded lumber and mounted them on old poles. Crude? Yes, but those boys by meeting their need learned more than basketball, they learned to meet life's problems. What more can be asked of any school system?

Again it's said that we must redistrict to save our small high schools. If our tax burden, as earlier stated, was better distributed the problem would be partly solved. Why confuse the issue? Our high school problem is not the grade school problem. High school students are better able to go greater distances by bus or their own car. Let's keep grade school students where they do not need to ride busses.

The final test is a product of the school. Are rural students inferior to town students? A check of honors in high schools will show that rural students earn their fair share of honors. Since by the final test, rural schools are not yet passé, we of the countryside must oppose redistricting if we would keep our rural schools. I believe the rural school, a time-honored institution, still has its place in the state.

Following the granting in April, 1957, of a year's extension, the residents of the community initiated plans for improving the school's program. On July 19th the secretary of the Windsor Board of Education informed the State Superintendent of Schools that the following steps had been taken to remedy the local school situation:

(1) In the way of redistricting, we have petitions being circulated in five outside districts; (2) We have two qualified teachers contracted for the ensuing year; (3) We are also considering the purchase

of science equipment enough for the basic sciences and have provided for the teaching of this subject; (4) No immediate plans have
been made for a new school building.

The problem of increasing the size of the school district and of
providing additional facilities for the high school continued to be a
source of controversy over the next few months. The State Department of Education maintained that the school district had taken no
realistic steps to solve the educational problems of the community.
The residents of the local school district countered this by saying that
the school board had been considering plans for reorganizing the entire district, but that "this takes a little time; it can't be done overnight."

On October 18, 1957, the secretary of the board reported to the
State Superintendent that three rural school districts with a total
assessed valuation of $1,600,000 had petitioned to join the Windsor
school district, and asked about the advisability of floating a bond
issue of $150,000 for a new school building. Two weeks later the State
Superintendent replied that the consolidation of three rural districts
with Windsor was a step in the right direction but was not enough.
With regard to the bond issue, the Superintendent stated that the
school enrollment in the district would not justify this expenditure,
and that it would be better to spend this money on the elementary
school facilities.

In opposing the proposed consolidation of school districts, some
people were reportedly suspicious that the people in Holden, where
the new high school would be located, were only interested in "gob-
bling up" all the smaller districts which surrounded it. Some were
quoted as saying, too, that the larger high school would force the "bad
influences of city life" upon the rural youngsters. They emphasized
that they believed a better education could be provided in a high
school of twenty pupils than in a high school of 1,500 pupils. There
was a strong feeling that the elimination of the high school at Windsor would serve only to increase taxes for the support of larger high
schools, and that in the long run local communities could not long
survive without the maintenance of the local high school.

*   *   *   *   *

The high school at Windsor was not permitted to operate in 1958–
59 as an approved school. The local residents seemed to believe that

they faced three possibilities among which they had to choose. One was to consolidate with the high school at Easton or the high school at Spencer. (Easton had a high school enrollment of thirty-seven, Spencer of fifty.) A second alternative was to form only an elementary school district and permit the high school students to attend an approved high school elsewhere in the county on a free-tuition basis. The third alternative was to contract with either Easton or Spencer for the education of Windsor High School students, but retain the high school district. It was argued that the third alternative would allow the residents of Windsor to reopen their school in the future.

The first of these alternatives soon appeared closed, since neither Easton nor Spencer indicated any interest in such a plan.

Several meetings of the patrons of the school at Windsor were then held to decide upon which of the two remaining alternatives to accept. First a vote was taken on a motion to form an elementary district and to permit students to go to an approved school of their choice on a free high school tuition basis. The motion did not receive the fifty-five per cent majority which the Chairman of the School Board ruled was needed for approval, and he declared the motion defeated. It was later discovered that only a simple majority was needed; nevertheless, a new vote was taken. On May 29, 1958, thirty-three voted in favor of contracting, and thirty-one in favor of forming an elementary district. This decision permitted Windsor to retain its high school district.

On June 23, 1958, several high school districts which the state had recently non-approved obtained from the District Court a temporary injunction against the State to prevent it from withholding free tuition money from non-approved schools.

In the spring of 1959 the District Court in the state's capital made the temporary injunction a permanent one. The Court held that the State Department of Education did not have the right to place schools on a non-approved list and deny them free high school tuition money. It held that the statute which gave the State Department of Education authority to

> . . . establish standards and procedures for classifying, approving and accrediting schools, including the establishment of minimum standards and procedures for approving the opening of new schools, the continued legal operation of all schools, and for the approval of high schools for the collection of free high school tuition money

was a delegation of "unregulated discretion" to the State Board of Education by the State Legislature, pointing out that the Legislature may not delegate unrestricted authority to any administrative agency. It declared the statute "invalid, unconstitutional and void."

The Court held also that the standards established by the Department of Education were of such a nature that:

> The vagueness, ambiguity, susceptibility of an incomprehensible range of interpretations, the inability of a citizen to determine any guides or controls as to the setting up of a school or what he should do from these regulations, clearly results in a situation in which there would be a complete abdication of the legislature and a possible assumption of dictatorship over the school system by an administrative board.

Meanwhile, in the 1958–1959 school year the residents of Windsor had provided for elementary education in the community and contracted with other high school districts in the county for the education of high school pupils. Three students attended high school in Easton, four in Spencer, and five in Holden.

The school district held its Annual Meeting in May, 1959, to make a final decision as to what action should be taken regarding the maintenance of a high school district. The district voted to organize only an elementary district and to continue to send high school students to other schools in the county. The vote was, in the words of one person present,

> . . . only won by a bare majority, so it was quite evenly divided and could have gone either way. As you well know in cases like these there is always bitterness of one sort or another. In my opinion, only my opinion, I believe that most of the people either have resigned themselves to not having a school in Windsor, or realize that it just doesn't seem feasible at this time. There is some talk of a reorganization plan to include several of the districts around and therefore having a school closer to Windsor. Whether this will materialize or not, I have no way of knowing.

The residents of Windsor had in effect voted to discontinue their high school.

SELECTED READINGS

Burke, Arvid J., *Financing Public Schools in the United States*, rev. ed. New York: Harper and Brothers, 1957.

Conant, James Bryant, *The American High School Today: A First Report to Interested Citizens*. New York: McGraw-Hill Book Company, 1959.

Kreitlow, Burton W., *Rural Education: Community Backgrounds*. New York: Harper and Brothers, 1954.

Loomis, Charles P., and J. Allan Beegle, *Rural Sociology: the Strategy of Change*. Englewood Cliffs, N.J.: Prentice-Hall, Inc., 1957.

Morlan, Robert, *Capitol, Courthouse, and City Hall: Readings in American State and Local Government*. Boston: Houghton Mifflin Company, 1954.

West, James, *Plainville, U.S.A.* New York: Columbia University Press, 1945.

CASE 18

Buckley: An Inadequate School System

In September, 1953, the Citizens Committee for Improving the Public Schools was formed in Buckley, a city of some 200,000 population. Mr. George S. Hampshire, a businessman who was a resident of Buckley, was Chairman of the Committee.

By 1954 the Citizens Committee was so disturbed over the conditions existing in the Buckley school system that it took the matter directly to Mr. Henry Stevens, State Superintendent of Schools, and complained to him of the following conditions in the Buckley schools: [1]

1. Classes were over-crowded.
2. There was a high teacher turn-over.
3. Per-pupil expenditure for the public schools was the lowest in the county.
4. Teachers were greatly underpaid.

---

[1] Article 5, Section 4, of the state constitution says: "The head of the department of education shall be the State Board of Education, which shall appoint and at pleasure remove a Superintendent of Schools to be the chief administrative officer of the department."

The Education Law states that the Superintendent shall "advise and guide the school officers of all districts and cities of the state in relation to their duties and the general management of the schools under their control."

5. School supplies were grossly inadequate.
6. Unsanitary conditions existed in some schools.

In beginning the investigation of the situation in Buckley, Mr. Stevens directed the Corporation Counsel of the City of Buckley, Mr. Herbert Leary, to answer the charges of the Citizens Committee. The substance of his reply of February 11, 1955, was as follows:

1. The children of Buckley "are, and at all times have been, accorded more than the basic minimum requirements of the Education Law."
2. The Superintendent's proposed investigation in Buckley was not "the answer to the financial problems of the City and the Board of Education."
3. The complaints were not specific enough to stand up in a court of law. They were "conclusions and opinions," and not statements of fact.
4. The charge was incorrect that the 1954 budget was insufficient to put teachers on the minimum salary scale provided by the state law. It was also incorrect that dissatisfaction and discouragement existed among the teachers, and that a heavy pupil load, as well as over-crowded conditions, were forcing many good teachers to leave.

In the course of the ensuing dispute over the Buckley schools public hearings were held. In April, 1955, in an action which he described as "uncommon" but not unprecedented, Superintendent Stevens said that by January 1, 1956, the Buckley Board of Education would have to submit to him "sufficient evidence of an adequate program, both in respect to its educational offerings and its building needs for the ensuing year." The Superintendent threatened to withhold further state aid unless the evidence were submitted.[2]

Buckley, stretching north and south along the Diablo River, grew in the nineteenth century as an industrial town quite separate and distinct from a big city neighbor. On the slopes leading to the river

---

[2] In 1953 the Superintendent had for many months withheld $500,000 in state aid to Buckley until the City had complied with the law and brought teacher salaries to the prescribed minimum. This action had been the result of a suit brought by Buckley teachers.

In 1954–55 Buckley had received $2,046,000 in regular state aid, and $231,000 as part of a state-wide emergency grant. Including state aid, the 1954–55 school operating budget was $5,731,000.

Joseph Square had developed as the center of business activity. In the days when most traffic was by boat, stagecoach, carriage, or horseback, it was logical that the center of business activity and of government should coincide. Joseph Square soon became the center of political activity in Buckley.

Between the Diablo River to the west and a smaller river to the east Buckley had a series of ridges running north and south. In the nineteenth century the city had developed as a group of little communities on the ridges or in the valleys. These communities, sometimes having little in common except city services, were frequently characterized by the existence of large numbers of one or another immigrant groups. There had long been a tradition in Buckley of separate "community" taxpayer associations, the chief activity of which had been the protection of local financial vested interests. As a confederation of small enclaves, Buckley citizens early developed great skill in making the pressures of local opinion felt among the politicians of the Joseph Square area.

It was not only geography which gave Buckley a north-south axis. Transportation moved in the same direction. The railroad ran north and south parallel to the river. A recently constructed multi-lane state parkway ran north and south through the eastern part of the city, and another parkway ran north and south along the boundary line between Buckley and its neighbors to the east.

These developments in Buckley had concentrated both industry and population in what came to be, in 1908, wards one through eight. Lack of any natural geographical passage to the east, together with the existing north-south transportation routes, meant that the Buckley "hinterlands"—roughly speaking, wards nine through twelve—were rather slow in their growth. It was not until about the time of the second world war, when the exodus to the suburbs became a major pattern in American life, that the eastern wards of Buckley began their immense growth in population. In 1940 three-quarters of the people of Buckley still lived in "old town," but this was no longer true by 1950. Yet in 1955 three of the four police stations were still in "old town." Between 1945 and 1954 Buckley increased in population by 19,381, and most of these people moved into wards nine through twelve.

The sprawling Harris Carpet Company, located in "old town," had grown over the years to become one of the world's largest carpet factories. Run by men who had learned their trade in Scotland, the plant was owned by people who had a paternalistic approach toward their workers. Their only significant industrial rival in Buckley was the Jones Elevator Company. In fact, however, Harris Carpet dominated the industrial scene thoroughly, and in the nineteenth century successive waves of immigrants had come to it in the following order:

1. Irish
2. Polish
3. Russian (mostly Ukrainian)
4. Italian

During the nineteenth century it had not been uncommon for Harris Carpet to send a ship directly to Ellis Island in New York City to recruit labor for the factory. Many immigrants who settled in Buckley had never been through New York City. For many years there had been entire Buckley wards where the language most commonly spoken had been Polish or Italian.[3]

The Harris Carpet and Jones companies prospered for many years. Employment at Harris Carpet reached its peak in the early forties, but post-war difficulties abounded, and by the spring of 1954 the plant had closed its doors, leaving Buckley with many temporarily unemployed.[4] Possessing a sprawling plant, the obsolescence of which proved to be very costly, the company was also the victim of consumer demand change. In 1954, with a production capacity of one hundred million square yards of wool carpet, it had sold only fifty million. The public had turned to cotton and synthetics. The plant moved to Alabama, where, with the aid of a $5,000,000 municipal bond issue, the city had built for the company an air-conditioned one-floor plant designed by the company's own engineers.

Having just lost its largest business, and having consequently suf-

---

[3] The U.S. census of 1950 showed the Buckley population to be 152,798. Of these, 147,782 were whites, and of these whites, 25,695 were foreign born. There follows a list, in the proper order, of the nine countries from which most of these foreign born had come.

1.	Italy	—6,041	6.	Scotland	—1,790
2.	Poland	—2,393	7.	USSR	—1,503
3.	Germany	—2,326	8.	England & Wales	—1,319
4.	Ireland	—2,317	9.	Czechoslovakia	—1,132
5.	Austria	—1,913			

[4] Of the 4,841 persons let out by Harris Carpet after March, 1952, jobs had been found for 2,489 by March 1, 1955.

fered a sizable cut in its tax roll, Buckley was soon threatened with another crisis. The Jones Elevator Company announced in early 1954 that it would invest substantially in modernizing the Buckley plant and equipment upon "satisfactory arrangements with city authorities on proposals which the company will make." The company then asked the city permanently to close four streets intersecting its Buckley plant and, further, asked for relief from "unwarrantably high tax assessments." With the closing of the streets, great savings could be had from reduction in costs of guarding the premises, simplification of intra-plant transportation, improved flexibility of lay-out, and use of land previously wasted.

Later Jones asked the city to reduce the assessed valuation of its plant for 1952, 1953, 1954, and 1955. The 1955 valuation was $3,010,-250, and the company asked that it be reduced to $2,265,280. In January, 1955, the company received from the city a refund of $91,-915.27 on taxes for 1947–51, as a result of settlement by the city of claims to force a reduction in tax bills.

The alternative which Jones offered was to move to a more modern plant in the Middle West. Approximately two thousand jobs were at stake. The fact that Jones for all practical purposes got what it wanted and did eventually invest heavily in its Buckley plant did not change the fact that, at a time when public education was in need of much more money from the city, the latter was faced with an industrial move if the tax relief were not granted.

The events connected with the Harris Carpet and Jones companies were sobering. That they were not disastrous was due in large part to the opening in April, 1954, of a giant shopping center in the eastern part of the city. This center, with its parking facilities for 5,140 cars and employed staff of approximately 3,000, was at the time one of the world's largest suburban mercantile marts. Its effect on Buckley promised to be great, but the precise nature of the problems and blessings it would bring nobody could foresee.

It was in the middle of these developments that Superintendent Stevens threatened to cut off state aid unless Buckley showed that it could produce an "adequate program" for its public schools.

At the time the Superintendent gave his warning, he also said that he was aware that Buckley was perilously close to its constitutional tax limit, but he added that it "is not clear" that "moneys may not be made available for educational purposes which are, perhaps, being diverted to other less important uses." Exactly what money was referred to was difficult to know, but that money was needed could scarcely be denied. By any standards Buckley schools were in bad shape.

In April, 1955, the Greater Metropolitan Area School Study Council, an affiliate of the Institute of Administrative Research at Teachers College, Columbia University, New York, reported that a survey showed schools in the area were spending an average of $400 per pupil, compared to a national average of $260. By the standards of the county, however, the Buckley figure of $299.34 was low, as Table I shows.

Table I

School Enrollment, Tax Rate and Cost per Pupil
In Eight Districts

Community	Enrollment Jan., 1955	School Tax Rate 1954–55	Cost/Pupil 1953–54
Buckley	21,694	11.99 ('54) 11.75 ('55)	$299.34
A	8,786	17.20	436.65
B	10,885	20.10	408.32
C	7,764	19.60	474.12
D	1,228	18.63	700.04
E	1,497	22.98	453.35
F	3,228	24.59	567.79
G	942	23.54	523.32

In 1939–40 Buckley had spent $160 per weighted pupil.[5] In 1957, experts calculated, $450 would have been needed to buy the same kind of education.

In early 1955 a beginning teacher who had completed four years of college was paid $3200 by the City of Buckley. Table II shows the relationship between this salary and the salaries being paid by neighboring communities in the county.

---

[5] The method used to compute the allocation of state aid to local school districts provided for differential weighting for pupils in kindergarten, grades one through six and grades seven through twelve. The weights were ½ for half-day kindergarten pupils, 1 for full day kindergartners and those in grades one through six, and 1¼ for those in grades seven through twelve.

Table II

Minimum and Maximum Salaries Paid to Teachers
in Buckley and Neighboring Districts, 1955

Community	Minimum	Maximum
Buckley	$3,200	$6,400
A	3,700	7,700
B	3,500	7,100
C	3,800	8,600
H	3,500	6,500
I	3,400	6,600

On April 15, 1955, the *Buckley News* contained an article relating, in the following terms, the facts about overcrowded conditions in the elementary classes.

Number of Classes	Size in number of pupils
7	40 or more
94	35–39
131	30–34
146	25–29
4	20–24
8	15–19
10	Less than 15

Mr. August Kulsky, Superintendent of Schools in Buckley, estimated early in 1955 that it would take between $10,000,000 and $15,000,000 in the next five to ten years to put the Buckley schools in order. He added that the city could raise $150,000 more and still be within the 2% tax limit imposed by the state.

Over the years the value of taxable property in Buckley had increased far less rapidly than the cost of operating its schools. But the state had made available certain taxes which localities might use for raising revenue. Theoretically, Buckley might have used any of the following taxes, in addition to the usual real estate levy.

1. A retail sales tax
2. A 5% tax on restaurant meals over $1.00
3. A theater admissions tax of 5%
4. A 3% tax on consumer utility bills
5. An automobile use tax
6. A tax on hotel rooms for transients
7. A tax on liquor store licenses
8. A tax on coin-operated amusement devices.

In 1955 the only non-property revenue in Buckley came from a tax on admissions to harness racing and a 1% tax on gross earnings of public utility companies. Other taxes which Buckley might have used to raise some extra revenue were, needless to say, unpopular. When the new shopping center was dedicated, Buckley residents rejoiced over the probability that a great many non-residents would come over the sales tax boundary line to buy in the county's tax-free area. Is it any wonder that talk of a sales tax in Buckley aroused little enthusiasm? In December, 1955, City Manager Kennedy told the annual public budget hearing that only a retail sales tax would effectively provide extra school money, and that he opposed it.

State Senator John F. James, Republican of Buckley, speaking on the floor of the state senate on January 7, 1956, said that a sales tax would be unworkable in Buckley, and that auto or restaurant taxes would be insufficient to meet school needs. He did not mention the other five non-property taxes available to the city.

Early in 1956 the City of Buckley requested that the state share its revenues from the Buckley Raceway, and it was suggested that this would be a long-term solution to the school finance problem. City Manager Kennedy specifically proposed at the state capital that the city take over the state's 15% tax on admissions to the harness track and share in the sliding scale levy on the pari-mutuel betting. Other proposals were made.

Dr. Philip Potter, a member of the City Council, was sponsor of a resolution to tap the local raceway for funds. The Governor was asked to summon a special legislative session which would empower Buckley to impose a 2% sales tax on the pari-mutuel take at the raceway.[6]

The raceway proposals had many political overtones. Designed to secure the aid of the state in the school crisis, they received no immediate positive attention and brought no immediate solutions to the problems facing the people of Buckley. It was contended that Buckley, composed of many different "communities," and governed by a City Council composed of one Councilman from each ward, found that its Councilmen simply did not want to vote for new taxes, largely for political reasons.

The activities of the Parent-Teacher organizations and several other groups in 1955 indicated that interest in the schools was high.[7] How-

---

[6] No attempt can here be made to assess the role of the raceway in Buckley politics. However, it should be pointed out that on January 6, 1954, a contribution of $100,000 for civic purposes was made by the raceway corporation to the city.

[7] In April, 1955, the Council of Parent-Teacher Associations reported a membership of 12,545. A two hundred per cent gain in one decade had come at a time when the school population rose only fifteen per cent. Of 639 teachers eligible for membership in 1955, 540 had joined.

The Council also reported that it spent $13,000 on textbooks, visual-aids material, and library books in 1953–54. This money came from fund-raising events in the schools.

ever, civic pride and community feeling for the most part lacked an outlet for expression. Buckley, divided between "old town" and the newer eastern areas, could not coordinate its efforts.[8]

As Buckley had grown in the post-war era, and an ever larger proportion of its people had come to live in the eastern part of the city, new problems had arisen. Many of the new residents worked in a nearby city to the south and had no contact with either the merchants or the politicians of Joseph Square. Leading the lives of commuters, they found that one inducement to settle in Buckley was the low tax rate. Transportation for these commuters was in a north-south direction, and their business was in the city, not in Joseph Square.

The post-war "newcomers" soon came to represent a great deal of the wealth of Buckley, but their voting power in the City Council was in no manner proportionate to either their wealth or their numbers. Faced with a situation in which the "newcomers" began asserting themselves, the "old towners" were reportedly rather ingenious at devising methods for the preservation of existing advantages.

In 1954 the Republicans of Buckley decided to try to alter the structure of the city government. In April the Republican City Committee voted, 182 to 7, in favor of a November referendum on the question of eliminating the election of Councilmen by wards and reducing the size of the Council from twelve to six. As one letter to the *Buckley News* expressed the problem, "At present Buckley is a confederacy of twelve wards, with all the weaknesses inherent in a confederacy."

The system by which Buckley was governed had much to do, it was asserted, with the plight of the schools. Otto Lenz, Chairman of the South Buckley Citizens Committee for Citywide Elections, said that American cities which had changed from the ward system to city-wide elections reported greater support of school programs. The Republican City Chairman said the ward system tended to disrupt civic unity.

The disproportionate representative system in Buckley is demon-

---

[8] Report No. 1 of the Buckley School Survey, published in 1957 by the State Department of Education, recommended that ". . . a full-time administrative assistant to the superintendent for community affairs be appointed." His job would be to inform the public "about education through every route possible and the performance of an honest listening function to know what the public wants in the public schools." Presumably it would be through this agent that orderly means would be provided for hearing from the community.

strated by the figures for the city at election-time, 1954, shown in Table III.

Table III

Registered Voters in Buckley by Wards, 1954

Ward	Reg. Voters	Approx. % Reg. Voters
First	3,786	5.3
Second	2,694	3.8
Third	6,641	9.5
Fourth	6,381	9.3
Fifth	4,744	6.7
Sixth	6,548	9.2
Seventh	3,111	4.4
Eighth	5,891	8.3
Ninth	8,498	12.0
Tenth	5,998	8.5
Eleventh	7,851	11.0
Twelfth	8,576	12.0

The City of Buckley had time after time shown a Republican majority for state and federal offices. However, in 1953 ten of the twelve Councilmen in the municipal government were Democrats. The strength of the Democratic party was in "old town," and Republicans who lived there were as under-represented in the Council as the Democrats who lived in the eastern areas of the City. Although this disproportionate representation was a political problem, it brought with it many sociological problems as well. The demand for school reform came to a very large extent from the "newcomers" of the eastern areas of town. Under the existing ward system, however, these people felt unable to express their beliefs in the form of proper political action.

In the November referendum the people of Buckley voted 25,897 to 19,110 in favor of retaining the existing ward system.

Another factor, the influence of which was not clear, was the attitude of the people of Buckley to the parochial schools. In 1954, when the public school enrollment was approximately 23,000, the parochial school enrollment stood at about 10,000 students, the majority in elementary schools.

Approximately $6,000,000 in church-related construction was planned, begun, or completed in Buckley in 1955. Heading the list was the Catherine Watson school building, with its Harriet Henderson

Baker auditorium, in Ward Three. Conducted by the Sisters of Charity of Mount Saint Vincent, this school was built for an enrollment of over 200 and included the most modern facilities for dramatic production and for training students in television technique.

Another large Buckley school project was completed in the spring of 1955, the St. Peter's Roman Catholic elementary school with facilities for 950 boys and girls. Built in the First Ward, this school cost approximately $1,400,000.

In 1955 the Church of Christ the King, in the Third Ward, began construction of an eight-classroom parish elementary school building. The projected cost, including a convent for teaching sisters of the school, was approximately $500,000.

At another location in the Third Ward priests of the Roman Catholic Capuchin-Franciscan Order completed a building project at Sacred Heart High School. Finished at a cost of over $400,000, this project meant that the school now had a total of 24 classrooms and two study halls accommodating more than 200 students each.

Growth of the parish school in the Polish-speaking area served by St. Casimir's Church brought completion in the spring of 1955 of a new $350,000 convent for the school's teaching sisters. This was in Ward Two.

The parish elementary school of St. Denis Roman Catholic Church in the Eighth Ward started construction, in 1955, of a $250,000 addition to the existing school, and St. Michael's Seminary, the major seminary of the archdiocese, dedicated a new chapel, a new classroom, and new living quarters in October, 1955.[9]

All this construction, and the interest which had brought it about, were the result of unprecedented prosperity and increasing population in Buckley. The enrollment in the parochial schools increased by 3,500 in the seven years from 1948 to 1955. It is perhaps worth noting that most of the construction of schools was in "old town," whose inhabitants carried more than their share of political power at Joseph Square.

While it was a fact that the wards having the largest Protestant and Jewish populations were the ones which lacked political power

---

[9] No accurate figure for the religious affiliations of the people of Buckley can be given. Not all groups follow the same calendar year or count membership in the same manner. The indications are, however, that Buckley in 1955 was about one half Roman Catholic. The Protestant and Jewish faiths shared in the construction boom, but most of their buildings were churches, parish houses, or Sunday School buildings.

at Joseph Square, it is not easy to ascertain the relation between the
religious situation and the school problems. Mr. Hampshire, Chairman of the Citizens Committee for Improving the Public Schools,
once stated that any new member of the Board of Education ought to
have children of his own in the Buckley schools. Arthur A. Flanagan,
Democratic boss, said that this was "vicious" and constituted an in-
jection of the "religious issue" into public discussion of the schools.
William A. Bader, Republican boss, felt the same way and seemed
outraged when he found that some persons had questioned whether
the fact that ten of the Buckley Councilmen were Roman Catholic
had anything to do with their votes for or against funds for the public
schools. The truth of such a charge could never be sustained. At least
one observer claimed that it was not a matter of the "religious issue"
having been injected into politics, but rather of politics having been
injected into a religious dispute.

It was true that since early 1955 only one member of the Mayor-
appointed nine-member Board of Education had had a child in public
school. It was also true that Fourth Ward Democratic Councilman
Dr. Philip Potter, a prominent Roman Catholic surgeon, was an able
champion of the cause of the public schools. So also was Mr. Richard
Johnson, a Roman Catholic who was School Business Administrator.
When in November, 1955, the Citizens Committee held a rally, the
first annual award of the Committee was presented to Dr. Potter. He
was hailed for his courageous efforts in behalf of public education in
the City of Buckley.

Over and over again Buckley officials had complained that the primary reason for their not spending more money on the schools was the
state law. It was true that when Superintendent Stevens made his decision with respect to Buckley he spoke of that city as being perilously
close to the debt limit and the tax limit imposed upon it by the state.
The City of Buckley had, however, reached only one half of its debt
limit and had some reserves in the budget.

It was said in many quarters that "fiscal independence" for the
Board of Education was the answer to the education problem in Buckley. That is, by constitutional amendment the legally defined taxing
and borrowing capacities should be divided equitably between the general municipal government and the school district government. The
proposal to give the Board of Education such independence was opposed by the Council of Civic and Taxpayers Associations. But it had

the support of the Board itself and was to be part of the State Education Department's plan for a long-range solution to the fiscal problems facing the school system. The Superintendent's plan would have amended the state constitution to permit Buckley, as well as several other cities, to establish an independent city school district after approval by the city's voters in a referendum. The existing law, which imposed a tax limit of 2% of the average assessed valuation of real property over a five-year period, was to be altered so that it would impose a limit of 1.15% on the proposed school district, and 1.35% on the city, thus raising the total levy to 2.5%.[10]

The plan did not, however, win approval in the legislature in the spring of 1956.

*   *   *   *   *

In Buckley the City Manager framed his budget recommendations to the City Council and submitted them by October 15th. The Council was not permitted to increase them, but it could reduce them or send them back to the Manager for further consideration.

When in the autumn of 1955 Buckley had a look at the proposed new budget, it appeared that the Board of Education would receive $700,000 more than in the previous year. In spite of this increase, however, the total sum allocated to the Board was approximately $800,000 short of what the Board had requested.

The proposed new budget did include an increase of $105,000 in contributions to the Teacher Retirement Fund, an extra $214,170 in debt service for education, and $8,000 for higher pension costs for Board of Education employees other than teachers. These items accounted for 59.5% of the total increase of the 1956 budget over the 1955 budget.

Reaction to the proposed new budget was immediate.

1. The City Manager told the annual public budget hearing that only a retail sales tax would provide extra school money, and that he opposed such a tax. He said the school problem

---

10 In 1952 two bills which would have given fiscal independence to the Buckley Board of Education had been before the legislature. The first had called for a split in the spending, with 1.1% for City Hall and .9% for the Board of Education. The second would have provided 1.35% for the city and 1.15% for the schools. Both bills had been killed.

resided in constitutional tax restrictions over which Buckley had no control.

2. The Board of Education unanimously adopted the new budget, after having cancelled proposed salary increases for teachers, and at the same time labeled it inadequate.

3. Mr. Hampshire and Mr. Herbert D'Antonio, Chairman and Co-Chairman respectively of the Citizens Committee for Improving the Public Schools, demanded that the State withhold further aid to Buckley.

4. Salary raises for teachers having been cancelled, the Buckley Teachers Association threatened to carry out a program of "minimum services"—that is, to protest by refusing to perform extra-curricular duties.[11] The Chamber of Delegates of the Association passed a resolution in January, 1956, to "adopt a teaching program shorn of after-school activities" and to set up emergency committees to carry out the program.

As part of a teacher campaign to force a 5% raise in salary, the threat of a "minimum program" was made at a most opportune time. However, the Board of Education told the teachers they would be "well advised" to withhold any action until the Superintendent's decision had been rendered. This the teachers agreed to do.

At the end of 1955 the Buckley Board of Education made its report to the new State Superintendent, Charles L. Martin. The inadequacy of the budget was blamed on the City Council; the Board felt the Council could still meet some of the critical needs by approving requests of $189,950 for supplies and $281,415 for a 5% salary increase for all school employees. That would still leave the Board in need of over $300,000 for operating outlays, and the Superintendent was asked "to use every means within his power" to make a special emergency grant if he were satisfied that the Council could not meet these requests.[12] The Board informed Mr. Martin that the inadequate

---

[11] It will be recalled that Superintendent Stevens had instructed Buckley to submit to him evidence of an adequate program "both in respect to its educational offerings and its building needs." With this in mind the Board of Education voted to transfer money designed for salary raises and use it for supplies, equipment and other needs.

[12] The raceway, always the center of political controversy, was again in the news. At the end of December, Senators Robert R. Jackson, Republican, and George P. Donahue, Democrat, sponsored a bill which would have turned over to the City of Buckley about $250,000 in raceway admissions taxes, at that time collected by the State.

budget had made it impossible to recruit new teachers and thus to reduce elementary school classes to thirty-five or fewer pupils.

What had Buckley actually done with regard to its school construction and maintenance program during the year 1955?

The School Business Administrator, Richard T. Johnson, had written in his operational report for 1955 that the Buckley school system had never "inaugurated and accomplished so vast a building and reconstruction program as in 1955." He listed the following accomplishments.

1. During the year the Board of Education had awarded 126 contracts valued at $6,002,699.41 (not including architects' fees).

2. The maintenance mechanic staff had been enlarged, and "no other single action has produced so much for the monies expended." The new staff, increased in number from 5 to 14, "will enable the Department to make many repairs not possible previously." The former crew of 7 painters was increased to 12, and it was anticipated that the painting cycle, which had been 12 years, could now be reduced to 8.

In January, 1956, ground was broken for the completion of the Southeastern Buckley Junior-Senior High School. The finishing of this school, at a cost not to exceed $5,000,000, had been voted by the City Council in mid-summer, 1955.[13]

In spite of the building program for 1955 a budget in which 94% of the funds went for salaries and wages had left little room for other items. Dr. Watrina Copeland, Director of the Health Service of the Public Schools, had reported in April, 1955, the existence of 7,280 cases of defective teeth in a total of 19,378 students examined. Furthermore, Dr. Copeland said the state recommended that there be 21 nurses in the Buckley schools, instead of 10, and 10 dental hygienists instead of one.

---

[13] This school, already partially completed and in use by 1955, was planned by more than 2000 persons, organized into 23 major committees. According to an article in a national professional journal, "The group planning approach was adopted as a matter of policy by the Board of Education. It resulted in determining to employ an educational consultant, and in establishing criteria for the selection of the architect. High on the list of architectural qualifications was the ability to work with consultants and groups in the long-drawn-out, but highly important, preliminary planning program."

Except for coaching fees and salaries, not a penny had been budgeted in 1955 for high school athletics.

A special survey revealed in the spring of 1955 that of the 37 public schools in the City of Buckley, 7 had libraries which met the minimum standards set by the State Board of Education and the American Library Association. Marjorie A. Burke, Supervisor of School Libraries, stated that it would take 31,027 books, as well as annual replacements and additions, to get the Buckley schools to meet the minimum requirements.

In May, 1955, the Principal of Madison High School said he had received no library books or magazines for more than three years.

THE SUPERINTENDENT'S DECISION

After the Buckley Board of Education had reported to the Superintendent, public hearings were held at the state capital. Mr. Hampshire of the Citizens Committee said there was no jubilation in the ranks of his group. Former Superintendent Stevens, he said, had given the city fathers and politicians an opportunity to redeem themselves, and they ought to have seized the chance. Members of his Committee told the Superintendent that in their opinion the case was now closed, because the Board of Education had itself termed the new budget inadequate. Their attitude was that nothing remained to be done except to take corrective and/or punitive action.

At the public hearing the Board of Education and the City took different stands. Mr. Hampshire questioned the propriety of the City's action in hiring special counsel to represent it, while the City's own corporation counsel represented the Board of Education.

Immediately after the hearings in early February, all interested parties began the preparation of briefs and rebuttals. These were to be completed within the 17 days, allowed by the State Superintendent. Events moved swiftly:

1. The Buckley City Council authorized four bond issues, totaling $775,626 to be issued at the call of the Board of Education. Nearly $500,000 was for new equipment. Nearly $200,000 was to be used for textbooks and replacement. Over $51,000 was for furniture, and $33,800 was to go for

window shades and drapes. The President of the Buckley Board of Education said he thought the State Superintendent would consider this favorably. It showed, he said, that the city was doing something.

2. At the state capital a bi-partisan bill was introduced to give Buckley and some other cities special contributions of state funds with which to pay probable mandatory teacher salary increases in September.

3. A series of 11 bills, designed to carry out recommendations of the state's Temporary Commission on Educational Finance, were introduced into the legislature with bi-partisan support on February 13, a few days before the due date for the briefs and rebuttals.[15]

In its brief submitted at the end of February, 1956, the City of Buckley charged that the State Superintendent was "without power" to withhold state aid from any municipality simply because in his judgment the over-all educational program of that area was inadequate. The city attorneys argued that Buckley was not accused of violating any law, and that the State Superintendent could not set up standards as to what was "adequate" without authority from the legislature. They claimed that neither Superintendent Stevens nor the state education laws offered any definition of "adequate," and that there were no standards by which to judge "adequacy."

The Buckley Board of Education objected to some of the figures given the Superintendent by the City, claiming they were "not supported by the facts."

On March 15, 1956, the state legislature passed without dissent a measure providing for a Supreme Court review of decisions of the State Superintendent in cases such as the existing one. There were public expressions of doubt that the administrators should have so much power over the disbursement of state funds. The bill was designed to take effect in September.

---

[15] The Commission's 342-page report, presented to the Governor and Legislature, had been the result of a study begun in August, 1954. Among other things, the report recommended increased state aid for education and held that the county within which Buckley lay could have raised $13,000,000 from taxes other than real estate (using 1954 figures). Of this, $11,800,000 could have come from a 2% sales tax, with food exempted. From a tax on motor vehicles $1,400,000 could have been realized, and from a 25% share of state retail liquor license fees $182,000 could have been obtained. Another $332,000 could have come from a 5% tax on admissions.

About one week later the Senate passed the same bill, again by unanimous vote. It went to the Governor, who vetoed it.

Meanwhile, Superintendent Martin had made his decision. In announcing his order to pay full state aid to the City of Buckley, the Superintendent said that the proposed program for 1956 would bring about "substantial improvements in the school system," but that the evidence was not sufficiently conclusive "to support a final determination of the adequacy" of the Buckley school program. Mr. Stevens, he said, had suggested a survey as a means of ascertaining the true facts about education in Buckley, and this was again recommended. Such a survey, said Mr. Martin, should be broad enough to "review the administrative and fiscal relationship between the city school district and the city government." The Superintendent indicated that he felt the permanent solution lay in a fiscally independent Board of Education.

In a very real sense the Superintendent's decision represented the beginning, not the end, of a chapter in the history of education in Buckley. The suggested survey was carried out, with the aid of about one hundred specialists from the State Education Department and 1,200 local residents. Seven reports resulted from the survey, and the public school system was indicted on many fronts. Evidence in the ensuing months suggested that as a result of the survey the plight of the Buckley school system was gradually being eased, and by the autumn of 1957 teacher salaries had increased to a range of $4,200 to $8,500.

SELECTED READINGS

Burke, Arvid J., *Financing Public Schools in the United States*, rev. ed. New York: Harper and Brothers, 1957.

Groves, Harold M., *Financing Government*, rev. ed. New York: Henry Holt and Company, 1954.

Hales, Dawson, *Federal Control of Public Education*. New York: Teachers College, Columbia University, Bureau of Publications, 1954.

Hatt, Paul K., and Albert J. Reiss, Jr., eds., *Cities and Society: the Revised Reader in Urban Sociology*. Glencoe: The Free Press, 1957.

Morlan, Robert, *Capitol, Courthouse, and City Hall: Readings in American State and Local Government*. Boston: Houghton Mifflin Company, 1954.

Queen, Stuart A., and David B. Carpenter, *The American City*. New York: McGraw-Hill Book Company, 1953.

Moral and Spiritual Values in the Limelight

CASE 19

At its meeting of November 30, 1951, the state Board of Education, affirming its desire to provide "the best security against the dangers of these difficult days," and voicing dissatisfaction with the lack of attention to religious values in the schools, adopted a "Statement of Moral and Spiritual Training in the Schools." Members of the Board included persons affiliated with Protestant, Roman Catholic, and Jewish religious groups, with the Protestants in the majority. The resolution recommended to local school boards that at the beginning of every school day the Pledge of Allegiance to the flag "might well be joined" with the recitation of the following non-sectarian prayer.

Almighty God, we acknowledge our dependence on Thee, and we beg Thy blessings upon us, our parents, our teachers and our country.

The statement further suggested:

We believe that the school day thus started might well include specific programs stressing the moral and spiritual heritage which is America's, the trust which our pioneering ancestors placed in Al-
310

mighty God, their gratitude to Him from whom they freely and frequently acknowledged came their blessings and their freedom and their abiding belief in the free way of life and in the universal brotherhood of man based upon their acknowledgement of the fatherhood of their Creator, Almighty God, whom they loved and reverenced in diverse ways.

Lawrence Keith, a Protestant, was Superintendent of Schools in Gulf City, the biggest city in the state and one of the biggest in the country. It was a city in which there were three large religious groups— the Roman Catholic, the Protestant, and the Jewish—and a large group of persons apparently agnostic or atheistic. The city Board of Education always included members of each of the religious groups, with none having a majority. Board members were generally regarded as being deeply involved in city politics.

Early in 1952, at Superintendent Keith's request representatives of the three major faiths in the city began meeting to consider the feasibility of implementing the suggestions contained in the statement of the state Board of Education. These representatives came from the Protestant Council of Gulf City, the Roman Catholic Archdiocese of Gulf City, and the Gulf City Board of Rabbis. They met virtually on a bi-monthly basis over a two-year period in an attempt to find some common area of agreement.

In the middle of this period, at a meeting on January 15, 1953, the Gulf City Board of Education adopted two resolutions, in the introduction to which it declared that it

. . . desires to fulfill the objectives of the State Board in seeking to nurture the moral and spiritual fiber of our children, stimulating thereby that love of God and country which springs from a wholesome home environment.

The first resolution directed what was then considered a compromise for the suggested daily prayer, namely,

. . . that at the commencement of each school day, the Pledge of Allegiance to the Flag be followed by the singing in unison of the fourth stanza of *America*:

Our Fathers' God, to Thee,
Author of Liberty,

> To Thee we sing:
> Long may our land be bright,
> With freedom's holy light;
> Protect us by Thy might,
> Great God, our King.

The second resolution requested the Superintendent of Schools to review the curriculum of the schools

> . . . with a view towards insuring that such curriculum includes appropriate programs of instruction emphasizing the spiritual interest and patriotic motivations of our pioneering ancestors, the devotion and self-sacrifice of the Founding Fathers and their abiding belief in the principles of democracy.

The attempt to implement these resolutions, particularly the second one, produced debate and disagreement among the representatives of the three major faiths. No generally acceptable solution could be found. In May, 1954, the three groups submitted to Gulf City education officials separate statements on "Implementation of State Board of Education's Proposal."

The statement of the Roman Catholic Archdiocese of Gulf City was issued on May 11, 1954, and was signed by its Secretary of Education, Monsignor Joseph F. Schmidt. It reviewed the official acts of the State Board in 1951 and the Gulf City Board in 1953. It then quoted the reiteration made by the State Board, at the anniversary convocation held in April, 1954, that the school day might well begin with "the proposed Act of Reverence to God," and that this might be supplemented by the development of additional programs, because

> . . . these troubled times, perhaps more than ever before, call for the teaching of "Piety and Virtue" in the schools and of that dependence upon Almighty God so clearly recognized in the Declaration of Independence, the Constitution of the United States, the Constitution of the State, and in the pronouncements of the great leaders of our Country . . . all of which are the very essence of our heritage and give fundamental significance to our educational efforts.

As an initial step, the Roman Catholic statement advocated that the City Board of Education provide for its professional employees

. . . a clear statement of what may and should be taught in the public schools concerning what the State Board of Education has called the basic truth of our existence, namely, "belief in and dependence upon Almighty God."

It quoted a recent Supreme Court declaration which said, "We are a religious people whose institutions presuppose a Supreme Being." It added that "the time has come for the enunciation of policy which will promote that recognition of God which is proper to our American educational institutions," and that it

. . . is indeed folly to attempt on the one hand a new emphasis on moral and spiritual values in public education while denying admission into the classroom of those religious principles upon which these moral values depend.

Thus, in addition to the daily recitation of the Act of Reverence recommended by the State Board, the Roman Catholic statement advocated that children

. . . should also learn the following basic and fundamental truths:

1. The existence of God;
2. Man's condition as creature dependent on his Creator;
3. God, the source of the inalienable rights of man;
4. The fundamental purpose of our laws—the protection of these God-given rights;
5. The basic equality of all men under God;
6. The dignity of man and sacredness of human life;
7. Man's responsibility to the moral law as formulated in the Ten Commandments.

Emphasizing the importance of the "search for a solution to the problem of secularism in modern education," the statement ended with a call to "those who plan and conduct the educational programs of our public schools in Gulf City" to implement the recommendations of the State Board, trusting that

. . . its most timely resolution of 1951 outlining its suggestions for the place of moral and spiritual values in the curriculum of the schools will neither be minimized by the Board of Education nor

watered down to a point where there is little or no resemblance to the
State Board's proposals.

In its statement issued three days later the Gulf City Board of Rabbis announced that it "is unable to accept the proposals of the State
Board." After indicating a dedication "to the service to God," a devotion "to the extension and enrichment of facilities for the religious
education of our children," and an admission that "we can never be
fully satisfied that we have achieved our mission as religious educators" in spite of the progress being made in that direction, the Board
of Rabbis asserted:

> . . . We are firm in our conviction that the delegation of respon-
> sibility to the public schools, recommended by the State Board, is
> ill-considered. We cannot accord to our public schools, or any other
> creature of the state, in whole or in part, the task of predisposing our
> children to follow in the faith of their parents. We must insist that
> the intrusion of the state into matters of religious education and train-
> ing, which have long been recognized as the exclusive responsibility
> of the home, the synagogue and the church, would violate the basic
> guarantees of religious freedom.

While granting that the State Board's intention was to avoid "a
sectarian emphasis," the Jewish statement pointed out:

> This, in turn, would require the Board of Education to provide the
> teaching staff with a framework of theological principles within which
> to conduct themselves in the classroom. Such a framework must, of
> necessity, be acceptable to all in the population. Even if this were
> possible of achievement, which is doubtful; even though most, if not
> all, of the members of the Gulf City Board of Rabbis would accept
> such abstractions for themselves, insuperable difficulties would re-
> main. As the teacher seeks to clarify these doctrines to the children,
> widely divergent interpretations, often wholly unacceptable to one
> group or another, are likely to develop. How and by whom these
> views are expounded in the classroom are, to us, not matters of mere
> detail, but of the utmost importance.
> . . . The teachers in the public schools are not trained as teachers
> of religion. They cannot possibly be qualified to instruct our children
> in the unique religious standards and traditions of the many religions
> in our land. We want nothing introduced in the public school cur-

riculum which could have the effect of challenging the religious loyalties of our children.

In answer to the question of "the role of the public schools in this most difficult and controversial area of life," the belief was stated that "it should be the continuation of the role they already play with considerable effectiveness, and which experience and tradition have assigned to them."

The statement then listed, with some commentary, five principles and limitations upon which this role should be based:

> In a nation with a heterogeneous population such as ours, the schools must maintain a complete impartiality in the realm of religion. . .
>
> Children should be taught the origins and meaning of religious freedom. . .
>
> Schools should include pertinent references to the role of religion in the teaching of history, the social studies, literature, art and other disciplines, whenever they are intrinsic to the lesson at hand. . .
>
> When the discussion of religious doctrine normally arises in the classroom, the teacher should refer the children to home, church or synagogue for interpretations of faith and belief. . .
>
> The schools should inculcate in children the moral and spiritual values which are basic to all religions.

In regard to the last, it cited "the memorandum of the Gulf City Board of Education on the *Teaching of Moral and Spiritual Values,* dated May, 1953, which we were privileged to see" and *"Moral and Spiritual Values in the Public Schools,* issued by the Educational Policies Commission of the National Education Association and the American Association of School Administrators, in 1951," as examples, "unlike the proposal of the State Board," of "a valid approach for the schools in which all the children of all the people are taught."

The statement pointed out that "while it has not been possible to achieve agreement in respect to the State Board's proposal, we do see many opportunities for fruitful cooperation among the religious groups in our community" and used as an illustration the suggestion made at the last meeting of the tri-faith group for joining forces for the promotion of Bible Week. But in such activities, it added, "we would do this with a full reliance on our own initiative and resources, and without the involvement of the public schools."

The statement concluded with complimentary remarks about the schools and "the dedicated service of the men and women who teach in them, most of whom are themselves products of our churches and synagogues." It stated that "the role of helping to mold the character of our youth" could certainly be entrusted to them, but insisted:

> We must emphatically oppose the delegation to these teachers of the emotion-laden task advanced by the State Board. This would mark a departure from our long established pattern and would inevitably embroil the schools once again in the sectarian conflict from which they have long been blessedly free.

The Protestant statement was submitted by Henry O. Simpson, Honorary Chairman, Department of Christian Education, Protestant Council of Gulf City, after consultation with Mrs. Maria Mackenzie and the Reverend Harry Webb, staff members of the Protestant Council. It began by asserting that the

> Protestant Church has given official recognition to the problem we are facing by the establishment of a Committee on Religion and Public Education within the Division of Christian Education of the National Council of Churches. This Committee is currently undertaking to discover just what agreement exists among Protestants in various parts of the country as to desired solutions of the problem. . . . A recent statement included the following:
>
> > The public school can declare, as the state itself declares, that the nation subsists under the governance of God and that it is not morally autonomous; that human, ethical and moral values have their ground and sanction in God.

In regard to a specific recommendation for the schools of Gulf City, it pointed out that "there will not be complete unanimity among Protestants." The following was then quoted from "a somewhat longer statement brought to our inter-faith committee":

> Public School education must take cognizance of religion as a powerful force in the lives of individuals and societal groups both past and present, and of its potential for the future of the world.
>
> Education in religion must avoid setting any child or group of children apart from or over against any other child or group of children, but rather it shall forward the full development of individuals and the harmony and meaningfulness of group living.

The atmosphere within the approach to religion as made in Public School, as elsewhere, seems to be as important as the concepts to be inculcated.

Basic in religious education would seem to be a carefully graded approach to such teachings as would help the child grow in his capacity:

For wonder and reverence;

For appreciative awareness of what is beautiful and true;

For thoughtful consideration of what is wrong and what is right;

For making decisions to act in the light of the highest values he can comprehend

The pervading purpose of religious education in the Public Schools should be the creation of such a climate of friendliness and eagerness to share in the search for values and meanings as will make the specific religious teachings and experiences of home and church relevant to life as the child experiences it in the Public Schools.

Children who present questions of doctrine and dogma, and often even those with behavior problems, should be referred to the priest, pastor or rabbi for help in the interpretation of religious sanctions and beliefs. Even the atheistic teacher can do this with such sympathy and understanding as will strengthen the hands of the religious leaders.

Those Protestants who "agree with the spirit of these proposals," the statement continued, would advise the Board of Education to continue its present policies and practices, saying that "to do more than this will raise serious problems within our democracy."

Other Protestants will say to the Board:

"This policy is inadequate and should be supplemented by a program which presents frankly and openly the religious faith of Americans, rooted in a common faith in God, the Creator, and in a recognition of our dependence upon Him. Less than this renders futile our best efforts to develop moral and spiritual values."

The statement closed by indicating that the latter point of view would be supported "in the specific Gulf City situation" by "many of the clergy and a considerable number of the laity," but that

[Some,] including members of the public school teaching staff, have expressed misgivings lest a public pronouncement calling upon the schools to include some more definite form of religious teaching should arouse such controversy as to defeat its real purpose.

In conclusion the statement asserted that "this report is not a statement officially approved by any Protestant body in the Gulf City area, but is an effort to present, as fairly as possible, the local Protestant attitude."

On June 14, 1955, the School Administrative Council of Gulf City, the highest professional body in the city public school system, adopted for presentation to the Board of Education, "A Guiding Statement for Supervisors and Teachers" on the subject of "Moral and Spiritual Values and the Schools." This document was divided into three major sections.

The first section, entitled "Moral and Spiritual Values in our American Way of Life," began with an assertion that the "American people are, characteristically, a religious people who derive their accepted moral and spiritual values from religion" and quoted the 1951 State Board of Education's statement that "belief in and dependence upon Almighty God was the cornerstone of the nation." The statement further asserted that commitment to basic moral and spiritual values has been a key to the quality of American life and that all the institutions of American life must contribute toward their inculcation.

"The Responsibility of Home and Church," as developed in the second section, lay in creating an everyday family life based upon devotion to human dignity, truth, loyalty, cooperation, morality, and brotherhood, and in "the family's commitment to the Creator and acceptance and practice of a religion." Morality and religion, it said, were interrelated.

> The greatest possible effectiveness of interrelating morality and religion can be achieved in the home and in the house of worship. Here . . . chiefly, is where sectarianism is properly taught, where religious instruction that advocates or prefers a given creed is properly given.

The major section of the statement was devoted to "The Responsibility of the Public Schools." This responsibility implied that "the public school must use every means properly at its disposal to develop in its pupils the cultivation" of moral and spiritual values. "It implies, further, that the program of the public schools must reinforce the program of the home and church in strengthening belief in God," while, at the same time, cultivating "a respect for adherents of different religions and beliefs."

According to the statement, "all courses of study in the public schools indicate in their statements of aims and objectives a realization of the importance of moral and spiritual values in the program of teaching."

The American teacher, it stated, "has a profound influence in building the character of children." He is "religious in character, in action, and in belief . . . belongs to a church or synagogue," and "should exemplify moral and spiritual values."

> Methods employed, materials of instruction available, and activities provide many opportunities for fostering desirable moral and spiritual attitudes . . . The teacher finds many opportunities to affect the lives, character and attitudes of pupils in countless positive and constructive ways. It is our experience that this is a better way of reaching our objective than through specific courses of study or separate periods of instruction.

"In all curriculum development work," it continued, "a significant criterion is the degree to which the result tends to strengthen moral and spiritual values." In all areas of instruction "opportunities are available for placing religion and religious institutions in appropriate context as phases of American culture."

The statement then went on "to cite only representative instances . . . that are peculiarly resident in each area of the curriculum," indicating that the experienced teacher will "recognize the possibilities of multiplying these instances many times in the subject fields in which he works."

In the field of social studies, for example, the study of historic documents, such as the Mayflower Compact and the Declaration of Independence, brings forth numerous references to God and thus can lead the school children to see the spiritual foundations of our nation. The language arts present a good opportunity in this area, because "good literature owes its greatness to the fact that it inevitably deals with matters of good and evil, life and death," and because "man's activities from time immemorial have been God-related."

Illustrations were given showing that science and mathematics present similar opportunities. "The study of science and mathematics is an eternal process of discerning order and system . . . Scientists and mathematicians conceive of the universe as a logical, orderly, predictable place." The consideration of the wonders of science "cannot do other than lead to humbleness before God's handiwork."

The fine arts, too, present an opportunity to inculcate moral and spiritual values. "In all types of music the spiritual and, indeed, the religious motif is most often prominent. Art, as well as music, can bring an awareness and appreciation of beauty in one's surroundings." In like manner, examples were used indicating the ever-present opportunities in industrial arts, in home economics and family living, in health and physical education, and in related areas.

Included in the summary on the curriculum was the statement that the public schools encourage the belief in God, recognizing the simple fact that ours is a religious nation, but they leave, and even refer, to the home and to the church the interpretation of God and of revelations. At appropriate levels and in appropriate contexts the public schools teach the role of religion and encourage factual study about religion, but they do not undertake religious instruction. They teach the moral code and identify God as the ultimate source of natural and moral law. They encourage children to discover and develop their own relationship to God, and they

> . . . Maintain a climate favorable to religion without making value judgments about any particular religions. Thus, the public schools devote their primary efforts to the development of the values and objectives of our American democracy recognizing their spiritual and religious activations.

Reactions to this statement were varied. It was endorsed by the Roman Catholic Archdiocese of Gulf City. According to the *Gulf City Courier* for December 16, 1955, Monsignor Joseph F. Schmidt, Secretary of Education for the Archdiocese, hailed the statement as a "forward-looking" document that would "do much to provide an atmosphere and environment friendly and favorable to religion without in any way indoctrinating the pupils in the tenets of any particular religion." He said that the statement agreed with his church's desire

> . . . for our schools to reflect the spirit of America by recognizing God's existence—Father, Creator and Law-Giver—as the only sound and generally recognized basis on which to build convictions and habits essential to moral living.

Monsignor Schmidt stated that keeping religion out of the classroom would, in effect, amount to teaching atheism.

At a convention of the National Catholic Educational Association held in April, 1956, a plea was made for adoption of the statement by the Gulf City Board of Education, and the comment was offered that this document could serve as a model for the rest of the country.

The Catholic Teachers Association of East Gulf City urged speedy adoption of the statement. The association, according to the February 4, 1956, issue of the *Catholic Herald* of East Gulf City, noted:

> We are gravely disturbed that the proposition that "the program of the public schools must reinforce the program of the home and church in strengthening belief in God," as "Moral and Spiritual Values and the Schools" puts it, should meet with such opposition. Can it be maintained that the program of the public schools must be designed to weaken belief in God? Yet, the studious avoidance and deliberate understatement of the religious functions of our democracy must inevitably have a debilitating effect. Long continued, such a policy must eventually undermine and ultimately destroy the faith in God of many of the children in our schools who would be subject to it.
>
> Such considerations have always required that our public schools give due weight to what the old "Course of Study in Moral Education" referred to as "reverence—dependence on a Higher Power." And as that same Course of Study noted, the development of true character is essentially different from merely refining the concept of self-interest. It involves "the will to be true to the right because it is right, whatever the consequences, to act with firmness in the right as God gives us to see the right."
>
> "Moral and Spiritual Values and the Schools" continues the tradition of our American public schools. It does not presume to teach specific religions, nor—at the other extreme— to kill religion through a subtle process of intellectual attrition. As in the past, it would have the public schools "encourage the belief in God, recognizing the simple fact that ours is a religious nation . . . teach the moral code and identify God as the ultimate source of natural and moral law."

The Protestant Council of Gulf City commended the administrators for their concern with the subject but urged revision of the document in line with the following principles:

> The statement should take proper account of the rights of those teachers, parents and others in the community who take a non-theistic position with respect to ethical and moral values, and should provide adequate safeguards against conscious propagation of sectar-

ian doctrines. As the public schools are for the children of all Americans, regardless of their creedal beliefs, we are not disposed, as great as is our concern that education should meet the needs of the whole child, to advocate measures which a minority of our fellow citizens regard as an infringement upon their freedom.

The document seems to imply that all the material of the curriculum is to be a vehicle for the teaching of moral and spiritual values. This seems to us to be a dangerous encroachment of the integrity of the respective disciplines or subject areas, for the primary function of the public schools is to provide the opportunity for teachers to train minds to use the skills and concepts of those disciplines and subject areas. But there is an area wherein the statement clearly recognizes that moral and spiritual values of the Hebraic-Christian tradition may be legitimately and appropriately dealt with. For example: The great political documents of our heritage reveal common convictions concerning human worth, individual dignity, liberty and justice, and the religious basis of our institutions. As the State Board of Education has pointed out, these documents should be intensively studied by all pupils. This we hold to be a legitimate area of instruction for all children.

The function of the teacher in the area of moral and spiritual values is, as the School Administrative Council recognizes, of pivotal and strategic importance. Insofar as the guiding statement places upon the public school teachers the duties of teaching religion which they may not be trained or qualified to discharge, we believe that the statement stands in need of revision. For the teacher can fulfill his primary task only it he feels himself unhampered either by specific prohibitions or by directives with respect to the use of relevant religious and ethical perspectives and insights, barring equally sectarianism or destructive negativism. We believe that the majority of teachers are in fact mediating moral and spiritual values of the Judeo-Christian tradition and we think they can be trusted to continue to interpret and apply these values in such a manner as they deem relevant to their respective disciplines.

Ultimately, however, it is the task of the home and the church, even more than of the school, to lead the child into a strong abiding faith. We welcome, therefore, the statements contained in the document which point to the basic importance of the church and the home.

According to reports in the *Gulf City Tribune* for December 19, 1955, and May 7, 1956, the Right Reverend Samuel T. Herring,

Bishop of the Protestant Episcopal Diocese of Gulf City, declared that in a "pluralistic" society, public education could not be used as a "vehicle" for the teaching of religion or of a "religiously grounded ethic. No one faith or denominational teaching can be chosen as the basis of the instruction," he said,

> . . . Nor can even a general theistic belief be promulgated without a violation of the rights of teachers, children and parents who have chosen an atheistic or secularistic way—much as we might wish that they had not.

A Presbyterian case against religious training in the public schools was made by the Reverend Dr. Charles A. McDougal. Recalling that since colonial days the Presbyterian Church had favored separation of church and state, Dr. McDougal declared that he was against religious influence in the public school system. He said, "I'm against turning over the public schools to any religious group, including Presbyterians." Dr. McDougal said that there were two places for a child to receive religious instruction—the home and the church.

The Society for Ethical Culture voiced its opposition to the proposed statement, saying, "Adoption of the statement would prove divisive and would, in fact, make the attainment of moral values more rather than less difficult." Warren Holmes, Chairman of the Metropolitan Council of Ethical Leaders, wrote to School Superintendent Lawrence Keith. Holmes' letter said the proposed statement would violate the principle of separation of church and state, ignore the forty per cent of Gulf City residents who do not belong to any of the three major faiths, and tend to bring religious standards into the selection of teachers and classroom materials.

The United Parents Association disapproved of the guide. It said that moral and spiritual values should be taught in the city's public schools, but they should not be interwoven with religious concepts or the teaching of godliness.

The Gulf City Civil Liberties Union also declared its opposition to the proposed statement.

The Jewish organizations in Gulf City were in unanimous agreement in opposing the guide. Although they issued separate statements, the reactions of the Gulf City Board of Rabbis, the American Jewish Committee, the American Jewish Congress, and the Anti-

Defamation League of B'nai B'rith were in fundamental agreement. All these agencies stressed that they were in favor of imbuing the young with moral and spiritual values and belief in God, but asserted that the inculcation of religious beliefs and values is the job of the home and the church or synagogue. Specifically, they declared that the term "moral and spiritual" as used in the guide is treated as synonymous with the term "religious." The weaving of religious values into teaching in public schools, they said, would violate the separation of church and state and thus threaten the integrity and non-sectarianism of the public school system. The door is opened to possible sectarian indoctrination, and disputes and friction within the community may be created.

The Jewish organizations stated that while the policy of "released time" merely sets aside a specific hour for religious instruction each day, the proposed guide would encourage the introduction of religion into every phase of school life and tend to make the public school teacher a full-time religious missionary. By providing for religious content in the curriculum, the statement would seem to recommend a program that might lead to a requirement that the public school teacher be a member of some religious faith. It could move in the direction of the questioning of applicants for teaching positions on their religious affiliations and beliefs; such a practice would violate the state law against discrimination and provisions of the state constitution. It would also violate the American tradition against religious tests for public office. Some of the Jewish organizations pointed out that the lack of standards and guides for the program would make it impossible for many teachers to resist the temptation to inculcate their own religious beliefs. Because of the emphasis upon the religious aspects of the subjects in the curriculum, the shaping and selection of teaching materials might become religious in significance and content.

Of importance, said this testimony, was the guide's assumption— which was untrue and unfair—that the public schools were not doing a good job in character training.

As a result of the widespread criticism of the School Administrative Council's statement, it was withdrawn for redrafting.

In July, 1956, the Council issued a revised statement entitled "The Development of Moral and Spiritual Ideals in the Public Schools." The new version began with a brief history, entitled "Background." This was followed by a section developing the universality of the concept of "Moral and Spiritual Ideals" and another discussing "Religion and Moral and Spiritual Values." It concluded with the main section on "The Curriculum and Moral and Spiritual Values." This last section was divided into three parts: "The Responsibility of the Public School," "The Curriculum," which contained illustrations from the subject matter areas, and a brief "Summary." The *Gulf City Tribune* for August 8, 1956, noted the significant changes from the 1955 statement.

Where the original stated that "the public schools encourage the belief in God," the revised report said:

> The teachers in the public schools know that while most pupils and their parents are affiliated with some church or synagogue, some are not; indeed, they also know that there are some children in the public schools whose parents give their allegiance to no religion.

Where the original version said that "The public schools must reinforce the program of the home and church in strengthening belief in God," the new report stated:

> Religious education and training are not functions of state-supported schools. It is, however, the function of the schools to be conscious of the various motivations that influence human behavior and to utilize those means and devices suitable at various age levels to support the efforts of the home and church in building good character in our children.

Another passage that had caused controversy in the original statement was the sentence, "The public schools identfy God as the ultimate source of natural and moral law." This was changed to the following: "This statement of policy recognizes that most children come to school with the belief in God and that the schools must not teach for or against the religious beliefs or disbeliefs of any group."

In the revised form the summary of the document declared:

> These, briefly stated, are some of the means and resources available to the teacher and the schools in discharging their responsibility for developing moral and spiritual values to the end that all boys and girls, regardless of their special abilities and skills, will become strong in character and worthy citizens of their country. These means become more fruitful and effective in the accomplishment of their

great objective when the teacher identifies these means and resources
with the primary purpose of the home, church and society. To the
extent that teachers utilize these opportunities and resources for
stressing moral and spiritual values, to that extent will the school, in
the language of the State Board of Education in 1951, "fulfill its
high function of supplementing the training of the home, ever intensifying in the child that love of God, for parents and for home,
which is the mark of true character training and the sure guarantee
of a country's welfare."

The reactions of organizations to the revised statement were again
in disagreement.

The Roman Catholic Archdiocese of Gulf City did not react officially. Lay Roman Catholic organizations once more gave approval.
The Coordinating Committee of Catholic Lay Organizations declared that the proposed code would bring about "an environment
friendly and favorable to religion without in any way indoctrinating
the pupils in the tenets of any particular religion." The Guild of
Catholic Lawyers of the Archdiocese of Gulf City and the Catholic
Lawyers Guild of the Diocese of East Gulf City deplored the attempts of some opponents to remove from the statement some references to God. They said that if this were done there could be no mention in class of the early prophets or the saints, "as they would be
meaningless unless they are linked to God. Why should there be a
spite fence between the church and state so that one cannot look at
the other?"

This time organized Protestants endorsed the guide. Speaking for
the Protestant Council of Gulf City, the Reverend John Christie,
Chairman of its Department of Christian Education, said: "While
there was some expression of concern that this statement is not as
strong as some might wish it to be, it is felt that it will prove generally
acceptable to the diverse elements of our religious community."

The Protestant Episcopal Diocese of Gulf City gave conditional
support to the proposed guide. Its statement, as reported in *The Gulf
City Tribune* for September 30, 1956, declared that "We agree with
the principles on which the document is based, but we have reservations about the interpretative and illustrative material."

Opposition to the adoption of the guide was continued by the
Gulf City Teachers Guild and the United Parents Association. In a
press release on September 14, 1956, the Teachers Guild expressed

its approval of "the effort which has been made to emphasize the time-honored American doctrine of the separation of church and state" but also its feeling that "some of the statements and references in the body of the report appear to violate these fundamental principles." It concluded that "this report in its present form would negate its basic purpose, and we therefore urge its modification or rejection."

The Jewish organizations were divided in their views.

The Gulf City Board of Rabbis commended the document for its improvement over the first draft, interpreted the new statement to mean that it did not "authorize new practices nor does it impose new imperatives on teachers" and that it forbade "certain sectarian or quasi-sectarian practices sometimes unfortunately found in our schools at present." Seven specific recommendations for change were made. The Board of Rabbis indicated that "If these changes are made, we would give our approval." Because the position of the Board of Rabbis seemed to be misinterpreted by the press, a further statement was released on October 2, 1956, saying that the proposal, "as it now stands is not acceptable to the Gulf City Board of Rabbis."

The Anti-Defamation League of B'nai B'rith approved the document on the basis of its interpretation and understanding of the statement. It said it regarded the statement as "essentially a summary of principles now generally followed," which did not "authorize or call for any new policies."

The American Jewish Committee regarded the document as "a significant advance." It pointed to the necessity that "every effort be made to assure that the actual practices in the classroom will in the future be in harmony with the basic principles enunciated." It urged the deletion of "a few inconsistent statements" and concluded with the "hope that, as the program unfolds, our schools will continue to sensitize children to the meaning of the Golden Rule, the sanctity of the individual, the codes of fair play, and the importance of judging their fellows according to individual worth."

In a telegram to the Board of Education the Jewish Labor Committee Panel on Gulf City Affairs voiced opposition on the grounds that "while the document states that religious education and training are the responsibility of the home, church and synagogue, its central theme is based on the premise that the public schools have a role in teaching religion." Implementation of the document would, therefore, "open the door to the teaching of sectarian and theological sanctions" and "would impair the necessary good relationship which exists between the school system and various religious groups in Gulf City."

The American Jewish Congress in a relatively long and explicit statement declared that it was "opposed to the present proposal of the School Administrative Council as we were opposed to the original one" because the "objections that we asserted to the original proposal . . . are still in large measure applicable to the present proposal." A primary difficulty, it claimed, was the premise that "the public school system has a responsibility for 'stimulating' or 'intensifying' in children 'a love of God.'" It asserted that as used in the statement "the term 'moral and spiritual' is synonymous with the term 'religious.'"

> The present proposal, as the former one, would unconstitutionally infringe upon the principle of the separation of church and state and would encourage if not make inevitable the introduction of religion into every phase of the school life. It could well lead to the imposition of a religious test for public school teachers. It lacks sufficient standards and guides to prevent the real danger of teachers inculcating the children with their own religious beliefs. Its adoption can only lead to competing pressures on the public schools by rival groups. Above all, it too is based upon the erroneous and unfair assumption that the public school has not been fulfilling its responsibilities in the building of character and training for citizenship and that our churches, synagogues and religious schools have not been fulfilling their sacred and unique responsibilities in the field of religious education.

On October 4, 1956, the Board of Education uanimously adopted the statement entitled "The Development of Moral and Spiritual Ideals in the Public Schools." According to the *Gulf City Herald's* report of this action, the Chairman of the Board stated his belief that the report "meets with the general approval of the general community and is endorsed in principle by the great majority of religious groups in our city as well as important civic associations." He went on to say that

> The Board recognizes that an important aspect of this program will be the manner in which it is applied in actual practice. We are

confident that the Superintendent of Schools and his competent supervising and teaching staffs will exercise the utmost care and discretion to insure that the implementation of the program will be in keeping with the spirit and intent of the statement.

The remarks of one member of the Board were noted in the *Herald*. He is reported to have said that while religious instruction in the schools was undesirable, "public schools have a responsibility for drawing attention to those religious and moral values which are common to all faiths."

SELECTED READINGS

Association for Supervision and Curriculum Development, *Forces Affecting American Education*, 1953 Yearbook. Washington: National Education Association, 1953.

Cogley, John, ed., *Religion in America: Original Essays on Religion in a Free Society*. New York: Meridian Books, 1958.

Cowan, Wayne H., ed., *Facing Protestant-Roman Catholic Tensions*. New York: Association Press, 1960.

Johnson, F. Ernest, et al., *The Study of Religion in the Public Schools: An Appraisal*. Washington: American Council on Education, 1958.

Konvitz, Milton R., *Bill of Rights Reader: Leading Court Cases*, rev. ed. Ithaca, N.Y.: Cornell University Press, 1960. Ch. 3.

O'Neill, J. M., *Religion and Education under the Constitution*. New York: Harper and Brothers, 1949.

Queen, Stuart A., and David B. Carpenter, *The American City*. New York: McGraw-Hill Book Company, 1953.

Redden, John D., and Francis A. Ryan, *Freedom through Education*. Milwaukee: The Bruce Publishing Company, 1944.

Thayer, V. T., *The Attack Upon the American Secular School*. Boston: The Beacon Press, 1951.

Religion, Science, and the Curriculum

In February, 1950, the state legislature unanimously passed the Stowe-Miles law, legislation which was specifically sought, advocated and sponsored by the Christian Science Church.[1] The law amended the State Education Law and provided that:

> Subject to rules and regulations of the state board of education, a pupil may be excused from such study of health and hygiene as conflicts with the religion of his parents or guardian. Such conflict must be certified by a proper representative of their religion as defined by section two of the religious corporations law.

Governor Ralph E. Hay, on the occasion of his signing the law stated:

> This bill would permit, subject to the rules and regulations of the Board of Education, the excusing of a pupil from such parts of

---

[1] Official membership figures are not available, because the church's policy forbids "the numbering of people and the reporting of such statistics for publication." The church is generally regarded, though, as comprising a distinct minority of the state's population.

330

study of health and hygiene as conflict with the religion of his parents and guardian.

The bill was advocated by the representatives of the Christian Science Church which finds the present teaching in the schools regarding diseases in conflict with its basic religious beliefs regarding man. The children of its members are required by the public schools to learn certain teachings and assert them in answers to examinations, even though these teachings are in fundamental contradiction with those of the religion of the child's parents.

This bill does not decide this conflict. It merely gives to the Board of Education the power to make such adjustment as it believes necessary to assure the religious liberty of the child and its parents consistent with the requirements of public education and public health.

This is not a matter of mingling religion with education. It is a delegation to a quasi-legislative body the power of clearly demarking the boundary *between* religion and education. The Board of Education as established under the State Constitution seems ideally designed for the resolution of such problems.

I believe it to be a simple fundamental of freedom of religion that the State shall compel no child to learn principles contrary to the basic tenets of his religious faith.

Practice followed in the state was for the State Education Law to define the general subject areas to be included in the various levels of education, and for the State Board of Education to adopt syllabi implementing the legislative mandates.

In August, 1950, the state Commissioner of Education, in an official bulletin to superintendents and principals, approved the exemption of the children of parents or guardians of the Christian Science faith from instruction in the units on Disease and Control as outlined in Bulletin 1371, entitled "Health Teaching Syllabus for the Junior and Senior High Schools." Among the subjects included in these units were the study and discussion of certain diseases, methods which aid in the control of disease, the importance of chest X-rays, governmental regulations relating to the control and prevention of infectious diseases, and the study of general facts about poliomyelitis and cancer. At the same time the Commissioner notified local superintendents and principals that:

Required sections of the state general examination, as well as the State Scholarship examinations, will be constructed so as not to penalize pupils who have been excused from instruction in the specified units of study.

The Commissioner also stressed the importance and the desirability of carrying out these procedures "in a way that will avoid causing embarrassment to any pupil or parent."

Prior to the passage of the Stowe-Miles law the State Board of Education had taken no position on the legislation but had requested the State Education Department to file a memorandum indicating the probable effects of the measure if enacted. This statement had been prepared and had read, in part, as follows:

> Under this bill parents may legally request that their children be excused from any part of the study claimed to conflict with the religion of parents or guardians. While, as noted above, the amendment has been sought by the Christian Science Church, the statute is general and would apply to adherents of any recognized religion. The statute on its face is permissive, but in my opinion the state Board may not properly refuse to act within its terms.
>
> It is our understanding that the principal objection of the Christian Scientists is to the part of the syllabus which develops information concerning the so-called "germ theory." They seek, therefore, the right to have their children excused from receiving such instruction. These children will, as a result, not be familiar with the danger of drinking water which has not been certified as free from typhoid germs. They will know little or nothing, as far as instruction is concerned, relative to germ warfare, nor about air conditioning as related to the germ theory, nor about ultra-violet light, etc. These are merely developed as examples and ramifications concerning the possible need for instruction in matters related to the germ theory.
>
> Other factors present themselves also in connection with the enactment of this legislation. If, as matter of law, members of the Christian Science Church are excused from instruction because it is alleged that such instruction conflicts with their views it is anticipated that other requests for similar legislation will be presented. For instance, the Mohammedans have already insisted that they should be excused from instruction on all Fridays because that conflicts with their religion. We have had innumerable requests from followers of various cults who do not want to participate in physical training because of the alleged misgarbing of students or because the parents objected to their children associating with other children who are

garbed as children are required to be in order to participate in these exercises.

If children are excused from instruction in the subject of health and hygiene the local Board of Education will of necessity have to make other arrangements for their instruction during such period.

Instruction concerning the germ theory is not new. It has been carried on in the school system for many years.

Among those who spoke out against the law after its passage were the state Association of Teachers of Biological Sciences, the state Association of Chairmen of Biological Sciences, the state Teachers Guild (AFL), the state Academy of Medicine, the Board of Directors of the American Civil Liberties Union, the United Parents Association, and a city Association of Teachers of Social Studies.

The most vigorous attack against the law came jointly from the associations of biology teachers and department chairmen. In their brief urging the repeal of the law, they declared:

Dr. Rufus N. Sealey, Commissioner of Education, has already approved the exemption of the children of parents or guardians of the Christian Science faith from instruction in the units of disease prevention and control and has indicated specifically which parts of the syllabus are to be omitted in their case. According to his ruling, these children will get no instruction in such areas as the building up of resistance to disease; the understanding of current health programs, both public and private; measures used to prevent the spread of communicable diseases; the importance of heart disease, cancer, diabetes, diphtheria, typhoid fever, tuberculosis, and infantile paralysis; the role of insects in the transmission of disease, a role which properly understood enabled the United States to build the Panama Canal after France had failed; the relation of the sanitary control of water and food to public health; war conditions and the problem of disease control and prevention; what bacteria are; the work of such eminent figures as Florence Nightingale, Louis Pasteur, Walter Reed, Robert Koch, and Alexander Fleming, the discoverer of penicillin; the home care of the sick; first aid treatment, and so on. This is only a sampling of the units of instruction that fall under the ban of law.

It is obvious from the mere listing of these topics that the law will deprive exempted children of invaluable information, but even more, the Commissioner goes on to state that "required sections of the state general examination as well as the State Scholarship examinations will be constructed so as not to penalize pupils who have been excused from instruction in the specified units of study." Thus, de-emphasis and virtual elimination of these topics looms up for all children, Christian Science or not. Even on a history examination, for example, no question may be asked about Louis Pasteur or Gen. William Gorgas, for these men were concerned with disease control.

This law and its method of implementation are so alarming from the point of view of the protection of the health of the individual and the community and from the point of view of the preservation of the State itself and its public education system, that a widespread demand for its repeal is in order. . . .

In addition to this general attack upon the law, the biology teachers and chairmen presented the following arguments.

1. The law weakened our military and civilian defense by keeping a section of our population ignorant of the basic facts about germ warfare.

2. The law threatened the integrity of public education by creating the opportunity for sectarian censorship of public education.

3. The law established, in essence, the principle that nothing can be presented in a public school to which some parents object.

4. The law separated physically along religious lines the students in a public school building.

5. The law was a threat to all children for it tended to deprive all children of health instruction. The argument here was that teachers would tend to minimize the topic of disease control and prevention because questions in this area would not be included in the state examinations.

6. Finally, the law made it a practical impossibility to teach effectively health education, biology, chemistry, physics, general science, civics, and other related subjects. According to the brief,

> It is impossible to carry out the intent of the law and at the same time present a course of health education, biology, chemistry, physics, general science, civics and other related subjects. References to diseases and their control occur at several times in all of these syllabi. A few examples will make this clear. In teaching about foods, such diseases as scurvy or rickets which are caused by a vitamin deficiency must be mentioned; appendicitis will be mentioned in connection with the digestive system; heart disease or high blood pressure in connection with work on the circulatory organs; anemia or

leukemia in connection with the blood; goiter and diabetes in connection with the endocrine system; dental caries in connection with
oral hygiene; and food poisoning in connection with food sanitation.
In the study of chemistry, antiseptics such as hydrogen peroxide or
plain soap or carbolic acid are discussed as well as the use of oxygen
as a germicide or of isotopes in medical research. In a physics course,
refrigeration to keep food free of germ growth, and heat and light
as sterilizing agents, are studied.

If a student were to be excused every time a disease is discussed,
he would have to leave the room for parts of the period at least
several times a week. In reality, such a student could not learn the
subjects named above with any degree of adequacy nor could anyone
teach them to him.

Moreover, the reading of textbooks is a form of instruction. A
teacher who issues a textbook which contains material on health is
violating the directive of the Commissioner of Education.

The state Teachers Guild (AFL) also conducted a lively campaign
against the law. Its arguments were substantially the same as those
presented by the biology teachers and chairmen. It placed great stress
on the contention that the law was a violation of the scientific attitude
and the scientific method. By permitting the religious creed of parents
to determine the nature of truth or falsity with reference to disease
prevention and control, said the Guild, the Stowe-Miles law violated
one of the basic tenets of the democratic way of life—respect for free
inquiry and objective research.

The Academy of Medicine argued as follows.

The very fact that some pupils are excused from the acquisition of
essential knowledge and from answering questions pertaining to it is
likely to have a bad effect on others. It tends to lower the level of
health and hygiene teaching throughout the state.

While the Delegate Assembly of the United Parents Association regarded the law as a threat to the health of the child and the community, the Executive Board of a city Association of Teachers of Social
Studies based its opposition strictly on the principle of separation of
church and state in public schools. The board of a local affiliate of the
American Civil Liberties Union voted 5–4 not to take any position on
this law on the ground that the issue did not involve civil liberties, but
the national Board of Directors of the American Civil Liberties Union

came to the opposite conclusion. By a vote of 10 to 1 it favored the repeal of the law on the ground that there was a distinction between the private right of religious conscience in such matters as ceremonies and the public principle of church-state separation in matters of curriculum.

The proponents of the Stowe-Miles law met their opponents with an armory of arguments of comparable force. The statement by the state Christian Science Committee on Publication to the American Civil Liberties Union was probably the most carefully argued defense of the law. It made three points.

1. The law was not a serious infringement upon academic freedom.

> The cause of academic freedom cannot prosper if there are encroachments upon it by either religion or the state. Time was when hygiene was taught under physiology in our public schools. Under this heading, we were taught concerning the proper care of the body and proper sanitary measures for ourselves and the community. We were not taught too much about the physical body as might lead adolescents to be concerned too much about it. We are vitally concerned with the more recent inclusion of medical education in our high schools because it is entirely contrary to the teaching which our children have in their homes and Sunday School. In the health and hygiene course, there is included in the "Health Teaching Syllabus for Junior and Senior High Schools" chapters entitled "Disease Prevention and Control." The opening paragraph of the one for seniors (Page 254) specifically states that health education rather than medical education should be taught in the schools but in practice the inclusion of this chapter causes high school teachers of junior and senior grades to teach disease symptomatology, processes and medical treatment. Such opportunity placed in inexpert hands is apt to be harmful.

2. The law did not endanger the protection of public health.

> Our students are taught the entire chapters of the curriculum entitled "Protection of Health in the Community" pages 103–107 and 244–253. Christian Scientists are vitally concerned as good citizens in the community with the protection of public health and they carefully observe the rules and laws laid down for the majority. We are particularly careful, for example, in the reporting of what might be communicable and infectious diseases to the health au-

thorities and we have not objected to the Syllabus provision which states that a health officer may talk to classes in health and hygiene regarding infectious and communicable diseases. Such medical officers are not apt to endeavor to impress high school students with their medical knowledge. Our children are also taught fully regarding first aid, narcotics, alcohol, and all hygienic and sanitary measures. In this respect we have the illustrious precedent of the Old Testament record in the Bible of the Jewish sanitary laws. What we do object to is the teaching of disease symptomatology, process and medical treatment, a specific example of which was the demand by a high school teacher to a 15-year old Christian Science girl that she go to the library and write an essay on cancer. Such an experience was difficult for a child on a Monday after she had been taught the day before in Sunday School truths concerning God and man emphasizing her well being as a child of God. The impregnation and indoctrination of such a child's thought with disease pictures could create a serious mental conflict. The old adage, "A little knowledge is a dangerous thing" is, in our opinion, especially applicable to the teaching by high school teachers of disease symptomatology, processes and medical treatment besides being directly contrary to the teachings and tenets of our church.

3. The law did not prevent either the teaching of the germ theory in the high schools or the inclusion of questions on this subject on state examinations.

The original claim of the Biology Teachers' Association that the germ theory was not being taught to Christian Scientists in the high schools and that questions on this subject were being omitted from examinations has been disproved by a recent official statement by Dr. Ernest Norman, deputy superintendent and head of the academic high school division of the Oldport Board of Education, in the *Oldport Times* of January 17, 1952, reading in part as follows:

> As a result of recent newspaper publicity many teachers of biology are under the impression that the state general examination in biology will not contain any questions concerning [the germ theory of] disease. I think it is proper for you to inform the teachers of biology that this impression is in error.

(This was confirmed in the same newspaper item by Dr. David M. Rich, Counsel for the State Department of Education.)

As a matter of fact, although our church does not subscribe to the germ theory as such, we are not objecting to our children being taught concerning the germ theory, especially as this relates to public health. Our position regarding examination questions is covered in a petition addressed by us to the Department of Education on April 16, 1951, which reads as follows:

> If, in the administration of the Education Law, Article 65, Section 3204, Division 5, there is any imposition or injustice to the students taking the full course of study in health and hygiene—insofar as the examinations are concerned—we would prefer to have the examination questions prepared irrespective of the fact that students of the Christian Science religious faith have been, under the laws, excused from study in prescribed areas for a period of approximately three to four weeks.

In other words, we are just as much concerned that no preference shall be given to a minority as we are that our students not be discriminated against in the forced study of subjects contrary to their religious beliefs and training at home and in Sunday School.

An eloquent defense of the law also appeared in *Education for Citizenship*, a bimonthly publication of a city Board of Education. Here, in the course of a debate, Mr. Frederick Thomas, principal of one of the high schools, answered the arguments of the associations of biology teachers and chairmen. Characterizing the law as "moderate in its requirements and justified in principle," Mr. Thomas pointed up what, in his opinion, was the fundamental principle involved.

> The issue is essentially a philosophical one. It involves the rights of parents in the education of their children and the extent, if at all, to which parental rights in education supersede those of the state. Furthermore it involves the right to religious freedom. Can an individual be constrained to study material offensive to his religious beliefs?
>
> God has endowed parents with fecundity, the principle of life, and correlatively has granted them the right to exercise authority over their children and to educate them for life. This right is also a duty and since the two are inseparably joined, the right is inalienable. It follows, then, that parental rights in education are anterior to those of the state.
>
> These rights are inviolable. Since parental power has the same origin as human life, it cannot be absorbed or destroyed by the state. Until such time as a child is able to provide for himself, the state cannot require anything of him against the will of his parents. This

does not mean that parental rights are absolute and despotic. They are subordinate to both natural and divine law and the ends for which man was created. But it does mean, among other things, that the civil government cannot violate parental authority by compelling a child to engage in activities against his parents' wishes. Parents have a God-given duty to keep the education of their children under their own control.

Another explanation of the Christian Science position appeared in the form of a letter to a national scientific journal. Arnold Prentis, a national leader of the Christian Science church, in answering the magazine's editorial comment on the Stowe-Miles law, said:

All we ask is exemption for our children from purely medical indoctrination through teaching of symptomatology and the depiction of the terrifying processes of certain diseases in movies, slides, or other instruction. Such teaching tends to undermine the religious teaching given Christian Science children in the home. In so doing it invalidates a right of individual conscience priceless to all free men.

. . . We ask the right to practice that intelligence which flows from a correct understanding of God and sincere love of him. Christian Scientists don't ask the right to be sick; they ask the right to use the spiritual resources they are profoundly convinced by their experience bring true healing.

The two-year public debate on the merits of the Stowe-Miles law finally had its repercussions in the legislative forum. In 1952 a bill was introduced to amend the law to read as follows:

Subject to rules and regulations of the state board of education, a pupil may, consistent with the requirements of public education and public health, be excused from such study of health and hygiene as conflicts with the religion of his parents or guardian. Such conflict must be certified by a proper representative of their religion as defined by section two of the religious corporations law.

In commenting on this proposal, the State Education Department declared:

This measure, of course, is sought by the Christian Scientists. It is their view that it obviates some of the objections which have been made in the program as adopted a couple of years ago. We are not altogether clear in our mind that the amendment will be a panacea but we think that it is a step certainly in the right direction. We recommend that the bill receive Executive approval.

On April 5, 1952, this bill became a law. In June, 1952, in order to clarify the meaning of this new legislation, the Commissioner of Education sent the following communication to all superintendents and principals:

This letter is an attempt to clarify the situation. This statute has no application to courses being given in biology. Consequently, any child who elects to take a course in biology is expected to complete that course in full.

The law pertains directly to the courses being given in the public schools in health education. It has already been pointed out that there is nothing in the health syllabus which anticipates that teachers will present the details of diagnosis and treatment of disease, which are functions of medical education and are not part of health education. However, where boards of education have authorized instruction in this area, children of Christian Science faith under the terms of the aforesaid statute are entitled to be excused from any instruction in either the details of diagnosis or treatment. This raises no question concerning the problem of either the state general examinations or the Scholarship Examinations for the reason that these examinations have not and do not include questions relating to the details of diagnosis or treatment of disease. The procedure for excusing children is contained in section 170 of the State Board Rules, which reads as follows:

A petition, duly verified, may be filed with the Commissioner by a proper person authorized to represent a religious group on a state-wide basis asking that the children of parents or guardians professing the religion of such group may be excused from such part of the study in health and hygiene as may be in conflict with the tenets of the religion of such group. Such petition shall contain a statement setting forth the specific area of health and hygiene where such conflict is deemed to exist. The Commissioner may consider such petition on the verified statements therein contained or he may direct a hearing thereon upon such notice as he may deem necessary and appropriate. If the Commissioner shall find that there is a conflict he shall make an order setting forth specifically such portion or area of study of health and hygiene as he shall deem in conflict with the tenets of such religion. The

Commissioner shall thereupon direct the local school authorities to excuse, upon written request, the child of any parent or guardian professing such religion from the study of that part of health and hygiene which the Commissioner found [sic] to be in conflict with such religion.

SELECTED READINGS

Association for Supervision and Curriculum Development, *Forces Affecting American Education*, 1953 Yearbook. Washington: National Education Association, 1953.

Ehlers, Henry, and Gordon C. Lee, eds., *Crucial Issues in Education: An Anthology*, rev. ed. New York: Henry Holt and Company, 1959. Part 2.

Johnson, Alvin W., and Frank H. Yost, *Separation of Church and State in the United States*. Minneapolis: University of Minnesota Press, 1948.

Konvitz, Milton R., *Fundamental Liberties of a Free People: Religion, Speech, Press, Assembly*. Ithaca, N.Y.: Cornell University Press, 1957. Chs. 5–9.

How Old Is a First-Grader?

At its meeting in the spring of 1955 the statewide Association of County Superintendents was considering a resolution on the subject of school entrance age.

The state compulsory school attendance law did not require children to attend school until they were seven. As a result of this law and of several other factors, the age at which children entered first grade varied widely within the state.

Some counties permitted any children who would be six by January 1st to enter the first grade the September before their sixth birthday; various others set the date at December 1st and November 1st respectively; and a very few set it at October 1st. One county school system allowed children who would be six before January 1st to enter in September, but required those with birthdays after October 1st to obtain medical certificates.

Not only did the earliest age at which children might enter first grade vary from county to county, but within a county it might vary from one year to the next. In some counties there had been a mushrooming of population caused by the movement, chiefly within the state, of rural people to urban and suburban areas. In other counties this had brought a striking shrinkage in population. Where enrollment was increasing, the cut-off date tended to be moved up; where

342

it was decreasing, the date tended to be moved back. Hence, beginning first graders in the state ranged in age from five years and nine months to seven years.

At the meeting of the superintendents there was some discussion of a proposal to base admission upon a child's mental age, with allowance for his stage of physical and emotional maturity. But many superintendents objected to basing admissions on test data, pointing out that their school systems lacked trained personnel who could administer the tests. (The state had recently appropriated a large sum to enable systems to buy standardized tests, but it had provided no funds for personnel trained in testing.)

There were indications that a number of superintendents were reluctant to take action on the question of school entrance age because they feared the reactions of parents. And a number made the point that fixing the entrance age would make it impossible for them to adjust the cut-off date in the light of fluctuations in enrollment.

The Association took no formal action.

At neither of the Association's next two spring meetings was the question of school entrance age formally raised. At the 1958 spring meeting, however, there were new expressions of concern over the lack of statewide uniformity, and a resolution on the subject was introduced. The arguments used three years earlier were reiterated. But this time the Association of County Superintendents passed a resolution asking the State Board of Education to fix a uniform statewide school entrance age. The resolution neither recommended nor suggested what that age should be.

In this southern state the money available in 1959 from state and local sources for the operation of the twelve-year public school program averaged approximately $200 per child per year, compared to the national average of more than $300. No state support was provided for kindergartens, and only a few of the larger cities had public kindergartens. In 1956 10,187 children attended kindergarten in the state, compared with 110,958 in the first grade and 101,280 in the second grade.

Children entering the first grade came to school with previous school experiences varying from none to excellent. For example, those living in the state's largest city might have attended a public school with a specially built kindergarten unit, with qualified teachers and excellent equipment. Here they might have enjoyed a year of useful learning, following a curriculum which included a planned program for developing readiness for first grade. Many other children would have attended private kindergartens without standards of operation and maintenance and without required certification for their teachers, conducted in churches or private homes. The equipment and supplies in such kindergartens would have been fair; the teachers might or might not have been trained for their work with children of this age. By prevailing standards daily programs would have been good in some respects and bad in others. Most children, however, would have entered the first grade with no school background at all.

Regardless of these differences in previous school experience, most first-grade children in the state were exposed to a course of study that emphasized the completion of a reading program, using one of the state-adopted basic reading series as its guide. Promotion to the second grade depended on the successful completion of this program.

The resolution adopted by the County Superintendents Association was presented to the State Board of Education for its consideration at its meeting on Monday, August 18, 1958. The minutes of this meeting report none of the discussion that went on. People who were present later disagreed as to how much consideration was given to the matter. One Board member contended that the pros and cons were thoroughly examined. Another maintained that the discussion had lasted about three minutes. In any case the State Board of Education voted to require that children entering the first grade be six years old by September 1st, to become effective in 1959. This action was a violation of the Board rule that a resolution must be tabled for a month before action. The Board's decision was published in newspapers throughout the state.

State Superintendent of Schools Louis E. Smith held a series of meetings with school people after the August board meeting and discussed the question of school entrance age with them. The school people he talked with told him they liked the idea but suggested that the state wait until 1960 to put it into effect.

In general, the public reacted unfavorably to the newspaper report of the Board's decision. The State Department of Education was swamped with telephone calls, letters, and telegrams concerning the new ruling. Those who telephoned were requested to express their views in writing. The State Department reported that between August 21st and September 12th it received 736 letters on the subject. Of these letters, 572 were against the September 1st deadline. Individual board members were also flooded with letters, telegrams, telephone calls, and visits—most of them against the September 1st cut-off date. The biggest objection expressed to the new rule was the fact that it was to go into effect in the school year beginning in September, 1959, one year hence. Many of the children who had already registered for kindergarten for the year now beginning would not be eligible to enter the first grade the next year. For these children there would be a lapse of one year between kindergarten and first grade.

The State Department of Education released to the capital city's major newspaper some of the comments of parents who objected to the new ruling. They were published in its issue of Sunday, September 21, 1958. Names were withheld, but places given.

> If we keep her out of school for two more school terms, we are afraid she'll have a complex for life.
>
> Our only solution will be to move out of the State, where we have lived all our lives.
>
> My little girl will be four September 30th. I deliberately planned her birthday to be in the fall.
>
> I was not started in school until I was seven. All my life I was bigger than any of the other children.
>
> We are a Protestant family, but before we will allow our child to remain out of school a year, we will try to enter him in a . . . Catholic school.
>
> The draft age 18 would get them before they even finish high school.
>
> Let's not be too hard with respect to the kids under six. It costs 17 cents an hour less to send a child to school than to hire a baby sitter.

A telegram from the former House Floor Leader of the State Legislature said the ruling was unfair to children and invaded the rights of local school boards. Comments such as these came from educators who did not feel the new ruling was necessary.

A suburban superintendent:

> It is obvious to educators that there is a difference in readiness of 5- and 6-year-olds for formal education. But the action of the state board wouldn't solve these problems. Actually there is reason to feel that the differences among first graders would be even greater than

now. No change should be made except on the basis of a long and careful study.

A big city superintendent:

> We don't have any trouble with administering the present rule. There has been much sound and fury. The thing to do is to let the teachers of young children get together and decide.

People who favored the September, 1959, cut-off date were quoted in the newspaper as having made these comments on the issue:

> Some mothers have pushed their babies into school too young.

> It means sadness and misunderstanding in the homes when children enter school too young.

> Long bus routes make a long school day and there are no facilities for babies to nap at school.

> After a brief period, when we'll all have time to adjust, even the "irate mothers" will be convinced of the wisdom of your decision.

State school officials who advocated the September cut-off date said they were concerned about the number of children who failed to pass the first grade. A study in one town had shown that 10 per cent of the first graders were failing.

The superintendent of an urban county had this to say about the new school entrance age: "All professional groups feel it is much more desirable for children to be six before entering school." He suggested "readiness" tests for children who were almost six.

On Monday morning, September 15, 1958, the State Board of Education met for further consideration of the new rule. The meeting was scheduled to be held in the State Board room, but it was moved to the Senate Chamber because so many people opposed to the rule attended. Many of them asked to be allowed to voice their objections. The minutes of the meeting report that four visitors were recognized to speak. Yet people who attended the meeting reported that many times that number of objectors spoke, and that they held the floor for about three hours. Most of them identified themselves as parents residing in the capital city area. Their objections were similar to those expressed by letter, telephone, and telegram.

To justify its position on the issue, the State Board cited the data it had collected concerning failures at the end of the first grade. The following information was quoted from the Superintendent's Annual Report for the school year 1957–58 concerning 199 local school systems:

	White	Negro
Enrolled in first grade 1957–58	71,255	41,801
Number below 6 years at entrance	15,093	5,072
Number not promoted to second grade	5,620	7,350

The ages of the children who were not promoted were not known. Board members and a member of the state department staff argued that when systems allowed immature children to enter school they were not able to complete the state-prescribed curriculum for the first grade. The high number of failures—and additional costs—were the result.

Members of the State Board also quoted from literature they had consulted in order to determine the optimal time of school entrance. In support of their August decision they referred to a study done in Austin, Texas, on "The Effect of Early School Entrance on the Scholastic Achievement of Elementary School Children in Austin Public Schools." [1] They said the study showed that 87 per cent of underage pupils did not match the scholastic achievement of normal-age pupils. A member of the State Education Department staff, displaying a copy of the 1950 edition of the *Encyclopedia of Educational Research*, referred to studies revealing the importance of sufficient mental maturity in those learning to read. After much debate, chiefly between the Board and the objectors, the member of the Ninth District moved that the Board put off until 1961 the effective date of the new rule. The motion was carried, 3 to 2. Another motion was also carried, directing the State Education Department to study the advisability of a testing program for selecting a minority of children almost six who might be allowed to enter. The Board member who had originally proposed the September 1st date said the delay just meant that the state would have three more classes of school children without the proper foundation.

On September 16, 1958, the following editorial appeared in the capital city's evening newspaper:

---

[1] Lowell B. Carter, *Journal of Educational Research*, Vol. 50, pp. 91–103 (October, 1956).

Is 12th Grade a Waste?

A new state policy on the age at which children will be permitted to start school got a good airing Monday before the State Board of Education.

The hearing was mainly one of protest by parents over a change authorized last month by the board. It provided that, beginning in 1959, a child would have to be 6 by September 1 to enter school.

After listening to the protests, the board postponed the effective date until 1961 and directed that a study of alternatives be made.

This issue, which has stirred such wide comment from both sides, may have triggered a great upsurge of public interest in the schools.

Also raised at the hearing was another question we would like to see pursued further. The reaction it got was especially intriguing.

When Board Member Mason M. Graham of Winchester stated that he favored doing away with the 12th grade, something he has never favored anyway, he was greeted with applause from the audience.

Is that the way the majority of parents in the state feel?

If the additional grade, which in effect is really the eighth grade, is doing little to beef up our program of education, we might as well do away with it and use the money to meet other school needs. Already we seem to be headed for higher school taxes.

Enough criticism has been directed at our present 12-grade program to encourage educators and the public to find out whether it's worth the money we're spending.

As a starter, why not hold a few public hearings to determine how well parents are satisfied with it?

On September 24, 1958, the State Superintendent wrote the following letter to all those who had written or wired him concerning their views on the school entrance age issue:

Dear Friend:

Thank you for writing me about the problem of how old a child must be to enter school. I am always glad to have your views.

I have delayed answering the letters I have received about this matter so that I may report the official action of the State Board of Education at its meeting on September 15, 1958.

The State Board of Education voted to delay until 1961 its rule that a child must be six before September 1 in order to enter the first grade.

The Department is making a study of research that shows what is best for the child in this matter, and will report its findings to the Board. The suggestion has been made that it may be well to allow those children whose sixth birthdays came between August 31 and January 1 to take a readiness test which would be used in deciding whether they are mature enough to enter school.

I hope you will always feel free to write me your views on any subject that concerns your child. We know that you have his best interest at heart, and we want you to know that we are interested in his welfare, too.

I wish this could be a personal letter, but I am sure you can understand that we have received many inquiries and communications about this matter, and we have—this time—to make this a mimeographed letter to you.

Sincerely yours,

Louis E. Smith
State Superintendent of Schools

Between the August and September Board meetings the staff of the State Department of Education had made a study of the literature dealing with the optimal time of school entrance. As a result of this study the following bulletin was published by the State Department of Education on September 30, 1958.

STATE DEPARTMENT OF EDUCATION
State Office Building
September 30, 1958

Division of Instruction   Louis E. Smith
In-Service Education   State Superintendent of Schools

CHRONOLOGICAL AGE AND SCHOOL EXPERIENCE

Many parents and professional education people in the state are concerned at this time over the most propitious age for children to begin school in order to insure their success. The Superintendent's Annual Reports for the school year 1957–1958 give the following information from the 199 local school systems:

	White	Negro
Enrolled in first grade 1957–58	71,255	41,801
Number below 6 years at entrance	15,093	5,072
Number not promoted to second grade	5,620	7,350

Figures on ages of first grade children and failures at the end of the first year, however, are not highly significant unless the ages of those individual children who failed could be known. At present that information has not been collected and tabulated. When information is tabulated on promotions and failures as related to age of individuals at entrance, the problem can be looked at more intelligently. There are very few controlled research studies which specially relate age at time of school entrance to success in school work. There was one such study, however, done in Austin, Texas and reported in the *Journal of Educational Research* in October 1956. This was done by Carter on "Effects of Early School Entrance on School Achievement of Elementary School Children in Austin Public Schools." Although Austin's policy is that children must be six years of age by September 1 when they enter school, and the beginner's curriculum is planned for children who are six years old or over, some parents secure admission of younger children on a tuition basis. The investigation by Carter involved a study of academic achievement of 50 children from seven elementary schools in Austin over a five year period. There were an equal number of boys and girls. They were treated as matched pairs as to intelligence—the invariable being whether or not they were six years of age at the time of starting school. Achievement in arithmetic, spelling, reading and English was measured by standardized tests. Although it was recognized that social, emotional and physical development are also objectives of schools, those factors did not enter into this particular study. Carter reached the following conclusions:

(1) The chronological older child appears to have the advantage in academic achievement when given the same school experience.

(2) In general the degree of school achievement attained on the first achievement test tends to remain constant throughout years of the elementary school.

(3) The under age pupils making lower scores on the first achievement test did not overcome this inferior position in the remaining years of elementary school.

(4) The factor of chronological age has more effect on boys in relation to academic achievement than on girls. The under age boys made lower scores and fewer high scores than the under age girls.

(5) Factors other than intelligence and chronological age appear to have operated in the case of some under age children to produce academic achievement equal to or superior to normal age children.

(6) Conversely factors other than intelligence and chronological age have operated in the case of some normal age children to retard normal academic achievement.

(7) In the subject areas most effectively taught the coefficient of significant differences tends to rise sharply. For instance, grade level achievement in arithmetic was consistently lower

than that of the other academic fields tested. The T test reveals no significant differences in the achievement of normal age girls and under age girls in arithmetic, but in spelling, reading and English the academic achievement of normal age girls was significantly higher than of under age girls.

Seventy-eight per cent of under age children do not equal the scholastic achievement of normal age children.

A number of authorities in the field of reading refer to chronological age as a factor in success in learning to read. In a brief description of types of pupils admitted to the first grade Betts includes: Those who have been admitted to school with chronological ages considerably below six years. When these children have normal intelligence or less, it appears that their chances of success with reading activities are appreciably fewer than those of older pupils. Furthermore, many of these pupils do not have needs that can be satisfied through reading. It is known that in learning to read, as in learning anything else, it is done to satisfy some conscious or unconscious need.

"The teaching of reading to beginners would be a less complex task if every child could meet these requirements: . . . a chronological age which would have made possible a general development of the organism sufficient to cope with reading activities, . . . motor control sufficiently developed to permit efficient eye movement."

Physical development is a process of maturation and is related to chronological age. Most reading authorities point to physical development as a factor in learning to read. Witty and Kopel refer to a study by Buswell of eye fixation as related to reading. Buswell found that the average number of eye fixations in reading a line of print decreases very rapidly from beginning first grade to the second year and that the same is true of regressive eye movement. ". . . one must conclude that reading progress in primary grades, as reflected in increased eye-movement efficiency, is to a considerable degree the product of physiological maturation."

Witty and Kopel also refer to "A Physiological Approach to the Analysis of Reading Disabilities" by Betts. This study is concerned with increase in head size with its resulting distance between the pupils of the eyes and the consequent adjustment that the child must make to achieve binocular vision. ". . . it would probably be between the sixth and seventh years, the first and second grades of school, when the greatest gain (increase in distance) is evidenced." From this conclusion is made ". . . that it may be well to delay presentation of silent reading materials until growth and maturation in this respect is relatively complete."

Children of the same chronological age differ widely in their mental ages. The term mental age denotes the relationship between a person's calendar (or chronological) age and his general intelligence or probable learning rate. A number of research studies have shown a definite relationship between mental age and success in beginning reading. Some of these show this optimum mental age to be not less than 76 months; some indicate six and a half years, others recommend more than that.

Gates says it has been found that it is impossible to designate the optimum mental age for all children with all kinds of teachers. Some programs in beginning reading are definitely more difficult than others and some teachers are clearly more skilled than others in teaching at the beginning stage. ". . . in one classroom a desirable mental age for the beginner might be as high as 6 years, 9 months— in very rare instances even higher—whereas in another it might be 6 years, 5 months, or 6 years and in very infrequent instances even lower."

Readiness for various school tasks is a factor which all good teachers recognize and toward which they work. Some aspects of readiness result from the general maturing which comes with age; some aspects come as a result of planned experiences. Those which come through maturation can not be hurried; those which come from rich experiences do not automatically come from simply waiting or postponing school entrance. Concerning readiness for reading Bond and Tinker say, "The child is ready to begin a specific reading program only when he has reached a certain stage of mental maturity, has a satisfactory emotional adjustment, and has acquired a satisfactory background in experiences and attitudes. Mental maturity, of course, comes only through natural growth, i.e., at its own pace." And again quoting Bond and Tinker, "Some aspects of reading readiness, as intelligence, come with inner maturation. But many important ingredients are learned and therefore are subject to guidance. . . . Reading disability is frequently caused by a child in a standard reading program before he has acquired the readiness which will insure success in classroom activities. . . . He may even come to hate reading and all persons connected with reading activities."

Anderson says, "After all is said and done, most failures in reading in the first grade can be put down to immaturity. . . . The resistance which many older children manifest toward reading can often be attributed to pressure to read before the child is ready for it. In a study of 83 disabled readers in Detroit schools, Whipple reports that 'in 59 cases . . . the evidence was indisputable that introducing the child to reading too soon was a major cause in his later reading difficulty.' "

Reading is essentially a process of getting meaning from symbols. Witty and Kopel say, "The most important elements in success in reading are intelligence and the degree of tendency to reverse and confuse symbols; the tendency to confuse symbols is generally characteristic of children having mental ages below six years, while reversals are usually absent in children who have attained a mental age of seven years (or more)."

"The reversals which characterize all poor readers reflect the combined contribution of immaturity, which leads to inadequate or faulty perception, and the consequent practice in confusion."

Witty and Kopel say that ". . . it is probable that attention has not been given sufficiently to the process of maturation, or inner growth, which doubtless affects group and individual differences in mental ability, reversal tendencies, perceptual span, and other factors essential in their interrelated and well developed functioning in successful reading." Boys are known to mature more slowly than girls. This is true in their overcoming reversal tendencies; it is true in increasing the "reading span." Reading span is defined as the number of words that can be grasped and immediately repeated after a three second exposure of reading material. "A reading span adequate for successful reading of word units is probably associated with the mental age of the average child at seven or eight years of age."

"It appears then that the intricate process of instruction in reading should be delayed until children's background of experiences and mental growth enable them to find meaning in the tasks presented them, and until this process of maturation has engendered a condition in which reversals are few and perception of letters, words, and other meaningful units is possible."

And finally, "we may soon look forward to a beginning reading program to spread over a three year period which the school will accept with as much ease as the home accepts the natural variations in children in cutting teeth, walking, and talking."

BIBLIOGRAPHY:

(1) Anderson, Irving H. and Walter F. Dearborn, *The Psychology of Teaching Reading*. New York: The Ronald Press Company, 1952.
(2) Betts, E. A., *Foundations of Reading Instruction*. New York: American Book Company, 1946.

(3) Betts, E. A., "A Physiological Approach to the Analysis of Reading Disabilities." *Educational Research Bulletin*, Vol. XIII, 1934.

(4) Bigelow, Elizabeth B. "School Progress of Under-Age Children," *Elementary School Journal*, XXXV (Nov. 1934).

(5) Bond, Guy L. and Milas A. Tinker, *Reading Difficulties; their Diagnosis and Correction*. New York: Appleton-Century-Crofts, Inc., 1957.

(6) Boney, C. DeWitt and Kate Agnew, "Periods of Awakening or Reading Readiness," *Elementary English Review*, XIV (May 1937).

(7) Buswell, G. T., "Fundamental Reading Habits." *Supplemental Education* Monographs No. 21, University of Chicago, 1922.

(8) Carter, "Effects of Early School Entrance on School Achievement of Elementary School Children in Austin Public Schools," *Journal of Educational Research* L (Oct. 1956).

(9) Gates, A. I., *The Improvement of Reading*. New York: The Macmillan Company, 1947.

(10) Witty, Paul and David Kopel, *Reading and the Educative Process*. New York: Ginn and Company, 1939.

* * * *

No further information concerning the problem of school entrance age was brought to the attention of the public for four months. Yet the wheels were quietly moving in an effort to head off the new rule.

On January 21, 1959, the state's House of Representatives gave the first reading to a bill which provided that children who were to be six years old before December 31st could start school in September. The representative who sponsored the bill said he had found "lots of support and no objections so far." The proposed bill was approved by the House Committee on Education on January 27th and was passed by the House on January 29th.

A committee of the state Senate changed the House bill by moving up the cut-off date to November 15th. The revised bill won committee approval by a vote of 22 to 17 and was presented to the Senate on February 5th. In the debate preceding the vote, senators presented their views. The Chairman of the Education Committee told the Senate that "Everyone is in agreement on the need for a uniform date throughout the state." The bill as it came from the House was praised by another senator. He said many parents from his county had complained about the action of the State Board. Another senator said he was against any legislature action fixing any specific date. He said the State Board of Education ought to be allowed to run school affairs. "If there is any heat, let 'em take it." One senator supported the House Committee's bill on the grounds that the December 31st deadline had been working well in his county since 1902. Another said he was against the bill, because he did not believe in making baby-sitters out of teachers. The September 1st date fixed by the State Board would help that situation, he said. "In our day and time too many mothers would like to get their children out from under their feet." Finally another senator asked for the passage of the bill. He said State Department of Education officials had asked the Education Committee to "give them a date." The bill was defeated by four votes.

The measure was reconsidered on February 9, 1959. In its final form the bill stipulated that any child who would be six years old by November 15th might enter the first grade in September, and any child who would be six by December 31st and who had attended an approved kindergarten might enter the first grade in September. In addition it allowed children who had not attended kindergarten to take a "readiness" test for admission to first grade. The bill passed both houses.

On March 18th the Governor said he was considering vetoing the bill. He pointed out that many towns in the state did not have kindergartens. He said school superintendents also had complained that there were no established standards for existing kindergartens.

In a special meeting that evening the Association of County School Superintendents called on the Governor to veto the bill. It asked that the Legislature refrain from setting a minimum age for first graders. The Association called on the State Board of Education to establish a new rule saying a child must be six on or before November 1st to enter school. Two members of the State Board of Education gave the legislature a verbal lashing for passing the bill in the first place.

On the following day the Governor vetoed the bill and said he hoped the State Board of Education would consider rescinding its regulation on the subject. He said he felt such matters should be left up to local authorities. "I don't think the state board can lay down rules that will govern every child in the state," he said.

On May 19, 1959, the State Board of Education, by a 7–1 vote, rescinded the September 1st cut-off rule scheduled to take effect in 1961, and turned the decision of how old a child should be when he entered school back to local school authorities. The Board left in force its September, 1958, resolution directing that a study be made of the school entrance age problem.

SELECTED READINGS

Bossard, James H. S., *The Sociology of Child Development,* rev. ed. New York: Harper and Brothers, 1954. Chs. 15–16, 20–24.

Gross, Neal C., *Who Runs Our Schools?* New York: John Wiley and Sons, 1958.

Hales, Dawson, *Federal Control of Public Education: A Critical Appraisal.* New York: Teachers College, Columbia University, Bureau of Publications, 1954.

Key, V. O., Jr., *Southern Politics in State and Nation.* New York: Alfred A. Knopf, 1950.

Swanson, Ernst W., and John A. Griffin, eds., *Public Education in the South Today and Tomorrow: A Statistical Survey.* Chapel Hill: The University of North Carolina Press, 1955.

CASE 22

The Ups
and Downs
of the
A-B-C Affair

Allison, Bloomfield, and Clayton had never had high schools of their own. For years they had paid for transportation and tuition to send their 9th, 10th, 11th, and 12th graders to school in the city nearby. But in the spring of 1952 the city, whose own school population was growing, informed the three communities that it would not be able to accommodate these tuition pupils much longer.

Members of the boards of education of the three communities had anticipated the problem, and during the preceding year and a half had met together informally several times with their superintendents to discuss it. The place of these meetings had rotated among the three communities. In 1941 the state had passed a "Consolidated School District Act," setting forth the conditions under which two or more communities might establish a consolidated high school district for the purpose of operating a public high school. With the thought of organizing such a consolidated high school district and building a single high school for all three communities, in August, 1952, the three towns formally organized a "Temporary Consolidated School Planning Committee" to study the question and make recommendations. In October this committee recommended the establishment of

357

a consolidated high school district. During the ensuing winter refer-
enda in all three towns endorsed the proposal, and on March 6, 1953,
a newly-elected board of education for the consolidated high school
district held its first meeting.

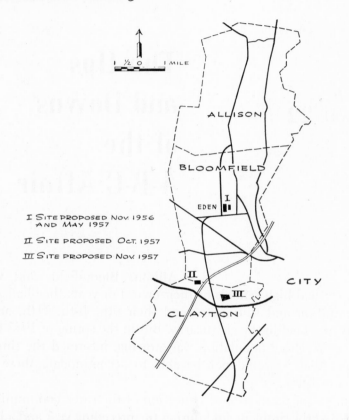

I SITE PROPOSED Nov. 1956
AND MAY 1957

II SITE PROPOSED Oct. 1957

III SITE PROPOSED Nov. 1957

The state consolidation law required that the members of such
boards be chosen by the already-existing boards of education in the
participating communities, and that each community have at least
one representative. In accordance with the planning committee's recommendations, the new board consisted of nine members, three each
from Allison, Bloomfield, and Clayton. Five had been members of the
planning committee, three of these also being members of the respective local boards of education.

The new board moved rapidly. By March 18th a 54-acre tract of
land close to the center of Bloomfield and in almost the exact center
of the area to be served was selected, and by March 20th an option

was taken on it. On April 10th an architectural firm was employed. On April 16th the board asked the State Department of Education to authorize the services of a superintendent for the consolidated district. In May the state and the Board agreed upon the appointment of Charles F. Lincoln as superintendent. Lincoln had been superintendent in Clayton; he retained that post and at the same time was made superintendent for the elementary schools of Allison and Bloomfield. At this time the state also approved the site that had been selected.

In June the Board presented progress reports to the three towns, called for a bond issue in the amount of $1,800,000, held public hearings on it in all three communities, and secured its approval by popular referendum. The vote was 762 to 28. The next months were devoted to such activities as the following: 1) the search for a principal for the new school—those given final consideration were all visited on their jobs; 2) the working out of a salary schedule; 3) the receipt and approval of bids on the bonds; 4) the completion and approval of the architect's plans; 5) the arrangement of contracts for the drilling of a well, for the rough grading of the site, and for the building of the building itself; and 6) the buying of furniture and equipment.

In October, 1953, Raymond H. Rivers was chosen to be principal of the new school. Mr. Rivers came from a neighboring state where he had been principal of a consolidated high school serving two communities with a total population of about 13,500. He had been in this position for four years. Before that he had been principal of a long-established consolidated school in another neighboring state, this one containing classes from the kindergarten through the 12th grade. During World War II Mr. Rivers had served in the Army and had attained the rank of lieutenant-colonel.

The Board had decided to open the school for pupils in the 7th, 8th, and 9th grades in September, 1954, and Mr. Rivers started serving as principal on December 1, 1953. He worked with the Board and the Superintendent on the technical matters of school building and the like. Under the general supervision of a board member who was on the faculty of a nearby private university, he devoted much of his attention to the planning of the school's six-year curriculum. He formed citizens' groups to deal with the course of study, the activities program, and the transportation problem. He called in a group of other administrators from the surrounding area to get their advice on the school program. He drew upon resource persons from the school of education at the state university. One of the most controversial questions to arise was that of the place of foreign languages in the program. The final decision in this matter was to offer a "full program" on an elective basis, starting with French and Spanish for grades VII and VIII, with Latin added for grade IX. Ninth graders were to have a choice of algebra or general mathematics, but all junior high pupils were to be required to take English, mathematics, social studies, and science in each grade.

Once the comparatively good salary schedule had been settled upon, Mr. Rivers began interviewing applicants for the faculty. The salary schedule, the position of the school close to an attractive city with excellent cultural and recreational resources, and the publicity which the new school had been given drew a large number of qualified applicants, and systematic recruiting proved to be hardly necessary. Mr. Rivers did the preliminary screening himself; Mr. Lincoln took part in the interviews of final candidates and made the formal recommendatons to the Board. Applicants who had been teaching in the 7th and 8th grades in the elementary schools of the three communities were given priority. Such teachers were among those who were visited in their classrooms before being selected. Mr. Rivers succeeded in his attempt to recruit a group of able teachers who would be a cross-section with respect to age, experience, and educational background. Eighteen teachers were appointed, together with one guidance counselor, a nurse, a secretary, and two custodians.

During these months Mr. Rivers visited the elementary schools from which the new school would be receiving its students. From members of the 7th and 8th grades in those schools he formed a student council, to be ready to go into operation the following September. He talked with the Council about what they wished in the new school and tried to involve them in the planning. He organized a competition among the school children of the district to settle upon a name for the new school. The winning name, selected by the Board just before the opening of the school, was based upon the name which the early settlers had used for this district but which had fallen into disuse: Eden Consolidated High School.

In May and June Mr. Rivers invited the citizens of the school district to meet to discuss the organizing of a Parent-Teacher Association.

Before the opening of school the PTA was in full swing; it was destined within three years to achieve a membership of 695.

Unusually good building weather made it possible for construction to move rapidly during the spring and summer, and on Monday, September 27, 1954, the doors of the junior high school wing of Eden Consolidated High School opened officially to the first pupils. The enrollment by towns is given in Table I.

Table I

Eden Enrollment, September, 1954

	VII	VIII	IX	Totals
Allison	23	24	19	66
Bloomfield	52	38	39	129
Clayton	86	66	48	200
Totals	161	128	106	395

The building, architecturally the most striking school building for miles around, was not yet finished. Sixteen classrooms were ready, but for most of the year there were to be no central facilities. Students and teachers brought sandwiches from home and ate them in the classrooms and corridors. According to one member of the staff "there was confusion, yes, but not misunderstanding," and the inadequate physical facilities resulted in a great deal of valuable informal communication. New patterns had to be established, and the 9th graders gladly assumed leadership. The new student council embarked formally on its duties. A school emblem was adopted. Editorial staffs began work on a newspaper, a magazine, and a yearbook. For the students, according to the principal, the experience was "sort of a lark."

Mr. Lincoln, the superintendent, was quoted as saying, "I want nothing to stand in the way of making this the finest school possible." Mr. Rivers reported that the morale of the teachers was the highest he had ever known.

Plans called for the new school to add a grade a year until it was a complete six-year school, and work on the building, including the senior high wing, continued through the academic year 1954–55. As it drew to a close, the building became adequate to house all six grades; indeed by state standards (classes of 25 pupils), its capacity was 1,119 students. The consolidated board of education now inclined to the view that not only next year's 10th graders, but 11th and 12th graders as well, should be required to attend the new school, rather than being transported to the city.

Some competition seemed to be developing between the new school and the city school for the enrollment of the prospective seniors; there was some public discussion of the matter, and mention of it appeared in the newspapers. The question most frequently raised was that of the effect of transfers upon students' chances of being admitted to colleges. This issue was settled to the parents' apparent satisfaction when the Principal and the Superintendent reported on conversations they had held with numerous college admissions officers at a meeting of the regional accrediting association.

On January 5, 1955, the Board devoted a public meeting to this subject, after which it adopted a new policy. Its decision that no help would be given to juniors whose parents continued to send them to the city school settled the matter for that group. The decision with respect to prospective seniors was as follows.

> The decision of the Board allows this year's 11th graders and their parents to make their own choice as to attendance at Eden or continuation of their present school plan. If a school other than Eden is chosen, tuition will be paid but the parents will have to provide transportation.

The Board requested that parents choose whether or not to register their children not later than February 9th.

All prospective seniors were invited to visit Eden on Monday morning, February 7th, before going on to school in the city. That evening their parents were invited to a meeting "to discuss registration from their viewpoint." Some half dozen leaders among the students decided to make the transfer, and the bulk of the others followed their lead. Arrangements were made for the students to preregister at the high school in the city. So far as school officials could tell, most parents had allowed their boys and girls to make this decision for themselves.

On September 7, 1955, Eden opened as a full-fledged six-year high school. It offered its students what it described as an "academic-general" curriculum, with no such separate tracks as the commercial, industrial arts, or college preparatory. In addition to subjects required for all students, there was considerable opportunity for electives chosen with rather extensive guidance from trained guidance counselors. Its teaching staff numbered forty. The enrollment was as follows:

Table II

Eden Enrollment, September, 1955

	VII	VIII	IX	X	XI	XII	VII–IX	X–XII	Totals
Allison	32	20	21	21	18	8	73	47	120
Bloomfield	83	54	45	44	25	24	182	93	275
Clayton	80	93	68	54	43	27	241	124	365
Totals	195	167	134	119	86	59	496	264	760

Before long the school found itself faced with problems which had not arisen the previous year. As the Principal expressed it, the faculty and the juniors and seniors seemed to have different "philosophies of education." There were numerous complaints from students that the faculty demanded too much of them, and assertions from the faculty that they must insist on a higher standard of homework.

Some students complained that "we don't have any freedom at Eden." When questioned about this, they referred to such facts as that lateness to class and unexcused absences were dealt with severely, and that they were not allowed to smoke on school property. (A student's first reported violation of the smoking rule led to a written warning to the parents, his second to one week's suspension.) Teachers reported that sometimes some ten or so students would gang up in a hallway, turn off the lights, and block the way of any teacher trying to get through. "This isn't what I'm used to," one offender said to Mr. Rivers. "There are times at MacDonald [the city school] when a faculty member doesn't dare go into the boys' room."

The Principal's response was to combine strictness in the enforcement of rules with the provision of outlets for students' ideas and energies. As the weeks went by students became deeply involved in Eden's activity program, including the Student Council, and they enjoyed the fact that they had a small part in the setting of school policies. They learned, as Mr. Rivers put it, that "they had freedoms here they didn't have at MacDonald," and they built up a lot of school spirit. " ' Feels Great to Score School's First TD' Says Eden's Cunningham," reported a newspaper headline in October.

On March 17, 1956, Eden Consolidated High School was formally dedicated. The school's concert band played, the a cappella choir sang, the Chairman of the Board welcomed those assembled, and a former board member who had in the meantime left town to become dean of a college in another state gave the address. The platform guests included the two United States senators, representatives of the state government, including the Department of Education, the President of the school's senior class, and many prominent local figures.

With its first year as a complete school drawing to a close, Eden seemed to be a well-established institution. Indeed there was already talk of a revision—presumably an improvement—in the curriculum. Late that spring Mr. Rivers drafted a plan for ability grouping, which was set forth in a four-page document bearing the title "Proposed Program for the Fast Learner," and a revised form of which, with faculty approval, was put into effect the following fall. The nearby university was making arrangements to place student teachers in the school for the fall. And in June Eden graduated its first class and took its place among the accepted secondary schools of the area.

*   *   *   *   *

The combined population of the three districts continued to grow rapidly; more so, in fact, than had been suggested by any of the formal predictions of a few years earlier. Tables III and IV tell the story.

Table III

1952 State Estimates of Enrollments

	VII–IX	X–XII	VII–XII
1954–55			
Allison	70	46	116
Bloomfield	111	75	186
Clayton	176	109	285
Totals	357	230	587
1955–56			
Allison	86	51	137
Bloomfield	129	75	204
Clayton	197	108	303
Totals	412	234	644
1956–57			
Allison	90	58	148
Bloomfield	126	71	197
Clayton	212	126	338
Totals	428	255	683

Table III (Continued)

1957–58

Allison	107	62	169
Bloomfield	130	87	217
Clayton	212	147	359
Totals	449	296	745

1958–59

Allison	121	76	197
Bloomfield	146	98	244
Clayton	244	161	405
Totals	511	335	846

1959–60

Allison	121	76	197
Bloomfield	171	97	268
Clayton	265	174	439
Totals	557	347	904

Table IV

1956 Consolidated Board's Estimates of Enrollments

	VII–IX	X–XII	VII–XII
1954–55 *			
Allison	66	38	104
Bloomfield	129	78	207
Clayton	200	104	304
Totals	395	220	615
1955–56 *			
Allison	73	47	120
Bloomfield	182	93	275
Clayton	241	124	365
Totals	496	264	760
1956–57 *			
Allison	85	54	139
Bloomfield	197	108	305
Clayton	286	169	455
Totals	568	331	899

Table IV (Continued)

1957–58

Allison	98	61	159
Bloomfield	203	148	351
Clayton	287	223	510
Totals	588	432	1,020

1958–59

Allison	106	82	188
Bloomfield	237	181	418
Clayton	315	257	572
Totals	658	520	1,178

1959–60

Allison	133	85	218
Bloomfield	271	197	468
Clayton	363	286	649
Totals	767	568	1,335

* Actual enrollments on October 1st.

In presenting to the public the figures given in Table IV, the consolidated board seemed to suggest that they were conservative.

These figures are based upon actual current enrollments and therefore do not reflect any estimates for such factors as families moving into or out of the area, drop-out rate, change of economic conditions, building rates, movement into or out of private schools, etc. In school planning, such factors must be considered, but since such estimates reflect, to a degree, differences of judgment, factual figures based on actual enrollments are therefore submitted to you.

Clayton, at least, expected a continuing influx of new families. In 1954 a study conducted by the Institute of Public Service at the state university had mentioned it as one of the four most rapidly growing communities in the state. The report of this study had stated that between 1945 and 1953 Clayton had experienced a 46.4% increase in population and that "indications are that this upward trend will continue, but at a rate somewhat lower than during the past decade." The report had pointed out that the population increase had been accompanied by an increase of more than 100% in public school enrollment.

Inevitably the thoughts of the public and of the consolidated board had turned to the question of building an addition to Eden. It was no surprise, therefore, when the Board, in November, 1956, presented to the people of the three communities "A Report from the Eden Consolidated High School Board of Education: Present Program and Future Plans," in which it put forward its view that "additional facilities will be needed not later than September 1959." The report, a seven-page printed pamphlet, said that the need for eventual expansion had been accepted ever since the Board had been formed, and that specific proposals had been under study since about a year earlier. It listed three possible courses of action.

1. Add to existing building.
2. Add to existing building to a limited degree only, as appears educationally and economically sound, and construct a nearby separate building for junior high school grades on the same site.
3. Build a separate junior high school building on a new site located with respect to population distribution and with such duplicate facilities as would maintain the quality of the present educational program.

The board rejected Plan 1 because of the inefficiency entailed in the operation of a large building. It rejected Plan 3 as being more expensive than Plan 2—costing $1,850,000 as compared with $1,193,000—and as sacrificing opportunities "for correlation and coordination of program with existing school, of special staff services, of extra- and co-curricular activities, of special instructional equipment, and others." Instead it favored opening, in September, 1959, a new 900-pupil junior high school building some 200 feet from the present school. It would make use of the existing auditorium, gymnasium, cafeteria, kitchen, library, homemaking and industrial arts rooms, administrative offices, mechanical and electrical services, water supply, and sewage disposal systems—expanding them wherever necessary.

It is not clear whether the Board was aware how vehement the opposition to the proposal would be. But its members already knew that there was strong feeling in Clayton, not only against the new construction proposal, but actually in favor of Clayton's withdrawing from the consolidated district altogether and building its own junior-senior high school instead. This suggestion had been made by Mr. Lincoln during the previous fall, the fall of Eden's first year of full-scale operation. That his view was shared by most, if not all, of the Clayton Board of Education had become clear later in the year, when the consolidated board had held joint meetings of all four boards serving the three towns. In April reference to "a clearly defined schism" over the "plan of gradual withdrawal from the regional set-up" had appeared in the press, and the Clayton board chairman had discussed the issue at a meeting of one of the elementary school PTA's. Thus, as the Clayton board had proceeded to engage in a study of the possibility of withdrawal, the consolidated board had become acquainted with the outlines of the plan being worked out and knew that it had become known as Plan II. Hence, on July 30th, it had included in its year-end report the following paragraphs:

1. We believe in the regional idea, adopted by all three towns three years ago and by no means discredited in practice. We believe that each town obtains by regional cooperation a better faculty and better facilities than it could command by itself. The regional board is wholly free from local political pressure and is so able to command the services of a better faculty and to maintain higher educational standards than a local board can. The better facilities consist of the laboratory equipment in the sciences; excellent library provision; adequate shop and homemaking equipment; better counselling and health supervision; an adequate gymnasium; cafeteria on a generous scale; proper provision for art and music development; extensive playing fields such as are usually associated with private schools.

2. We believe that the withdrawal of the largest number of the group before the regional venture is fairly underway could have a disheartening effect on both faculty and student body.

3. There would be a lesser but real damage done to the curricular planning which is based on the wider base represented by three communities.

4. This aspect of the wider base seems important to some of us. Our communities differ. Clayton furnishes more of the industrial and commercial element. If we want our children to be part of the whole American picture and not one-sided or prejudiced in any one direction, we should give them the broadest possible contacts in the most impressionable years of their lives. Our group has not too great diversity—to cut it down even to a small degree seems to some of us unwise.

5. Finally, the cost of Plan II (independent Clayton school) would be much greater to all three towns, especially to Clayton, and the Consolidated Board has heard of no additional values to be gained at this heavy cost.

Nonetheless it was something of a bombshell to many of the citizens of the three communities, when, almost simultaneously with the issuance of the consolidated board's November report on its plans for expanding Eden, the Clayton Board of Education published a much more ambitious report recommending Clayton's complete withdrawal from the consolidated district. This printed document, thirty pages long, was entitled "School Planning Report, Town of Clayton, Clayton Board of Education, November, 1956." It was offset-printed—at whose expense was never revealed—and contained eleven statistical tables. It was signed by the nine members of the Clayton Board of Education and mailed to all boxholders in Clayton. The first paragraphs of this report read as follows:

> The people of Clayton will soon be called upon to vote in favor of a plan for establishment of a Clayton High School, or to vote funds for expanding facilities at Eden Consolidated High School
>
> Because of the importance of this decision, and its far-reaching effects on the future of the town, the Clayton Board of Education submits the following report based on a year's study.

After sketching the general background of the Eden Consolidated High School and commenting on the unprecedented population growth, especially in Clayton, the report mentioned that since late 1955 the Clayton Board of Education had been studying the whole question. Its study had led the Board to favor a prompt start toward complete withdrawal from the consolidated district.

The report gave statistics on estimated enrollment, essentially the same as those in Table IV above, and predicted that for the indefinite future Clayton students would compose about half of Eden's enrollment. It referred briefly to the consolidated board's proposal and then discussed at some length, and enthusiastically, the alternative—to "adopt a long range plan for the creation of an independent Clayton junior-senior high school by building a junior-senior high school for occupancy by September 1959 and adding to it by September 1963 to meet anticipated student capacity requirements through the 1965–66 school year."

The report pointed out that four years earlier the planning committee which had recommended Clayton's original entrance into the consolidation had foreseen the need to make some such choice as this, quoting from that report the following:

> At this point it is impossible to predict what the growth of Clayton may be in the 1960's. On the other hand a consolidated junior-senior high school would have reached the approximate upper limit of economic size in 1962. If the population of the three towns tended toward stability at that time, there would be no problem. If the population continued to expand at current rate, there are two possibilities. Each town might provide its own junior high school, while the consolidated school would continue to be used as a consolidated senior high school, adequate for an indefinite period in the future. Alternatively, a new consolidated junior high school might be built, while the old consolidated school would be used entirely as a senior high school.

The unexpected rapidity with which the school population had grown would lead the issue to arise three years earlier than had been anticipated. All parties had agreed to reject the idea of separation of Clayton from the consolidation for the junior high grades only; consequently the report argued, Clayton should withdraw completely and promptly, except that students once enrolled at Eden should be allowed to graduate there.

Over thirteen pages of the report were devoted to technical presentations comparing the consolidated board's plan with the Clayton board's plan, and exploring the legal and financial issues. Details of the buildings proposed, the capital costs, the total costs to the various towns, and so on were presented. As soon as its students were no longer attending Eden, Clayton, it was pointed out, would not be liable for the Eden bonds, unless the other two communities should default on them, which was highly unlikely. At the same time, figures presented purported to show that because of their own expanding school population, the other two communities would benefit financially from Clayton's withdrawal. The report conceded that withdrawal would require Clayton to spend $32,801 more for secondary education over the period 1959–64 and would require the tax rate to be increased from 3.3 mills to 3.4 mills.

The report summed up the advantages of its withdrawal plan in the following twelve points.

1. This is a long range plan under which the regional school would serve Clayton in a diminishing degree until 1963. By that time, Clayton would have established its own high school with an estimated enrollment of 1094 students in grades 7–12, nearly 100 more than the present three-town enrollment at Eden Consolidated High School.

2. With a student population of 1094, Clayton would be able to offer an educational program comparable to the best high schools in the state. There would be no educational feature or item of plant which would not be possible if the people of Clayton wanted it.

3. With the children of Clayton attending a high school supervised by the same administration as the elementary schools, an overall philosophy of education could be carried through from kindergarten through twelfth grade.

4. Clayton residents would have a full voice in the decisions of the Board of Education regarding its secondary school as compared to the one-third vote now held on the Consolidated Board.

5. Financial control and responsibility would rest squarely with Clayton voters.

6. Sole ownership of plant would reside in Clayton.

7. All required buildings would be located in the town of Clayton with the result that Clayton would have facilities available for every type of community interest. This plan envisions facilities for an indefinite number of cultural pursuits, an adult education program, lectures, concerts, and the like, as well as playground and recreation areas for adults as well as school children.

   Faced with a population growth as indicated in the recently adopted Town Plan, Clayton community requirements will demand facilities provided by high school buildings. Normal elementary facilities would never fill this need.

8. There would be no detrimental effect on the continued successful operation of Eden Consolidated High School because it would be fully utilized on the basis of projected enrollments. Its location in Bloomfield makes it suitable for the exclusive use of the towns of Allison and Bloomfield after graduation of the last Clayton class in the spring of 1963.

9. The cost of borrowing money is approximately ¼ of 1% less.

10. Clayton students attending a local junior-senior high school would have greater opportunity to take part in extra-curricular activities. The problem of transportation during after-school hours would be greatly lessened.

11. Enrollment at Eden would be stabilized with the result that further expansion of that plant could be deferred for approximately 10 years.

12. The annual cost of transporting students would be substantially less.

The inside back cover of the Clayton report carried the following:

> On Thursday evening, November 1, 1956, this report was presented to the Consolidated Board of Education at a joint meeting with the Clayton Board called for the purpose.
>
> The report was further discussed by the Consolidated Board at its meeting of Tuesday, November 13, 1956.
>
> The following letter dated November 14, 1956 is reprinted in its entirety:

> Henry Kaufman, Jr., Chairman
> Clayton Board of Education
>
> Dear Hank:
>   The Board of Education of Eden Consolidated High School, has examined your report, to Clayton residents, of facts and figures pertaining to school facilities and plans for future needs.
>   There are so many discrepancies in this brochure that we cannot approve it. We would like this statement included in your report.
>   Thank you for your attention to this matter.
>   Very truly yours,
>   EDEN CONSOLIDATED HIGH SCHOOL
>
>   M. A. Clinton Lane
>   Chairman, Board of Education
>
>   Henrietta E. Levy
>   Secretary, Board of Education

In spite of the fact that Clayton had not concealed its intentions, the formal withdrawal proposal came as a surprise to most residents of the three communities and, to many of them, as a shock. With the exception of Mrs. Francis, whose husband was an active proponent of withdrawal, the reaction of the teachers at Eden seems to have been one of unanimous dismay. Some of them had moved to this area and bought homes; the uncertainty about the future of the consolidated school made them anxious.

Mr. Rivers expressed concern about the possibility that those favoring withdrawal would accuse the Eden faculty of indoctrinating the students, and called a special faculty meeting to pass on to the faculty the Board's instructions not to discuss the matter with the students.

But students, too, were worried. According to a member of the school staff, "You could hear them buzzing about 'What will happen if we get out?'" They expressed concern about the effect withdrawal would have on the athletic teams and dread of the possibility of losing access to the excellent gymnasium, science laboratories, and home economics equipment. Most of their parents are reported to have felt strongly one way or the other, the majority being for the consolidation.

There is no evidence that the high tension about the issue affected school affairs or the faculty directly; indeed the issue was not even mentioned in the school newspaper or the PTA newsletter. But a feeling of great uneasiness reportedly pervaded the institution, and the teachers, who had tried to build a good school, were said to have "a little feeling of discouragement" in spite of repeated assurances from members of the Clayton Board of Education that they were making no reflections on the school itself.

The reaction of the board of education of the consolidated district was to write immediately to the city fathers of Clayton, asking them "to do everything within your power to expedite the presentation of this issue to the townspeople of Clayton."

The Clayton Board, meanwhile, called a public hearing for December 6th at one of Clayton's elementary schools, to present its ideas and gauge the public support for them. Although there is no reason to believe that efforts were made to secure a large attendance, several hundred people came. According to some they were a cross-section of the people of Clayton; according to others they were mostly parents of Clayton students at Eden.

Reports of the meeting were diverse and confusing. According to one partisan of the consolidation it was a meeting full of "bitterness" and "fireworks," in which speakers lost their dignity and self-control and treated each other with disrespect. "Almost deliberate lies were told," he said. According to a partisan of withdrawal, the vast majority of participants in the meeting came already opposed to withdrawal and were represented by "skilled speakers," including a member of the consolidated board and Mr. Rivers himself.

The Clayton board conducted the meeting and presented the main arguments for withdrawal. Other issues, too, were brought out. One of their key speakers was Mr. Lincoln, who would presumably be the superintendent of the Clayton district if and when it built a high school. In response to questions about the staffing of a new school he replied that he could achieve it without difficulty, a statement which was challenged by his opponents. The opponents of withdrawal argued that the state law prohibited the community from borrowing money amounting to more than ten per cent of the total assessed valuation of property in the town. It seemed as though the Clayton board had not investigated this question, but some of its members spoke of the possibility of engaging in a reassessment of town property. According to one person present, this proposal "went over like a lead balloon." The opponents of withdrawal argued that consolidated schools received from the state a 50% reimbursement of money spent on transportation, and that a Clayton high school would have to carry all transportation costs out of local funds. They also pointed out that the state made additional building grants for consolidated district buildings. The probability of smaller classes at a Clayton high school would also mean higher per-pupil costs, the opponents said.

Whether or not it is true that speakers lost their tempers, it seems clear that the proponents, as one of their own number later said, "presented a miserable case." As the evening progressed, it appeared that the majority of those present favored Clayton's staying in the consolidation. Someone suggested that a vote be taken. Both the Chairman of the Board and Mr. Lincoln objected. A standing division was taken, however, which showed ten per cent or fewer of those present in sympathy with the withdrawal proposal. The meeting broke up.

What were the issues behind the pros and cons of withdrawal? The answers to this question given by different citizens of the three communities were conflicting.

The formal arguments for withdrawal, as they had been set forth in the Clayton board's pamphlet have already been presented. Other views, though, were espoused by, or imputed to, those favoring withdrawal. Some of them maintained that Clayton's schools had always been better than those of either Allison, a rural community which had neglected education, or Bloomfield, where there were extremes of wealth and poverty, and many of whose community leaders sent their children to private schools. This being the case, these persons reasoned, a separate Clayton high school would probably be better than one operated by a board two-thirds of whose members were from the other two communities.

Their opponents seemed to feel that under Mr. Rivers' leadership a high quality of secondary education was being offered which was if anything an improvement over that preferred by Mr. Lincoln and the others who had been in control of the elementary schools. Possibly there was some significance in the fact that the leaders of the withdrawal movement included a dean and two faculty members of a nearby state college devoted mainly to the preparation of elementary and junior high school teachers, while several members of Eden's board had close connections to the conservative, private university in the nearby city, which had recently inaugurated a Master of Arts in Teaching program. According to one Clayton resident, the state college people were jealous because of the number of university M.A.T. graduates who had been appointed to Eden's staff during its first year of operation as a senior high school, as compared to the number of state college graduates. At any rate there had been open disagreements about educational policy between Mr. Brooks on the one hand and Mr. Lincoln and one of his state college associates on the other. Mr. Lincoln was on the state payroll: a Bloomfield resident said "the state people always stick together."

Despite the Clayton Board's official disclaimers of objections to Eden itself, there were suggestions from some persons that "pretty bad things are going on" there. There were rumors to the effect that students from Clayton were having "a tough time," that standards had been raised "erratically" and "unpleasantly." The parents of one Clayton boy who had been suspended said they felt they had had a most unsympathetic reception from Mr. Rivers. Mr. Francis, the dean of the state college and a leader in the withdrawal fight, was said to have received from his wife, an Eden teacher, reports of "horrendous" conditions at Eden, including constant disagreements on educational policy. (Mrs. Francis' reports were discounted by colleagues, who, behind her back, circulated reports alleging that she was emotionally unstable.)

Although criticism of the school was never voiced openly at any meeting, the teachers reportedly felt that they were being sniped at privately by persons too polite to criticize them publicly.

Opponents of the withdrawal made much of what they felt were Eden's strengths. As they had been listed by Eden's board, these included:

1. A broad program of studies which can be enlarged further with increased enrollment.
2. Provision for a transition from elementary to senior high school through combined subject-area core teaching at the junior high school level—for example, related teaching of English and Social Studies under one teacher. . .
3. . . . Grouping of students in lower grades to provide for individual rates of learning.
4. A broad and varied program in the junior high school leading to preparation for wise selection of courses at the senior high school level.
5. A fast-learner program in both junior and senior high schools.
6. . . . Remedial services.
7. . . . A sound academic program enriched by co-curricular and extra-curricular activities. . .

Reportedly the high quality of Eden's staff and equipment was frequently cited during the debate.

Some of the proponents of the plan attached importance to such matters as the age span in the school and the size of the school. A lot of people, one reported, were afraid that the younger pupils were learning fast habits from the older ones on school buses, and that being together with senior high pupils would hamper the proper development of the younger ones. Many people favored "smaller, more intimate" schools. They may have been among those who preferred to return the 7th and 8th grades to the Clayton elementary schools.

An underlying question on which there was disagreement was that of the desirability of localism as against regionalism. On this question two social scientists from the nearby university, friends and fellow citizens of Clayton, found themselves in opposite camps. One, a sociologist, argued that public institutions should be close to the local community and subject to local control; the other, a historian turned professor of education, argued that localism was outmoded, and that higher standards and greater effectiveness required the relative strengthening of regional, if not state, or even national, authority. The latter argued that the consolidated board was less susceptible to political pressures.

What part did outright local pride play in the withdrawal movement? Many of the opponents of withdrawal argued that it was the whole basis of the movement. According to a Clayton citizen opposed to withdrawal, "There was no evidence of lack of satisfaction with the school. It was a matter of the selfish, jealous, community pride of the local elementary school board." Those who knew the members of the board well refused to accept this statement as true of them all. On the other hand, a Clayton resident who favored withdrawal said that there was a "general local autonomy feeling." One resident said that many of Clayton's political leaders had always disliked the idea of consolidation but had in 1954 realized that there was no choice. A Bloomfield resident said the issue was one of "naked power."

Participants in the controversy, when asked about it later, frequently accused their opponents of using inappropriate, if not unfair procedures. The Eden board made much of the fact that it was "charged by law with the responsibility for the proper education of children in the towns of Allison, Bloomfield, and Clayton in Grades 7 through 12." This being so, board members maintained, the Clayton board had no mandate to concern itself with secondary education; initiative for withdrawal could properly come only from the regular town authorities.

Members of the withdrawal group, on the other hand, criticized the consolidated board for trying to put across its expansion plan through agreements between leaders without consulting the people. In turn, it was asserted that the Clayton Board of Education had isolated itself by working behind closed doors.

As to the complicated financial aspects of the question, there was never full agreement on what was involved. A well-informed supporter of consolidation said that "the withdrawal people were newer settlers, not aware of the tax situation." A well-informed person on the other side, however, said that "the old-timers, who might be expected to oppose tax increases, and so on, argued, 'Let's get the best, even if it does cost a little more.'" Several supporters of withdrawal, when confronted with the state formulae providing for larger grants to consolidated schools, retorted that "in the end you pay the taxes anyway."

Perhaps at this point it is well to glance briefly at the three communities themselves.

Of the three, Allison was the community farthest geographically from the city which dominated the area. It had always been a rocky, hilly, agricultural township, with a sparse population, estimated in 1955 as 1,600. In the 1930's enterprising city-dwellers had slowly started moving out "to the country," where land was cheap, and where they could have some of the pleasures of country living without being far from the attractions of the city. Until recently Allison had had no zoning, although it now was no longer primarily agricultural. With the influx of professional people, notably university professors, it was now regarded as a liberal community, in spite of the fact that politically it was almost solidly Republican.

Bloomfield, the center community of the three, had also been rural, but it had received a large migration from the nearby city, which it adjoined. The section of the city closest to Bloomfield was a solidly middle class section which in the 1920's and 1930's had come to be characterized as the Jewish section of the city, as the members of that group had worked their way up from the ghetto-like slums where their parents had started life in America. It was from this same section that most of Bloomfield's in-migrants reputedly came, and well-to-do Jews played a large part in the social and political life of Bloomfield. Except for a part of the township devoted to truck farming, where a few hundred obviously poor families lived, Bloomfield was regarded as a wealthy place. This impression was substantiated by the zoning regulation which required new residential lots to consist of at least two acres of land. The estimated population of Bloomfield in 1955 was 3,400. At the time of these events, it had become fairly stable.

Clayton lay athwart the main highway entering the city. It had a small ribbon development of light industry, wholesale warehouses, and the like. Primarily, though, it was a residential community, with its people working either in the nearby city or in a smaller city lying in the opposite direction. Its population growth is shown in Table V.

Table V

Population of Clayton

1945	2,527
1950	3,032
1955 (est.)	4,700

Note: Of the change between 1950 and 1955 13% was attributed to natural increase and 87% to net migration.

According to a 1956 report of the town planning and zoning commission, the occupations of Clayton residents were as follows:

Table VI

Occupations of Clayton Residents, 1954

	Numbers	Per cent
Professional, technical, etc.	252	25.3
Managers, Prop's, Officials (not farm)	176	17.7
Craftsmen, Foremen (not farm)	168	16.9
Clerical, etc.	141	14.2
Sales	97	9.7
Operatives, etc.	75	7.5
Service Workers	35	3.5
Farmers, Farm Managers	26	2.6
Laborers (not farm)	6	0.6
Private Household	4	0.4
Occupations not reported (no data)	. . .	. . .
	996	100

Ever since Clayton had come to be a home for persons working in the nearby cities, it had had a small Roman Catholic minority. This group had experienced a relative growth with the influx during the preceding decade of numbers of persons of Italian descent. Jewish people moving to Clayton, on the other hand, had tended not to feel welcome, and cases had been known where such persons had moved on to Bloomfield.

According to a Clayton resident, who was active in civic affairs and a trained observer, the typical Clayton home was five or six years old, on a one-acre lot, a one-story ranch house with three bedrooms and a two-car garage, a two-tone house with matching two-tone car. According to this observer Clayton was "very homogeneously middle class."

* * * * *

In the weeks after the stormy meeting of December 6, 1956, tension in the three communities and at Eden subsided. No further public meetings on the subject were held; there was no referendum; no new statements were issued. Perhaps with the activities of the Christmas season moving to the forefront of their lives, most people found it easier to regard the issue of withdrawal as settled—at least temporarily. The Clayton Board of Education seemed to drop the issue. Early in the spring, at that board's recommendation, the town council of Clayton appointed a Land Purchase Committee and Long-Range Planning Committee. The latter committee was asked to make recommendations about the future location of Clayton schools, but none of the key leaders of the withdrawal movement were included in its membership; and, as time went by, it actually invited the Clayton members of the consolidated board to meet with it.

In February, 1957, a 45-member state evaluation team visited the high school as planned. Among other things its report said this:

> Eden is one of the finest educational developments in the state. . . . The faculty, students and future of Eden is [sic] unusually fine, and the school's growing pains, inevitable in any school which grows, are being handled expertly and with great foresight.

The consolidated board, which had delayed pressing its building plans until the withdrawal issue had been settled, now moved ahead to present a concrete proposal. In May it mailed to all boxholders in the three towns a ten-page printed pamphlet entitled "School Building Plan, Eden Consolidated High School Board of Education, May 1957." This report expanded on the November one, presenting extensive cost data for a new school and architects' plans. As had been envisaged in November, the new school was to be just behind Eden and was to house all 7th, 8th, and 9th grades, while the original building was to become a three-year senior high school.

> Educationally we shall profit mightily by this plan as compared with the other possibilities. We can establish a real Junior High School with its own program and procedures but still closely knit to the program and procedures of the Senior High. We shall be able to maintain the high level of morale already existing in both teaching staff and student body without danger of a damaging break between Junior and Senior units. . . .

> We of the Consolidated Board are convinced that this plan is educationally and financially advantageous. It provides conservative expansion and permits future flexibility.

Two public hearings were announced in the report, both to be held at the Eden building—one on Monday evening, May 27th, the other on Tuesday evening, May 28th. A referendum in all of the three towns was announced for Monday, June 3rd.

At the hearings on the new junior high school building the consolidated board again encountered opposition. Opponents of the bond issue argued that the proposed 2000-pupil complex on the one site would be in effect a single school and as such would be too big to be educationally sound. They stated that there would likely be a serious water supply problem. And they pointed out that the center of population of the Allison-Bloomfield-Clayton region was considerably further south—closer to the center of Clayton.

Mr. Rivers was quoted in the newspaper as saying that "the continual disagreement and controversy, however sincere on the part of the people involved, will in time take the heart out of the existing consolidated school."

Dean Francis of the state college was quoted as saying, "For the first time in my career in public education I am out of sympathy with a bond issue for educational purposes." Mr. Francis and one of his colleagues who served on the Clayton Board of Education still spoke of the desirability of Clayton's withdrawing from the consolidation. (One Eden parent was heard to comment later, "If this is the caliber of state college, I'll withdrawn my daughter's application.")

Some of the Eden staff seemed to be quite upset by the hearings, and a university faculty member who had spoken strongly for the bond issue said later that the way in which the Principal and several teachers had thanked him for his remarks was "almost pathetic."

Later in the week the press carried a statement signed by two Bloomfield residents claiming to be "spokemen for a citizens' group of Allison, Bloomfield, and Clayton residents who have banded together to endorse the Eden Consolidated Board of Education proposal."

> We recommend the proposed Eden expansion because (1) the State Board of Education feels that consolidated schools offer the best and most economical form of education; the State building grant

awaiting the Governor's signature provides $100 extra per pupil in consolidated districts only and this will mean approximately $100,000 in additional State aid to Eden. (2) It should be clear that two separate schools on the same site are being proposed. (3) It should be known that this running controversy on withdrawal has impaired teacher-recruitment, no easy task these days. (4) Towns in consolidated districts benefit from additional State aid for transportation of high school pupils to the amount of 40% rebate. (5) When a third school is necessary, the consolidated board has stated that it will build another junior high school in the center of population which is Clayton at present.

Another statement appearing in the press on the same day confirmed the impression that opposition to the bond issue was not confined to Clayton. A prominent citizen of Bloomfield had this to say:

> The proposition before Allison, Bloomfield, and Clayton at next Monday's referendum boils down to a few basic factors. (1) It is contrary to the concept of consolidation to have one town, Clayton in this case, dominate by numbers and contribute more than one-half. (2) There exists a serious health hazard due to very poor sewage, drainage, and possible water contamination on the present site. The report read at Tuesday's hearing, the engineering report of the State Health Department, states that areas such as the proposed location are generally avoided. (3) The proposed plan is not a result of cooperative planning between the towns: it is rather a plan evolved by the Consolidated Board without consulting the towns. (4) It's a 'take it or leave it' proposition; there's no opportunity to express a preference of one plan over another.

By all reports this was a week during which the holding of informal meetings, the distribution of statements, and the canvassing of voters reached a peak. Reportedly members of the state college faculty were especially active. There was disagreement as to the extent to which the Eden teachers who were residents of the communities busied themselves likewise. It was, however, reported that the students at Eden became involved through being asked to carry literature home.

On Monday, June 3rd, the referendum was held and the bond proposal defeated. The results are shown in Table VII.

Table VII

Results of Referendum, June 3, 1957

	For	Against
Allison	164	114
Bloomfield	276	676
Clayton	628	752
Totals	1,068	1,542

According to most observers the withdrawal issue had probably been crucial in the defeat of the proposal, but it could not have been decisive without the usual vested interests and opposition to outlay for schools.

Mr. Rivers regarded the moment of defeat as a critical one for the school. The recruitment of teachers was always especially urgent at Eden because of the larger than usual turn-over in a school which employed many recent college graduates and many wives of professional persons. Recruitment for the fall of 1957 had already been badly hurt. Another observer said that the outcome of the referendum "came close to doing great harm" to the school and quoted others as having said that it would "disrupt" the school.

The consolidated board moved quickly. On June 6th it wrote to the Chairman of the Clayton Board of Education as follows.

> The Board of Education of Eden Consolidated High School is presently considering what ought to be its next recommendation to the region for the education of the children for whom it is responsible.
>
> To assist in that consideration, it has called a meeting at Eden School at 8 p.m. on Wednesday, June 19, 1957, of various town officials, those having an official interest in education and representatives of groups which took a public position for or against the most recent recommendation of the regional board. It is our hope that from such a meeting our board will be able to derive a better understanding of the views of the people as expressed in the recent referendum.
>
> Judging from the comments made at the recent public hearings and those most prevalent since the recent referendum, one of the most determining factors in the vote was the uncertainty in the minds of the voters engendered by the sequence of positions taken by the Clayton Board of Education within the past year.
>
> You will recall that under the date of November 14, 1956, this

Board notified the Boards of Selectmen and of Education in Clayton that plans must proceed promptly if the admitted need for additional junior-senior high school facilities was to be met by September, 1959. It was quite apparent that the necessary planning would be basically dependent upon whether Clayton voted to withdraw from the region as your Board advocated or remained a part of the region and worked co-operatively toward the solution of the problem within the regional concept. Clayton authorities were requested to expedite the answer to this fundamental question. No reply has as yet been received from the Clayton Board of Selectmen.

In December, 1956, your Board conducted a public hearing on this question at which those present voted decisively in favor of the region. Following that vote, your Board notified this Board, by letter dated December 17, 1956, of its official decision "not to call a town meeting to vote on the establishment of a Clayton junior-senior high school system." Consequently, planning on a regional basis was actively pursued.

Notwithstanding your decision in December, 1956, your Board caused to be published a statement of policy in the newspaper issue of May 26, 1957, that, in your opinion, "it would be a mistake for Clayton to continue to pay money into a school in Bloomfield when Clayton will soon have a secondary school population large enough to support its own junior-senior high school."

. . . We respectfully suggest that the Clayton Board of Education has the duty to determine unequivocally its position on the following questions:

1. Will it, in the forseeable future, request a town meeting in Clayton to vote, whether, pursuant to statute, it should ask a referendum on the question of its withdrawal?

2. If so, when does it contemplate that such a town meeting will be held?

3. If not, what are the recommendations of your Board with reference to providing the needed facilities within the region?

We cordially invite two representatives from your Board to meet with us on June 19. We hope that your representatives will feel free to discuss this matter openly with us and to express the views of your Board on the general question and on the specific questions set forth above so that we might all fulfill our respective duties to provide those educational facilities whose need is undisputed in a manner which will be in the best interests of the children and most acceptable to the townspeople.

To the same meeting the Board invited 26 other residents of the three communities, a broadly representative group of leaders in PTA's and civic and religious groups.

The meeting on June 19th came to be known as the "harmony meeting." According to the newspaper, the date had been set "to give those invited ample time to prepare suggestions, proposals, questions and answers." Proponents of various plans who attended the harmony meeting later said it was a good one and made constructive headway. One of the withdrawal leaders urged the Clayton board chairman to drop the fight because of the effect it might have on the morale of the pupils. It is not clear who proposed the idea, but there was essential agreement on a plan to build a new junior high school serving all three communities but located close to Clayton. The location would have the advantage that in the event of subsequent withdrawal, Clayton could take with it a considerable amount of the school plant built during its participation in the consolidated district. It was agreed that the consolidated board should work on this new plan.

At a second harmony meeting in the early fall, the Board reported its progress with the plan. It had decided that the new school would be a two-year junior high school housing all 7th and 8th graders in the consolidated district. At this meeting—likewise characterized by participants as a good one—several members of the Clayton Board of Education pledged themselves not to propose Clayton's withdrawal from the consolidation during the time work was in progress on the new building.

On October 19th the consolidated board released to the press the following statement.

> The June 3 referendum vote by the three towns . . . rejected the proposal of the regional board to build a junior high school adjacent to the present building. Taking this vote in conjunction with many discussions and conferences held since that time, it is clear that many citizens are in favor of a new school built in Clayton.
>
> The Eden board has therefore undertaken to determine, from that point of view, the best plan for meeting the crisis of numbers which we shall face in the fall of 1959. . . .
>
> The consolidated board has an option on a site in Clayton.
>
> There will be three open meetings to discuss the expansion plans. They are to be held Tuesday in the auditorium of Mary O. Tracy

School, Clayton, at 8 p.m.; Wednesday in the auditorium of Allison
Community School at 8 p.m.; and Thursday in the cafeteria of
Bloomfield Center School at 8 p.m.

. . . A referendum is tentatively planned for Tuesday, November
19.

On Sunday, October 20th, there appeared a report in the local
newspaper to the effect that on the preceding Sunday, October 13th,
about 50 property owners of Bloomfield and Clayton had met at the
home of Joe Salerno to discuss the proposed site for the new school.
The paper said that according to a real estate agent and property
owner in the area who had attended the meeting—

> People attending Sunday's meeting voiced strenuous objections to
> the proposed site because the site has limited access and the school
> building would be located in the back yards of many homes now en-
> circling the site. It is located in an area depending on well-water. Two
> cases have been reported of wells going dry in the area this past
> summer.
> Other objections expressed to the choice of the site were its ir-
> regular shape and the fact that it crosses town boundaries.

A physician at the meeting was quoted as having especially stressed
the health hazard involved in the possibility that sewage leeching
fields would be close to a reservoir.

> Present at the meeting were some persons whose property adjoins
> the proposed site. They advised the group that litigation would be
> started immediately to prevent the sale of this property to the con-
> solidated board.

Again the consolidated board moved quickly. Within two weeks it
announced that it had taken an option on another site, 50 acres of
land in Clayton owned by the water company serving the nearby city.

The board then issued a new ten-page printed pamphlet setting
forth its revised plan, and announcing a single public hearing, to be
held at Eden on November 20th, and a referendum on a new $1,700,-
000 bond issue to be held on November 26th.

> The Board believes that the plan here submitted meets the crisis
> in numbers in accord with the desires of the voters of the three towns
> and with a minimum of disturbance in the operation of the Junior-

Senior High School under the consolidation concept in which the towns have expressed their belief. . . .

This plan allows for the greatest flexibility. Estimates of future enrollments are at best intelligent guesses. Our towns, however, are growing, and it cannot be many years before there is another crisis of numbers. By adopting the recommended plan we shall, when that crisis occurs, be in the best position to expand: by enlarging the new school in Clayton, by building a second Junior High in another location, or by enlarging to a limited extent the present building in Bloomfield. . . . If by that time there should be a decision to abandon the present regional alliance, we should be in the best position to facilitate a fair adjustment among the towns.

On November 12th the Clayton Board of Education passed the following resolution.

The Board supports the general principle of building a junior high school in Clayton as part of the Consolidated High School system. The construction of this building is compatible with Clayton plans if and when an independent Clayton school system becomes necessary.

But there was a good deal of concern on the part of the supporters of the new proposal about the lack of public interest in the forthcoming referendum. The day after the hearing a newspaper headline reported "Proposed Junior High School Unopposed at Eden Hearing." Four days later another headline said, "Supporters For New School Fear Complacency At Polls."

On November 26th the referendum was held and the bond issue approved. The vote is shown in Table VIII.

Table VIII

Results of Referendum, November 26, 1957

	For	Against
Allison	131	75
Bloomfield	346	29
Clayton	474	41
Totals	951	145

During the ensuing months work on the new junior high school got under way and formal discussion of Clayton's withdrawing from the consolidated district came to an end. Two of the leaders of the withdrawal movement receded somewhat from the center of the stage, as Mr. Lincoln resigned as superintendent of the consolidated district— reportedly under pressure from the Board—and the state college faculty member on the Clayton board was not renominated.

In March, 1958, at a consolidated district budget hearing, members of the Clayton Board of Education joined members of its Board of Finance in opposing adoption of a revised salary schedule which would have led to a substantial discrepancy between salaries in the consolidated district—including the junior high school it was building in Clayton—and the Clayton schools. The Clayton school board argued that "we should stay together."

However, on May 26th, Clayton's special committee on the town's educational needs submitted a report which contained no mention of a high school.

As the year wore on, Mr. Rivers and others reported that "the business of withdrawal has been with us ever since and keeps bobbing up." Applicants for teaching positions frequently asked about it. "It looks to me as though they plan eventually to withdraw," Mr. Rivers said during the summer. One observer who had stayed closely in touch with the events presented in the preceding pages said it was now his impression that most of the people of Clayton were glad to be in the consolidation, while the people of Allison and Bloomfield would prefer to have them out. Meanwhile the population of Clayton continued to grow.

SELECTED READINGS

Conant, James Bryant, *The American High School Today: A First Report to Interested Citizens.* New York: McGraw-Hill Book Company, 1959.

Kreitlow, Burton W., *Rural Education: Community Backgrounds.* New York: Harper and Brothers, 1954.

Morlan, Robert, *Capitol, Courthouse, and City Hall: Readings in American State and Local Government.* Boston: Houghton Mifflin Company, 1954.

Sargent, Cyril G., and Eugene L. Belisle, *Educational Administration: Cases and Concepts.* Boston: Houghton Mifflin Company, 1955.

Seely, John R., et al., *Crestwood Heights: A Study of the Culture of Suburban Life.* New York: Basic Books, 1956.

Whyte, William H., Jr., *The Organization Man.* New York: Simon and Schuster, 1956. Ch. 28.